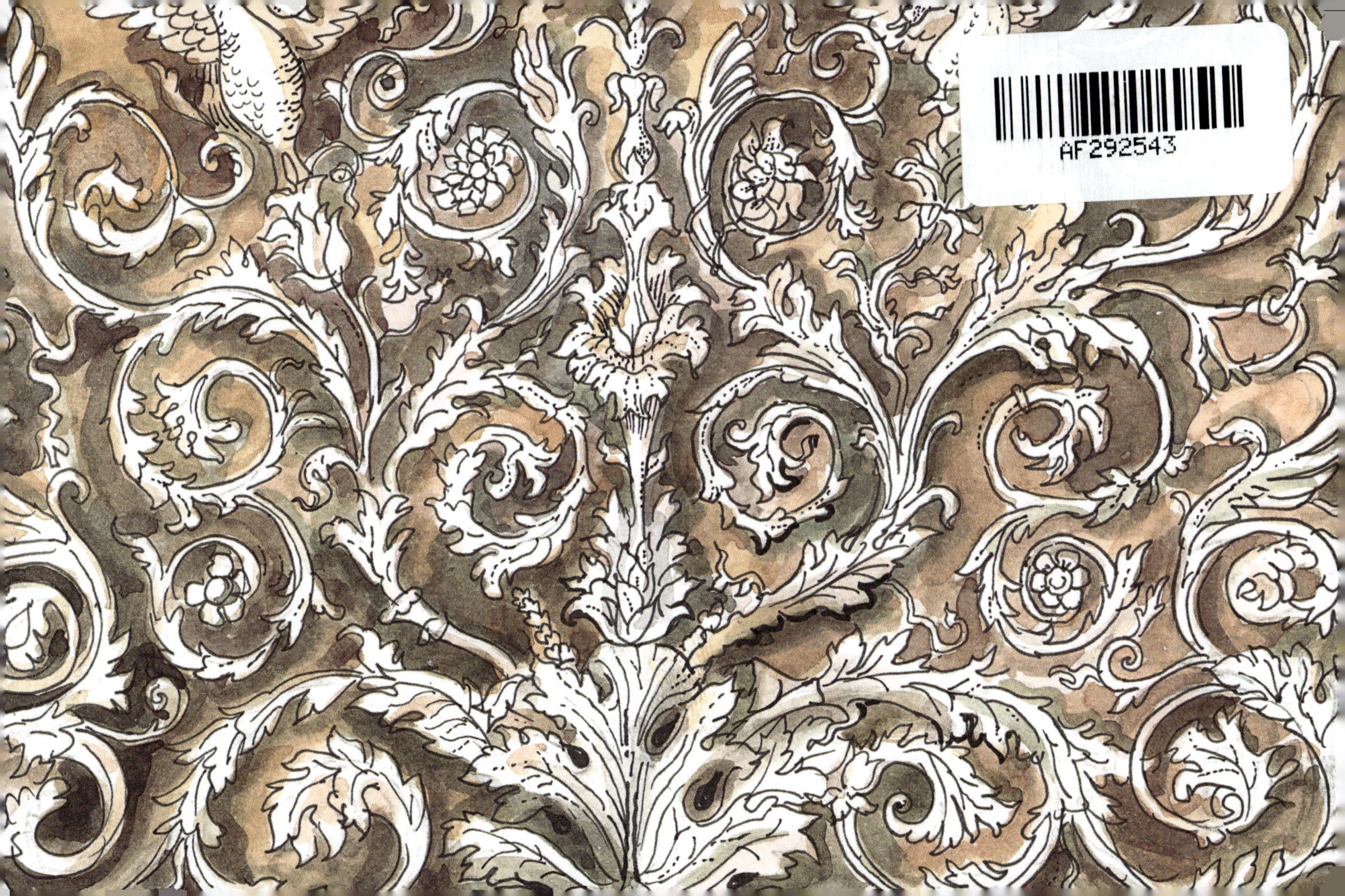
AF292543

ROME · A SKETCHBOOK

MATTHEW RICE

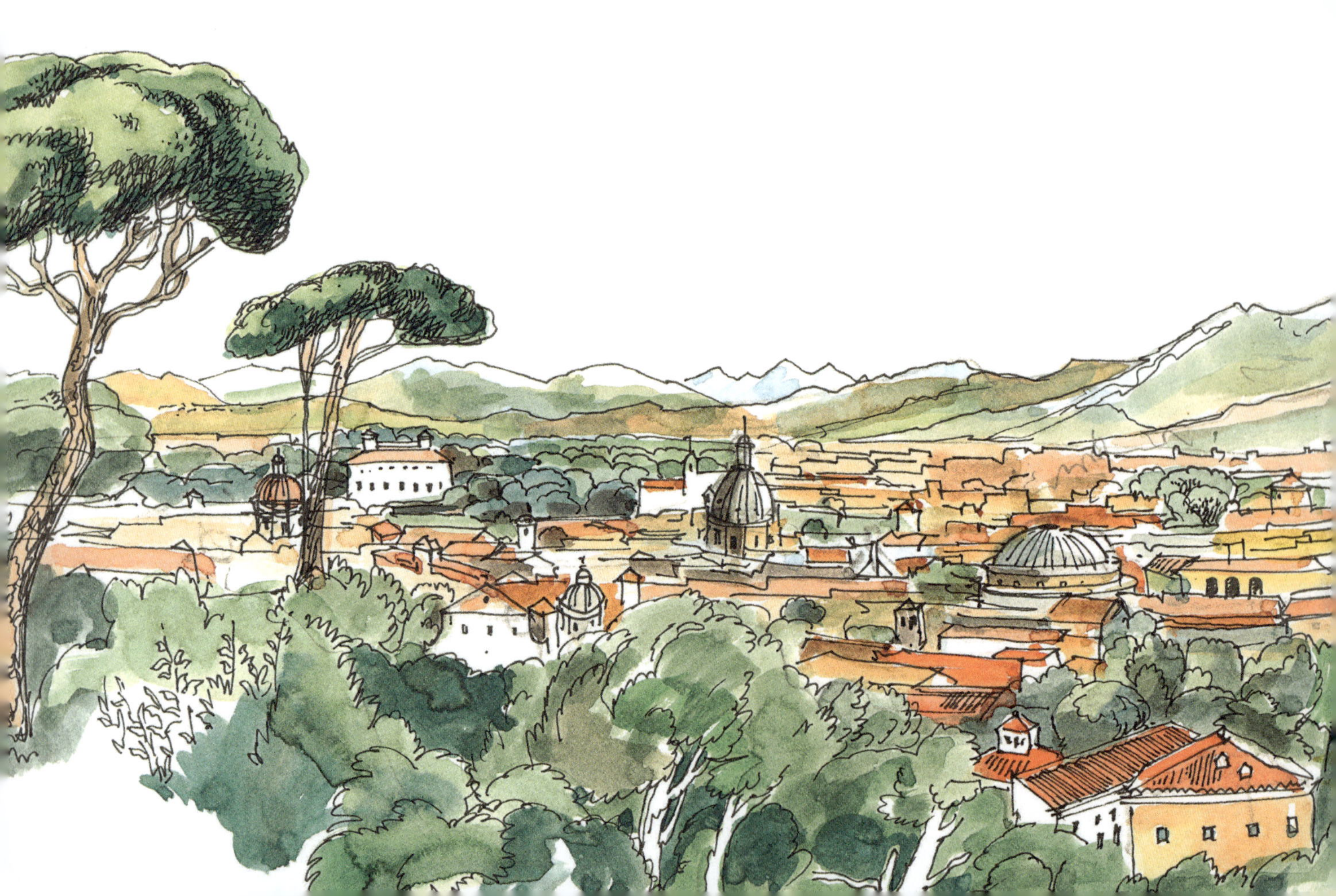

ROME

MATTHEW RICE

PARTICULAR BOOKS

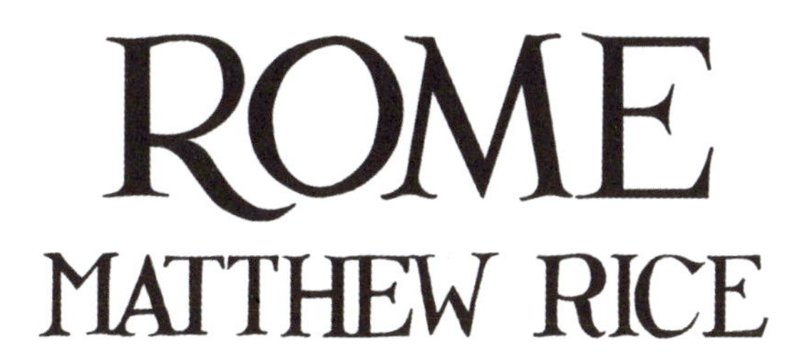
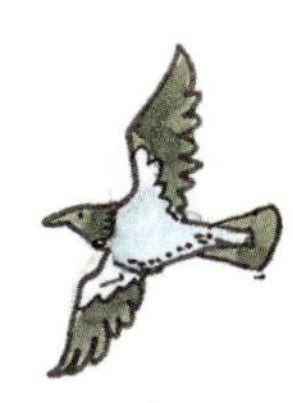

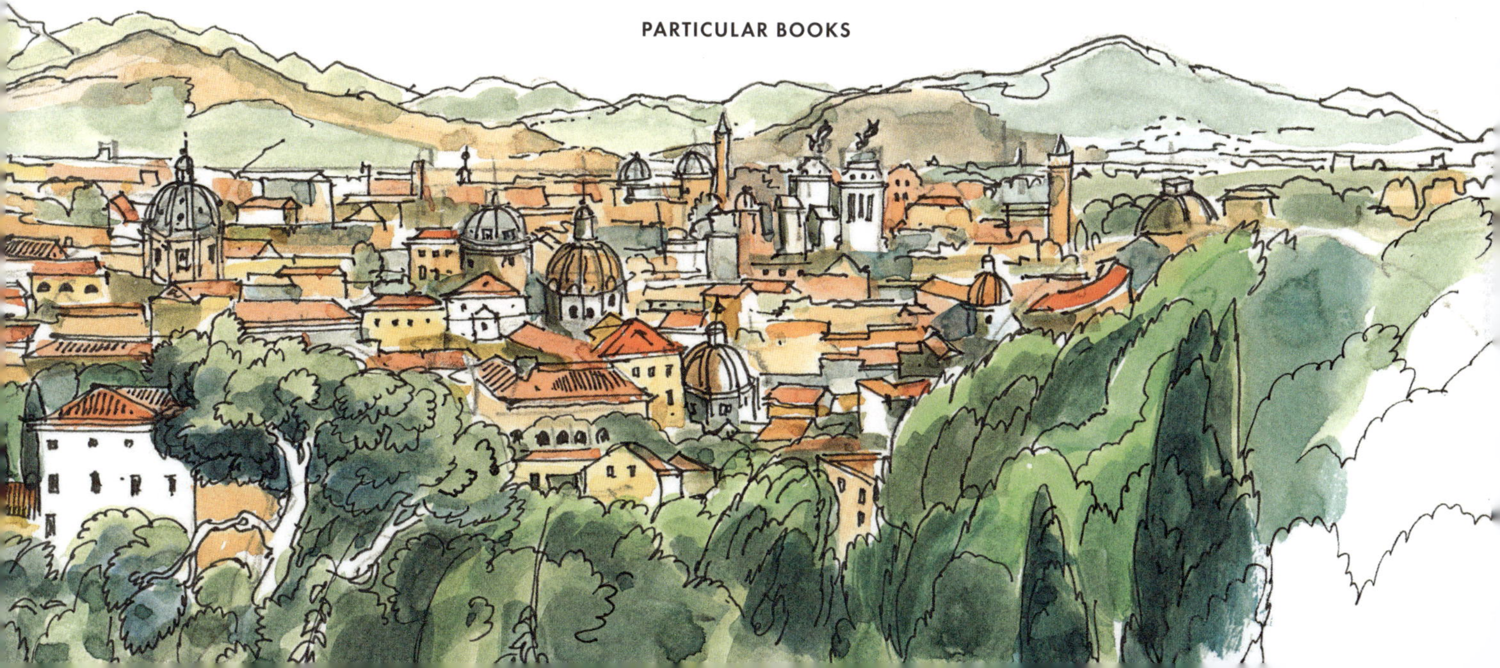

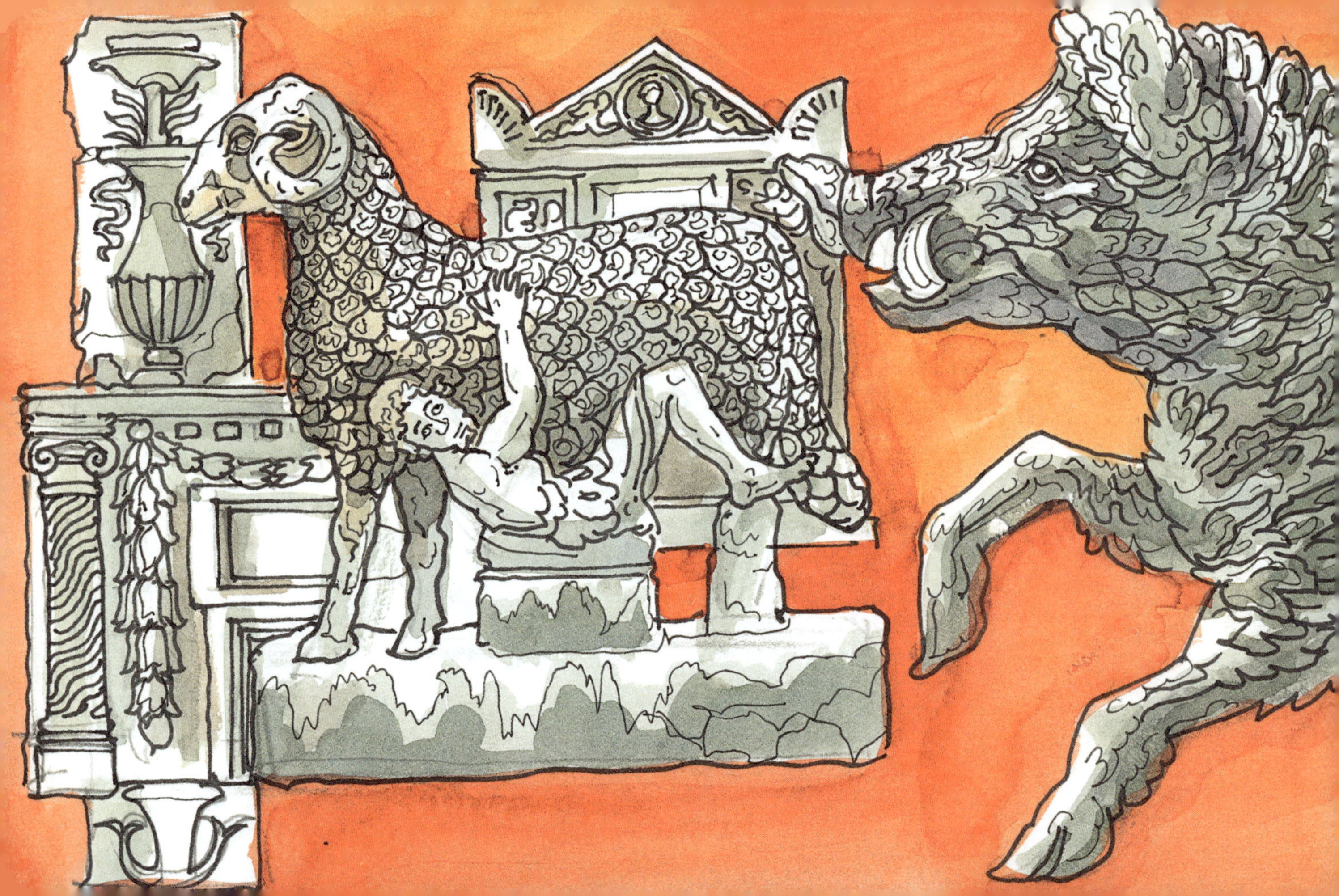

Contents

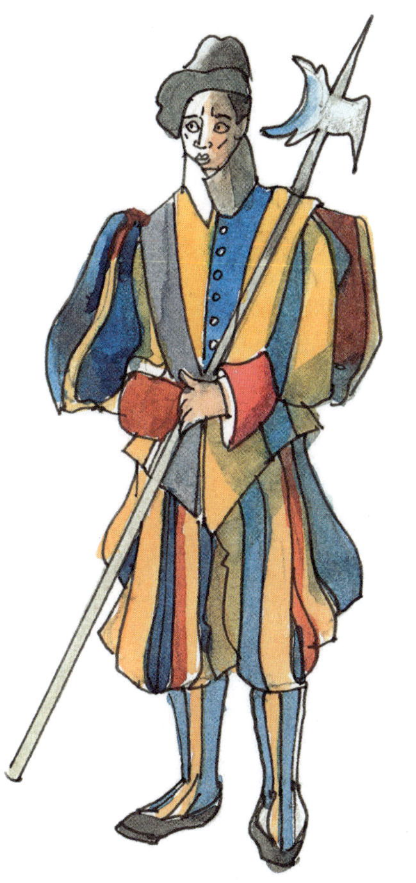

Rome with a paintbox

To find one of the BEST PLACES in the world, follow the Via Nomentana as it heads out of the centre of Rome, where the British Embassy rubs Brutalist shoulders with Michelangelo's strangely mannered Porta Pia. Leave the BAROQUE SPLENDOUR of the centre of town and forge through the nineteenth-century city extension, the Belle Époque and Art Nouveau fringes and on to the projects of Mussolini's modern city. To the west of the street is the modest Villa Ada Savoia, where the last King of Italy walked through the sombre pine and palm trees, eventually summoning Il Duce from his neo-Classical Villa Torlonia across the road for his ignominious dismissal in 1943.

A few hundred metres further out of town, an inconspicuous sign directs you to a pair of the most exciting places in Rome. Sant'Agnese fuori le Mura is a seventh-century Byzantine basilica, yet it is not the first of this name built over the saint's burial place. A fourth-century building once stood there, and part of that remains, too, in the small round church of Santa Costanza. She was a daughter of the Emperor Constantine I, who was the first to accept Christianity as an Imperial religion, and this late-Classical rotunda is one of the most remarkable survivals of ancient Rome.

The church is decorated with mosaic and is absurdly pretty, with elegant repeating patterns full of vines and olives, pheasants and partridges and more narrative scenes of late-Classical Rome. The ceiling is a microcosmic snapshot of a city that once controlled more of the world than any other. Santa Costanza is built over catacombs in a green and peaceful garden far enough from the Forum to illuminate how large the city was even then. It may be a relatively little-known building, but its architectural language is familiar throughout the Western world, the RAMPAGING TENTACLES of the Renaissance pushing their way into the drawing rooms of the Pennines or Vienna's Ringstrasse, the town halls of New England and the railway stations of Manhattan. An architectural vocabulary and cultural language that moulders in the

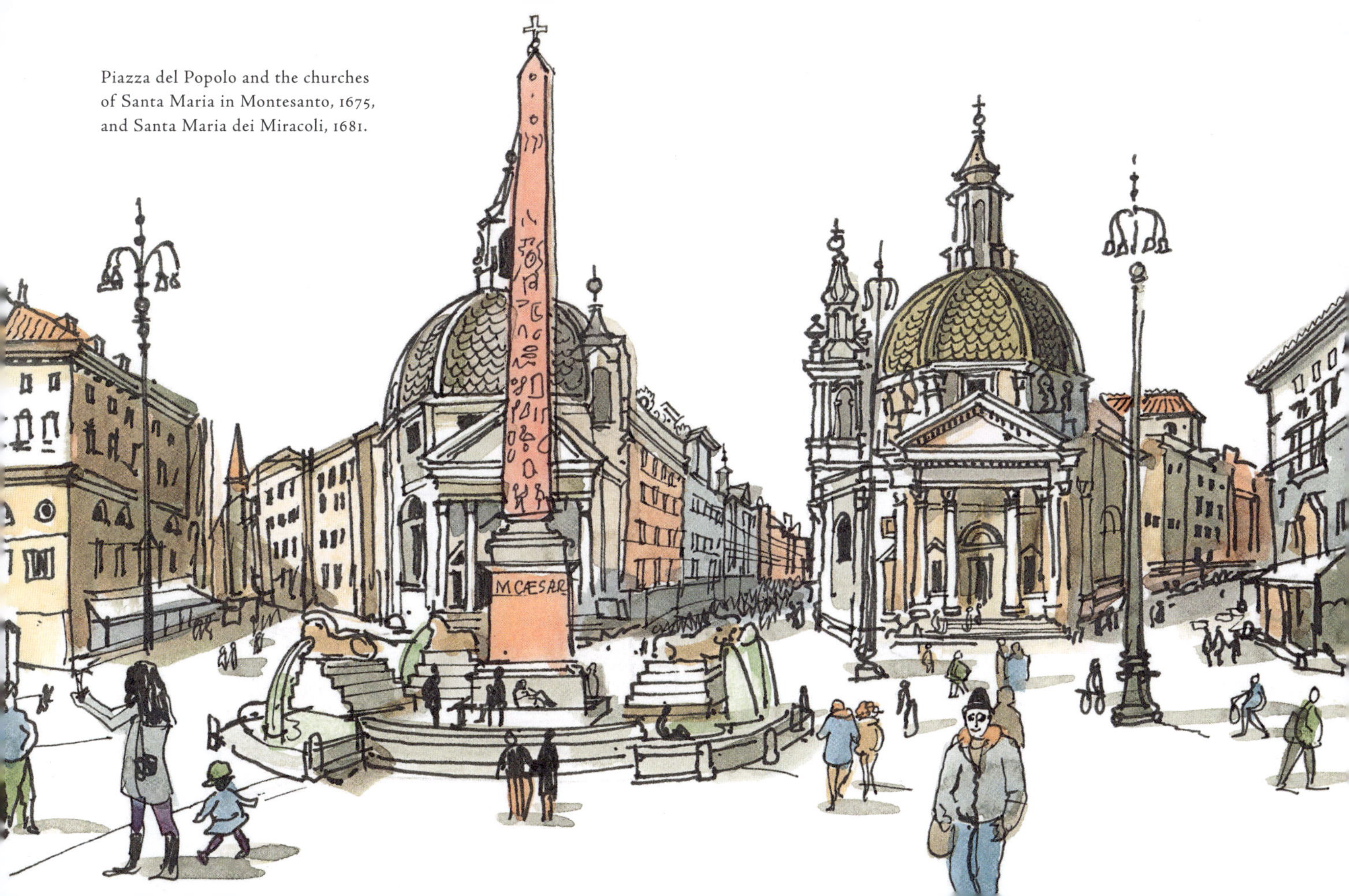

Piazza del Popolo and the churches
of Santa Maria in Montesanto, 1675,
and Santa Maria dei Miracoli, 1681.

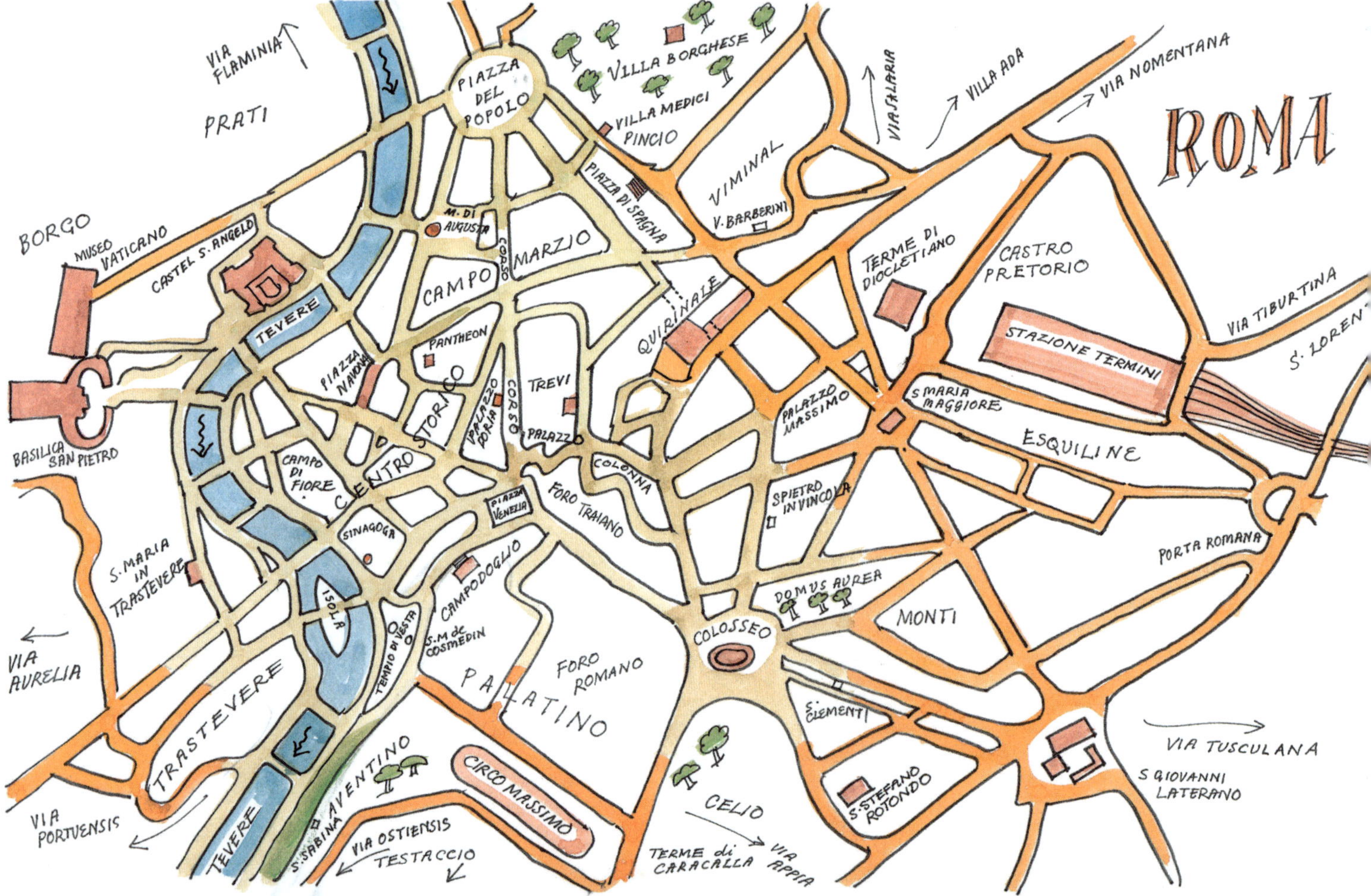

ROMA
VIA FLAMINIA
PRATI
BORGO
MUSEO VATICANO
CASTEL S. ANGELO
TEVERE
BASILICA SAN PIETRO
PIAZZA DEL POPOLO
VILLA BORGHESE
VILLA MEDICI
PINCIO
PIAZZA DI SPAGNA
M. DI AUGUSTA
CAMPO MARZIO
CORSO
PANTHEON
PIAZZA NAVONA
CENTRO STORICO
CAMPO DI FIORE
PALAZZO DORIA
CORSO
PALAZZ
TREVI
VIMINAL
V. BARBERINI
QUIRINALE
COLONNA
VIA SALARIA
VILLA ADA
VIA NOMENTANA
VIA TIBURTINA
S. LOREN
TERME DI DIOCLETIANO
CASTRO PRETORIO
STAZIONE TERMINI
S. MARIA MAGGIORE
ESQUILINE
PALAZZO MASSIMO
S. MARIA IN TRASTEVERE
SINAGOGA
PIAZZA VENEZIA
CAMPODOGLIO
FORO TRAIANO
SPIETRO IN VINCOLA
PORTA ROMANA
ISOLA
TEMPIO DI VESTA
S. M. de COSMEDIN
FORO ROMANO
PALATINO
DOMUS AUREA
MONTI
COLOSSEO
S. CLEMENTI
TRASTEVERE
VIA AURELIA
VIA PORTUENSIS
TEVERE
S. SABINA
AVENTINO
VIA OSTIENSIS
TESTACCIO
CIRCO MASSIMO
CELIO
TERME DI CARACALLA
VIA APPIA
S. STEFANO ROTONDO
S. GIOVANNI LATERANO
VIA TUSCULANA

jungles of Asia or Latin America, yet survives as the outward dress of Western colonial powers worldwide. Just as Latin is the language of global knowledge – how we name WILDFLOWERS or BIRDS, DISEASES or PLACES – so the visual language of ancient Rome represents power, culture, legal probity, longevity and military honour. And Rome, most excitingly, is still here, the temples and the forums, theatres and aqueducts. It is the epicentre, the trawling ground of European culture… and the weather and the pasta aren't bad either.

The best tip for Rome visitors comes from the novelist Elizabeth Bowen's *A Time in Rome*, which was written in 1960 but remains useful. Don't, she firmly suggests, take either taxis or the bus… just walk. It is a slightly counter-intuitive command when getting to know a large capital city, but it really works. By WALKING THE CITY, you gradually map its baffling complexities and understand its topography. Successive improvers, whether emperors, popes or invaders, made this easier by driving powerful straight avenues through the city that take you from one obelisk to another, two or three miles distant. These canyons, cutting through blocks of houses many hundreds of years old, utterly ignore the boundaries of *rioni* (boroughs or wards) and, in a city well known for its hills,

even fairly major topographic impediments. One of these dramatic changes in level is dealt with by the famous Spanish Steps, which take tourists or nuns, *carabinieri* or schoolchildren tumbling down from the lofty Pincian ridge to the fountains and narrow alleys of Trevi below.

Rome, nevertheless, remains extremely BIG – being an Imperial capital, a manifestation of papal power and a massive statement of nineteenth-century nationalism. All this makes those Bowen-inspired walks quite serious expeditions. Similarly, seeking out a particular Byzantine church or WRITHING BAROQUE ANGEL can turn into a five-mile round trip very easily, one offering such tempting diversions that the carefully planned route may need serious modifications. These might take the form of a glimpse of a glittering altar, an ice cream or, indeed, when exhaustion (or one o'clock) comes round… a *trattoria* with paper tablecloths, a short menu and a single remaining empty table beckoning one inside.

I arrived in Rome in early February, when, despite balmy, sunny days, all Romans were firmly wrapped up for winter, thick and fleecy or downright furry. They were well aware that, the minute the sun dropped, Rome would be subject to a real winter's chill. But in Italy, spring comes early – by the end of March, the wisteria was out and the turf in Hadrian's Villa and the Via Appia Antica was full of wildflowers. In the deep terraces of the Villa d'Este, wafts of thick-smelling violets carpeted the ground, and the southern spring sun was warm.

Walking out from San Lorenzo each morning to begin work, my coffee stop was a bar at the side of Santa Maria Maggiore. It is an all-day establishment, and by 7.30am there was a welcome and an espresso. Sitting and planning my day, I felt as if I was on the edge of a cliff, about to dive into Rome: that vast church marks the end of the rather generic buildings and parks of the nineteenth century and the beginning of the ancient city. This is ROME PROPER, the greatest concentration of architectural treasures anywhere on Earth. Santa Prassede, with its glittering mosaics and empty-faced sheep, is nearby, as well as the great Basilica itself, which was built from AD 432–40. In every direction are delicious treats of all sorts…

Rome and its iconic monuments have long been globally recognizable; some early-medieval Italian coins were struck with the Colosseum as a universally recognized symbol of the ancient city. There is almost no surprise at the first sight of that massive amphitheatre or, indeed, the unemotional backdrop of the Vittorio Emanuele II Monument. They garner a look of recognition, not discovery. But the other great familiar sights – the Pantheon, the Trevi Fountain, the Piazza Navona or Bernini's curving colonnade at St Peter's – are genuinely ASTONISHING, bigger, more dramatic or better preserved than a phone-sized photo ever prepares you for. THE TROOPERS of ancient and papal Baroque Rome are standard fare for the tourist, but the lesser-known architectural, historic and artistic treasures of the place outnumber these one hundred to one. A short visit requires an edit to be made before you even arrive: do you see Trastevere and Testaccio, the Vatican and Trevi, early Christian Rome or even the nearby out-of-town delights, Villa d'Este, Tivoli, Via Appia Antica and Ostia Antica? A weekend is never enough – and, at the Vatican and around Trevi, will also be impossibly crowded. A longer stay makes longer excursions not only possible, but desirable, and, as you plough resolutely up one hill or another to another great site, chance encounters along the way make the original target almost irrelevant.

Rome is also suffused with glamour. Of course, there is the romantic grandeur of faded greatness, but it is overlaid with a persistent mid-century chic based in no small part on a small clutch of films: *Roman Holiday* (1953),

Bernini's fountain in the Piazza Navona, 1648–51.

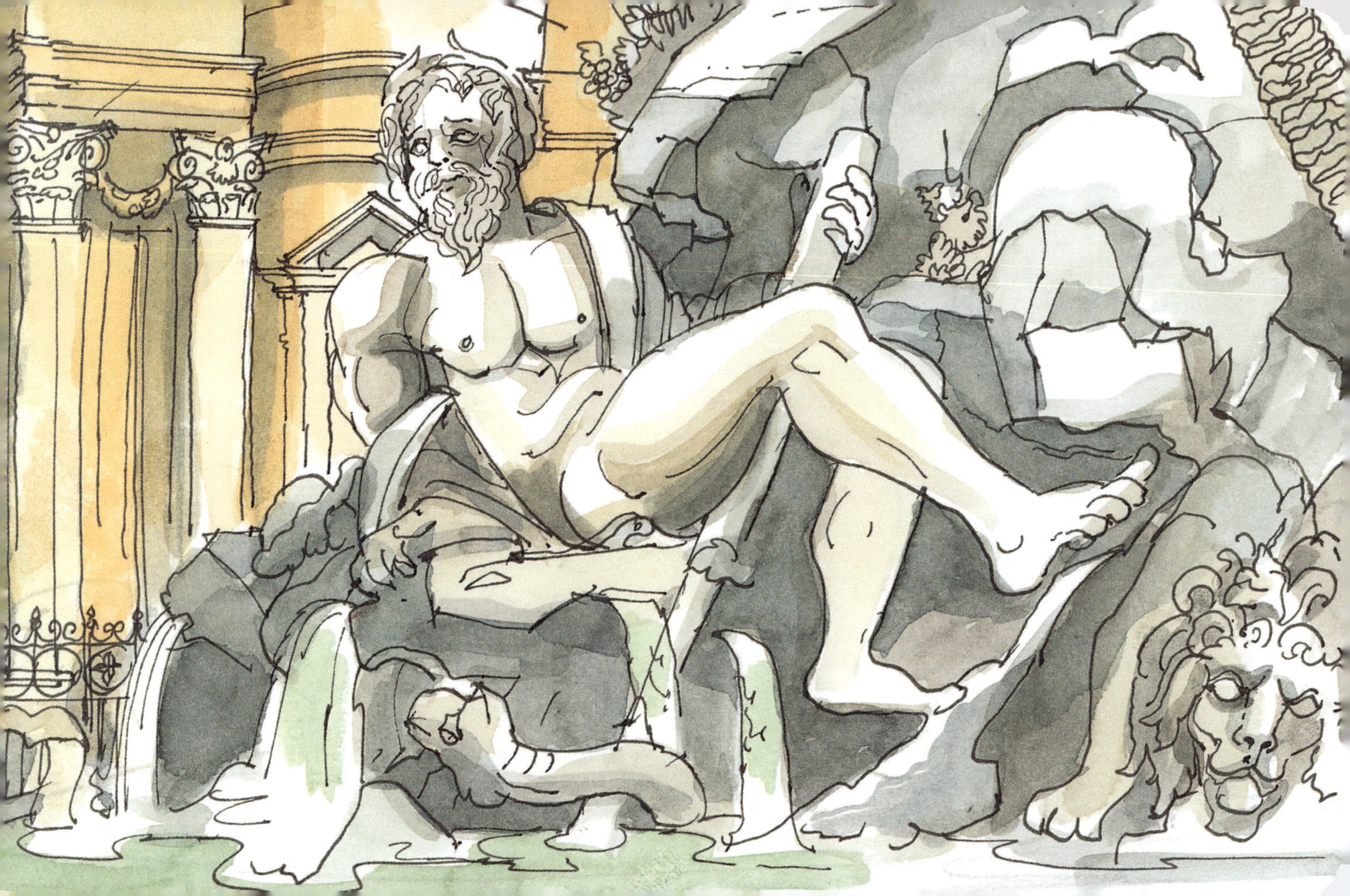

La Dolce Vita (1960) and, more recently, the much-admired *La Grande Bellezza* (2013). The first two coined a visual language through the lens by which we recognize Rome seventy years later. This is, in part, because the city has actually changed little – at any rate, not sufficiently for another filter to have been applied. Walking down the hill towards the Spanish Steps and passing the moss-encrusted gods of the Quattro Fontane, I saw a smart olive-green Fiat Cinquecento of the original shape. Admiring its economical lines and almost unthinkable smallness, I noticed it was followed by a 1950s Simca, a coincidence… Approaching the balcony at the top of the steps, I again spotted a couple of elegant old cars outside Hotel Hassler and registered the formally dressed clientele. Only at the snap of the clapperboard did I notice that I had intruded onto a film set and was being politely, but firmly, ushered out of shot and closeted with a small crowd of onlookers.

Drawing a city is a very particular way to see it. It is slow – even if, like me, you are a quick worker – but engraves a series of images so DEEPLY onto one's mind that they seem indelible. Even if you are a fabulously careful photographer, your most diligently composed iPhone picture will be taken in a tiny proportion of the time that is needed to make the most basic drawing. All the LOOKING and ANALYSIS and CALCULATION that goes into mapping a view or a building and converting them from three dimensions into two is disregarded in the blink of an eye. A friend once pointed out that all that care and attention is worthless if the picture doesn't feel like the thing you are drawing. I'd never really thought about that, but, now, I pause for a minute and actually think what is distinctive and interesting about the church, tree or hill. It's a useful tip to remember.

A city with hills is a city of views. Rome's seven hills – Palatine, Capitoline, Quirinal, Viminal, Esquiline, Caelian, Aventine – are a misnomer; there are a dozen or more ranged around the river plain. But the wide panoramas from vantage spots at all points of the compass are so extensive that they correlate easily with the map. Gradually, you learn to spy the landmarks. Some are obvious, such as the Vittorio Emanuele II Monument or St Peter's; others are less obvious, but are equally visible, like the brick masses of the remaining medieval towers around the ancient Forum. A particularly grand vantage point is the Gianicolo (the walk towards which is buoyed up by fifteen minutes spent admiring Bramante's faultless Renaissance masterpiece the Tempietto). From here, the city – or, at any rate,

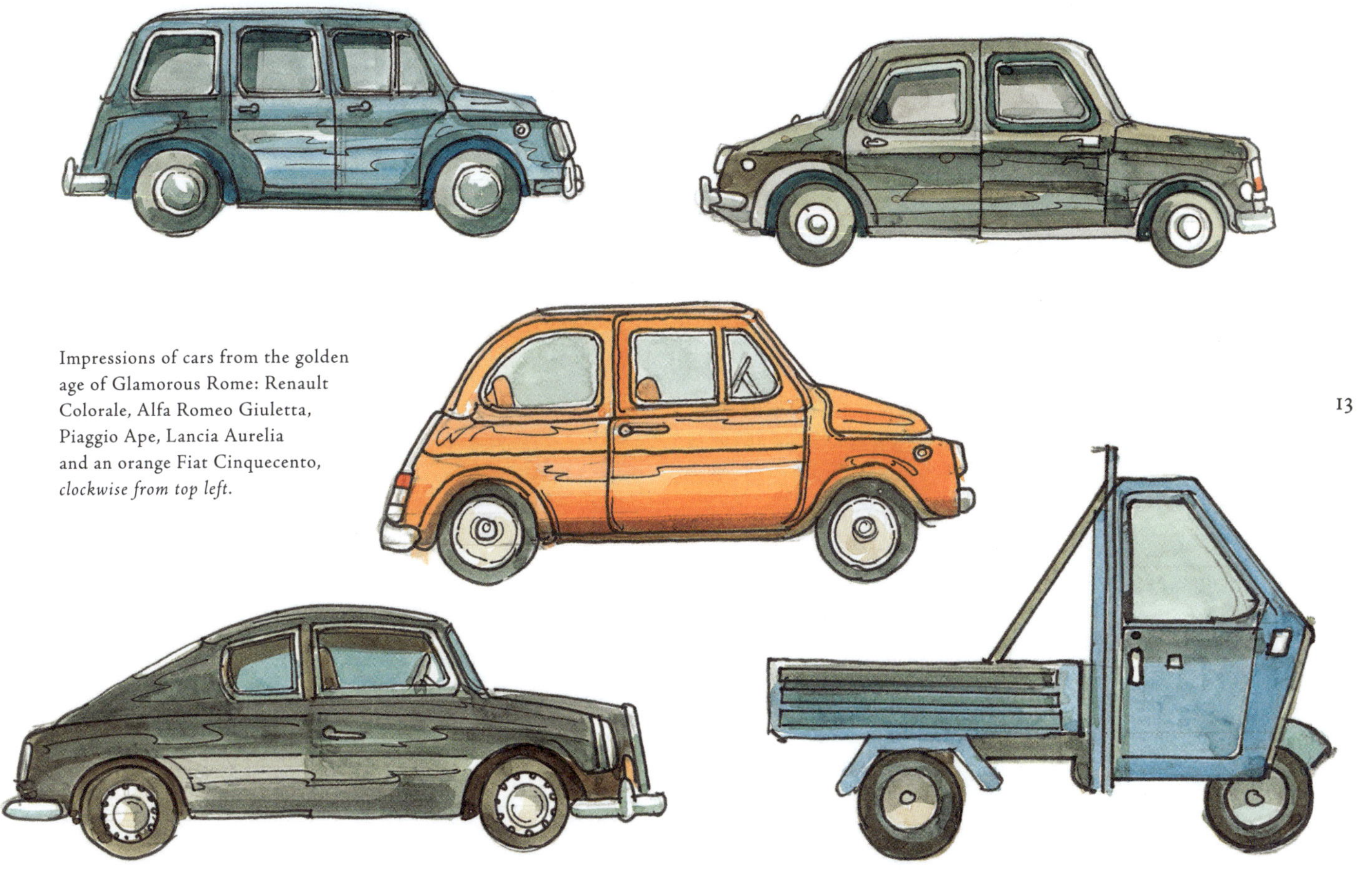

Impressions of cars from the golden age of Glamorous Rome: Renault Colorale, Alfa Romeo Giuletta, Piaggio Ape, Lancia Aurelia and an orange Fiat Cinquecento, *clockwise from top left.*

13

the ancient city – is spread out above the river from the Aventine to the Villa Borghese a mile or so distant. The opposite view from the orange grove beneath the pines on the Aventine itself is duller, but the backdrop is green and marvellously like an eighteenth-century engraving.

Another mapping walk is one that traces the ancient walls of the city. We are used to seeing Roman walls in many European cities, but this is the *Roman* Roman wall. It is remarkably well preserved, despite having been pierced with little hesitation whenever a new ingress or egress was required. The Aurelian walls were built in AD 275, when the rather overconfidently modest Servian walls of 575–535 BC seemed inadequate to stave off the incursions of Germanic tribes. Enclosing a much larger Imperial city and genuinely hard to tackle, these massive fortifications weave in and out of Old Rome, leaving plenty of the city OUTSIDE, as well as open space within.

Gates mark the old Roman roads that led from the Empire's centre to its furthest corners. In one way or another, all survive: the Via Appia, built in 312 BC, leads to Taranto and Brindisi; the Via Aurelia is now the SS Aurelia dual carriageway heading to Genoa; the Via Ostiense traces the ancient road to Rome's giant port of Ostia; the Via Flaminia heads across Italy to the Adriatic.

Via Tiburtina led and leads still to Tivoli, the rural pleasure grounds of the ancients where Hadrian's massive villa stands, looking back across the plain to the capital. The ancient gates are equally impressive. Some, like the complex Porta Maggiore or Porta San Giovanni, survive as potent manifestations of the greatness of the Empire, with massed columns and giant archways. Others, such as the abandoned Porta Tiburtina, are muscular, the bold white marble traced with lost inscriptions, revealed only by the ghosts of bronze rivets that once held the letters in place.

I tried colouring in the roads I had walked with a thin black pen on the map when I came home each evening, another Bowen trick. As I retraced my walks, the black net of recorded travels spread until it covered the sheet like a DRUNKEN SPIDER'S WEB. It started well, an inky colonization, but seemed increasingly pointless until, one morning, the pieces suddenly fell into place. The hills, the slopes and the roads coalesced into an undetailed but usable mental map, and I could begin to really concentrate on LOOKING and DRAWING.

By then, the spring had progressed by a couple of weeks, and it had become a pleasure unalloyed to sit or perch on a wall and, as I drew, to work out why Rome is the GREATEST CITY ON EARTH.

I first came to Rome as a teenager. I abandoned my grown-up travelling companions to find a schoolfriend, Askandar, and was thrilled to find that he had the keys to a dull orange Cinquecento – thrilled because we were sixteen and it was the object of greatest desire. We spun around the juddering cobbles, paying no attention to stop signals and learning the word *semaforo* for traffic lights. Although these days they seem mostly to be adhered to, we were not alone then in our *laissez-faire* approach to traffic controls. We saw the Colosseum from what felt like two wheels, then fell into a bar and pursued oblivion until rudely ejected by the owner, who, no doubt, had children of the same age and deplored our state. Later adult trips were quick weekends, visiting the principal sights from one or another central flat or hotel.

Now, with the untold luxury of two months and a wonderful flat in extramural San Lorenzo, the challenge of fixing the plan of my new city became unavoidable. For this, the paper map on my kitchen table was unbeatable. Although Rome was traditionally established around its seven hills, they are NOT a very good start for an exploration. For one thing, there are several other significant hills, such as Gianicolo (or Janiculum), and, anyway, Rome now spreads further afield than the original settlement. Within the city, bounded by the Aurelian wall, are the *rioni*. Although essentially

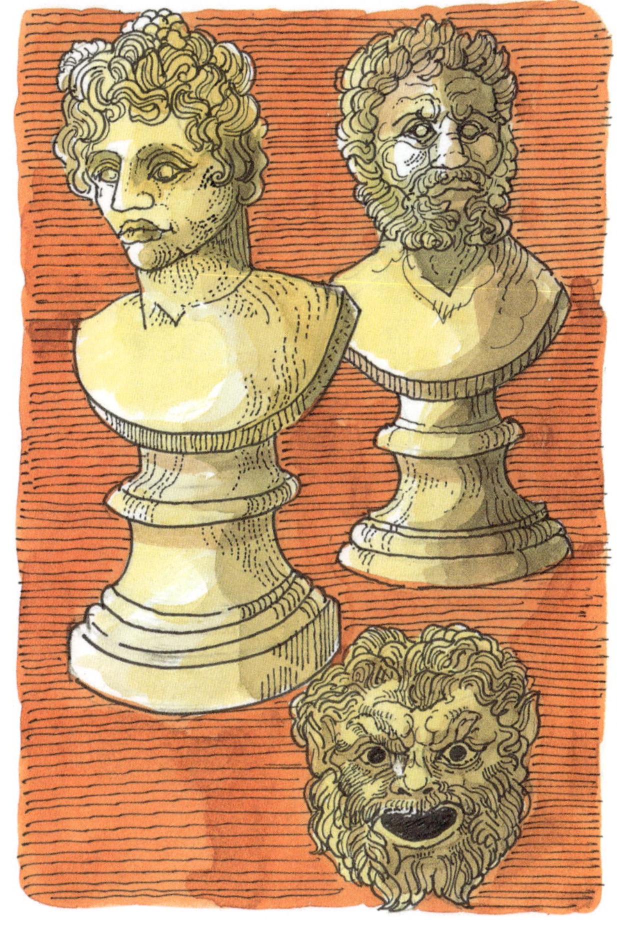

Two Imperial busts and a comic mask in the Capitoline Museums.

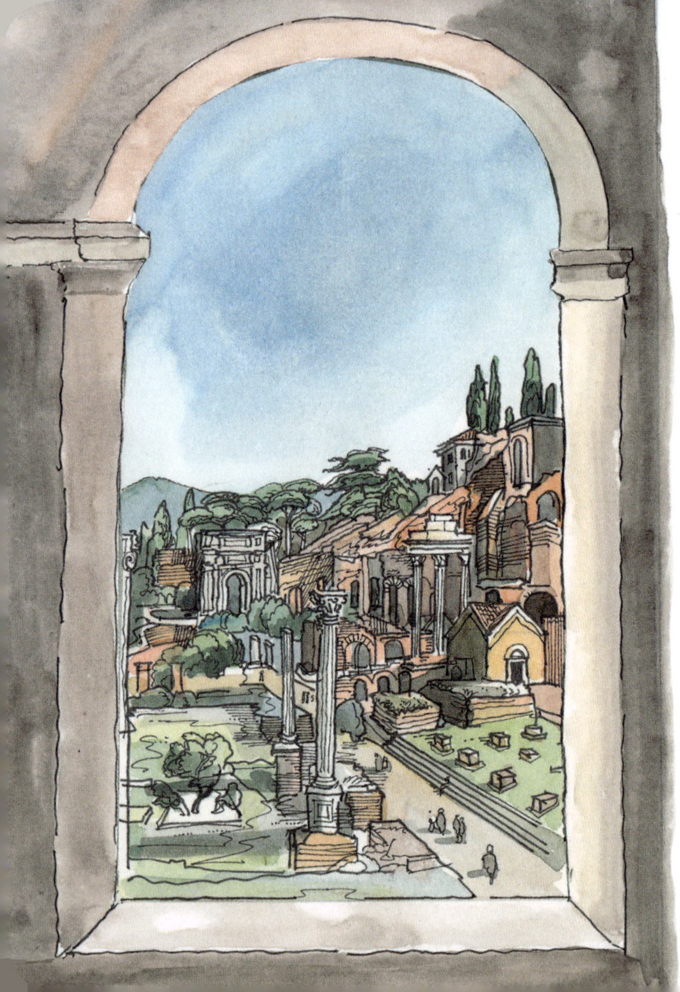

districts, like the *sestieri* of Venice or the *arrondissements* of Paris, there are twenty-two of them in the historic centre alone and we pass imperceptibly from one to another. The principal Imperial roads in and out of Rome still pierce the wall, offering an aid to orientation, so my plan was to follow some of the most obvious straight lines that bisect the city. These were often BRUSQUELY SMASHED through the existing urban fabric by successive popes eager to aggrandize or regularize their city, and walking for a mile or more along these dividing lines reveals its changing character as you forge in towards the inevitable Forum.

After the nineteenth-century *Risorgimento*, the capital of the newly unified Italy required boulevards and avenues to compete with the rest of the world. Further from the centre, the character of the streets becomes decreasingly specifically Roman and far more European, with grand arcaded residential and commercial blocks. Further still from the centre, Belle Époque villas and modern blocks of flats appear. Mussolini was as powerful a driver for this as any sixteenth-century pope, and his great neo-Imperial avenues set the tone of suburban Rome.

View of the Forum from the ancient Tabularium in the Capitoline Museums, *left*; a minimal remnant of aqueduct amid quite ordinary houses, *right*.

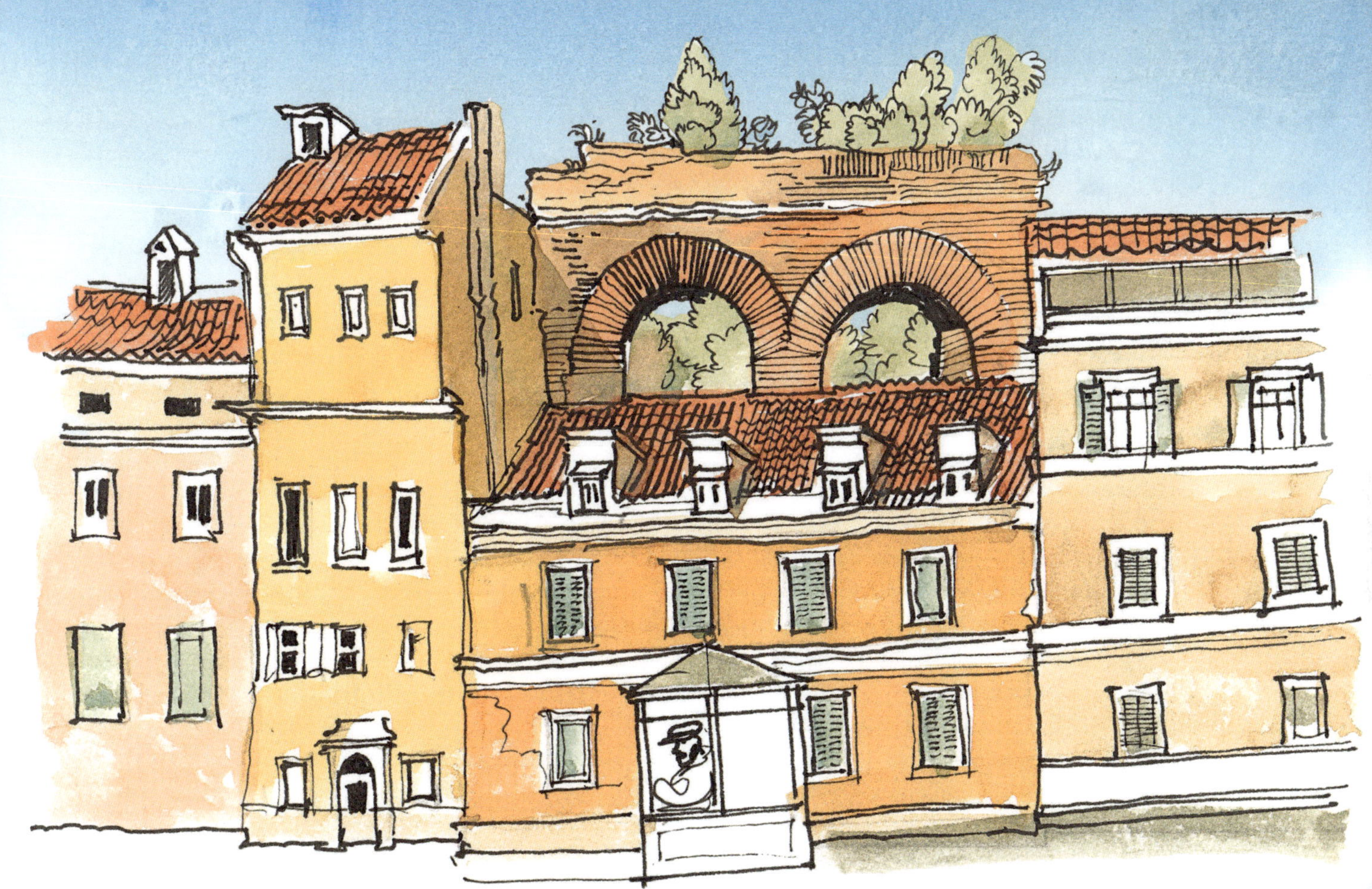

Forum

The utter incomprehensibility of the Forum is due to the fact that the most important things are the least clear, made even more so by the CONFUSION of it being a 2,400-year-old site. My children used to be devoted to a book called *A Slice Through a City*, in which it was shown how, over centuries of rising ground levels, the chapters of history were layered on top of each other. That imaginary settlement was admirably clear and, although some elements of one era survived to another, the ARCHAEOLOGICAL LASAGNE of buildings and roads was nevertheless manifest.

Not so in Rome, where a baffling number of forums, temples, road levels, baths, taverns, shops, monuments and churches seem to have been scrambled together. Looking down from the Palatine Hill to the Forum below, a plan starts to emerge, but it is confused by upstanding temples, columns and arches that are sometimes 1,000 years apart in age and muddled further by the Farnese gardens created by Cardinal Alessandro Farnese, the sixteenth-century owner of much of the hill, who built himself a villa and the first private botanical gardens in Europe in 1550.

What *is* clear is that a central Via Sacra, a processional route, led to a series of open spaces, around and among which the other monuments are scattered. To join the architectural dots further, you need to exercise your imagination and look at the extraordinary heritage of architectonic detritus reassembled in museums, galleries and villas around the city, then superimpose this supreme SOPHISTICATION on to the brick hulks still standing.

One giant that emerges through dint of its tremendous size and simple form is the Basilica of Maxentius, its three massive coffered vaults visible from most vantage points. It was completed by Constantine in AD 312, with a mighty nave that awed early travellers, but it partially collapsed in an earthquake in the ninth century. What we see today is only the north aisle, yet it still appears to be the work of giants. Better preserved through economical re-use is the church of San Lorenzo in Miranda. Entered from outside the Forum, this appears to be just another Baroque church and not one of the most exciting, despite

The Emperor Vespasian began the Colosseum around AD 70.

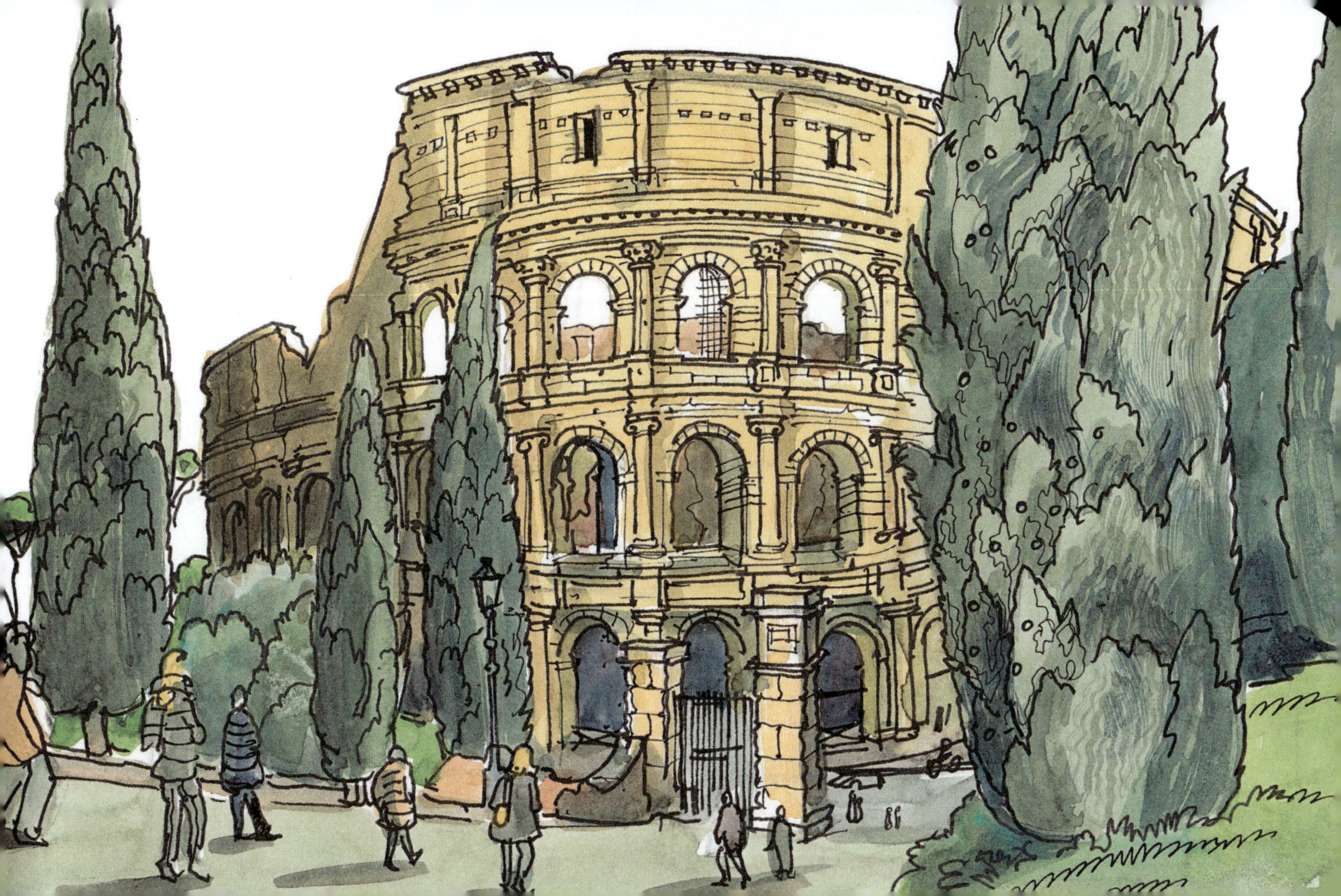

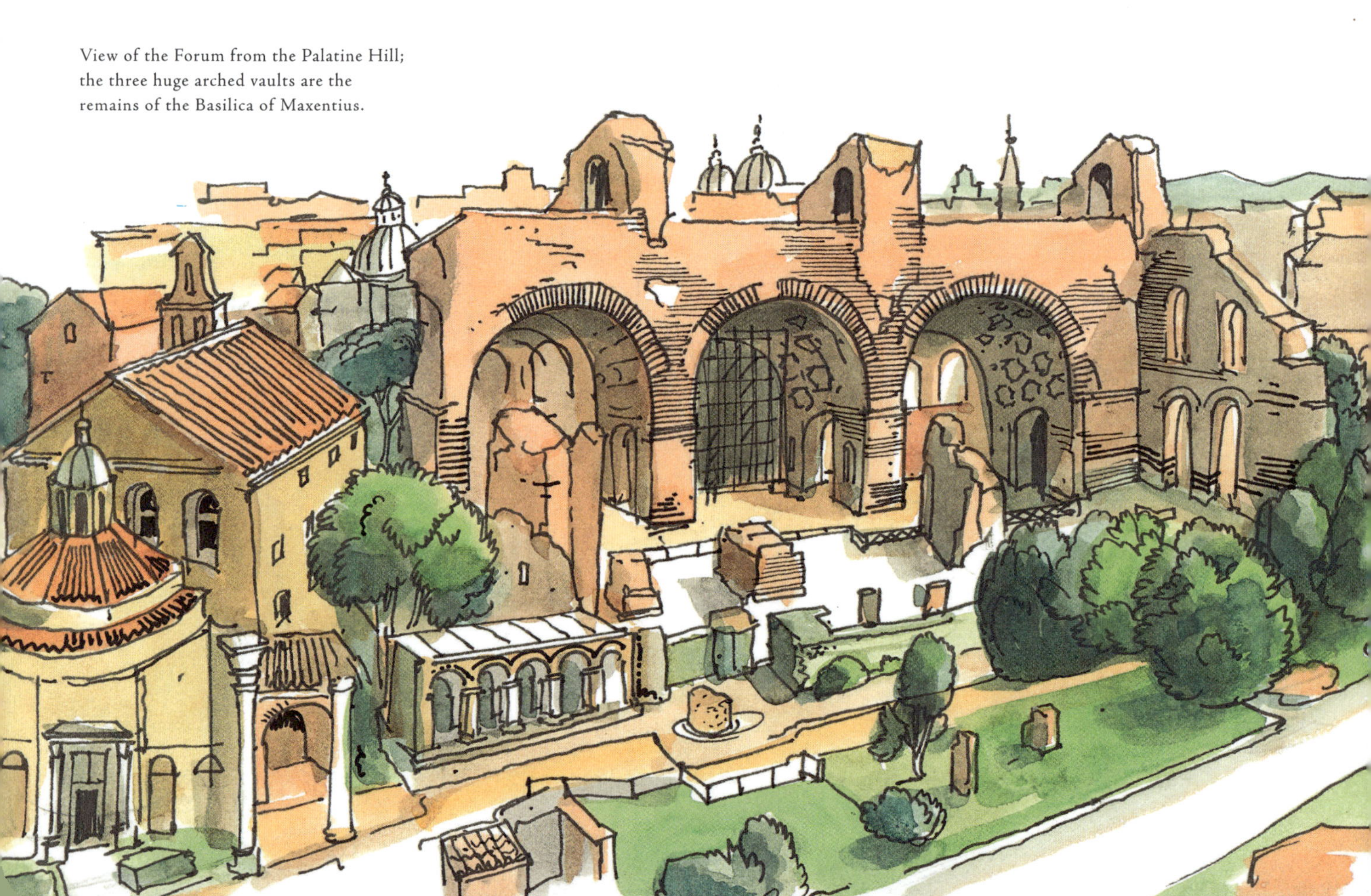

View of the Forum from the Palatine Hill;
the three huge arched vaults are the
remains of the Basilica of Maxentius.

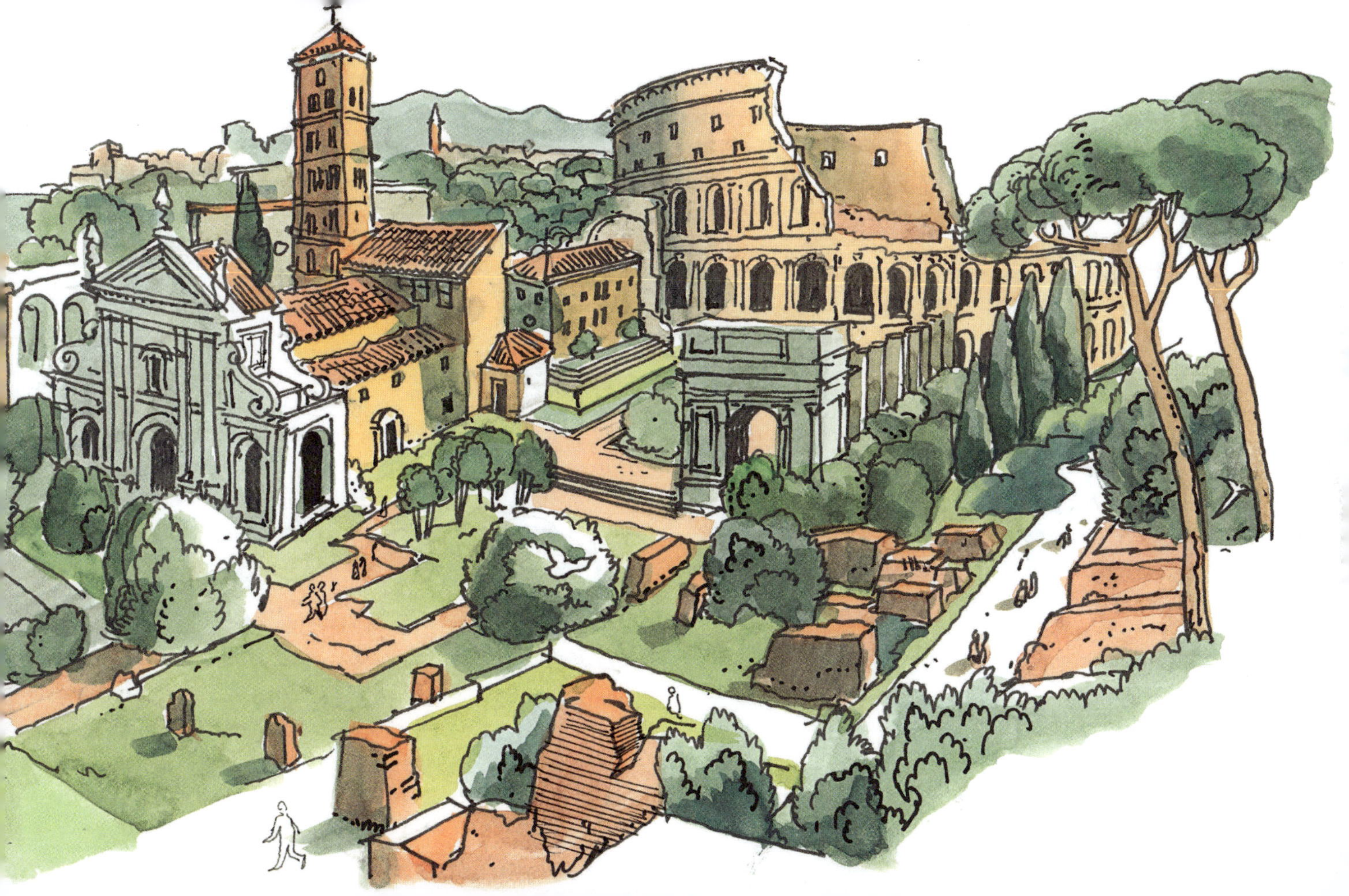

a small cloister nicely planted with geraniums. However, it is set within the ancient temple of the deified Emperor Antoninus and his wife, Faustina, built in AD 141, some 1,500 years before the church. As a result of this gap, the floor level of the church is a surprising six metres higher than that of its mother temple. Despite this apparent mismatch, the degree to which the Roman Baroque style drew on the legacy of its ancient predecessors allows for a synergy between the Forum-facing façade, adapted with a bold seventeenth-century pediment, and the sixteenth-century gilded interior. Similarly, Santi Cosma e Damiano was built into the temple of Valerius Romulus in AD 309, but by 527 it had been turned into a church. It is highly decorated inside with fine MOSAIC SHEEP and a figure of Christ of more recent style and dubious taste.

The spot from which you're admiring all this, the Palatine Hill, was named after Pallas, son of Evander, who was the son of the goddess Carmentis and the god Hermes and came from Pallantium, the ancient Arcadian city. Following its use by the Emperor Augustus as the site for his Imperial home, Palatine gave its name to all 'palaces' in European languages. Once a series of buildings of inconceivable grandeur, the palace is now reduced to baffling, clay-brown masonry mammoths that offer more the armature of buildings than any real indication of what it felt to walk into the palace, let alone to approach the Imperial presence.

Among the puzzling ruins is a museum hanging over the Palatine precipice, giving splendid views of the Circus Maximus around which the chariots once raced, but it is so thoroughly outshone by its near neighbour the Capitoline Museums complex as to preclude a visit unless it is raining and you are tired and cold. The latter is built on the facing hill of the same name, the site of a huge and massively significant Temple of Jupiter, destination of processions following the Via Sacra through the Forum. All the unfortunate captives, rich booty or triumphant generals made their way, heads bowed or swollen, to these giant columns. The Capitoline Hill was the sacred centre of Rome, encrusted with temples to which was added a further building, the Tabularium. Its original function was to house the state archives, but it had a later medieval iteration as the civic, secular and administrative centre of the city. Now, it is incorporated into the giant museums that cover the site.

Walking up the grand stairway, the Cordonata, you come to the CAMPIDOGLIO, an elegant *piazza* from which you enter an astonishing set of buildings housing

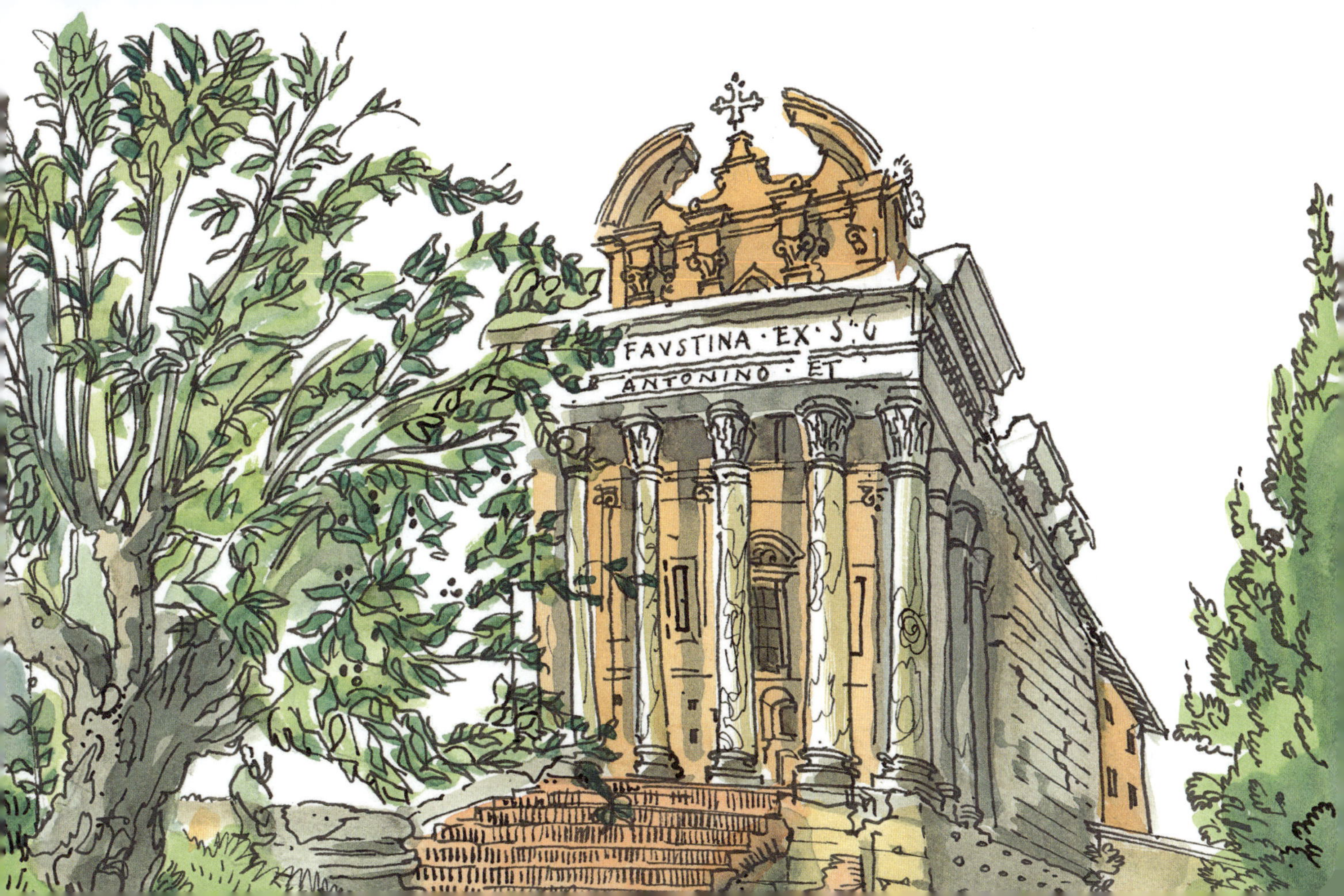

FAVSTINA · EX · S · C
ANTONINO · ET

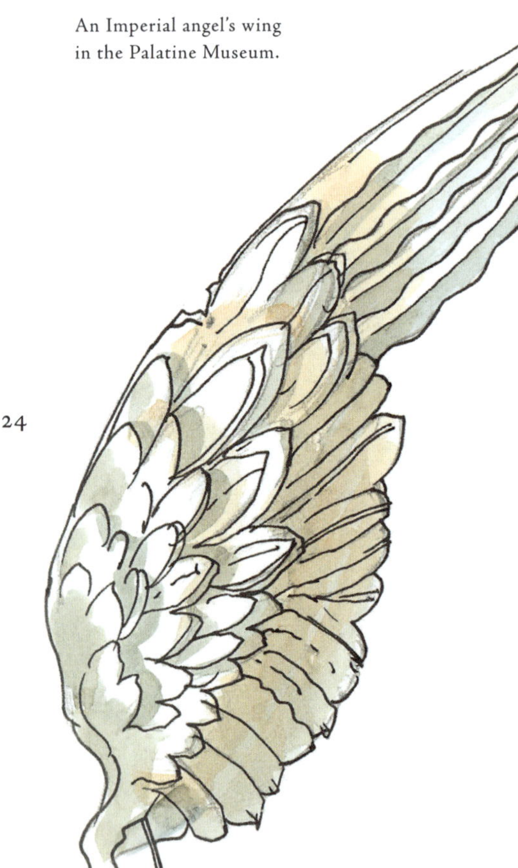

24

what may be among the oldest museums in the world, having been given to the city by Pope Sixtus IV in 1471. Among the treasures Sixtus transferred to the Capitoline Museums from the palace at St John Lateran, the oldest papal basilica, was the much-reproduced she-wolf that fed Romulus and Remus, as well as the enormous gilt-bronze equestrian statue of Marcus Aurelius, thought at the time to be Constantine, the first Christian emperor. In Imperial Rome, the Capitoline development looked towards the Forum, but by the Middle Ages it had swung round to face the Campus Martius below. As it became increasingly important as the seat of the city's government, it took on some of the characteristics of other Italian city halls, with crenellations and a tower. Then, in 1536, Paul III commissioned Michelangelo to re-design the complex, with work, after various delays, being completed by 1654. One great room leads to another full of familiar and unfamiliar statuary; one wing is connected to the other by a subterranean corridor.

The Colosseum dominates the eastern end of the Forum and, despite its being regularly used as a quarry throughout the Renaissance and Baroque periods, it has survived as one of the world's most famous buildings. Its superimposed colonnades in DORIC, IONIC and CORINTHIAN orders are instantly recognizable and are as well known as the gruesome, giraffe-killing, dwarf-fighting, Christian-martyring horrors that took place within. Immediately beyond, the atmosphere changes from monumental to domestic and you are in the parish of San Clemente. This is the ultimate palimpsest of a church built on top of a Mithraic temple, under which is a tiny and very early church. Nearer the surface, but still several feet beneath ground level, a flock of docile mosaic sheep graze under a vinous tree of life.

Climbing the hill towards St John Lateran, a rather martial-looking mass turns out to be Santi Quattro Coronati. This is again very early, with, supposedly, fourth-century foundations. It twice defended a pope against invading Normans or Germans, but when the papacy left St John Lateran for the Vatican, it lost its significance.

Heading further uphill along a most unprepossessing road blighted by ugly barracks and hospitals, a hairpin return takes you to the plain brick façade of Santo Stefano Rotondo. It is entered through a narthex supported by six ancient columns, which cannot prepare you for the sheer scale of the circular temple you enter. Originally, three concentric circles comprised this centrally planned church, which was built between AD 468 and AD 483, the period of time when Odoacer the German chief finally brought Barbarian power to the holy city. The outer ring has been lost, but this is still an extraordinary building. It is not a simple dome like the Pantheon, but rather is supported by a tripartite arch on two massive Corinthian columns. The profound visual calm induced by the regular repeating Ionic columns of the inner ring is UTTERLY RUINED by the lurid strip-cartoon series of frescos that line the outer walls, depicting one gory martyrdom after another: lions pull apart smiling neophytes, young nuns are subject to unspeakable and fatal indignities as male Christians in the time of persecution are butchered in ways increasingly violent and imaginative. I think there may be a case for a pot of whitewash…

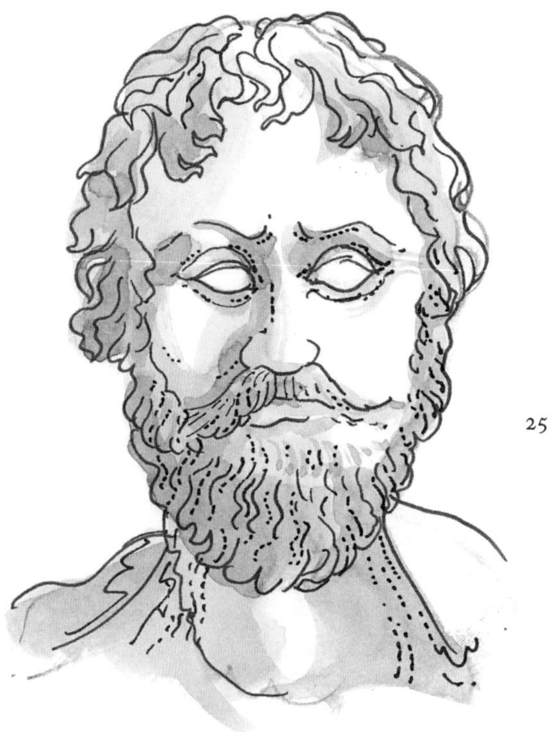

25

Bust in the Capitoline Museums, *above*;
the Arch of Constantine, built to celebrate the
Battle of Milvian Bridge in AD 312, and the courtyard
of San Clemente near the Colosseum, *overleaf.*

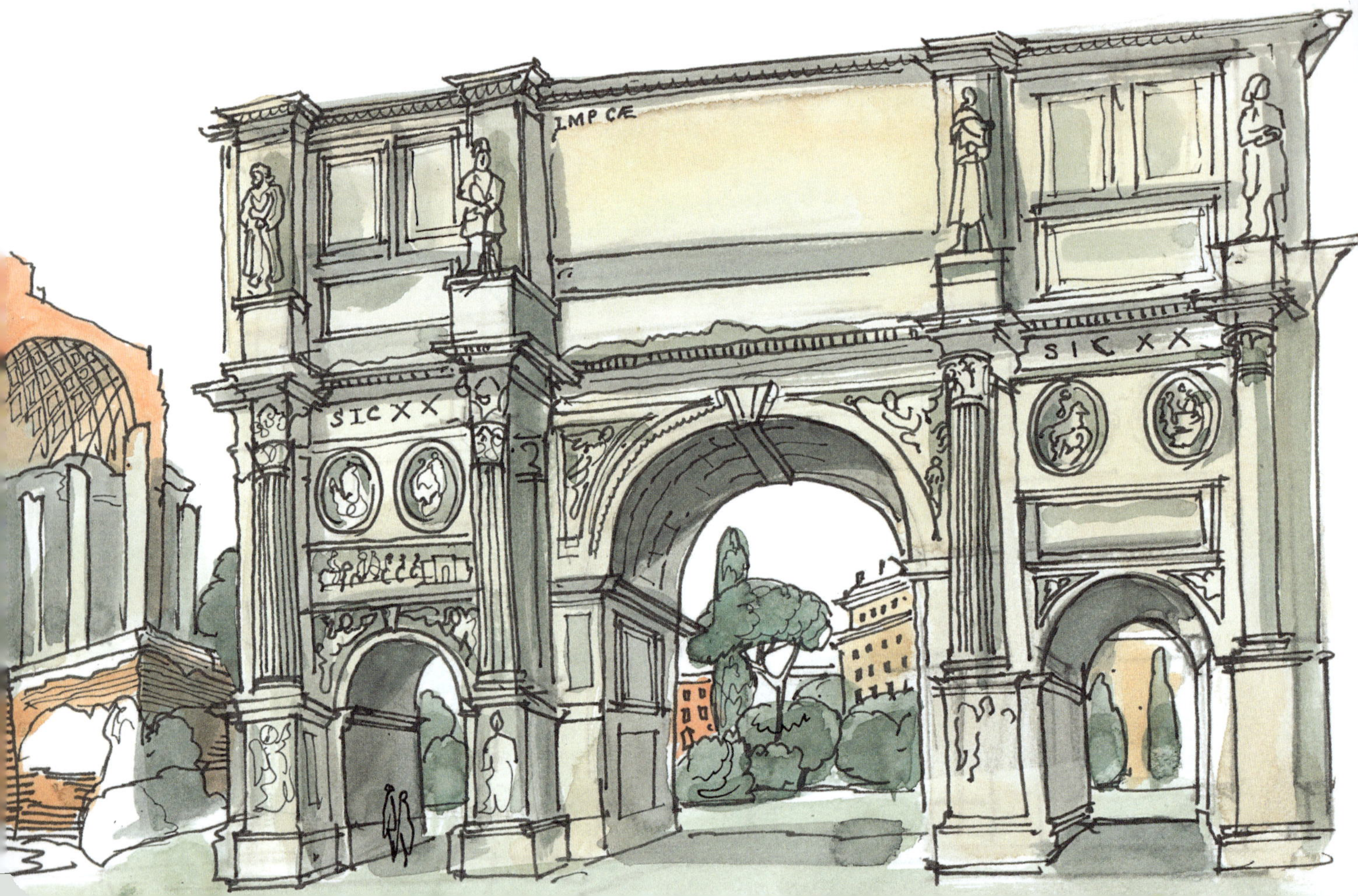
IMP CÆ
SIC XX
SIC XX

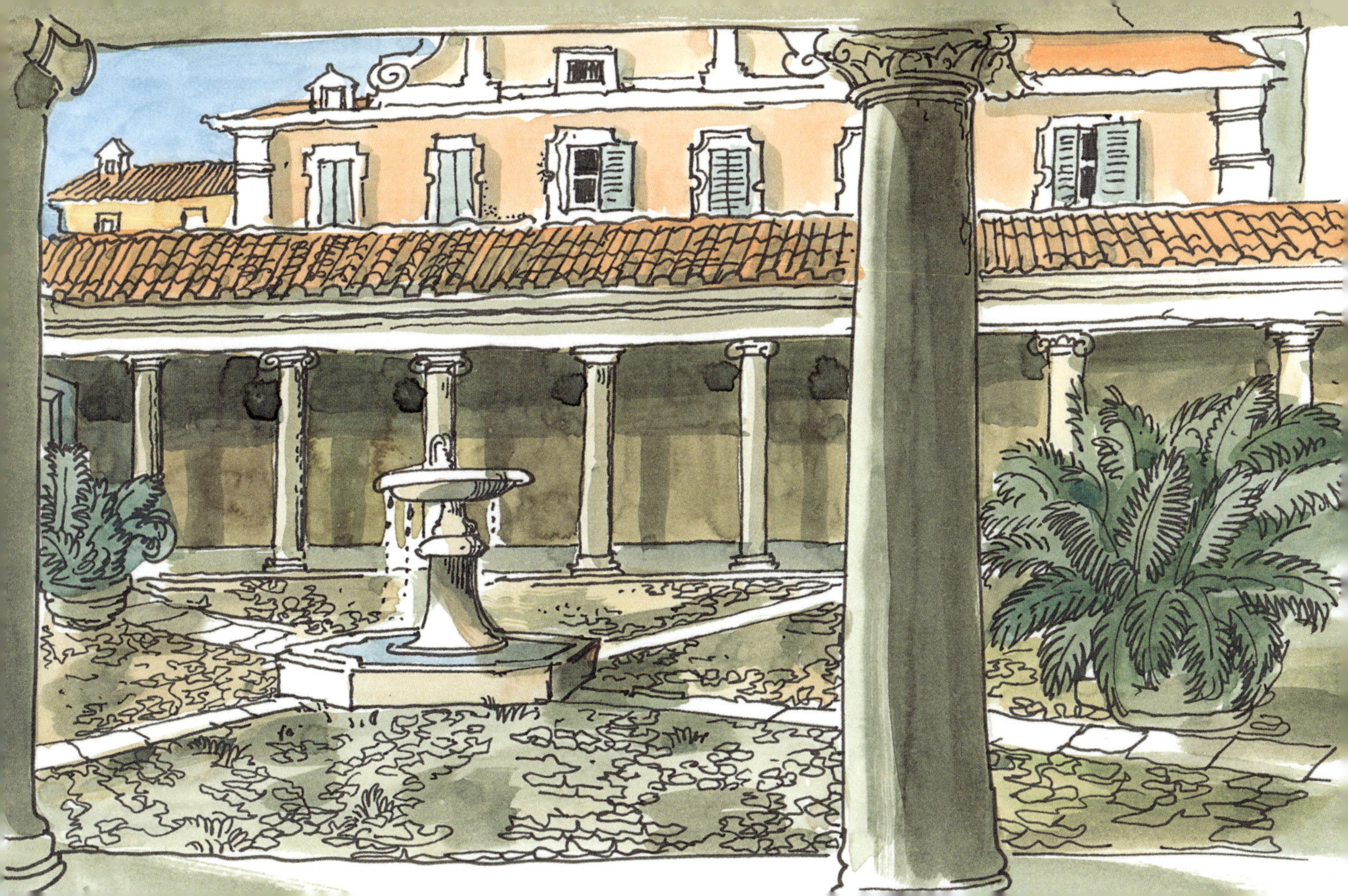

The Aventine

The advantage of a city with hills is that views change in a very short distance. The crows in Rome are the hooded variant, their smart ash-grey capes and breasts making them better dressed than the dowdy, black-suited English birds. As the smart crow flies, the shady, SOFT Aventine Hill is only a few hundred metres from bustling Testaccio, the tourist-crammed Forum or the busy traffic along the Tiber. Yet it is elevated, isolated from the noise. Below, the brown mammoth of the Baths of Caracalla is one of those monuments that challenges the imagination. It is almost impossible to see this as more than a monstrous pile of bricks, yet it was once full of bathers and sportsmen, and clad in marble, gilded and painted throughout. Now, it is hard to observe anything other than that it is HUGE. I shouldn't bother with it, but, rather, head on to the quiet Via di Santa Sabina, a ten-minute climb or a more strenuous one up the track from the riverside, which leads you up stone steps into another world of glossy orange trees, shady stone pines and green grass.

The church of Santa Sabina is the key to this gentler Rome. It is visible from Trastevere only as a plain brown hulk, yet its interior is as beautiful as any in the city. Although much restored, re-thought and adjusted, it remains in form and in atmosphere a simple late-fourth-century basilica and, in fact, is the oldest extant Christian basilica in Rome. Its monolithic columns once supported the portico of a Temple of Jupiter on the same – very commanding – site. It contains a pair of doors carved of cypress wood, which, astonishingly, have survived since its construction in AD 430–432. The doors are, unsurprisingly, late Classical in style and expressively carved with scenes from the life of Christ, including an early depiction of the Crucifixion with the two robbers. They are so well preserved that the work leaps across the centuries and makes very real the earliest years of Christian Europe. The apse is decorated with characteristic vertical bands of purple porphyry and carefully book-matched, pale, blue-grey marble. In front, the low, marble walled choir, the *schola cantorum*, is decorated with repeating patterns of a complex, twisting, almost Celtic design. When I visited,

The graceful, arched, fourth-century basilica of Santa Sabina, Aventine Hill.

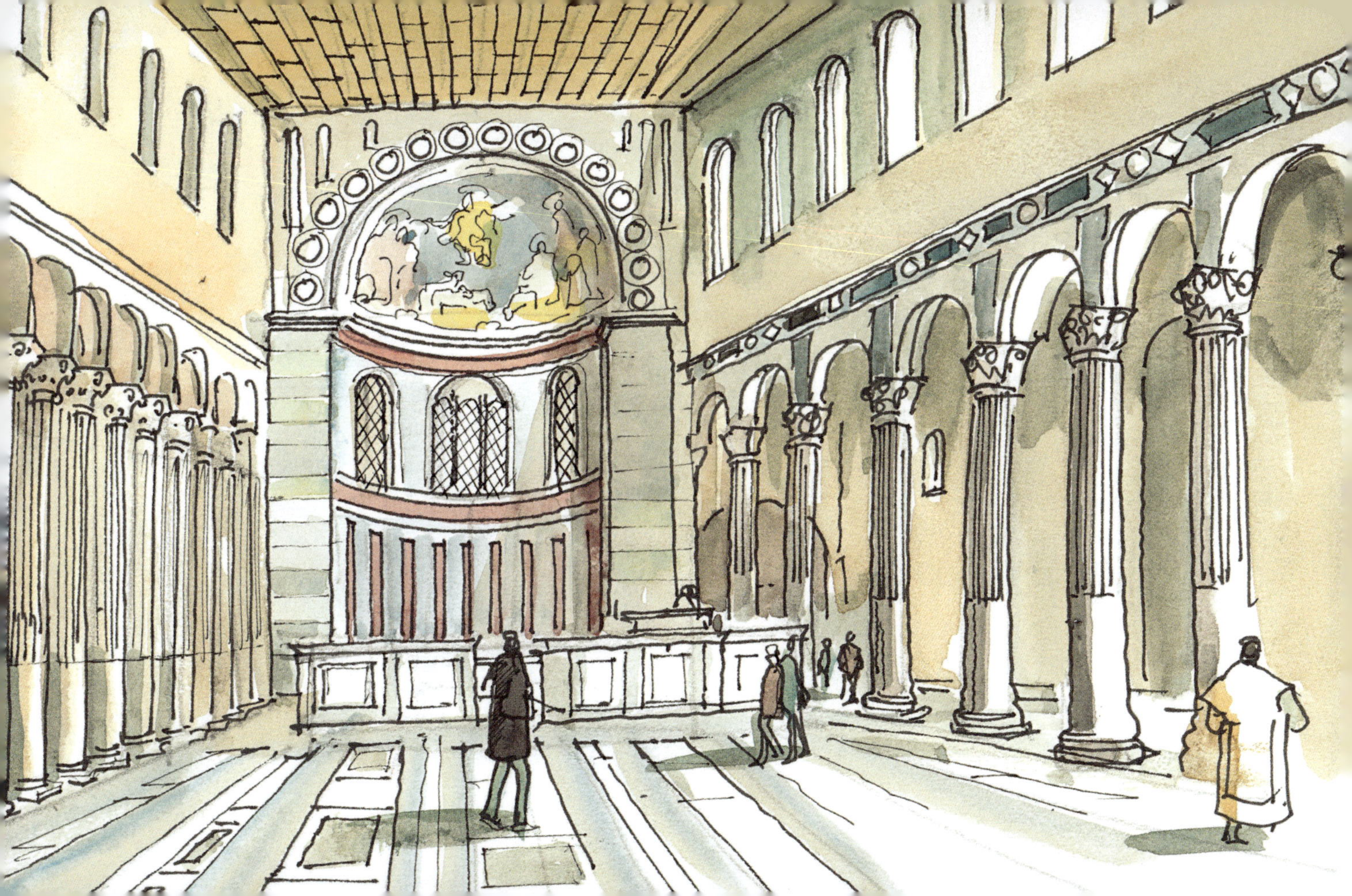

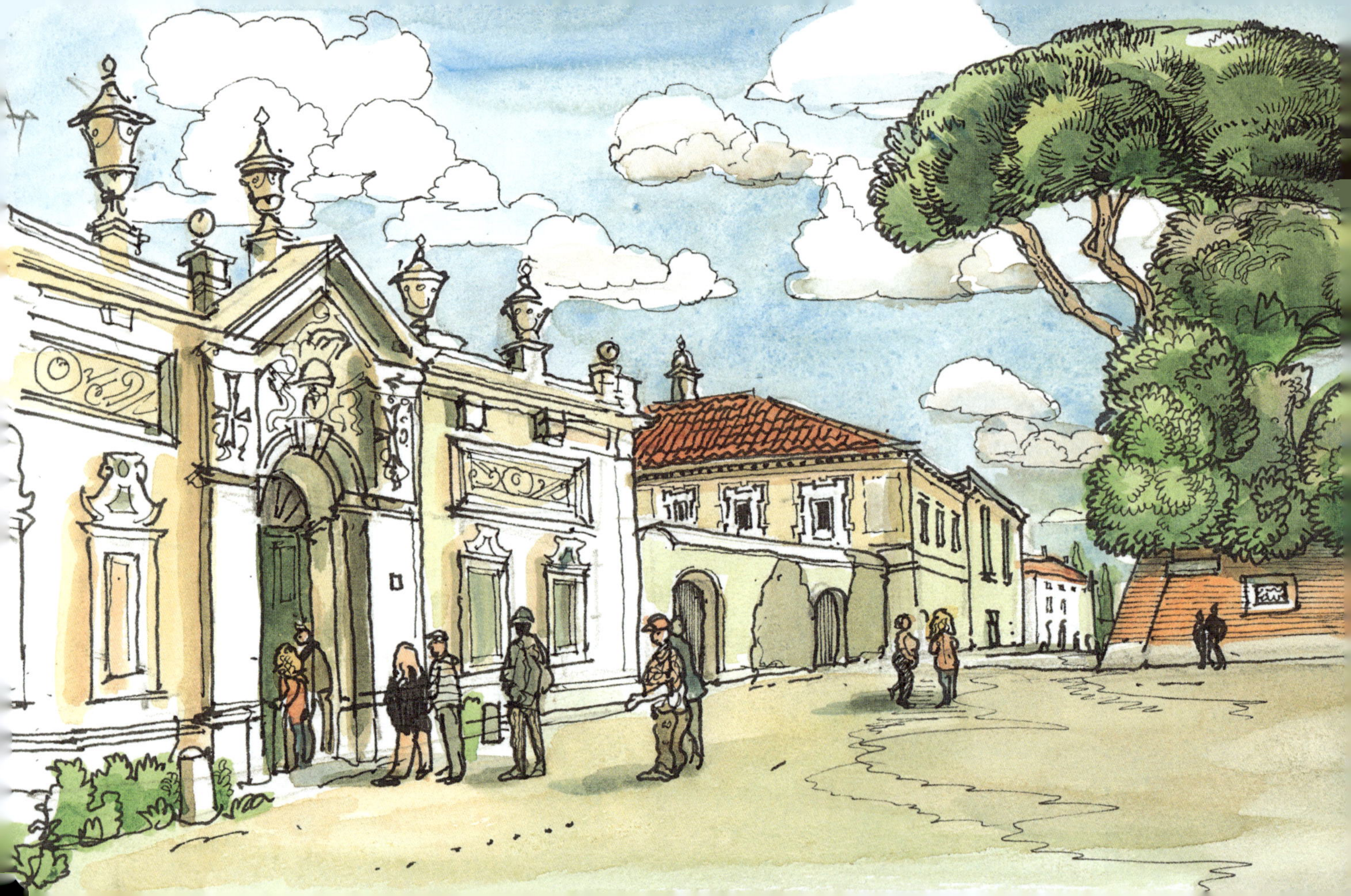

I could hear the organ from the courtyard outside: at the modern console, a very accomplished organ scholar freshly returned from a year in Germany was rattling through Bach preludes and fugues, lending the perfect soundtrack to this distinguished church. The large windows were re-made a century ago in an approximation of their imagined original form, with flat patterned stone tracery and with selenite, a creamy crystal, in place of glass, giving a warm, soft cast to the whole building.

Santa Sabina is the initial home of the Dominican order, its dark-cloaked brotherhood devoted to spreading the gospel in the wide world. They were known as the Blackfriars and had been instituted by St Dominic, in France in 1216. They were granted the church as head-quarters in 1219. The day I visited, the monastic scene was completed by the SWISHING HABITS of two friars crossing the shiny stone floor.

Further up the road, in front of a blank wall topped by urns and framed within a modest (by Roman standards) pediment, is a fairly desultory line of pilgrims waiting politely. Some are walking away from the queue to buy a *panino* or sustaining ice cream, as taxis disgorge new

Queuing to see St Peter's in miniature through the gate of the Knights of Malta.

recruits. At first, there is no explanation for the straggling line, the denizens of which appear only to be bowing slightly before rather a bathetic faded dark-green door of the Knights of Malta. The scene does look slightly peculiar, but it is happening for a reason. In the door is a keyhole through which, carefully planned and framed by bay and box in the garden within, is a flawless view of the dome of St Peter's. Whether it is the delayed gratification, the effect of the ice cream or the delicious miniaturization of such a mighty building, it is remarkably exciting.

Walking down the stone staircase overhung with figs and capers, the peace is drowned by traffic as you hit the riverside main drag, but you are faced by two perfect temples surviving in the old Forum Boarium. The first, the Temple of Hercules Victor, is circular in plan with a pantiled octagonal cap and, despite its great age – second century BC – its Corinthian columns are astonishingly well preserved. In geometric contrast is the similarly pleasing rectangular Ionic Temple of Portunus, while across the road is the much-visited jewelbox of Santa Maria in Cosmedin. This ancient church has a numinous and beautiful interior, but the Bocca della Verità is the main attraction. This slightly hideous face is housed in the medieval porch and is alleged to trap the hands of liars in its stony gob.

The Campus Martius

The Old City, between the ancient Forum and the Vatican, lies on the low ground beneath the ridge of the Pincian–Quirinal–Esquiline hills. It was in Imperial days called the Campus Martius. This area, north of the Capitoline, was outside Romulus's original city boundary, the *pomerium*. Initially an open space for gatherings and military tattoos, it was the site of the Villa Publica, where the census was taken. As the population grew, both residential and civic buildings began to be erected on this 600-acre site that runs from the theatres of Marcellus and Pompey to the Stadium of Domitian, a long oblong racetrack of the first century A D, on which the Piazza Navona now stands. This contains Bernini's most dramatic Fountain of the Four Rivers and the gently curving façade of Borromini's Sant'Agnese in Agone. (The term *in agone*, which led to the name 'navona', referred to the exertions of the competitors in races and other sports.) Nearby Campo de' Fiori was for centuries the site of the city's main food market, following its move from the Capitoline.

After the final Barbarian sackings of Rome, the vital aqueducts that sustained life in the city were destroyed in the sixth century. It was easier by far to starve out the city, rendering its citizens raving with thirst, than lay siege to its substantial walls. This made the hills of Rome uninhabitable, so the rump of the settlement moved down to the Campus Martius, where, although highly unpalatable and often downright dangerous to drink, the waters of the Tiber could be utilized. For centuries, pilgrims arriving at the city of St Peter, the very centre of Christianity and the Holy Catholic Church, were astonished to find the fabled metropolis reduced to a large medieval village interspersed with the hulk-like brick or stone fortresses of powerful families, housed either in classical ruins (the Frangipanis holed up in the Colosseum, the Pierleonis in the Theatre of Marcellus) or substantial brick towers, some of which survive in reduced form today.

With the rise of Renaissance Rome, this low-lying area became the commercial and residential centre of the city

Piazza Navona and one of Rome's many obelisks imported from Egypt. This one was in the Circus of Villa Maxentius on the Via Appia, *right*; writhing Tritons and waterhorses in the Trevi Fountain, by Salvi, *overleaf*.

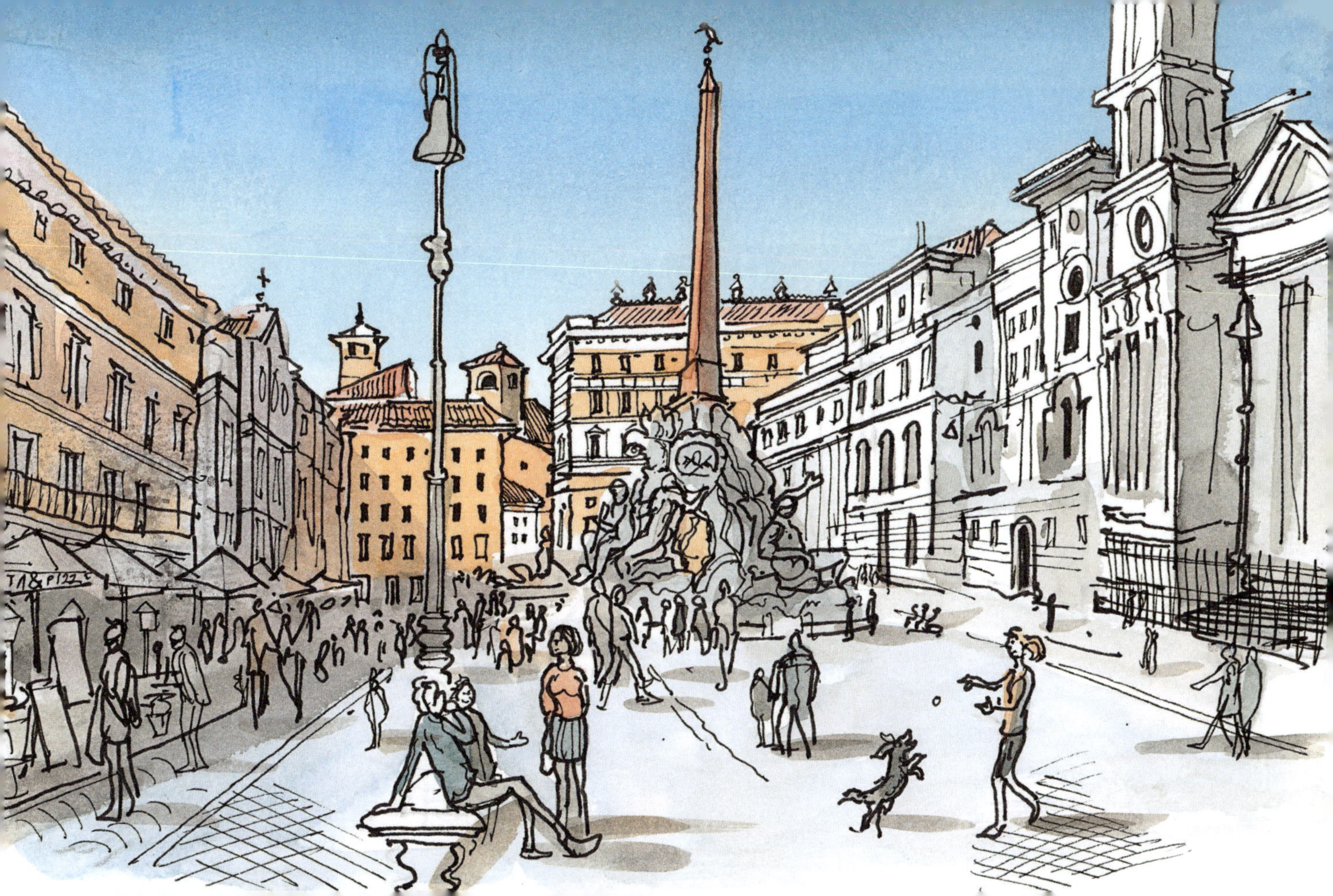
TAVL & PIZZA

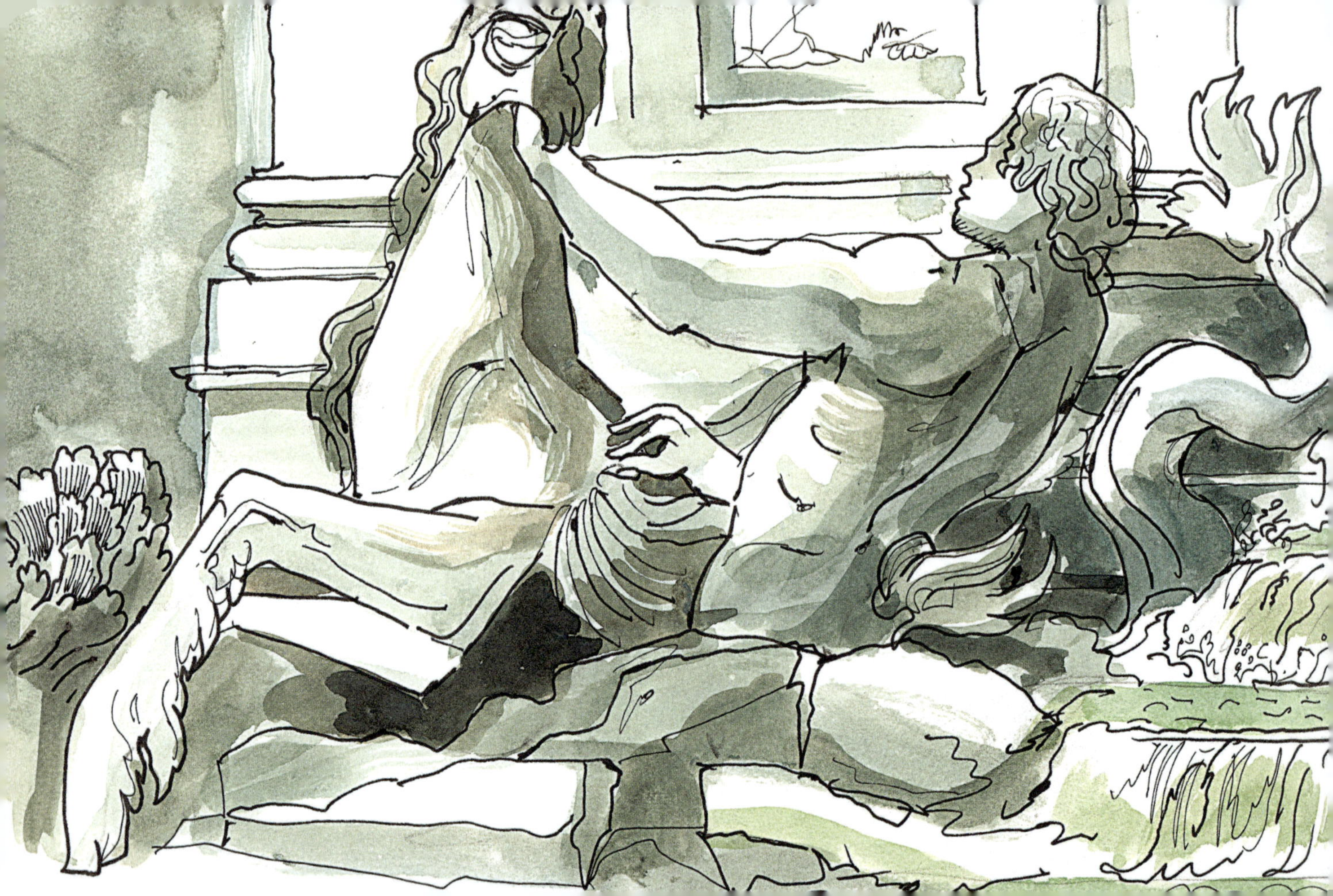

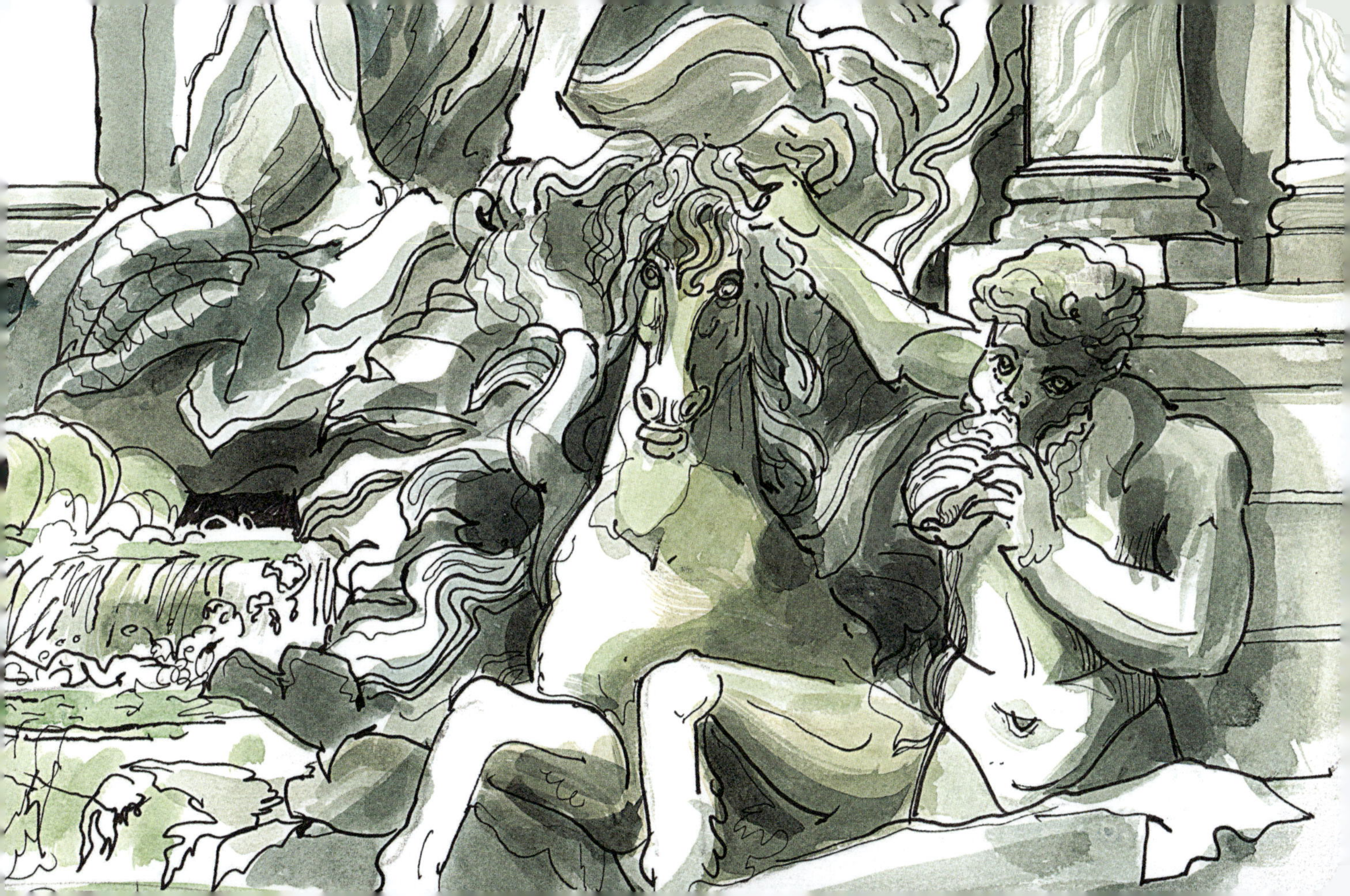

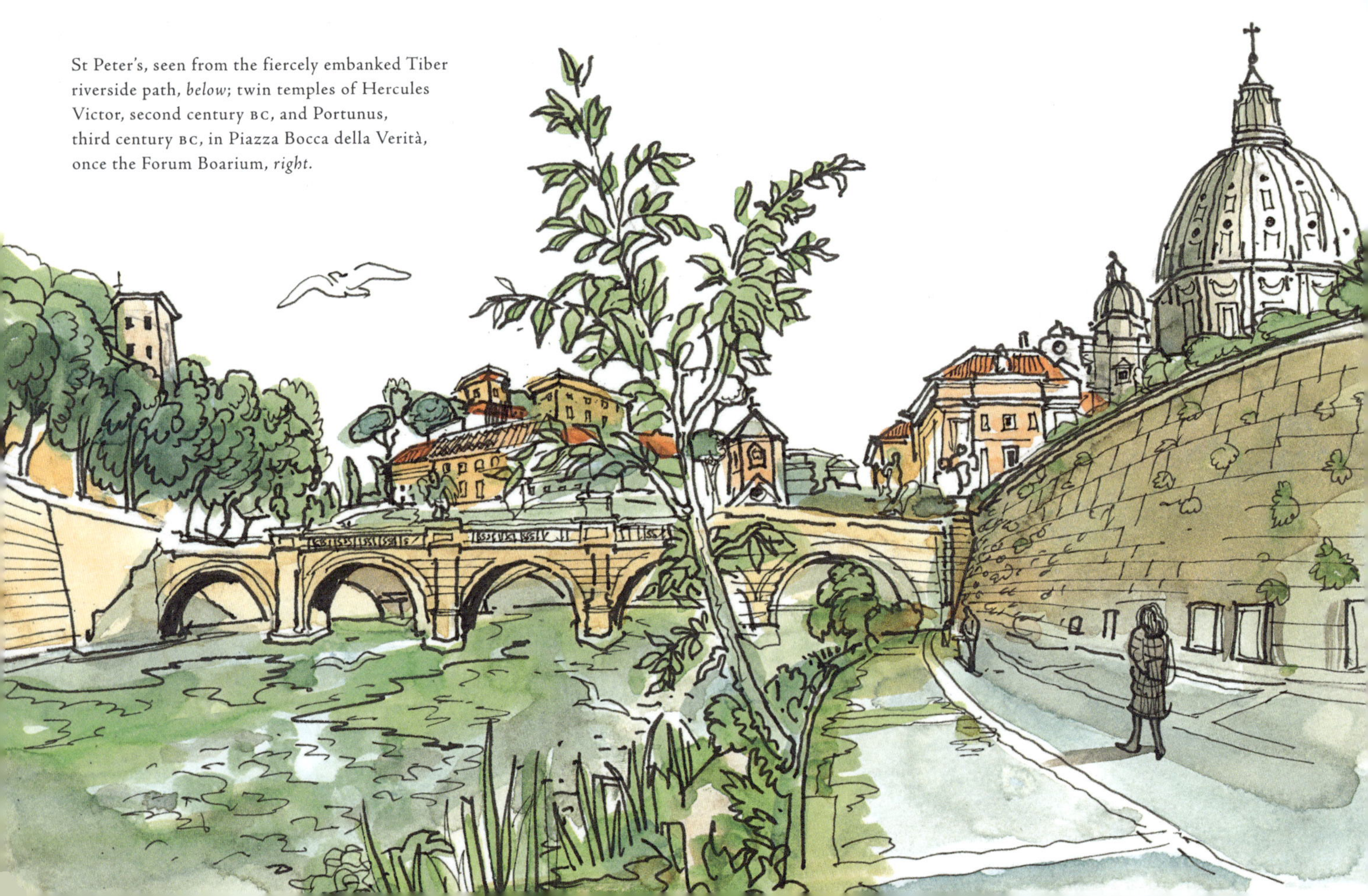

St Peter's, seen from the fiercely embanked Tiber riverside path, *below*; twin temples of Hercules Victor, second century BC, and Portunus, third century BC, in Piazza Bocca della Verità, once the Forum Boarium, *right*.

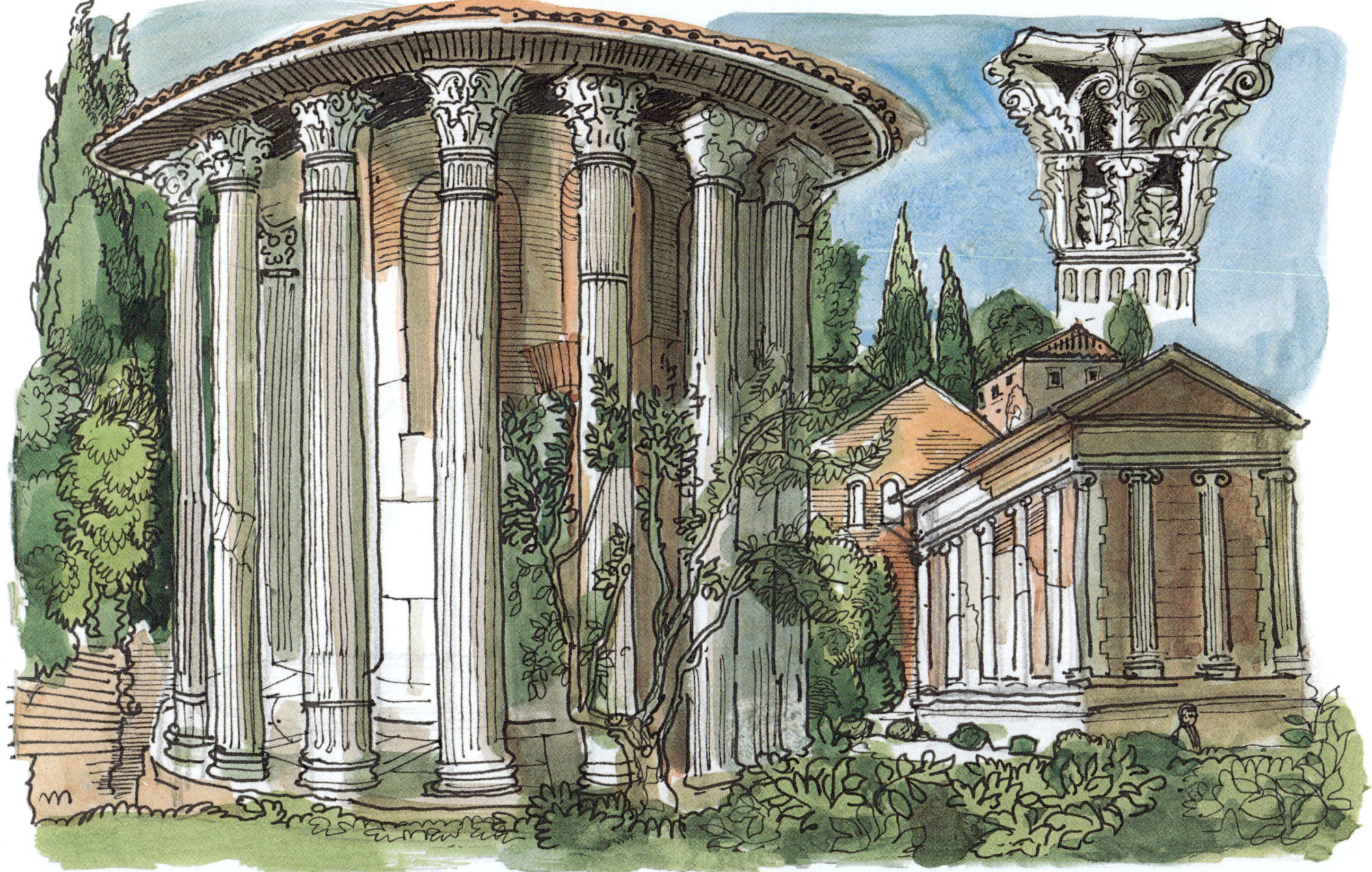

and, gradually, the low-rise medieval settlement turned back into a gracious European capital. The embankment of the Tiber in the nineteenth century cut the city off from its river, and what was once a tumble of riparian shacks and enterprises much favoured by painters seeking the picturesque became a limestone canyon with no connection to the surrounding city.

Today, the Campus Martius is the centre of tourist Rome. It is sliced in half by the Via del Corso, which connects the Piazza Venezia to the Piazza del Popolo. The street was once a racetrack with large crowds of high-spirited Romans encouraging or jeering contests that would not have been entirely to our tastes: the long-awaited races of the Jews or the prostitutes – happily, it is now mainly pedestrianized and full of smart shops.

The Piazza Navona, Pantheon and the Trevi Fountain are genuinely unmissable treats, and it is worth engineering early-morning glimpses for uninterrupted views. Yet even on a dawn expedition you will not be alone, for the fountains will already be lined with the utterly charming phenomenon of the insta-boyfriend carefully styling his partner in front of a world-famous view. It's become a key part of Roman-fountain-tourism – and why not, as the water creates a pale-emerald aqueous background that is hard to beat.

The Pantheon is the great intact relict of Imperial Rome. Built first as a temple by General Marcus Agrippa (son-in-law of Augustus) from 27 BC–AD 14, it was burnt down and then rebuilt by Hadrian in AD 126. As with so many other repurposed temples, its HEATHEN ORIGINS were forgotten, and it has been a church, of Santa Maria ad Martyres, since the seventh century. It is to that conversion that it owes its remarkable survival, although its bronze roof was removed in AD 663 by the Emperor Constans II. Further north, the streets take on a business-like atmosphere, and the police-military presence is ratchetted up as suited diners fill the cafés, revealing that this quarter is the seat of the Italian parliament.

There are smaller *piazze*, too, each with its *trattorie* and bars, as well as a series of churches and fountains, including Santa Maria sopra Minerva, the only Gothic church of note. In front of it, one of Rome's smaller Egyptian obelisks rests on the broad back of a charming elephant. At the northernmost end of the Via del Corso is the Piazza del Popolo, a huge neo-Classical wasteland.

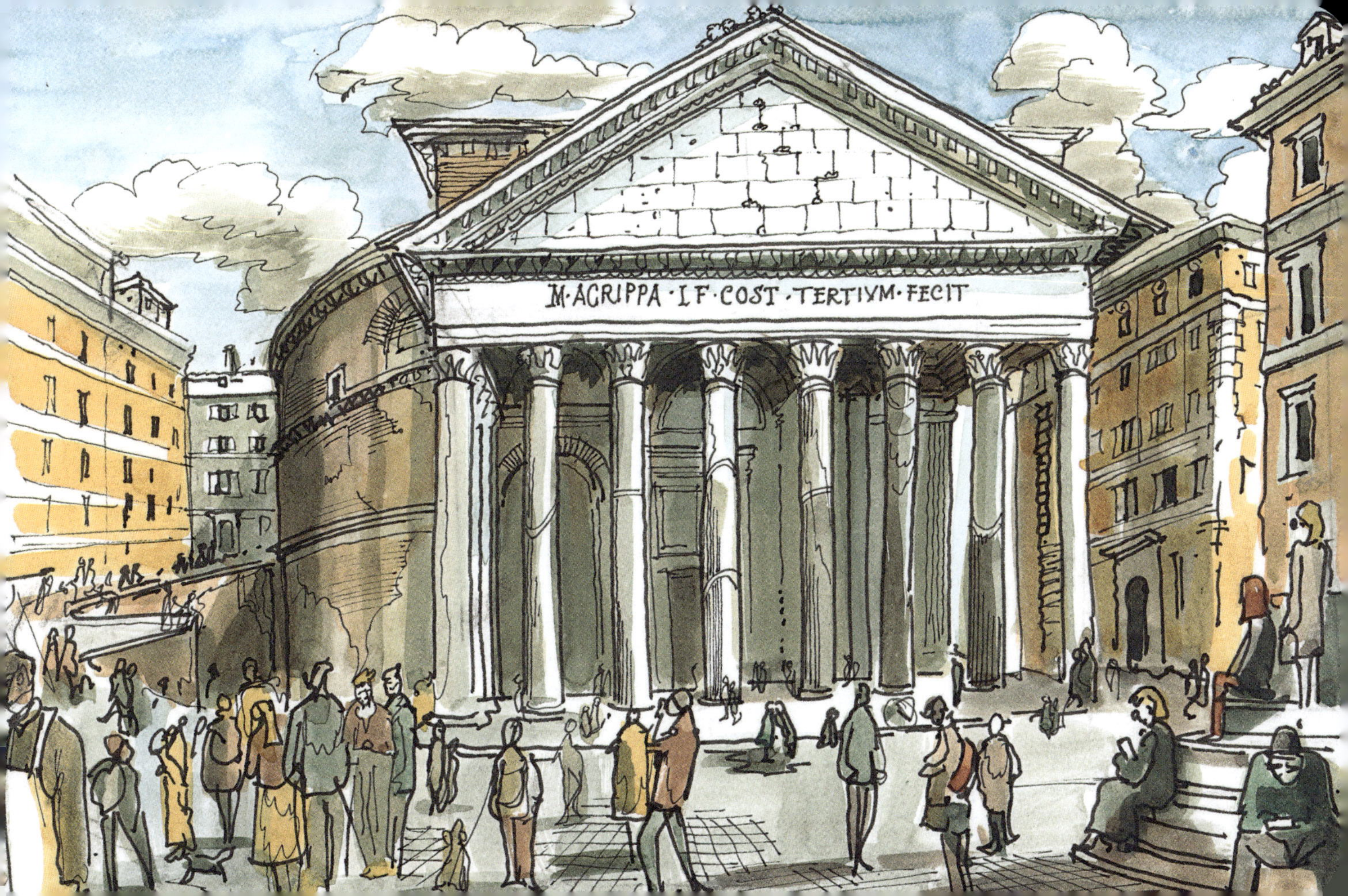

M·AGRIPPA · L·F·COST · TERTIVM·FECIT

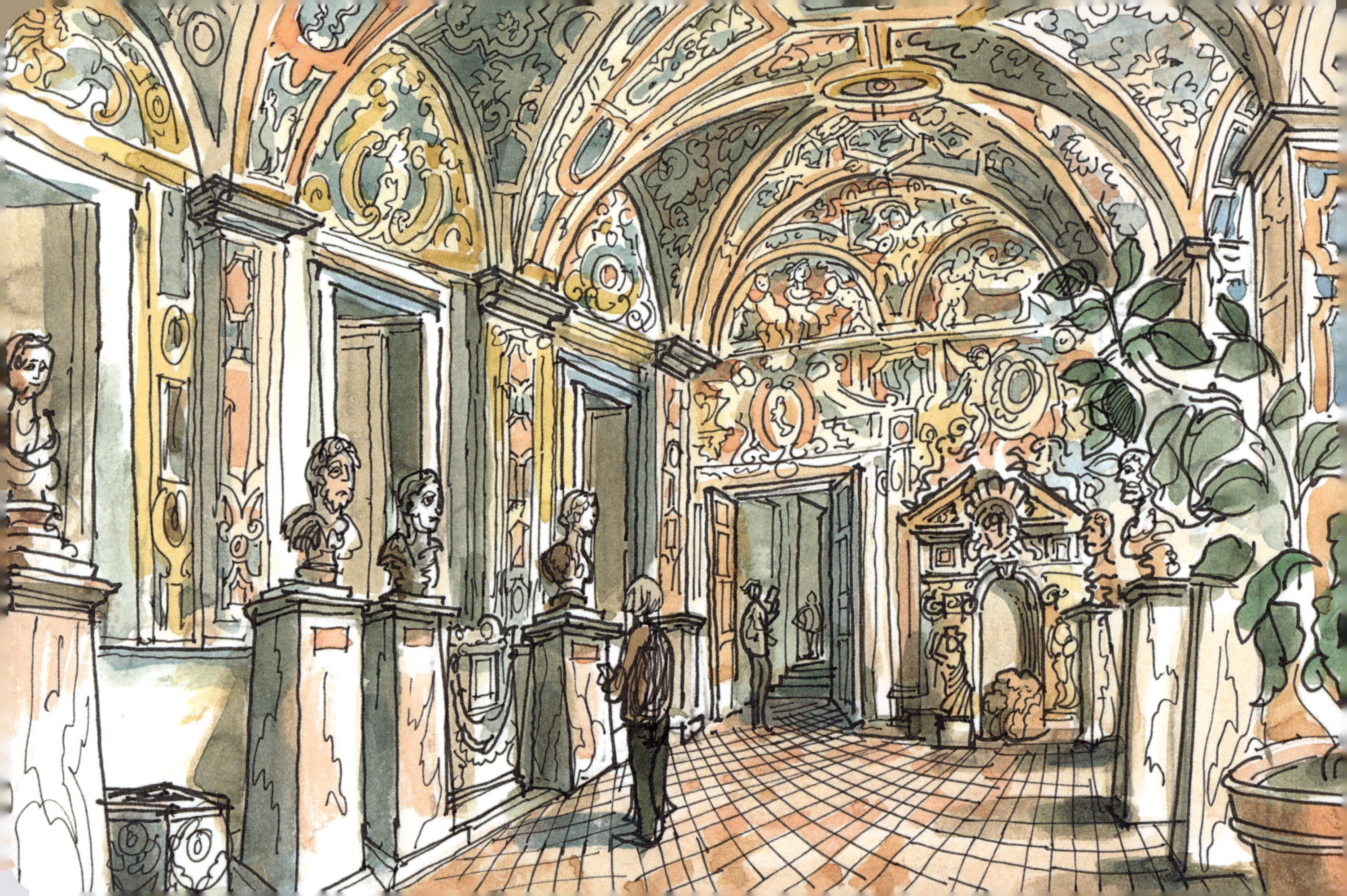

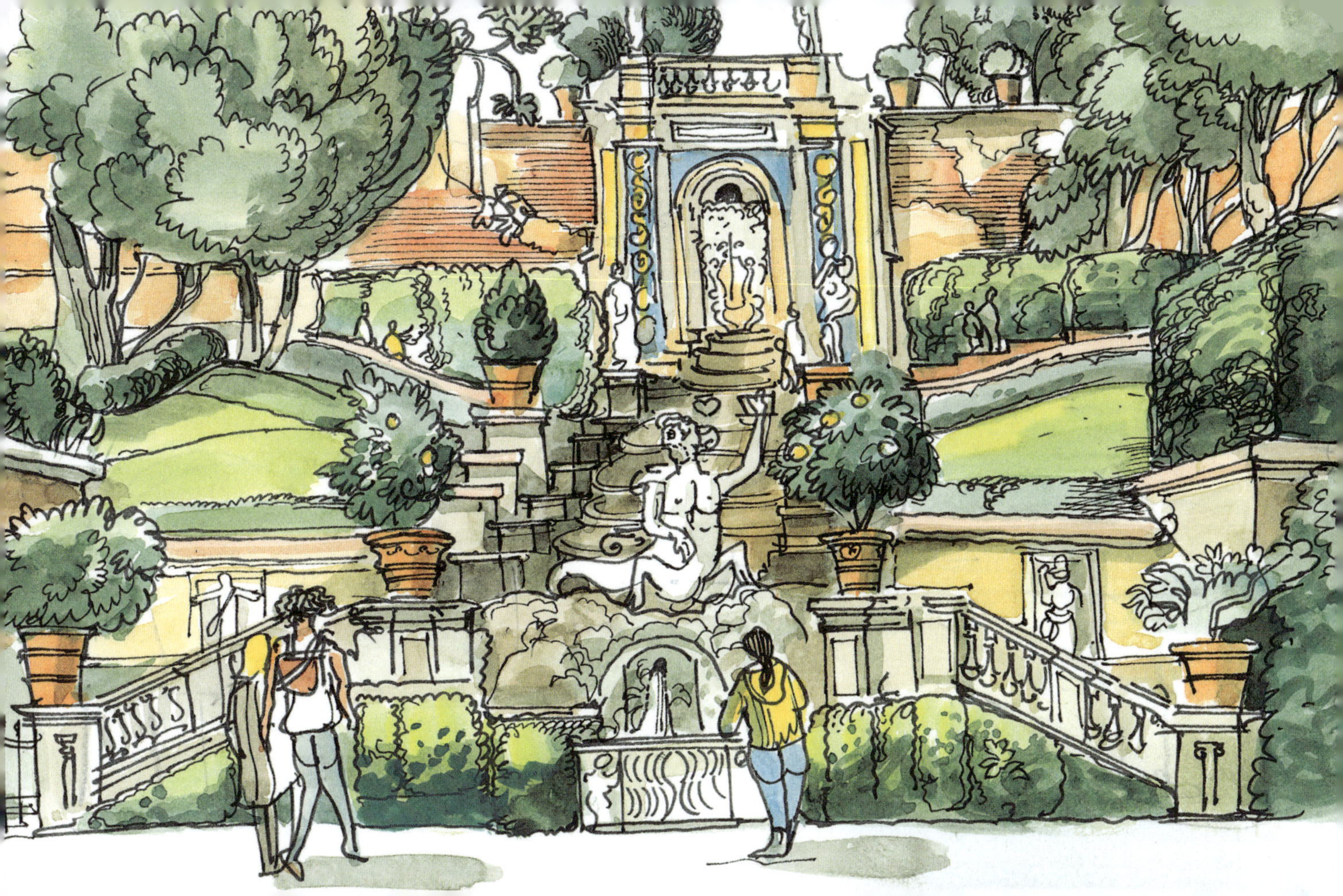

Two nearly matching domed churches face a complex arched gate giving onto (via a death-dealing inner ring road) the Borghese gardens. A little way to the south on the bank of the Tiber is a large site comprising the burial site of the God-emperor Augustus, a huge and ruined concrete drum, with, immediately alongside, the Ara Pacis, an altar to Augustus. Housed in a modern glass box – and rather hot, be warned – this *tour de force* is a heavily carved narrative work, the walls decorated with a repeating arabesque pattern below reliefs illustrating the story of Augustus's life. The deification of emperors feels implausible, but the Roman concept of a god in a pantheistic world makes it more reasonable. In any case, here it is, built in marble and surviving for 2,000 years… and you can walk into it.

Nearer the river, the character of the streets changes. International brands disappear as all roads lead to Campo de'Fiori. At the height of its counter-reformational powers, the Catholic church took a hard line on its opponents, among the most notable being Giordano Bruno. His heretical views included doubts about the Trinity and a deep mistrust of the veracity of the virgin birth. He was duly burnt on a pile of crackling faggots, but, two centuries later, a kinder age commemorated him with a cowled bronze statue in the middle of the square previously known for its executions and pilgrim hotels. Now, a large fountain is surrounded with flower sellers, and the market, selling vegetables and cheeses, is cleared in the afternoon to allow smart bars to face one another across the void.

Only a street away is the Palazzo Farnese, one of Michelangelo's greatest buildings. Its regular, pared-back form and first-floor windows with alternating curved and pointed pediments were repeated in clubs and civic buildings throughout nineteenth-century Europe and America. IT IS A SEMINAL BUILDING. Nearby is the Palazzo Spada, with its famed *trompe-l'oeil* colonnaded passage and remarkable collection of paintings.

Tight against the Theatre of Marcellus is the Roman ghetto. There have been Jews in Rome for more than 2,000 years, with many arriving after the fall of Jerusalem following the first Jewish revolt in AD 70. The Via del Portico d'Ottavia is at the centre of the old ghetto and is lined with kosher restaurants. The Roman Jews were powerful among European Jewry in the Middle Ages owing to the longevity of their residence and the generally agreed purity of their liturgy and manifestation of the faith.

Soldiers in camouflage guard the marigolds in the Campo de'Fiori.

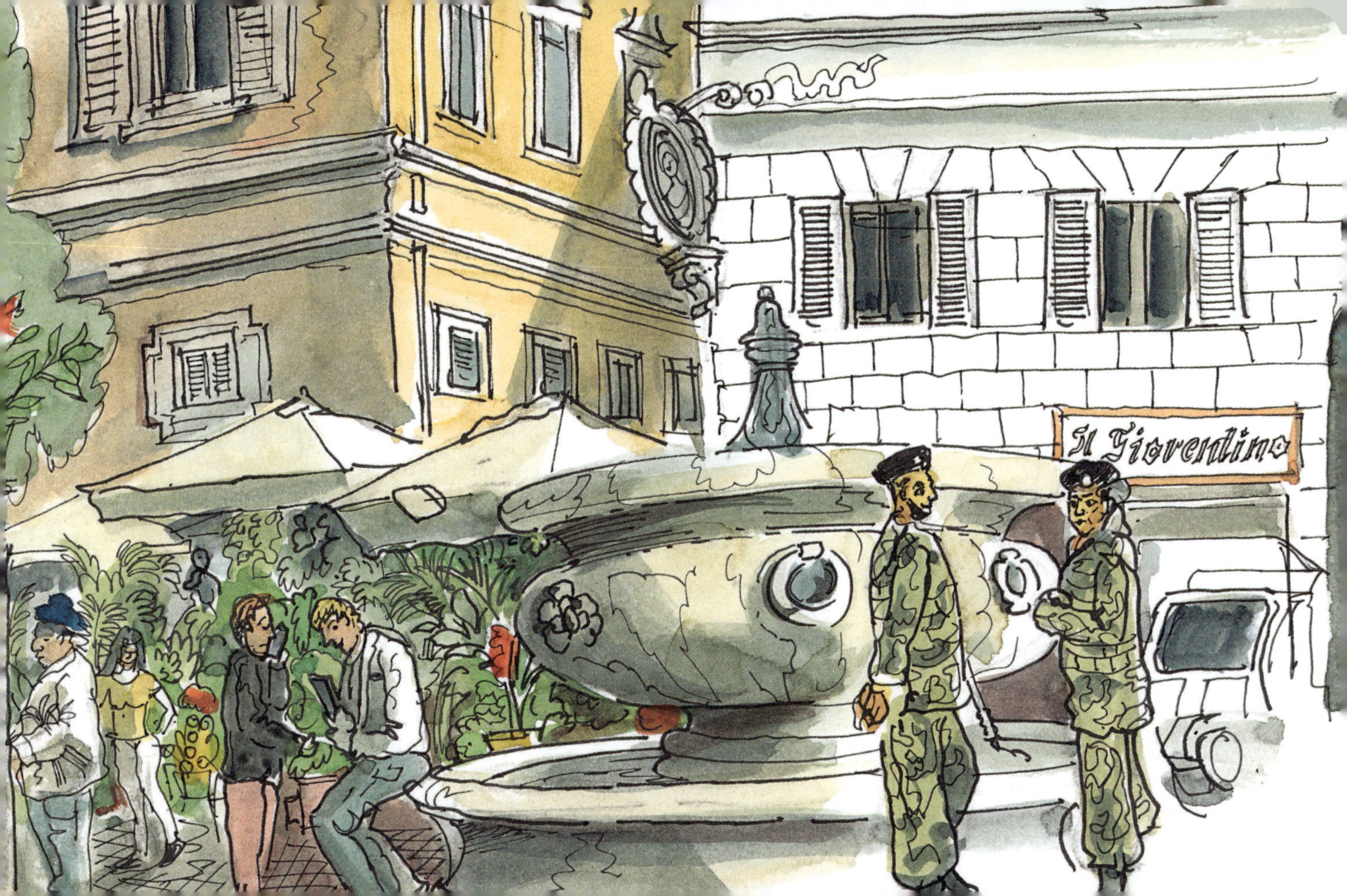
Il Fiorentino

The Hills

Of the hills that make up a great part of historic Rome, some are blatantly expressed and some are occluded. Among the most obvious is the Pincian Hill with its flight of Spanish Steps, which was built in 1725 to regularize the steep incline. The Steps also served to connect the Spanish embassy and French church on the hill to the Piazza di Spagna below, with its naval fountain by Bernini (*père et fils*). This is also, famously, where John Keats lived and died, his bed right up against the window to allow the sweetest view of the Steps. From them, a deceptively gentle slope takes you gradually up the Via Sistina to the Piazza Barberini and the *palazzo* of that name. The great lantern-bearing atlantids around the *palazzo* give only a whiff of the treats inside, for the Barberini pope, Urban VIII, was building in the grandest yet lightest of styles.

The two bravura staircases test the most accomplished draughtsman. One rectangular in plan, by Bernini, and the other Borromini's oval, or helicoidal, they rise through several storeys of interrelated columns and pilasters linked by a strong and sinuous rail and comfortably gentle steps. Looking through, or, indeed, up or down, is the ultimate Baroque architectural experience. They are full of movement and incident, without a hint of seasickness, and might make you want to abandon your visit, sated after ascending the first flight. Luckily, you have to see the whole gallery before you can descend the second. Two great paintings might be all you need, one of which is Raphael's serious and sexy portrait *La Fornarina*, the baker's girl. It feels as if she was, indeed, the painter's lover, to have totally engaged his attention. It is the most powerful painting, as, clasping the thinnest SCRUMPLE OF MUSLIN between her breasts, she fixes the viewer with an intense and level stare.

A no less powerful record of the MALE GAZE is Caravaggio's *Judith Beheading Holofernes*. The murderous protagonist is meditatively forcing her sword deep into the agonized neck of her subject, his body wrenched from sleep by this rudest of shocks. Her wrinkled maidservant stands by in attentive horror with a gloomy hessian

The church of Trinità dei Monti at the top of the Spanish Steps, *right*; parterres and glasshouses behind the Palazzo Barberini, 1625–33, and the park of the Villa Borghese, given to the people of Rome in 1903, *overleaf*.

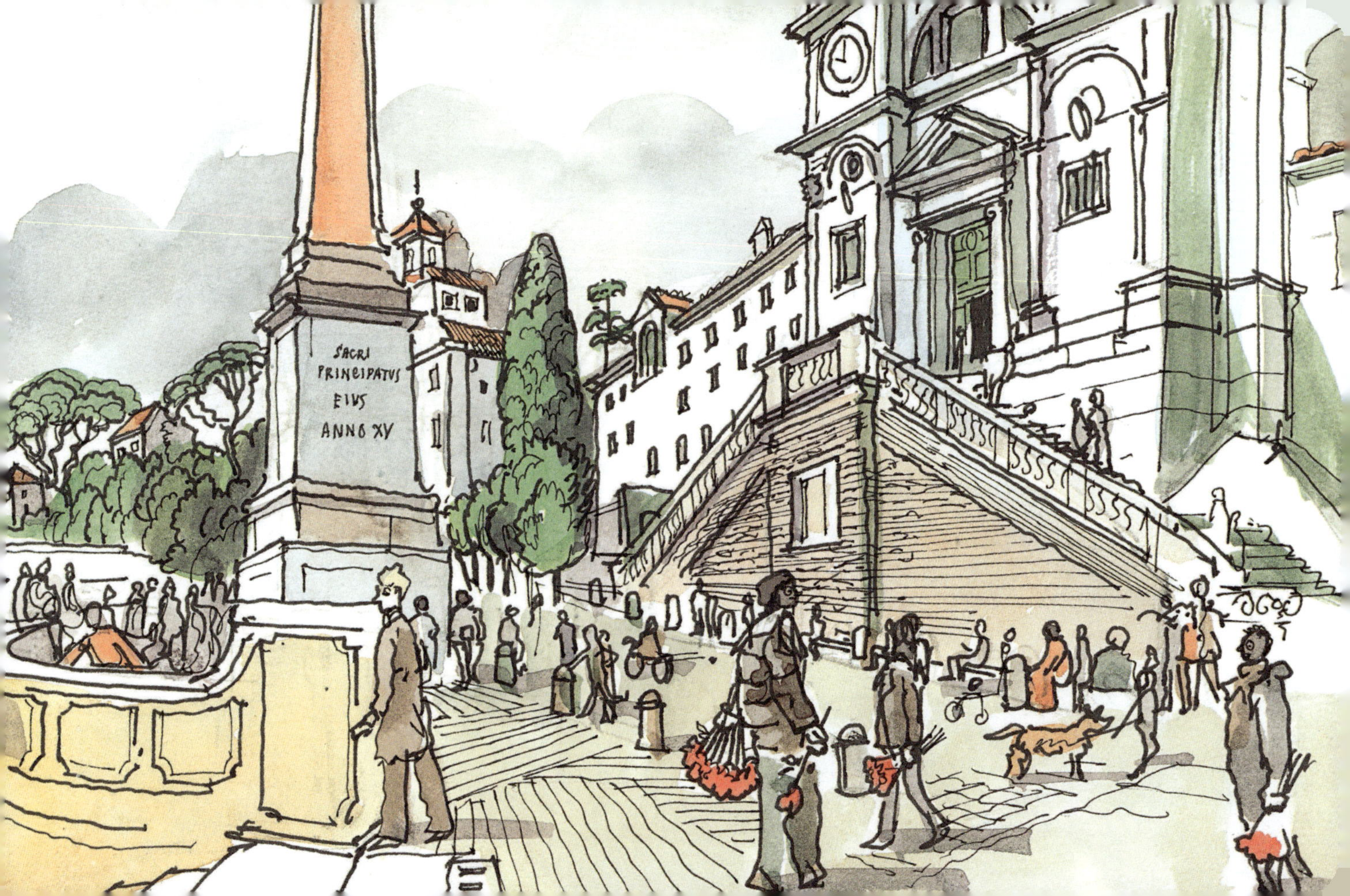

SACRI
PRINCIPATVS
EIVS
ANNO XV

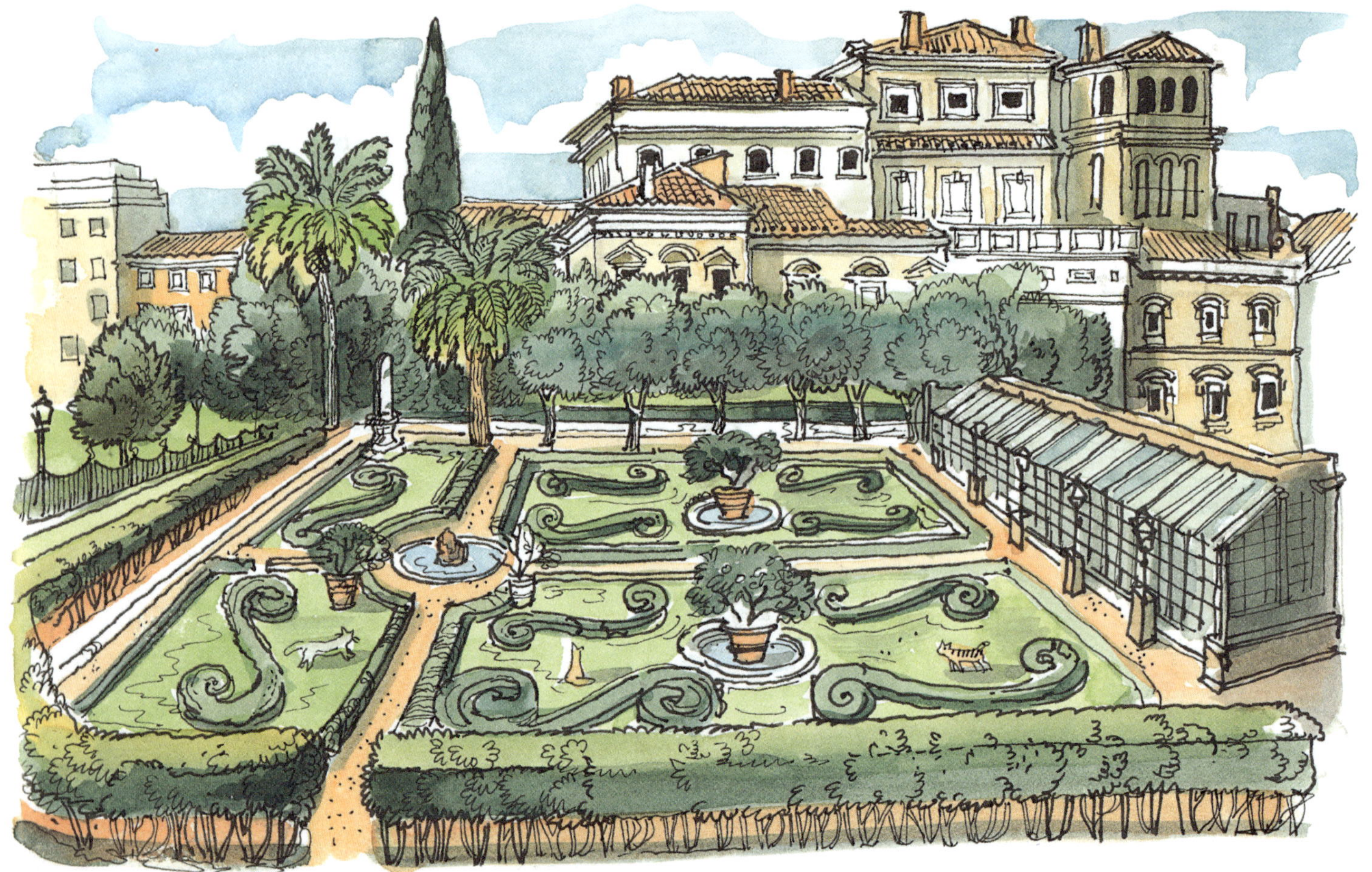

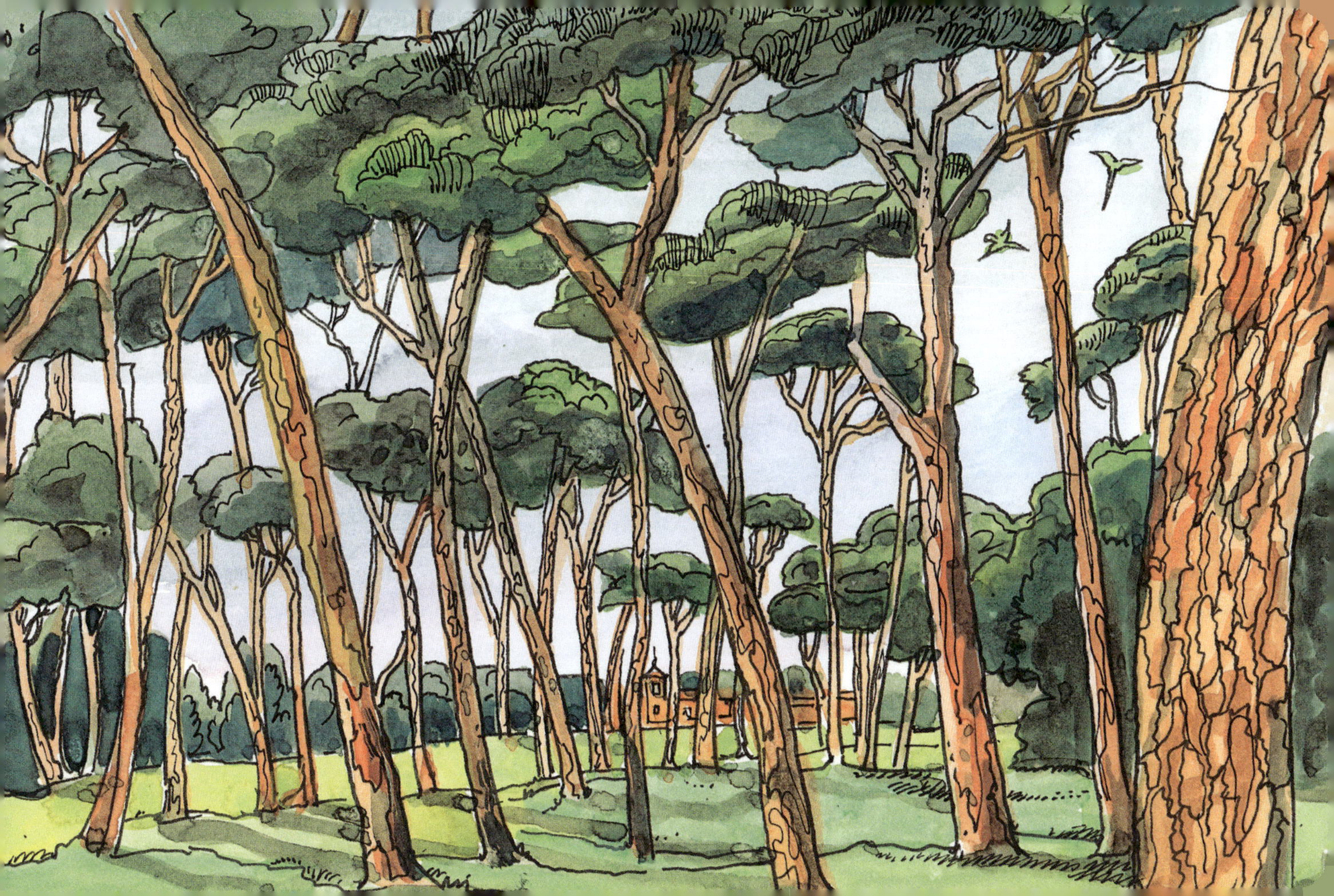

receptacle as Judith herself performs the felony in the most revealing shirt she could have chosen, thrown into stark contrast by the attendant crone. These two extraordinary paintings hang among hundreds of others and a grand collection of ancient sculpture. Climb the splendid central stair to find a raised parterre, an enviable greenhouse and a colony of the most GLOSSY ROMAN CATS lounging happily against the warming walls.

Monti is the *rione* that covers the area leading up from the Colosseum by way of San Pietro in Vincoli and on to Santa Maria Maggiore. Halfway up the rather steep main drag, the Via Panisperna, is a somewhat forbidding wall (also visible from nearby Via Nazionale). Cuttings like this chiselled into the hills urbanize a bumpy topography, but, in so doing, create narrow canyons that amplify the traffic noise and funnel walkers up the hills, as here, on the Quirinal. An almost invisible street between the two main roads, the Via Mazzarino, takes you up a flight of brick stairs strewn with human detritus and past non-specific slices of ancient remains until, with a breath of relief, you enter the Giardini Aldobrandini attached to the villa of that name. Built by a cardinal who amassed a great collection, now absorbed into the Pamphilj holding, the villa and garden moved into public ownership in 1929. It is the last and most exhausted shred of a moth-eaten botanic garden much visited by dogs and their owners. The place is dusty, a little unloved, and the scrappy lawns have long since lost their aspirations to velvet green, but it remains a secret, still place in the middle of the city, a welcome respite for the trudging visitor. It has statuesque cypresses, umbrella pines, figs, olive trees and tall palms, with enough unusual specimens to remind you that this was once a real botanic garden. With tumbledown statuary, the odd fallen capital and pretty abandoned pavilions, it has a TRISTE CHARM.

Make your way to the far end of the Giardini Aldobrandini for a splendid view of the Forum, domes, lanterns and one of the tall brick towers that once characterized medieval Rome, with as backdrop the rather unloved Vittorio Emanuele II Monument. The defenders of this edifice claim it is the only building in the Forum that gives an impression of the grandeur of the ancient city, whereas less sympathetic pedants say it is too white for Roman marble. Ill-scaled and domineering, it diminishes the extraordinary architectural set piece of the Capitoline, but appears to be a desirable background for photos that require life-threatening traffic-dodging in the Piazza Venezia.

Rectangular staircase in the Palazzo Barberini, designed by Bernini in 1630.

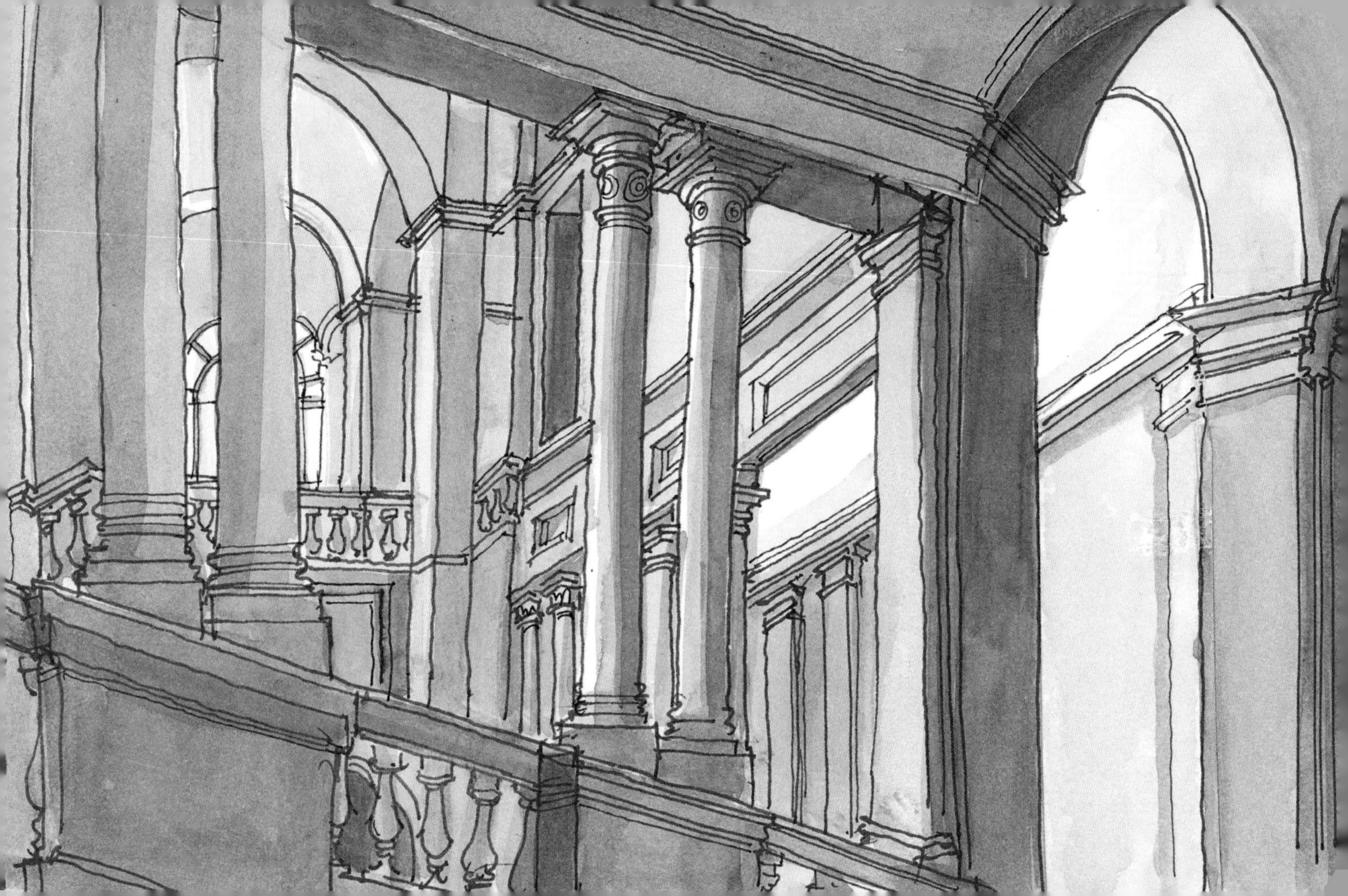

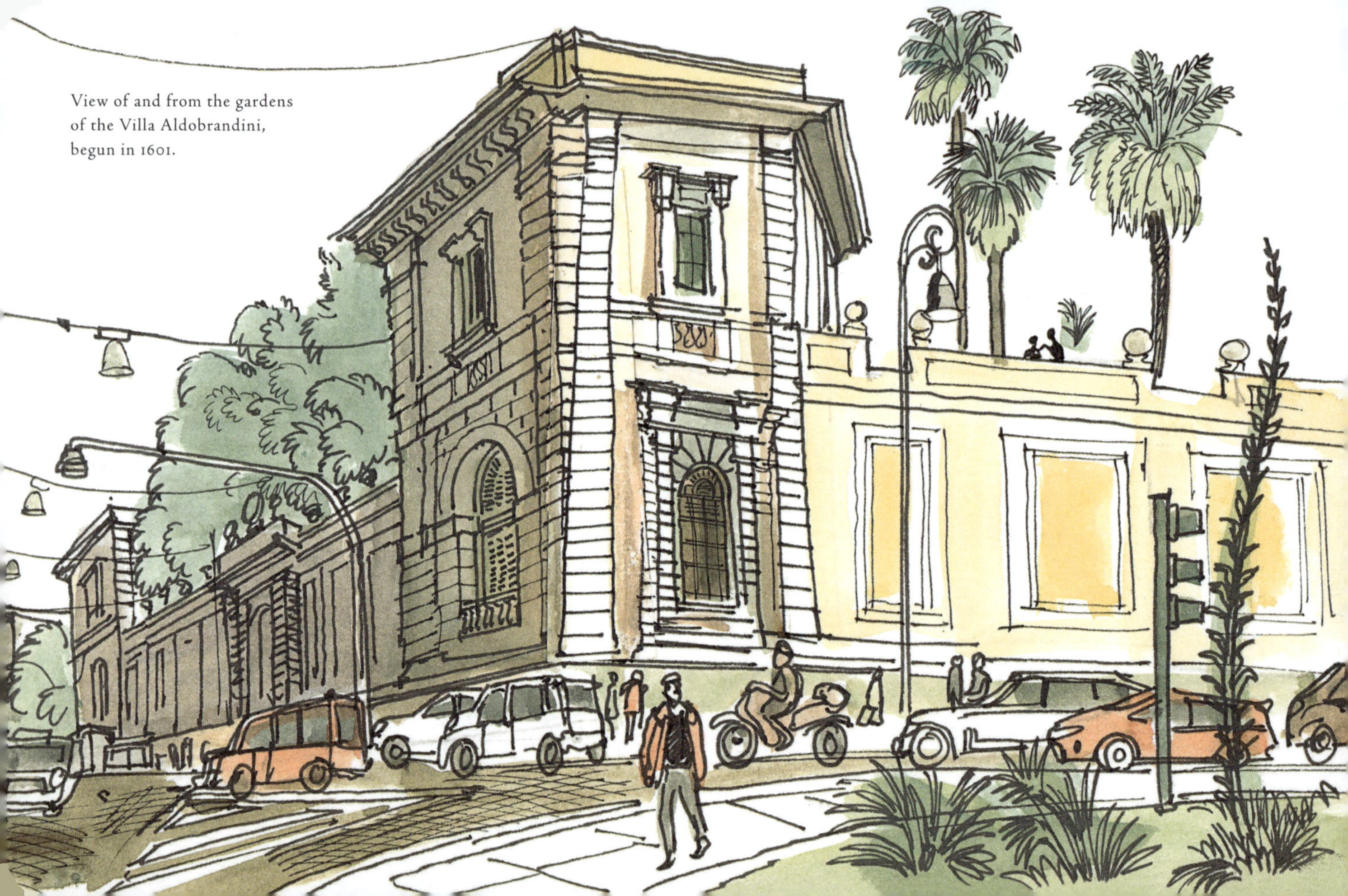

View of and from the gardens
of the Villa Aldobrandini,
begun in 1601.

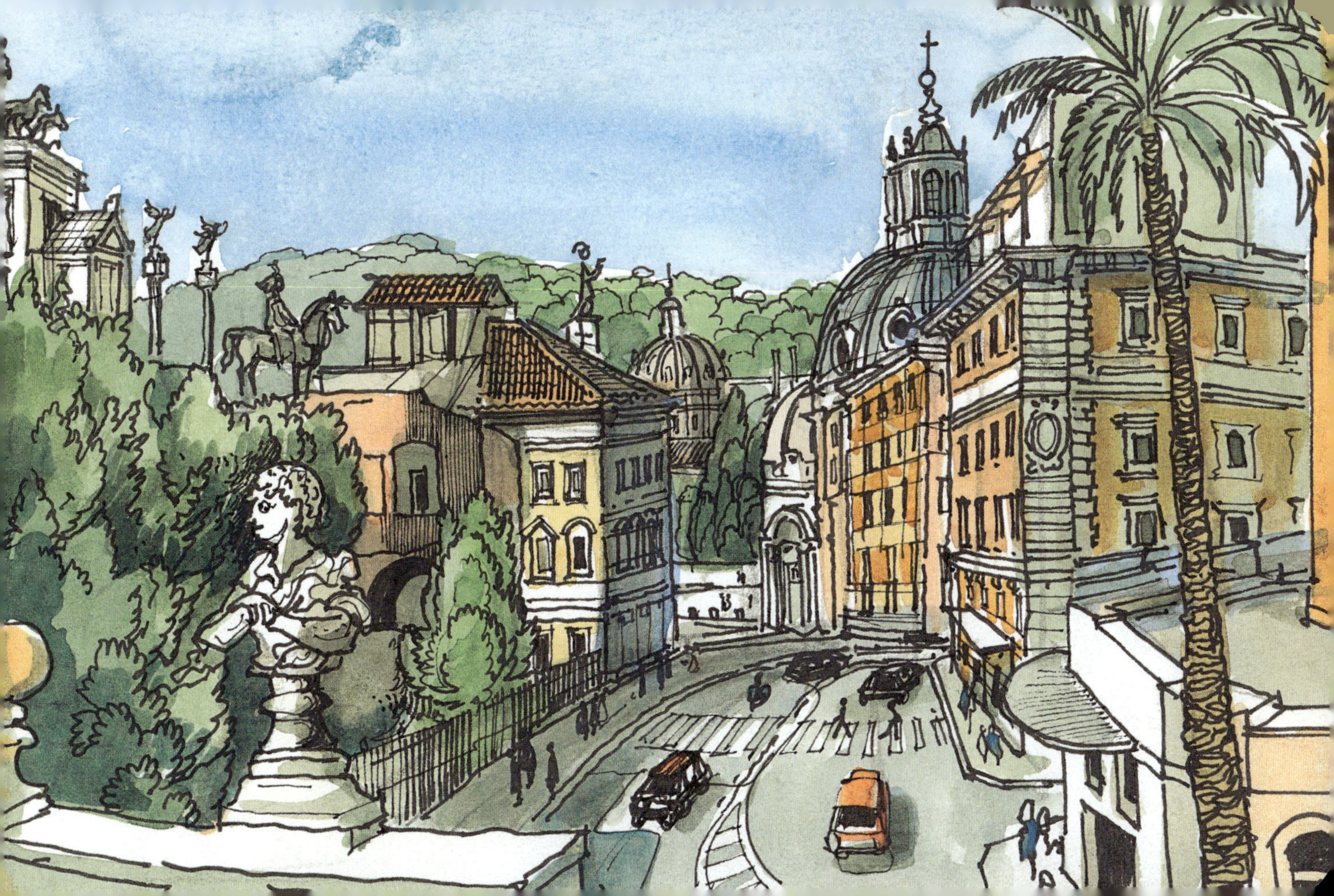

Over the left wall of the Giardini, the church of Santi Domenico e Sisto is a brilliant exercise in site-specific architecture. Perched on top of an urban cliff, its necessarily tall façade forms a prominent feature, visited by hurrying nuns and young priests from all over the world attending the neighbouring Pontifical University of St Thomas Aquinas. The cemetery of the San Lorenzo district, the Verano, is approached down a rough avenue of tin shacks, each housing a brightly coloured flower stall. Napoleon decreed there should be no more burials inside the city, so this graveyard was founded in 1804, outside the walls and over ancient catacombs. Rome is not a city lacking in temples, columns or other architectonic components, yet this cemetery, as in London, Paris and Venice, picks up the gauntlet with odder and odder aedicules, architectural compositions in miniature, from tiny temples to craggy sandstone cliffs and Egyptian kiosks – Egyptian just *is* the international language of Death – to the most strenuous exercises in free-style eclecticism. These reach a nadir in the memorials of great men and their wives who entered the nether world when Mussolini was expressing Fascism in a particularly loveless and massive stony language. The dictator's moll, Clara Petacci, who met a particularly violent death with Il Duce at the hands of the *partigiani* in 1945, was laid to rest here with her family. Ronald Firbank, the exquisite aesthete, is also in the throng, albeit beneath a slab curiously austere for a man whose novels abounded in pink cardinals and poodles. It is a commonplace that great cemeteries are

The Dying Gaul, a first/second-century AD Roman copy of a third-century BC Greek original.

oases of calm, yet they seem to have more in common with one another than with the cities in which they lie. The silent avenues, lowering evergreen trees and, everywhere, a cloying gloom and sadness. The Verano does have exceptionally good cypresses, cedars and pines, and there is an unusual level of care and general kemptness about the place. But in the tower-block insulae of the dead, where lesser souls lie guarded by a stone pot of flowers and a simple ceramic portrait-tile, the unspeakable sadness of dying does make you wish you could fly out and not walk sedately past the grieving widows and sisters as you head back to the lilies.

Climbing higher above Trastevere, one is tempted like ORPHEUS to turn, to admire the panorama, but you should persevere. Stone steps may release you from toiling around hairpin bends of shallow, sloping road, but they are nevertheless steep. As you ascend through banks of acanthus and bay, the view gradually emerges behind you. There is a tempting pause at the

first-level *piazza* in front of San Pietro in Montorio, but push on. Passing the colossal temple to water that is the Fontana dell'Aqua Paola, you emerge on the flattened peak of the highest of the Roman hills, Gianicolo. Walk to the balustrade, where the panorama of Rome from the Aventine to the Borghese is stretched across the widest of views, with the dramatic snow-capped hills of the Abruzzi beyond. The Vatican, one component too many, is modestly hidden behind an outcrop of inky pines. From the amorphous texture of pan-tiled roofs, rendered walls and pine trees, project the city's landmarks, laid out so clearly that all the pieces suddenly fall together.

53

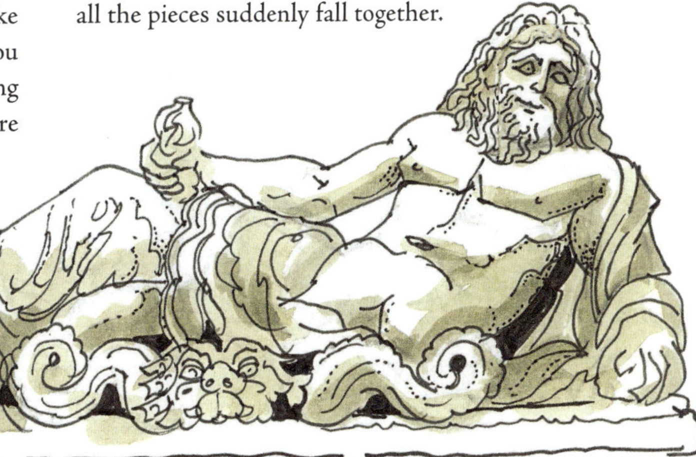

Marforio, one of the six 'talking statues of Rome', once thought to represent the River Tiber or, perhaps, Neptune.

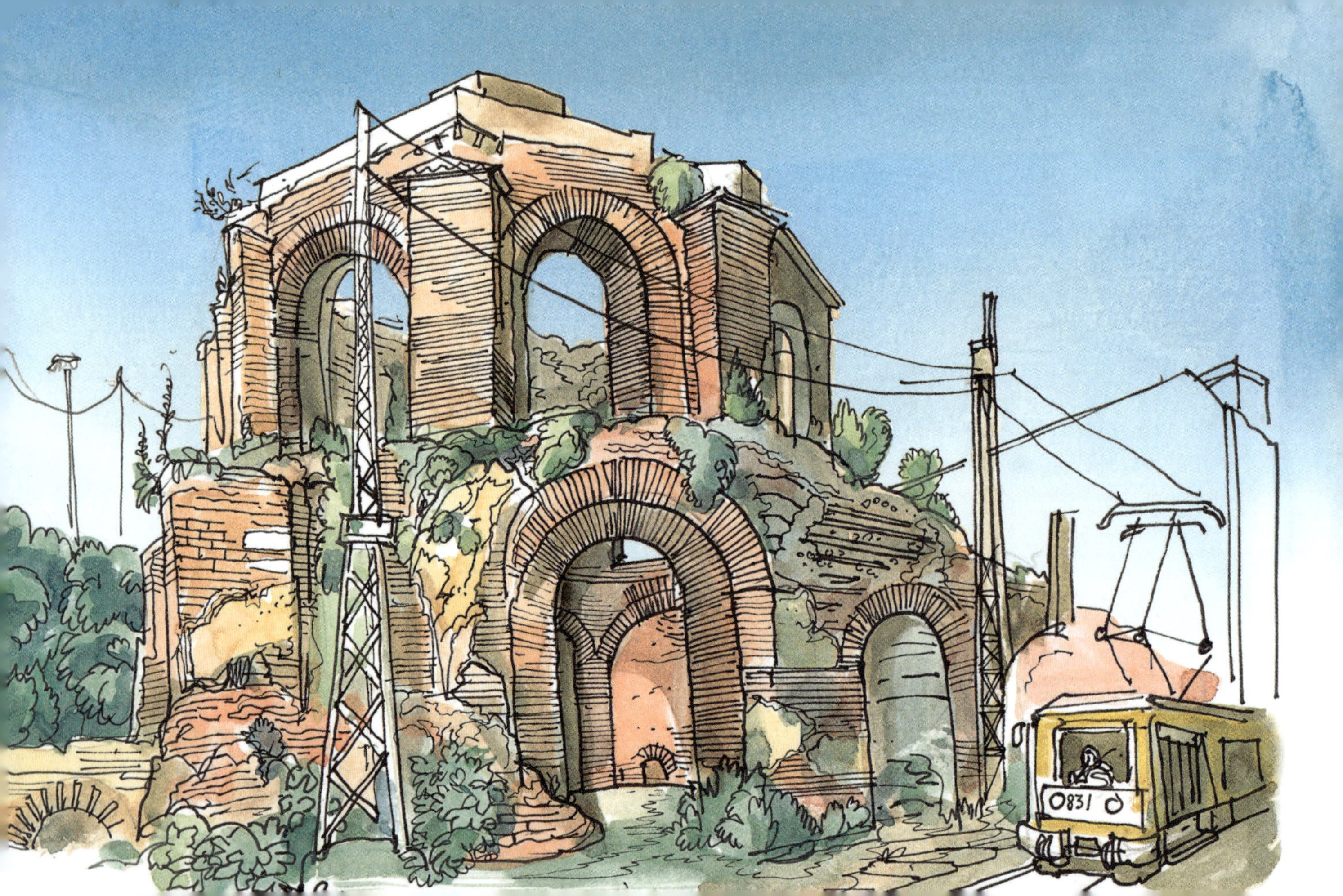
0831

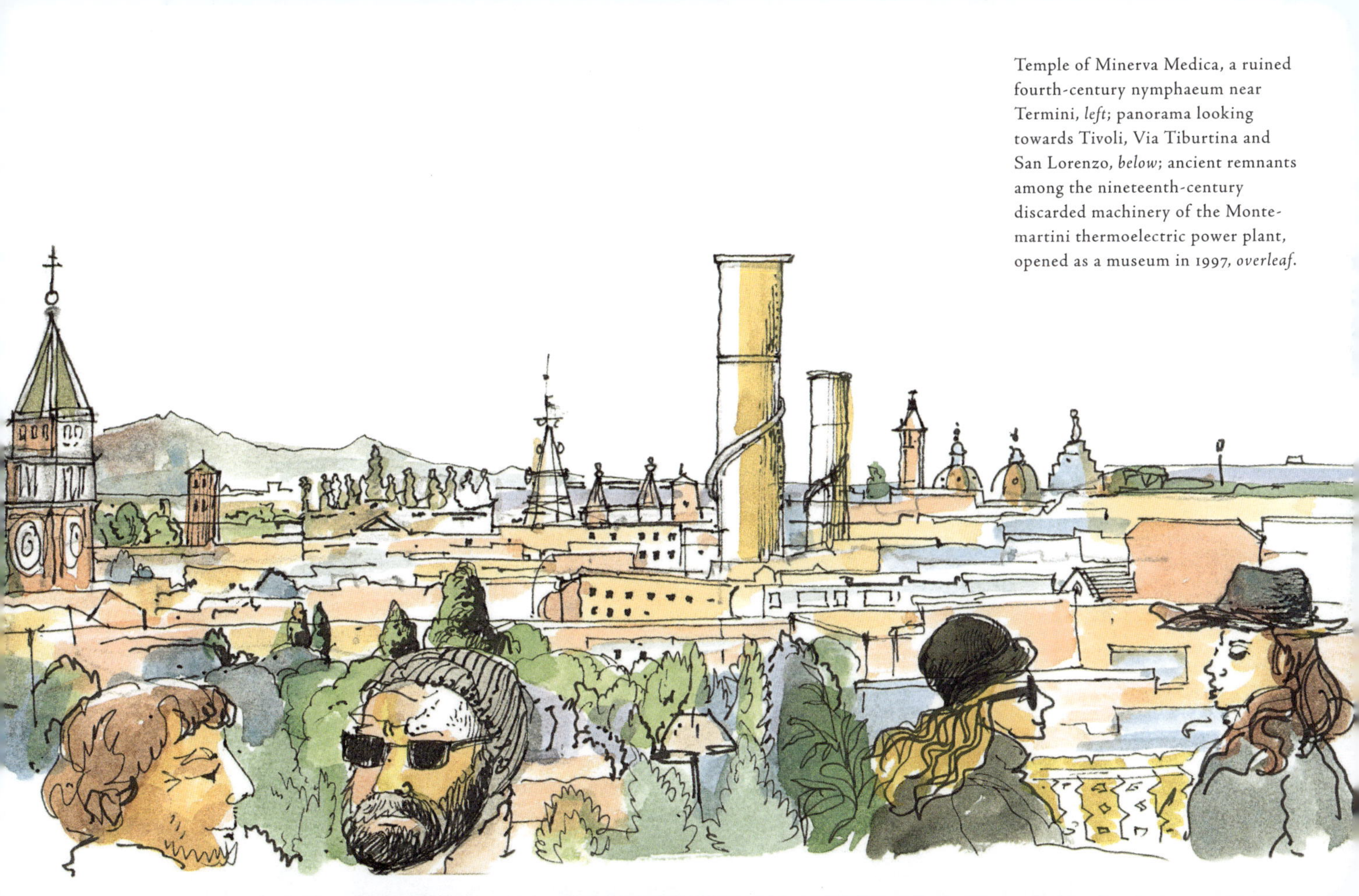

Temple of Minerva Medica, a ruined fourth-century nymphaeum near Termini, *left*; panorama looking towards Tivoli, Via Tiburtina and San Lorenzo, *below*; ancient remnants among the nineteenth-century discarded machinery of the Montemartini thermoelectric power plant, opened as a museum in 1997, *overleaf*.

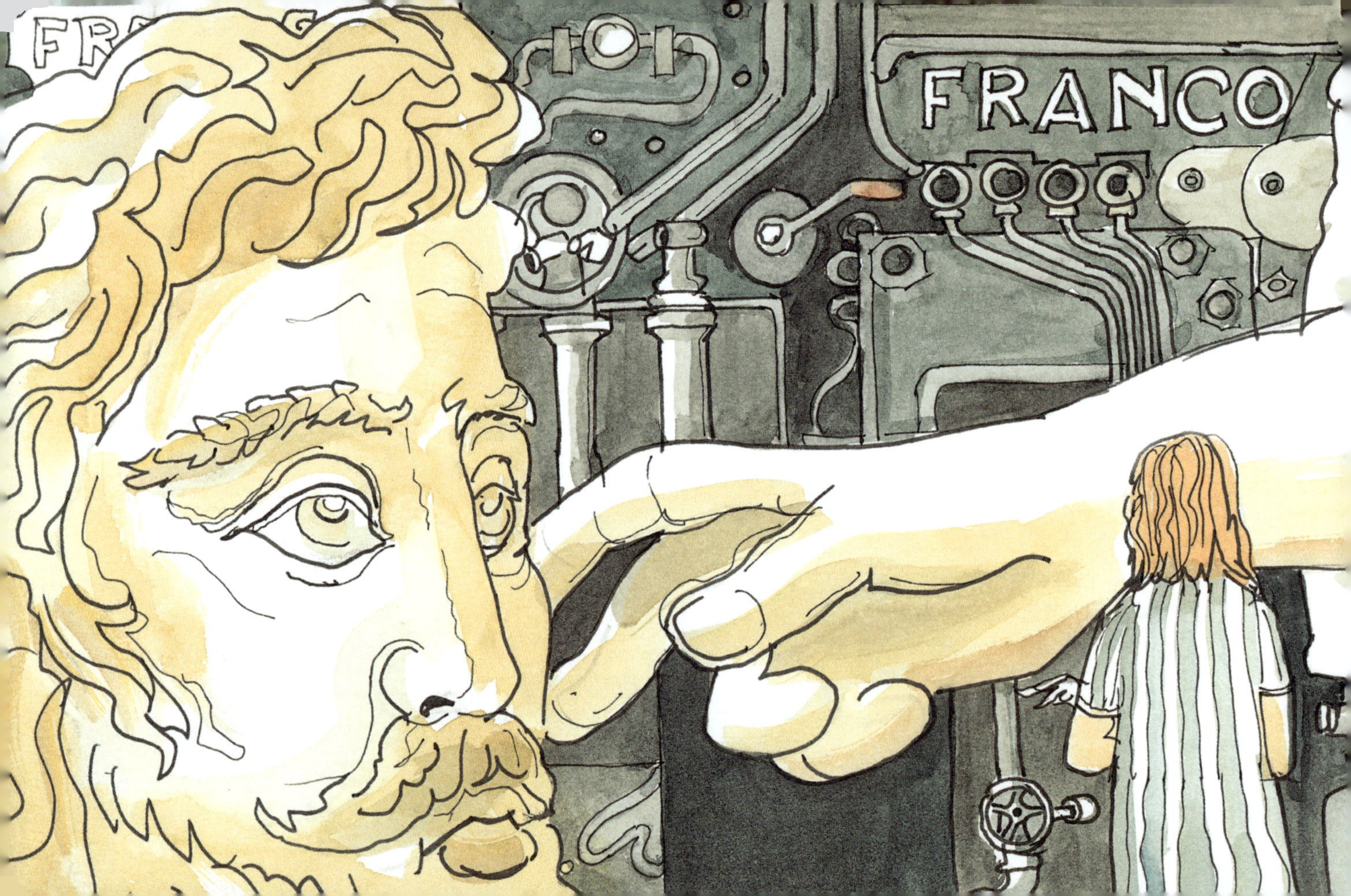

FRA
FRANCO

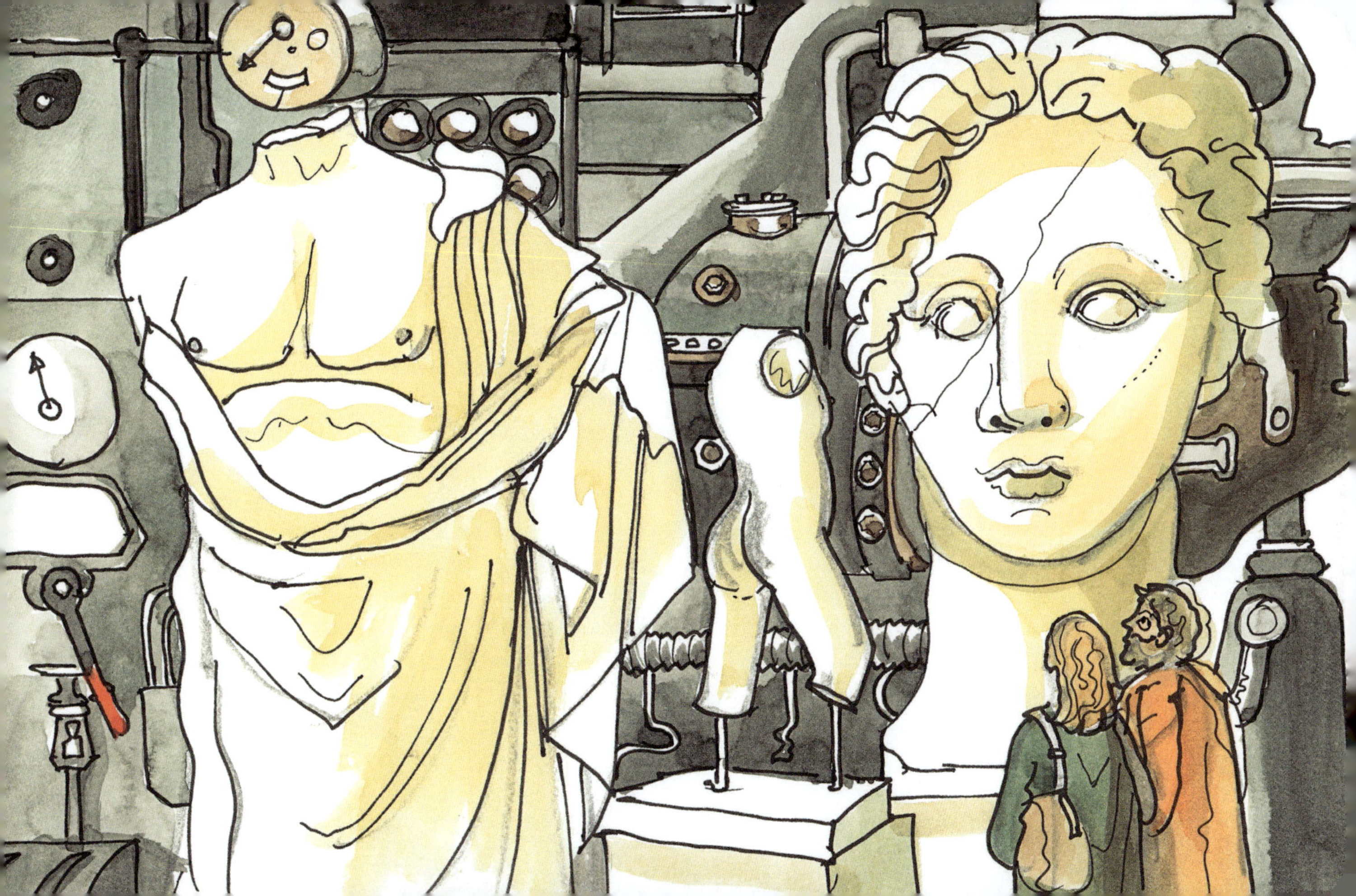

The Vatican, Trastevere (and Testaccio)

The banal avenue from the Tiber towards St Peter's is grandiose, but architecturally plodding. Instead, approach the head and heart of the Catholic Church sideways on, through the Via dei Penitenzieri and Borgo Santo Spirito, and be bowled over when you enter the ENFOLDING ARMS of Gian Lorenzo Bernini's colonnade of 1656–67.

The great church, dedicated to the first Bishop of Rome, stands on this spot thanks to a curious incident towards the end of his life. A rival preacher, Simon Magus, set himself up as leader of the Christian faith in Rome and began to compete for proof of his magical holiness. Peter really pulled the cat out of the bag, as it were, making a dog speak, a child talk with a man's voice and, in what seems now a less than religious act, bringing to life a tuna fish. Not to be outdone, Simon flew high over the city, but the ambitious wizard was brought tumbling to the ground by Peter and broke his leg in three places. A Roman beauty, Xanthippe, mistress of a great patrician, was inspired by these high jinks and converted to Christianity, taking a vow of chastity at the same ceremony. Albinus, her lover, caused Peter's death in his anger. The apostle was crucified

and his remains buried ON THE VATICAN, at which spot this church, in its original form, was built.

Bernini's colonnade is decorated with the symbol of the Chigi family, one of whom was named pope as Alexander VII and became one of the architect's great patrons. He commissioned many major projects, culminating in the obelisk-bearing elephant in the Piazza della Minerva. At St Peter's, the master of the Baroque built a colonnade of 284 Doric columns made of stone from quarries at Tivoli. Now, pilgrims and secular sightseers perch on the generous steps, plucking up courage to join the queue to see inside the church. It is worth the wait, for no better reason than to be bowled over by the astounding scale of the giant piers that support the roof, each as big as a small parish church. The interior is the size of a city square and full of incident, human and architectural.

The Vatican museum has one of the greatest collections in the world, not to mention the most famous frescos, in the Sistine Chapel. Built by Pope Sixtus IV – hence the name – in 1481–82, it was lavishly decorated in a series of the very best murals by Botticelli, Perugino, Pinturicchio,

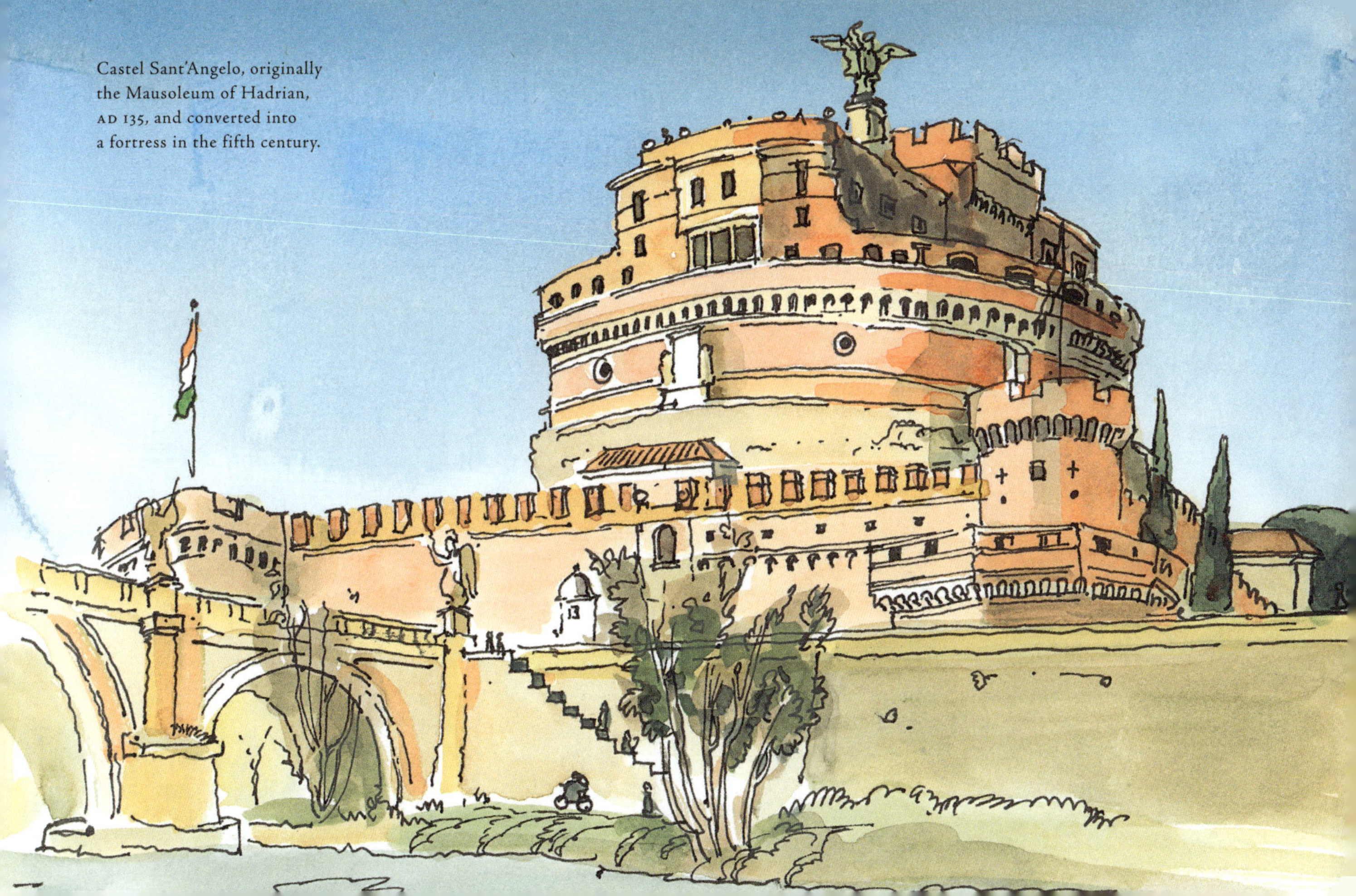

Castel Sant'Angelo, originally
the Mausoleum of Hadrian,
AD 135, and converted into
a fortress in the fifth century.

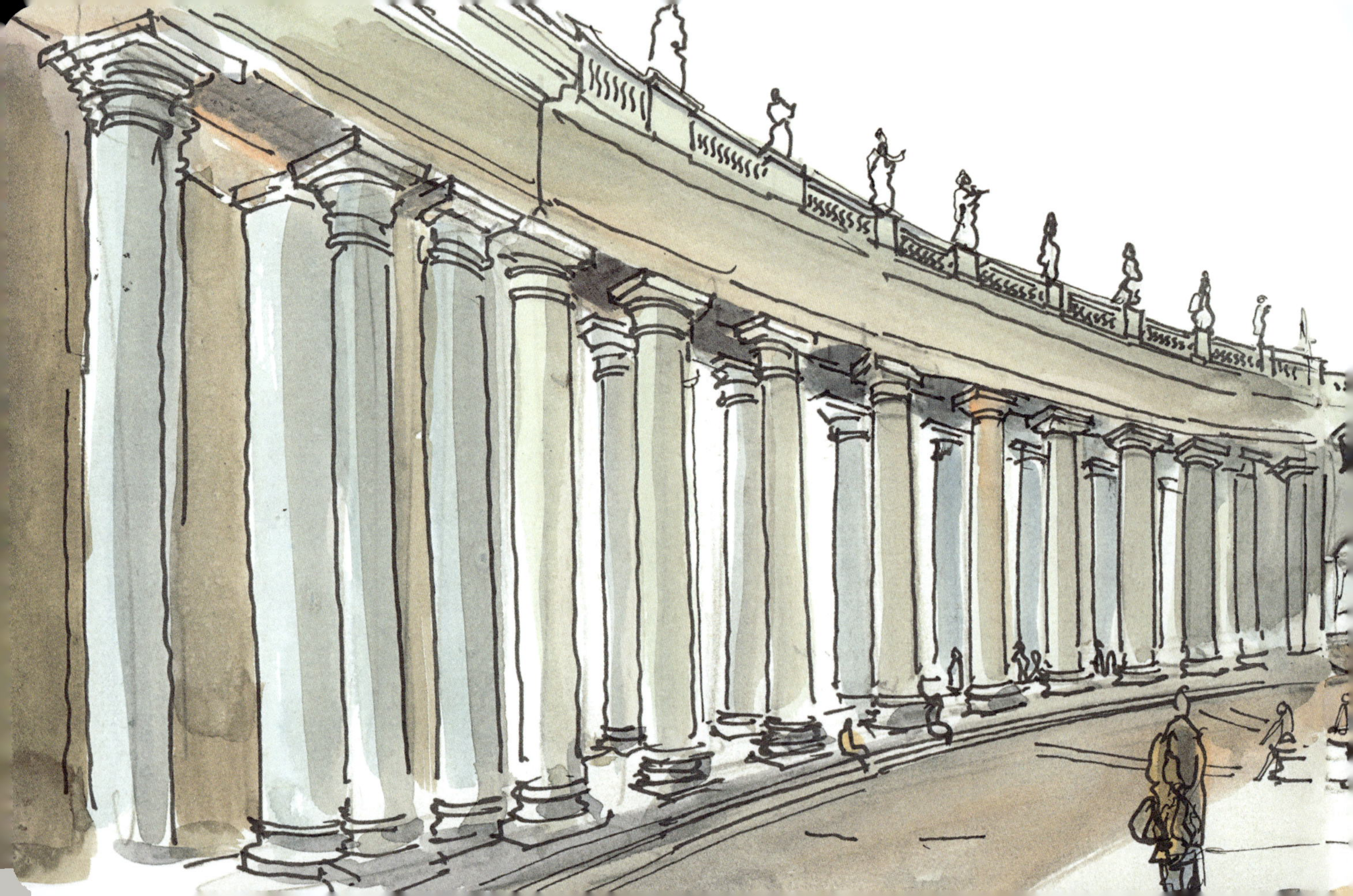

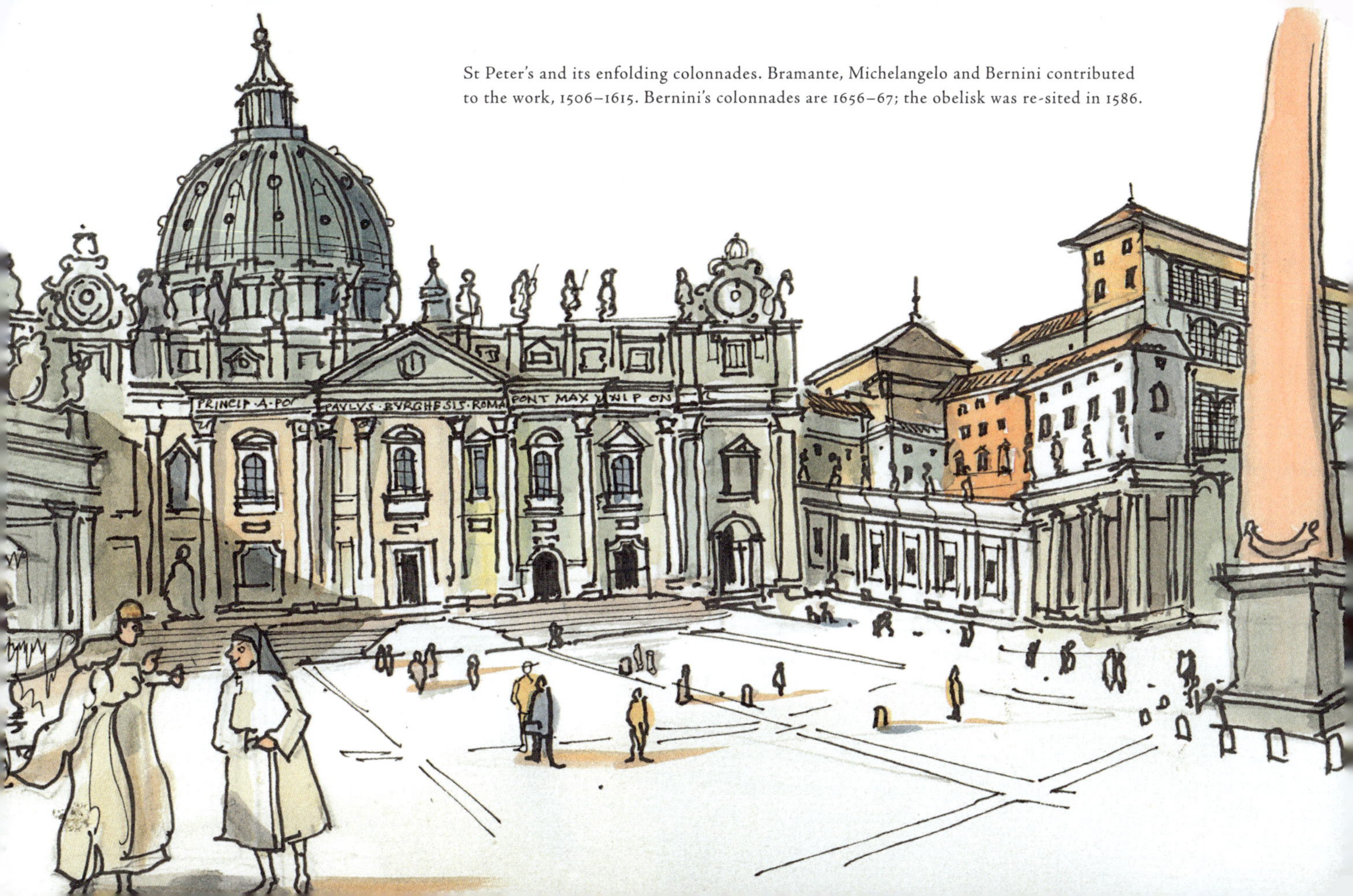

St Peter's and its enfolding colonnades. Bramante, Michelangelo and Bernini contributed to the work, 1506–1615. Bernini's colonnades are 1656–67; the obelisk was re-sited in 1586.

Ghirlandaio and, eventually, the great Michelangelo, who painted the famous *Creation of Man* ceiling from 1508–12.

There is near-folkloric horror of the Vatican tour. Tales of queues hours long and of sardine-packed tourists in the Sistine Chapel are universal. In fact, a pre-booked and inexpensive ticket gets you quickly marched in to where the richest collection in the world is laid out in a relaxed and immediate way. The collection is Imperial in scale and extremely varied: sculptures, papal carriages, sedan chairs and cars, early Gothic paintings, mummies and sphinxes in the blackest basalt and more marble busts than tourists. There are treasures from Peru and the South Pacific (no mention of their provenance) and a collection of Italian paintings that makes most national galleries look like the church fête. The route shuffles you past these treasures (including the Hall of Animals, filled with marble goats and bulls, dogs, rabbits, birds and a stout and modern-looking pig) in an inexorable line toward the Sistine Chapel. Ropes prolong and complicate the progress, but, in due course, you arrive via the Raphael Rooms at THE GREAT PLACE itself.

One's first impression is of a long and splendid space, with ceilings like an endless strip cartoon. The Michelangelo wall is either the greatest painting ever, or a lot of naked folk scattered against a rather gloomy sort of blue sky. It's a matter of taste. (Here follows a rare warning: beware the 'Bistrot breakfast' in the Vatican café. This stacking of American-inspired breakfast goods is of such whole-hearted gluttony and generosity that, were you to finish this gargantuan feast, you would NOT get further than the first cracked marble arm.)

Back at the riverside is the Castel Sant'Angelo, over the ramparts of which Verdi's fictitious heroine Tosca leapt to her death. This giant drum began life as the Mausoleum of Hadrian, but it has several times served as redoubt for beleaguered popes. Most notably, Clement VII hid here, under fire with dwindling supplies, as troops of the Holy Roman Empire sacked the city in 1527.

To the south is Trastevere, on the bank of the Tiber. This part of Rome, informal, full of happy American students and relaxed tourists, is a Left Bank-ish contrast to the Campus Martius and is reached by the most picturesque compilation of bridges: Sisto, Garibaldi, Cestio, Fabricio and Palatino – as well as Isola Tiberina. Around that island's base, a stone apron is splattered with sunbathers and general idlers. Trastevere proper radiates from the ancient

A characteristically domestic scene in Via Titta Scarpetta, Trastevere.

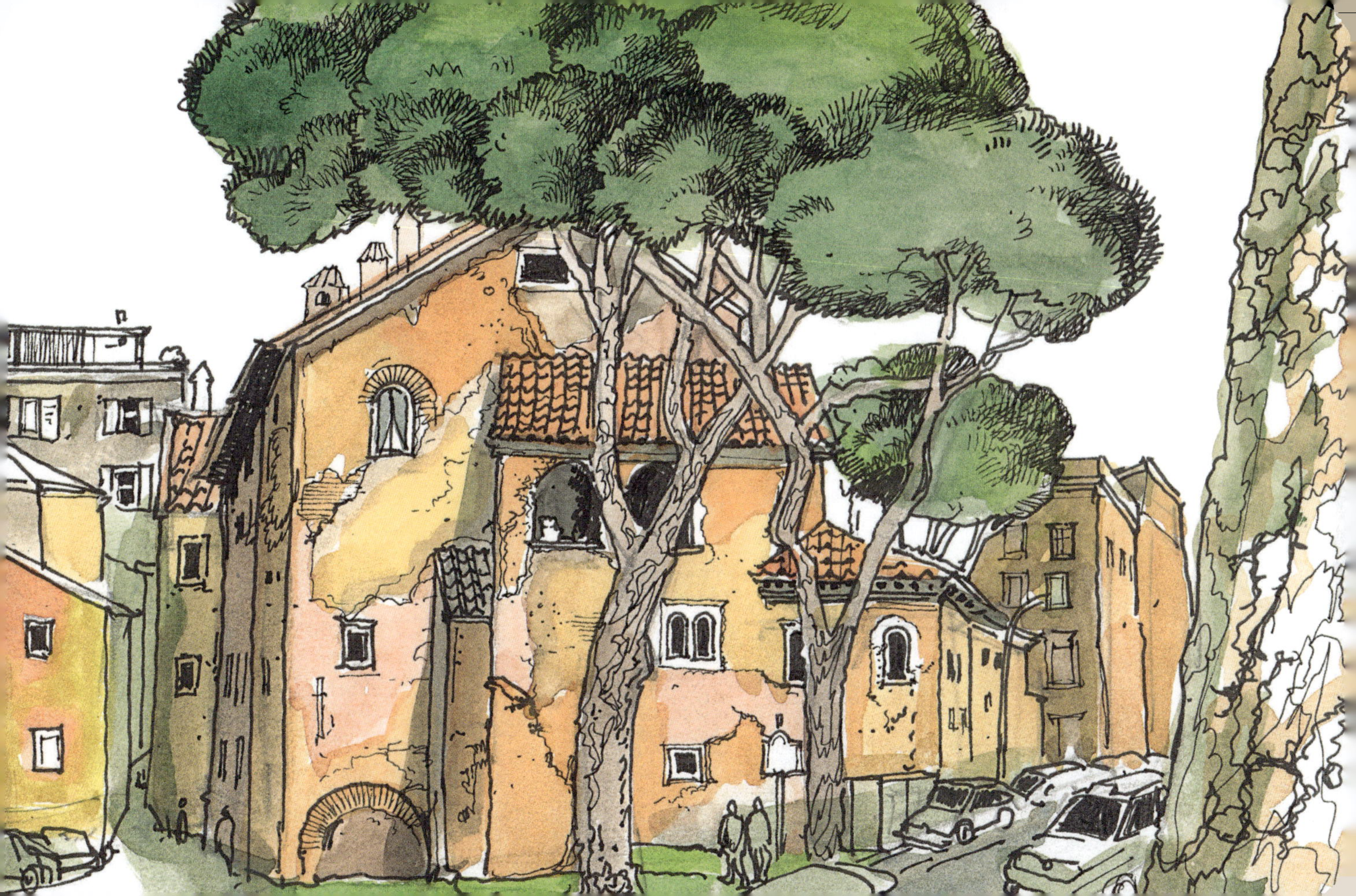

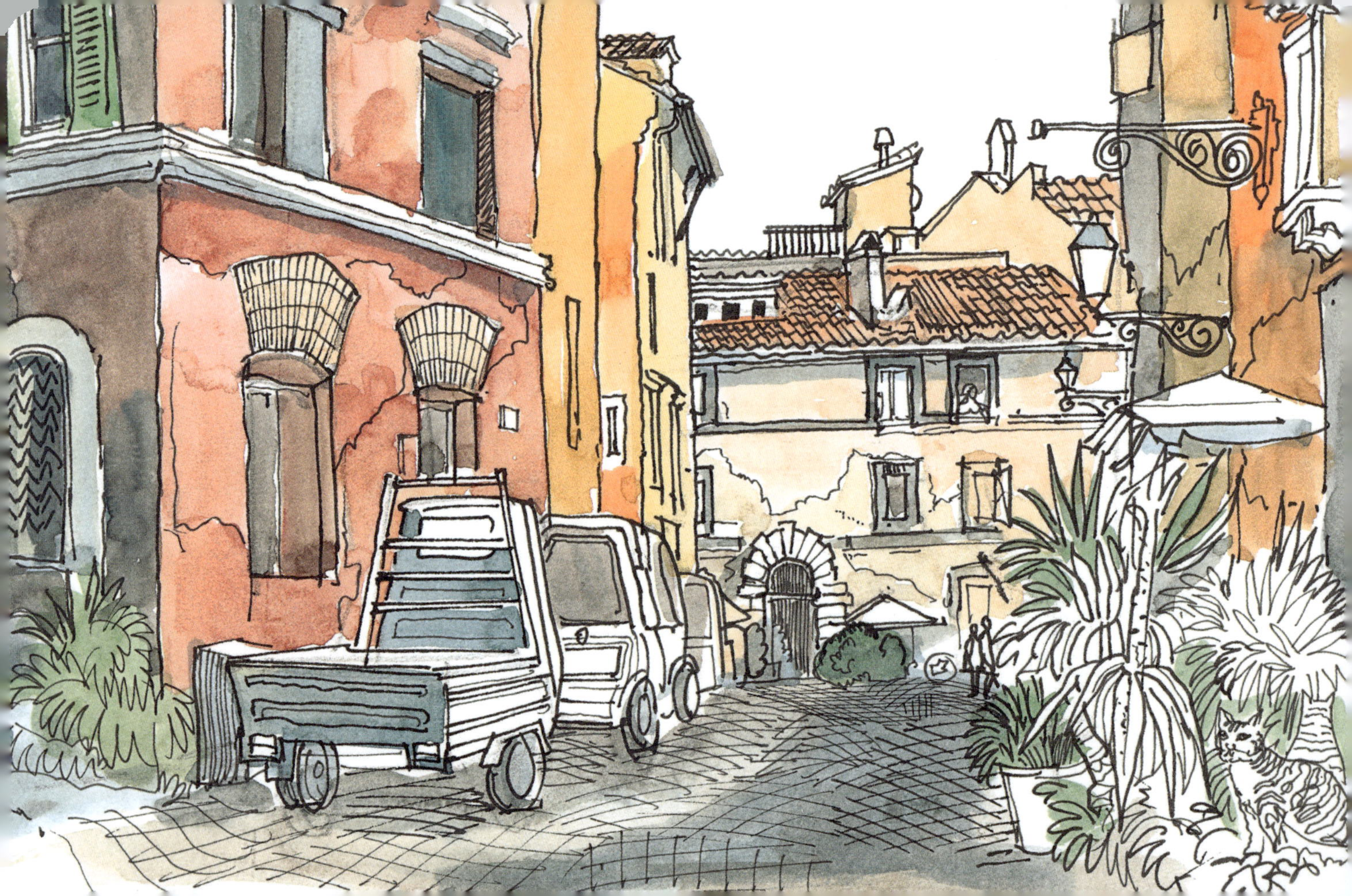

church of Santa Maria. In its narthex is a whole collection of late-Classical inscriptions, set into the plaster walls.

A few picturesque and bar-filled streets to the east is Santa Cecilia. Entered through a pretty courtyard with a threadbare garden, it has a rather plain white façade but a sumptuous gilded interior. The remains of the saint and her husband are kept in the ninth-century crypt, which is lavishly decorated with mosaic-covered columns and vaults. Nearer the river, one or two really medieval blocks give a fleeting impression of an earlier Rome. Back along the water towards St Peter's is the Villa Farnesina, its once-splendid Tiberside gardens shorn away by the late-nineteenth-century embanking, although a formal courtyard of orange trees remains. The house itself, built for Sienese banker Agostino Chigi, and the first of the city's suburban aristocratic villas, is richly adorned, not least by Raphael, whose *Triumph of Galatea* hangs upstairs. On the ground floor, a whole series of his most wonderful paintings decorates an equally entrancing room, the loggia of CUPID AND PSYCHE. The artist, a friend of Chigi's, designed the elegant structure and, with his studio and circle of close friends, embellished it for their patron's wedding, in a welter

Architectural informality in Via delle Luce, Trastevere.

of clouds, breasts and angel wings. The whole scheme is bordered with exquisite flower- and fruit-studded swags.

Across the Tiber in the working-class district of Testaccio, a cherub TUSSLES CHARMINGLY with a long-horned ox above the entablature of the entrance to the Mattatoio. This was the city's main slaughterhouse and the ineffable sadness of the abattoir lingers in the cattle pens, which have incomprehensibly been retained in the forecourt to what are now two grand art galleries. Solid, built to foil the escape attempts of a terrified steer, they impose a feeling of prison-camp desperation on to a place that requires the willing suspension of the knowledge that it was a place of violent death. Like the meat-packing districts of New York or Copenhagen, the surrounding area has turned into a food-filled pleasure dome. Street-food stalls, cafés and *trattorie* throng the market, which sells every conceivable Roman ingredient, particularly offal, harking back to the area's origins, in abundance.

Further out, a planned suburb of good-looking blocks of model housing was built to accommodate the workers needed to contract a new Rome. The capital city of a young country, unified in 1871, required parliaments, courts and civil offices, so the last decades of the nineteenth century saw a building boom that transformed Rome. In Testaccio,

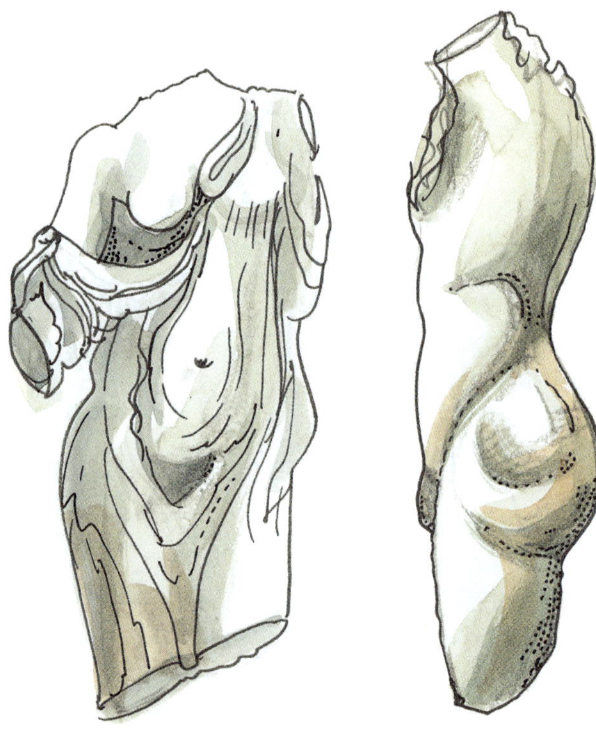

Even such truncated torsos as these are still expressive and reveal
the deep sophistication of ancient Roman sculptural works.

streets surround a recently restored square, in the middle of which is a large pyramid comprised of a carved confection of stacked amphorae. These echo the hill that rises modestly and tree-covered a few blocks south, a man-made mountain created entirely of discarded terracotta oil and wine vessels. This ancient dump of one-use ceramics is a birdsong-filled slagheap and a symbol of long-standing conspicuous consumption. Amphorae were made in VAST NUMBERS and were the most popular containers of the day. Oil was both the main cooking medium and the lighting fuel burned in fine bronze standard lamps in great villas, or in tiny earthenware lamps in the more modest tower blocks, or *insulae*, in which the PLEBS lived less glamorous lives.

Centrale Montemartini is the city's redundant main electricity-generating power station, now converted into a stylish museum of antique marbles, a deep trawl of Classical finds from sarcophagi to headless torsos and graceful (intact) ornamental statuary, as well as a massive arm, a head and other body parts dispersed among the no-less-sculptural black iron machinery. Although one longs for a bold and MORE IMPISH CURATOR to have made a few light-hearted decisions, perhaps a naked bottom or breast peeking out through the manifolds and

boilers, or a titan hand emerging to grasp a giant spanner, it is still visually very exciting. Also striking is the trio of papal railway carriages, one dull green and pontifically sombre, the other two adorned with cheaply gilded barley-sugar columns and cresting to give rather more of a circus-menagerie wagon theme. It is hard to get a taxi here, so be patient or be prepared to walk a rather dull mile back past the old wholesale markets into town.

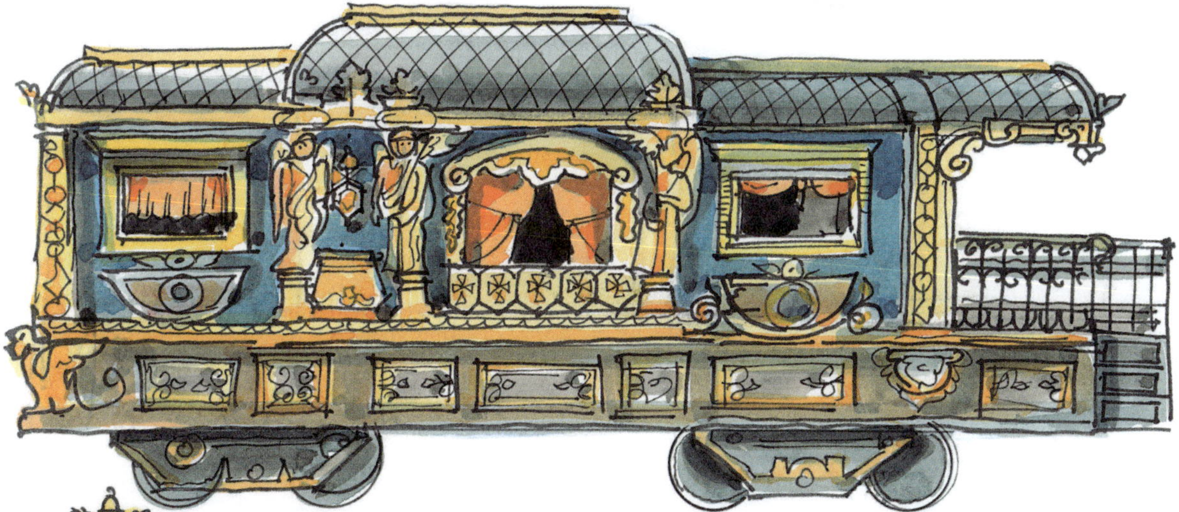

The Via Appia

On a hot day, when you long for greenery, set off for the Via Appia Antica, about twenty minutes' drive from the Forum. Make sure your taxi drops you a good way down at San Sebastian, as this cuts out the least interesting mile of cobbled racetrack and delivers you at the beginning of the most beautiful walk from city to country. Within an hour, you will be watching lambs bouncing around on ancient masonry against a backdrop of the Alban Hills. The first of the great Roman roads to be built, this vital arterial road to Brindisi and the south was begun by Appius Claudius astonishingly early, in 312 BC. Shaded by cypresses and pines, it is interspersed with the remains of tombs that once lined the route.

The Villa of Maxentius was built by that emperor in the fourth century AD, on the site of an earlier grandee's house. A picturesque ruin today, its circus and towers remain in a flowery meadow. The spine of the emperor's private racetrack has been excavated, but its granite-obelisk centrepiece has been removed and now crowns Bernini's Four Rivers fountain in the Piazza Navona. Passing a very pretty Roman farmhouse surrounded by plum trees and with a winning dog in its garden, you approach the mausoleum of Maxentius's son Romulus. A large farmhouse is now attached to this impressive circular plinth, beneath which is a wonderful circular vault. Rather horrifyingly, there was a lime kiln built into this structure to turn the salvaged marbles of the villa into plaster in the sixteenth and seventeenth centuries. This quarry function was the sad fate of so much ancient statuary in a period when pre-Christian buildings were not merely undervalued, but also despised for their secular, heathen subject matter.

Further down the road is a massive and obviously Roman white drum of a building, with medieval crenellations. This is the tomb of Caecilia Metella, a consul's daughter, whose son built it in 30 BC. It has well-preserved and highly decorative grand swags around its frieze between oxen's heads (BUCRANIA). The battlements are a reminder of the mausoleum's conversion into a castle of the Caetani family, who bought the surrounding land in

Umbrella pines and Sunday walkers on the Via Appia Antica.

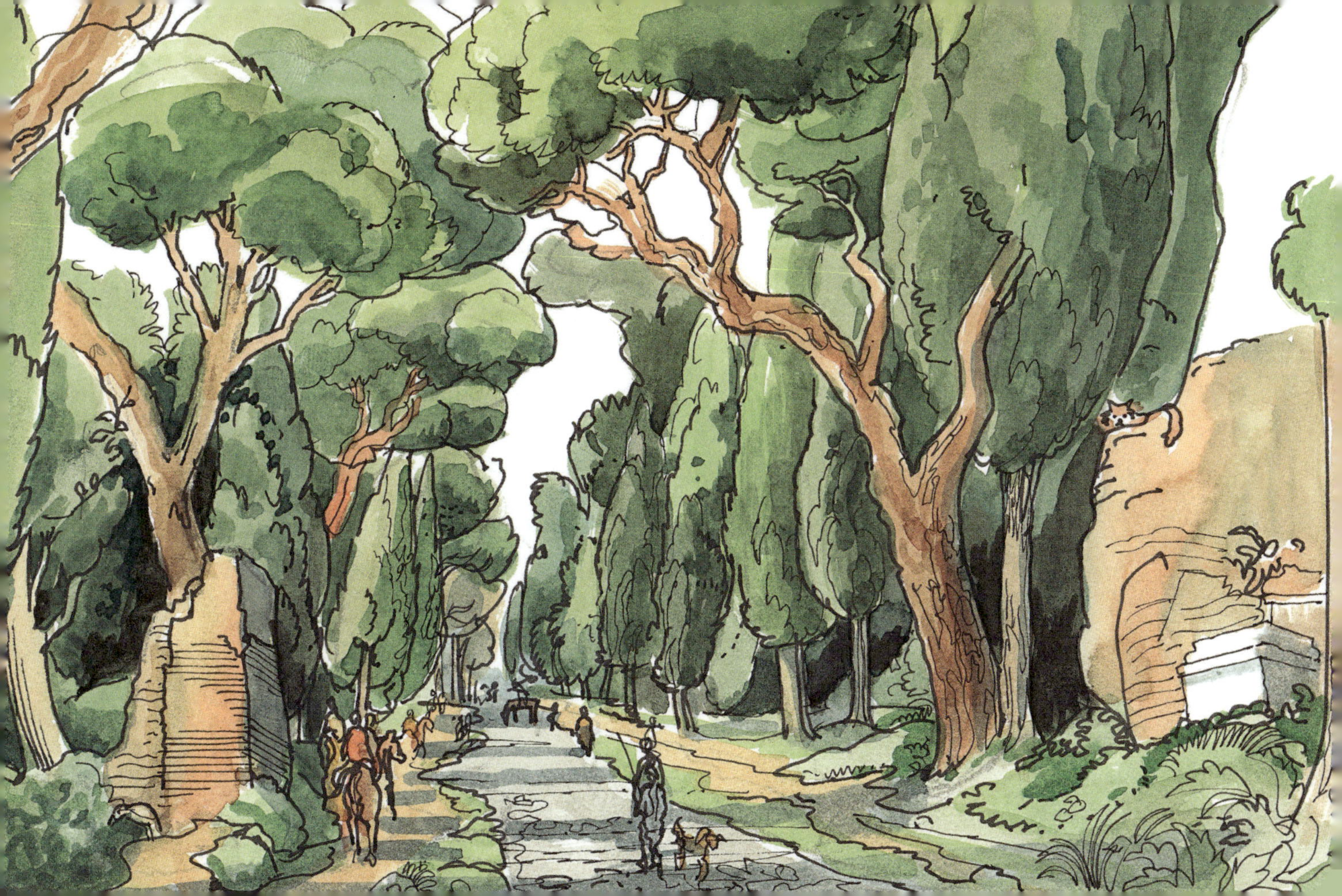

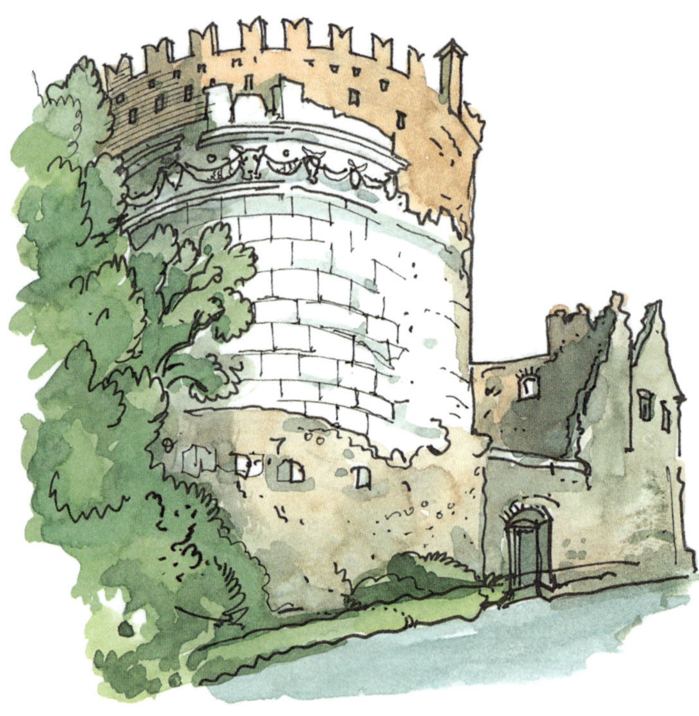

Tomb of Caecilia Metella, first century BC, Via Appia, *above*;
farmhouse in the grounds of Villa Maxentius, *right*.

1302 and used it to control the road and exact tolls on passing traffic. Today, they would be dunning a selection of off-road cyclists, plodding pony riders and a few four-wheel-drive cars braving the uneven road. The principal traffic is pedestrian, especially on a sunny weekend, when the restaurants and cafés that stud the road are a popular lunch destination, with delicious smells of grilling meat and tempting tables under the umbrella pines.

A museum and visitor centre set back from the road at Capo di Bove are rather underwhelming, but persevere because, inside, you can see three aerial photographs, taken in 1958, 1975 and 2006, that show the changes to this landscape in recent times. Like so many parts of the world with marginal agricultural application, the area has become progressively more wooded and scrubby over the decades. Grass and other herbage once considered valuable to feed a hutch of fattening rabbits, a donkey or goats are now felt by an urbanized population to be of no commercial interest, so there is increasing wildness. Old photographs of the tomb of Caecilia show it in stark isolation, yet, covered in ivy and roses, it is still recognizable from Piranesi's engraving of 1762. Further up the road, the fields are empty on either side and sheep and cattle graze, watched by slouching rural cats draped over the ruined monuments.

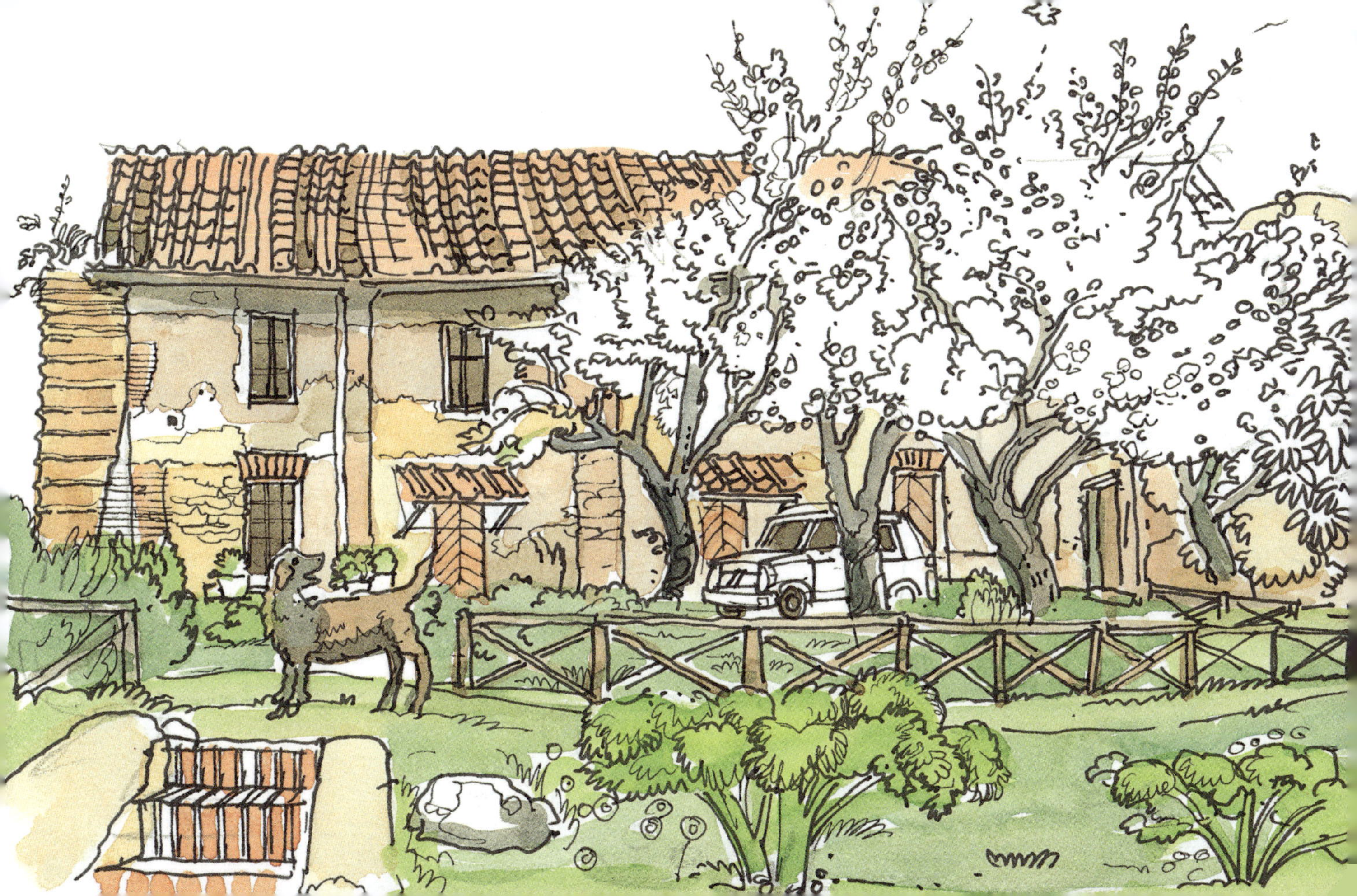

Ostia

One might decide not to visit OSTIA ANTICA. It might seem like an out-of-town trip too far, another train or taxi ride and a day wasted out of Rome. But that would be to miss a great treat, not least because so many visitors DO NOT make the effort, which means that this large and beautiful site – about 175 acres of excavated city and port, civil buildings and *insulae*, temples, warehouses and a theatre – is wonderfully empty.

Ostia stands at the mouth of the Tiber, the obvious place to build a sea port, and was developed as the fledgling city state became a superpower. By the third century BC, the *castrum* or camp had been built. At this early stage, the port was focused on military activity, and the PUNIC WARS with rival power Carthage, which raged from 264–146 BC, made equipping the Roman fleet an imperative. Later, as the Empire grew and the population of Rome swelled, so the need for bread increased. The *quaestores* or public officials originally responsible for Ostia were military, but now they became the GRAIN QUAESTORS.

Cargoes, initially coming from Sicily and Sardinia and later from North Africa, were landed here. River barges tugged upstream by slaves and oxen transported wheat to the capital, along with French wine and Spanish oil. Warehouses – *horrea* – were ubiquitous, but this was no small-town outpost. By 12 BC, Ostia had a 3,000-seat theatre and the first synagogue to be founded in Rome, indeed in Europe. Augustus inaugurated the first forum, and temples were built at either end. Trajan, realizing that the actual harbour was at risk of storm damage, constructed a large, hexagonal safe harbour, which still survives. The port required regular dredging to allow large vessels to dock and, by the second century, the city, which was prone to flooding, was being built upon higher foundations. As Rome prospered, so Ostia, too, grew in size, wealth and sophistication. A local patrician aristocracy emerged and, with it, a series of atrium houses of high quality, with mosaics, wall paintings and statuary.

Silting and the various vicissitudes afflicting Rome took their toll in the fifth century. Ostia became less a port than a safe and semi-rural suburb, until, finally, a series of

Reconstructed and rescued ruins of Via della Foce, Ostia.

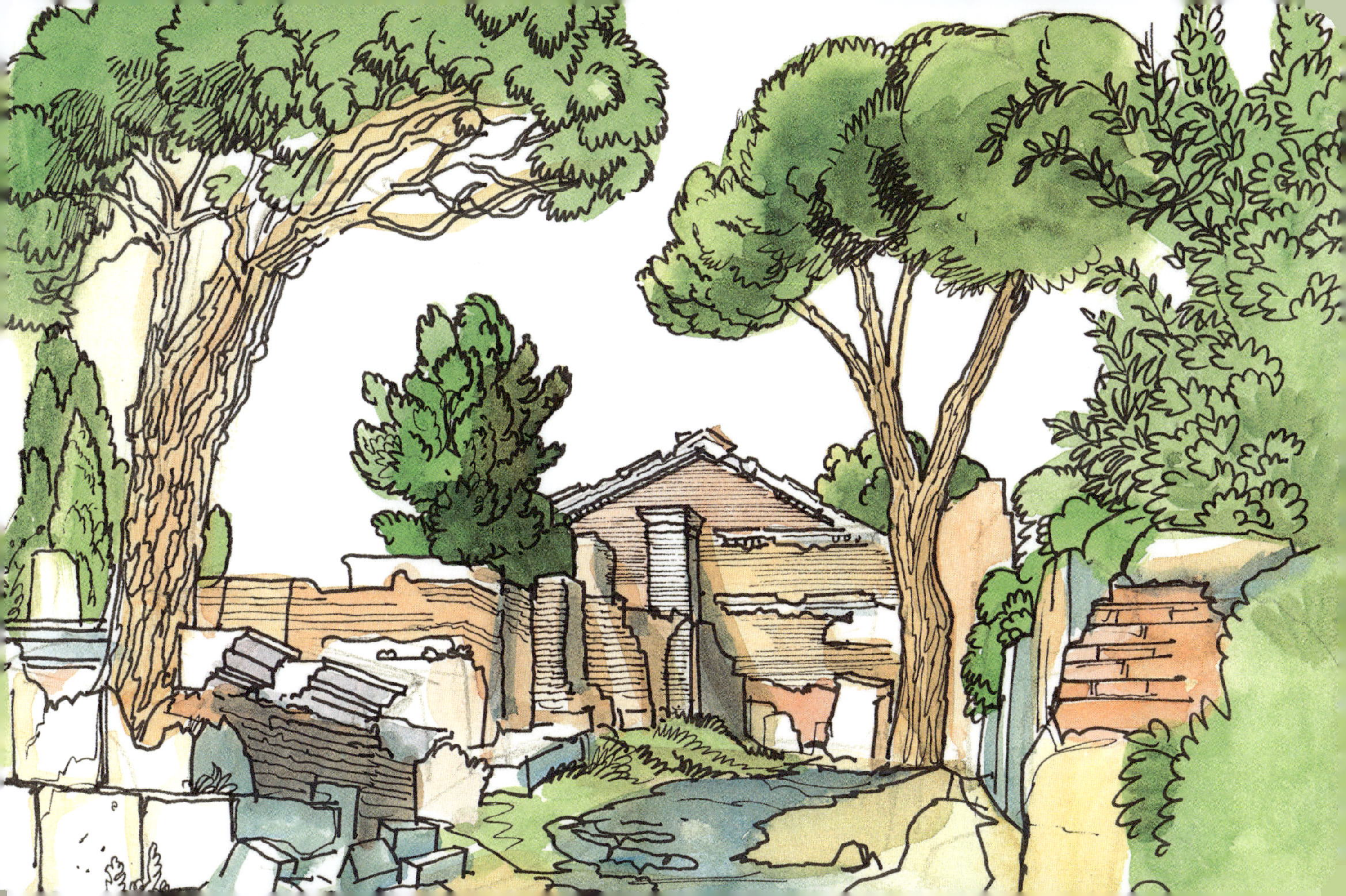

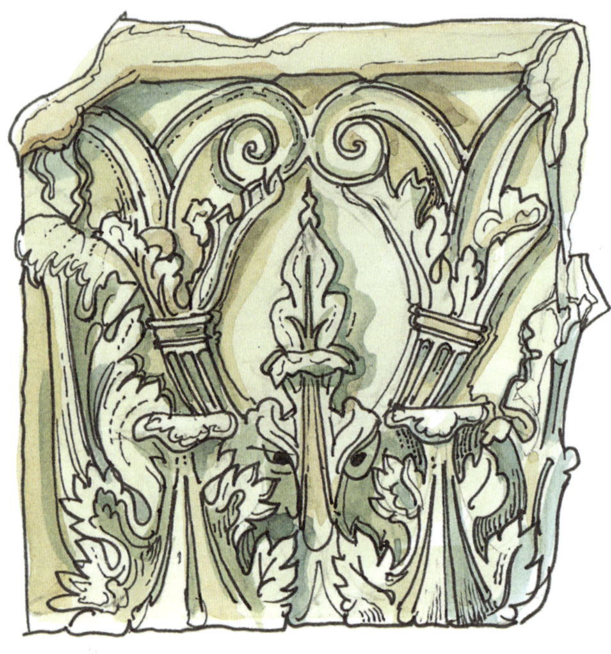

Graceful and imaginative dancing on a composite
capital, Ostia, *above*; theatre, 19–12 BC, rebuilt AD 196
and excavated by Mussolini, *right*.

Saracen attacks ended its status as a world port. By the
Middle Ages, Ostia was a quarry, with marble and other
stone being stripped from the great buildings to be re-used
in cathedrals and other structures as far away as Florence,
Siena, Pisa and Orvieto. Elsewhere, lime kilns were established to turn marble statuary and fragments into mortar.
By the fifteenth century, the city was ruined, apparently
stripped of everything of value, at the mercy of looters and,
presently, those searching for antiquities, too. By this time,
even the Great Forum of Rome, a political centre con-
trolling most of Europe, had turned into meadow.

The eighteenth-century grand tourists may have stim-
ulated early archaeological activity, but it was not until
1930 that Mussolini began a more systematic approach to
digging up the ruins of ancient Ostia, which intensified
as the international expo of 1943 approached. Notwith-
standing the exigencies of the Second World War, Il Duce
continued the dig, intent on providing evidence of his
cultured and historically inspired regime. Even so, today,
most of the city is still several metres below a field on
which long-legged sheep are grazed, and we are able to
see only part of the picture when walking into the site.
(Warning, the rather military-seeming visitor centre is far
from welcoming. Don't be put off!)

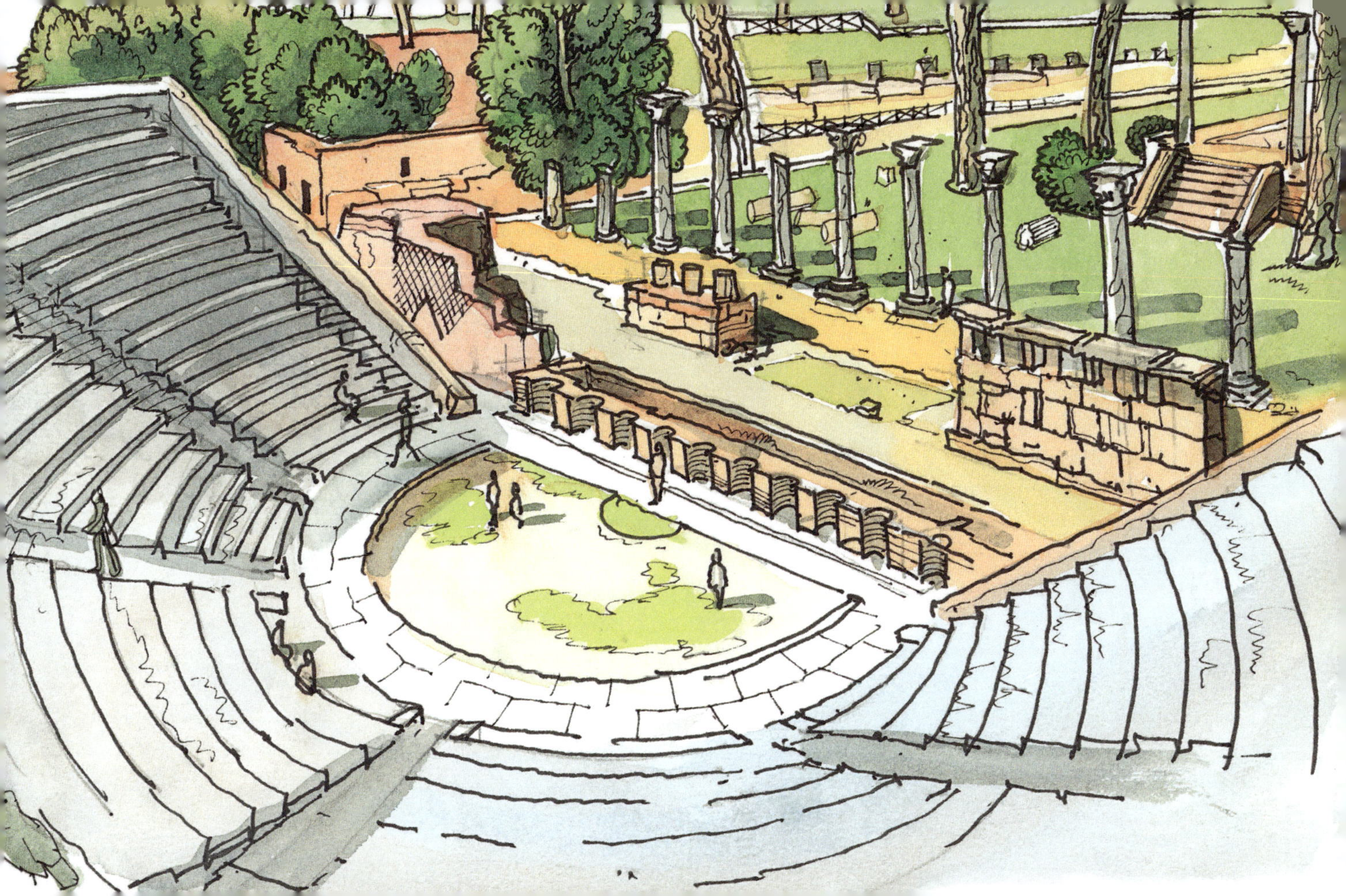

Tivoli

Ancient Rome was MALODOROUS. Although there was, indeed, a drainage system that was the envy of the Western world and a supply of clean, safe drinking water, it was still by any standards unhealthy. Even the best-paved roads were not improved by a layer of domestic waste, and, however elegant the tiled courtyards and tinkling pools may have been within, the tsunami of filth that greeted the greatest senator made summer a challenge.

The wooded hills beckoned, and the nearest were at Tivoli where, centuries before, a rival power had built an acropolis. After a disastrous alliance with the Gauls, TIBUR, as the area was then called, was absorbed by Rome and became a popular resort. The poets Catullus and Horace, and Caesar's assassin Brutus, built villas here, drawn by the precipitous river valley that created a landscape of great romance. Temples and nymphaea sprouted up, and the Emperor Hadrian built his villa complex within easy reach of the city. Most glamorous of all is the villa built in 1550 by Cardinal Ippolito d'Este, heavily and beautifully decorated with bright frescos that anywhere else would alone justify the visit. Here, however, they can be briskly passed by on the way to a series of terraces dropping more than a hundred feet. Long tanks of water grottos and complex Baroque fountain heads in nymphaea lie between soaring black-green cypresses and bay and myrtle hedges, while a row of lion and monkey heads and rivulets between mossy rocks send water to feed cool channels connecting the tanks, statuary and urns.

These gardens and villas were the focus of much Grand Tour interest throughout the eighteenth and nineteenth centuries, which was amplified when Pope Gregory XVI created his own landscape at the Villa Gregoriana. Taking advantage of the natural havoc wreaked by a recent landslide in the Aniene valley, a series of paths hug the contours among the ancient Roman contributions and the luscious forest, pausing either at the mouth of a suggestive cave or grotto or to look across the valley at the villa opposite, Sant'Antonio. The noisy cascade can be enjoyed at certain times of day, completing this most romantic of landscapes.

The Temple of Vesta, first century BC, *right*; the cascades and tanks of the Villa d'Este, Tivoli, 1560–70, with views towards Hadrian's Villa, *overleaf*.

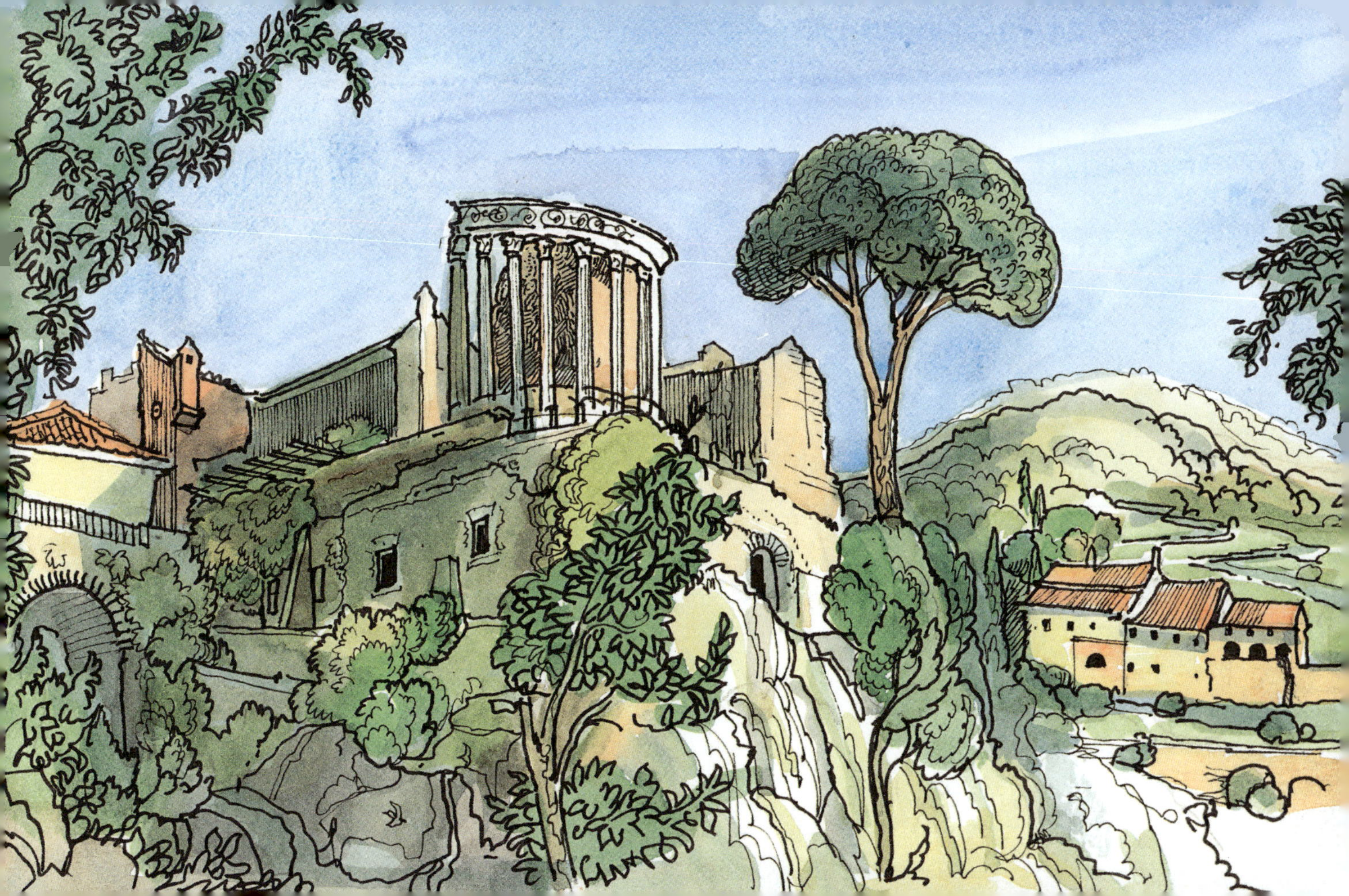

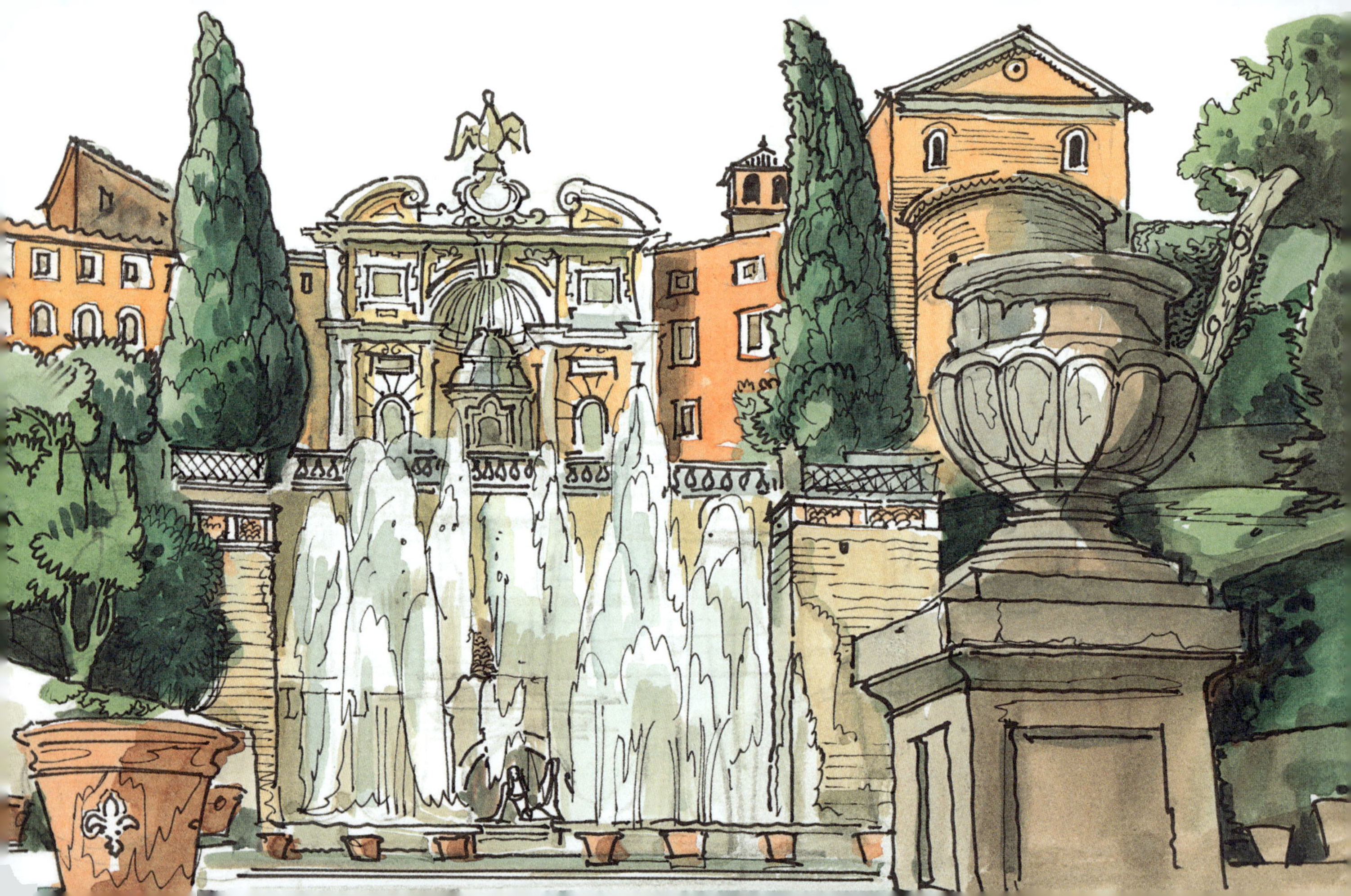

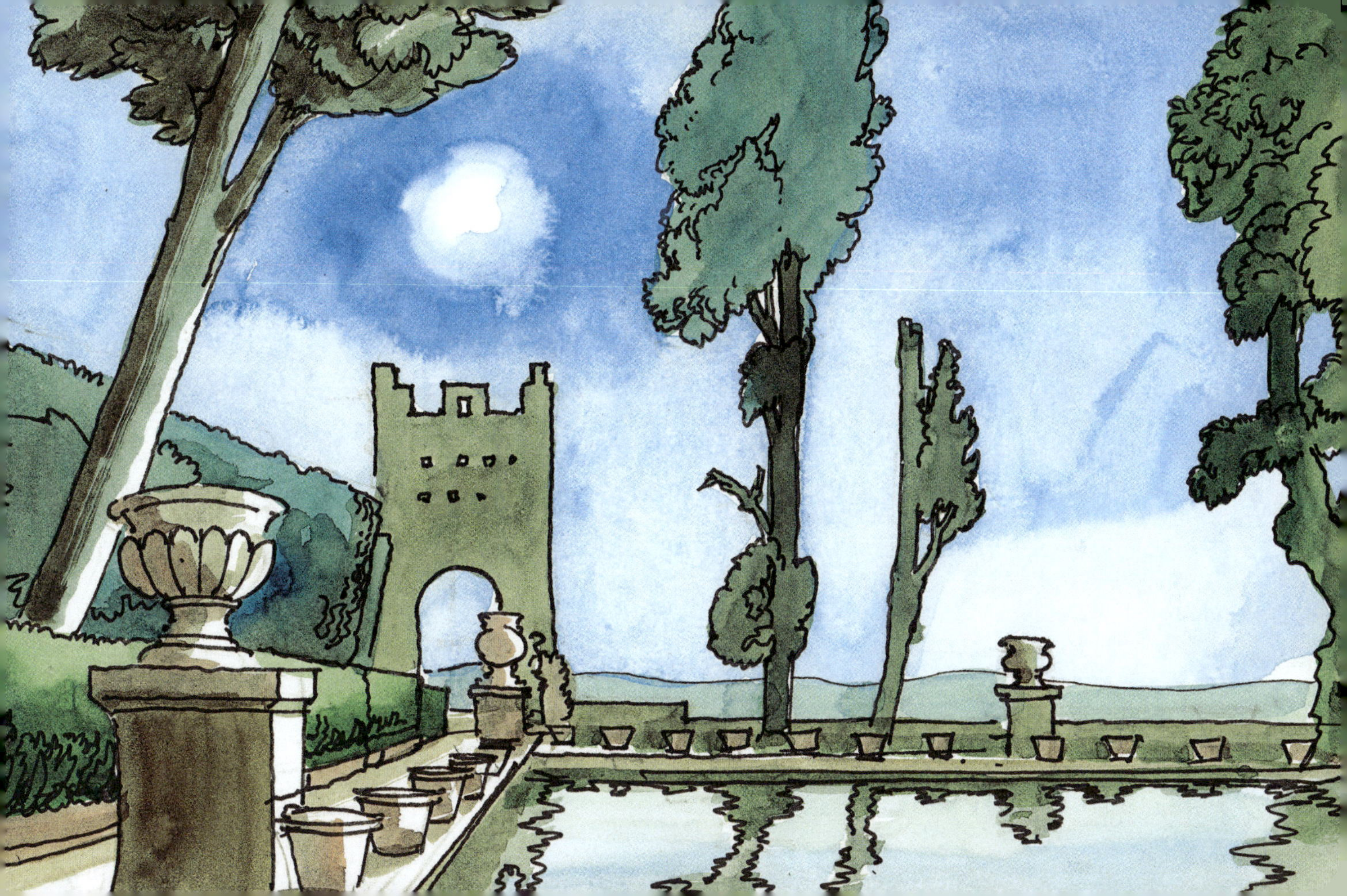

Hadrian's Villa

A short taxi ride from Tivoli, through the scrappy suburbs of the flatlands, there is no indication of the immense ruins of Hadrian's Villa (Villa Adriana) hiding in the olive groves. A brick wall some fifteen feet high defines the edge of the site, pierced by a modern and inconsequential opening. Inside, you leave the twenty-first century behind. Sit on a bench and listen to the thousands of bees that fill the rosemary hedge, which surrounds a long shallow tank two hundred metres long. At the far end, the land falls away between two sentinel cypresses to the misty plain that stretches twenty miles to the city. Honey was the sweetener of ancient Rome, so perhaps these busy workers are descendants of the Imperial bees of Hadrian's hives.

Calling this place a villa is a massive understatement. The site feels like an ancient city – it covers 200 acres and was larger than Pompeii – one comprised of the ruins of great and beautiful buildings: two sets of bath houses, theatres, libraries, dining halls and all the components of the principal rural palace of the ruler of the Western world. As the entire court would be installed here along with the emperor who, incidentally, ruled the whole Empire from this site from AD 128, it was temporary home to thousands: courtiers, politicians and guests of the great man, as well as an army of slaves to look after them.

Hadrian's Villa is one of the easier ancient remains to understand, with a visible skeleton well-enough preserved to clothe with ideas of an Imperial PLEASURE DOME. The Maritime Theatre is a subsection of the villa, and was probably reserved for the Emperor's personal use. It has canals dividing tiny stone islands that once housed studies, libraries and a small dining room. Surviving columns and fragments imply a place of deep sophistication and elegance. Today, on a quiet afternoon, small children and lawless grown-ups might disobey the fierce Keep Off notices and play a high-stakes game of pirates as they leap across the canals.

Most exciting of all is the *canopus*, a tank or lake, 120 metres long by 20 metres wide, surrounded by statuary that includes a GREENISH MARBLE CROCODILE. The original sculpture is kept safe in the adjacent small museum, but a good copy still lolls malevolently poolside. This whole complex was a memorial to the Emperor's lover

Antinous, who died in Alexandria in AD 130, hence the Egyptian croc. One end of the pool offers a magisterial viewpoint towards the capital. At the other is an ornate and extensive nymphaeum, containing a grand dining room from which Hadrian, the air around him cooled by jets of water playing on the artificial rocks, could look out over the glassy pool and sweetly remember Antinous.

Walking around Hadrian's Villa, you are sometimes aware of a secondary series of corridors behind the gracious colonnades, along which servants could move invisibly from place to place. Further subterranean passages carried enslaved humans and animals beneath the surface of the palace. The villa is a fifty-minute cab ride from central Rome – the final approaches wind through the least promising dusty suburbs of Tivoli – but it is well worth the not-insubstantial fare. Buy a picnic to eat in the beautiful olive grove, where a succession of spring flowers makes an absurdly pretty carpet. Thus you can lie, not in Classical grandeur in a painted *triclinium*, but among anemones and grape hyacinths, daisies, spurges and salvias that stud the bright-green early growth.

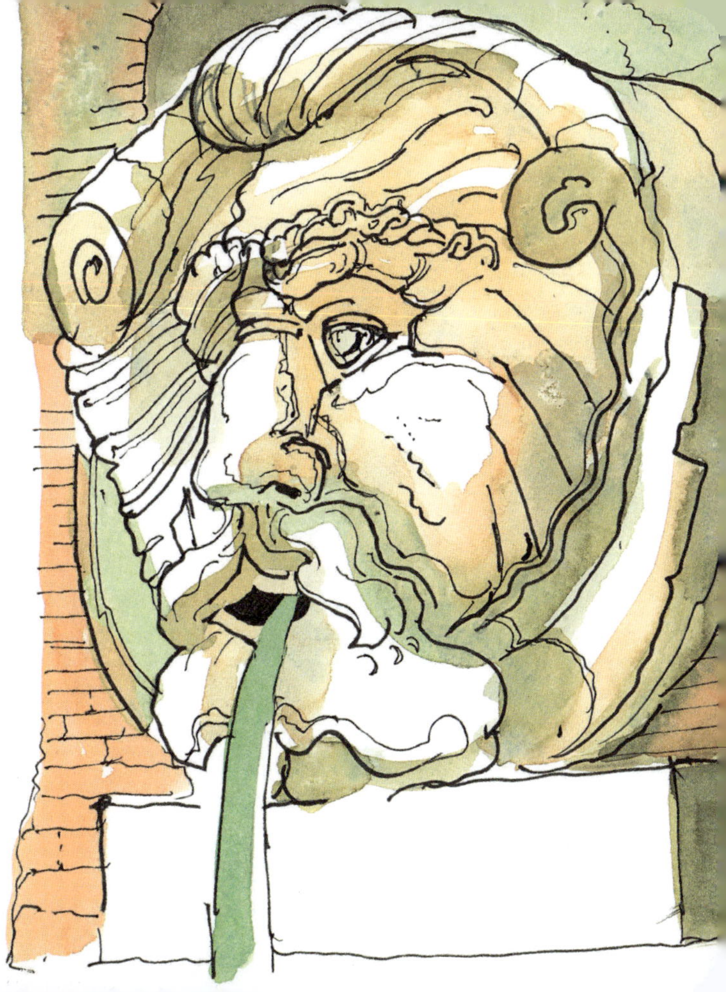

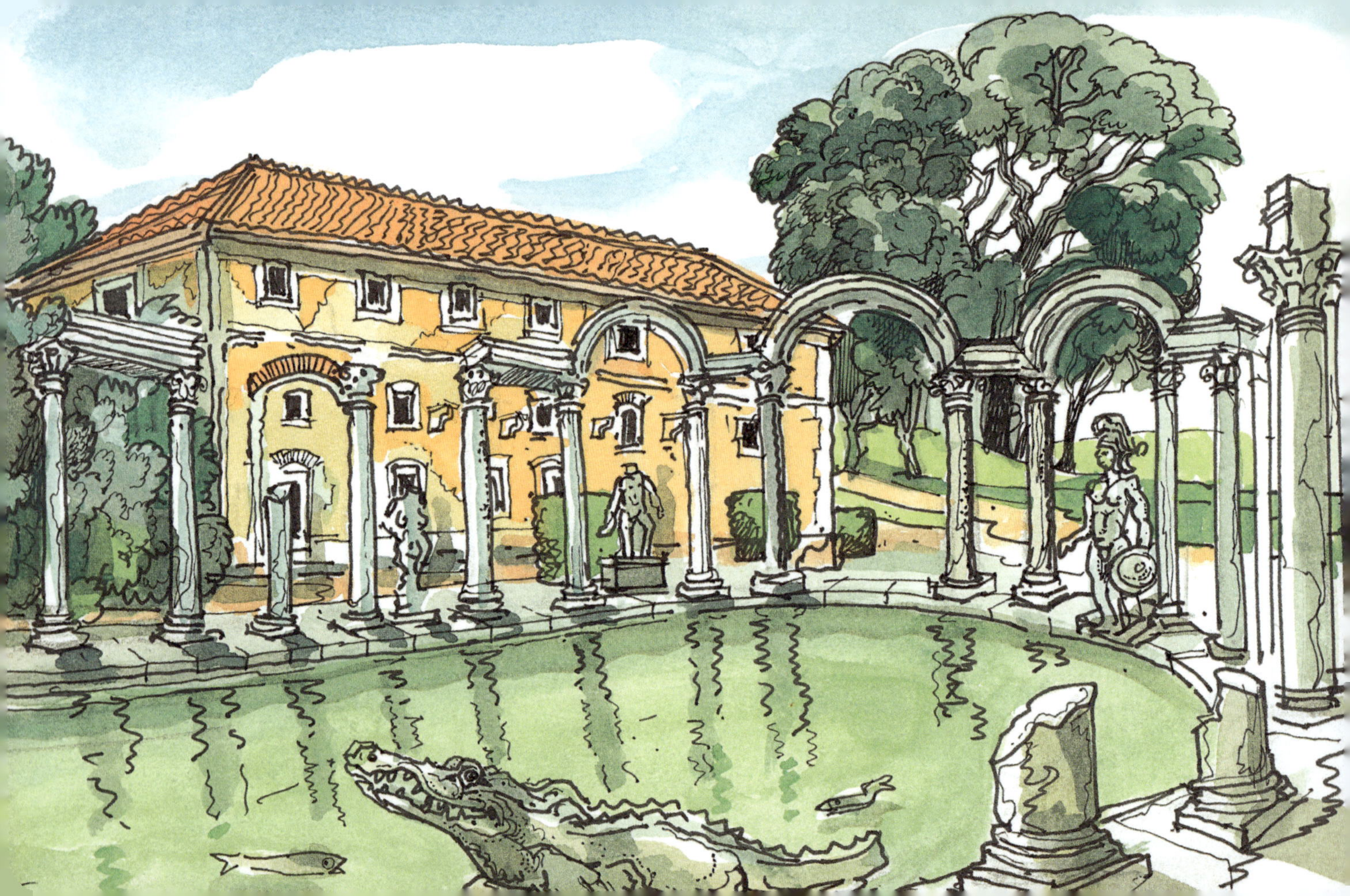

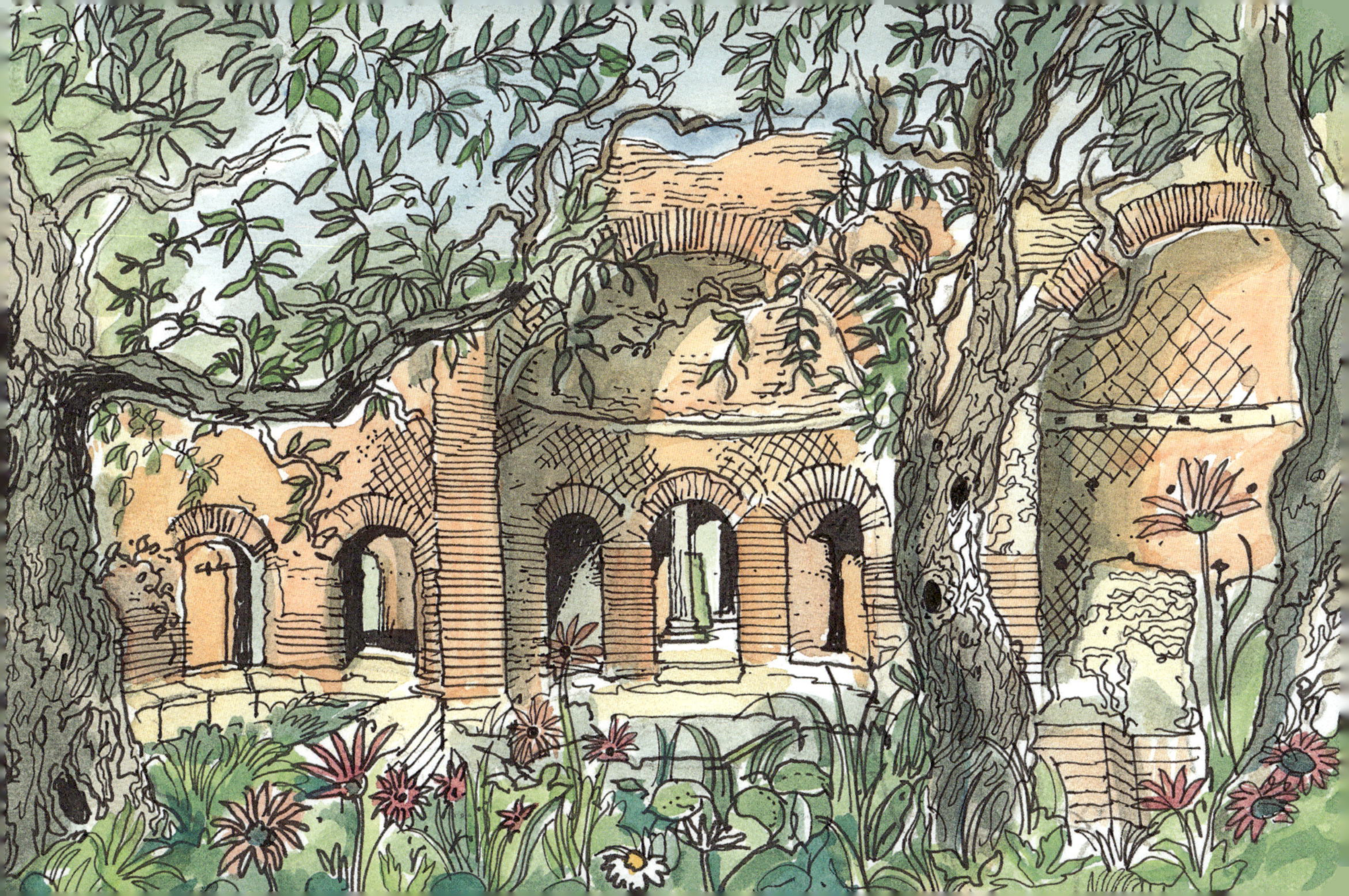

A concise history

ROME, like Istanbul or Palermo, has a history of great complexity and length, one full of mysteries and misunderstandings. The city's population has grown, shrunk and grown again over 2,500 years, and whole areas have fallen into ruination, only to re-emerge a few centuries later. Meanwhile, the macro-scale urban legend is as thoroughly researched as any in the world; historians from Livy during the first century BC to Gibbon in the eighteenth century have themselves become subjects of historical research. So multi-layered and SO LONG is the story that there is barely a stone unturned or a phrase unwritten.

Walking around Rome, the length of the story may be obvious, but the twists and turns of the plot are not. So obscured is the Forum that it defies historical analysis without a very patient guide on hand. Even then, without an open and orderly mind to absorb the facts, it quickly becomes a mere pile of Classical stones, slabs and acanthus scrolls. Although architecture can help reveal the true history of a place, the story of Rome is worth mapping out first, not only to understand the city, but to understand how it is so central to the story of Europe. Therefore, here is a very simple calendar, with ROUGH DATES.

750 – 500 BC Rome was founded, according to tradition, by demi-gods Romulus and Remus on 21 April, 753 BC. It became a local power in Italy, a country influenced by the Greeks, who had colonies on both the mainland and islands. The Romans and the Etruscans were near neighbours.

500 BC – 0 The Roman republic was established and became a Mediterranean empire. The city was big, but its buildings remained simple and, for the most part, were made of wood, terracotta and brick. In 390 BC, the Romans repelled the Gauls and realized that they must defend their city. The PUNIC WARS, 264–146 BC, saw the city of Carthage destroyed. Later, the fall of the Phoenician Empire in North Africa and the Mediterranean islands added rich territories to Rome and wealth to the city.

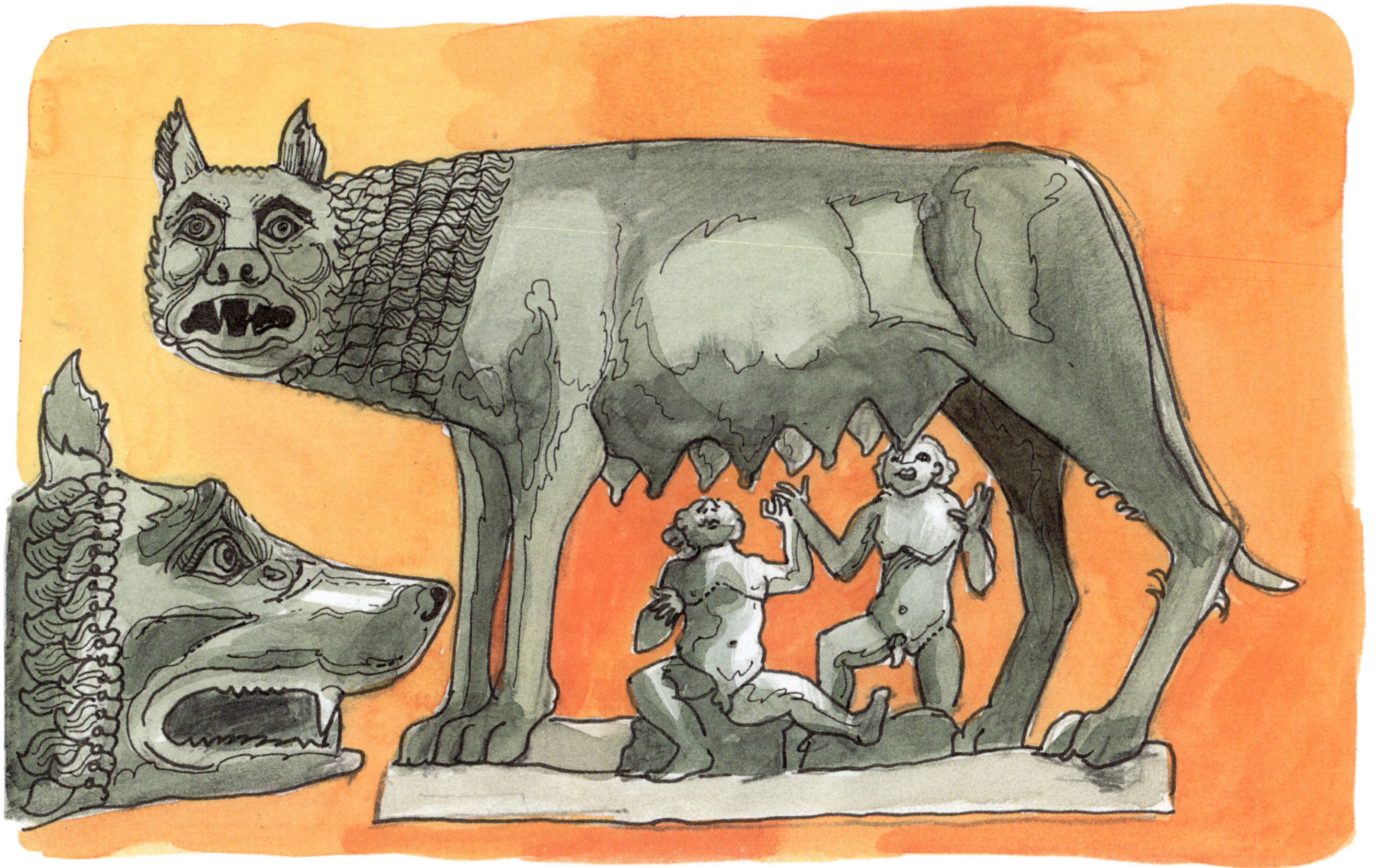

0 – 476 The Roman Empire. Emperors replaced the republican system and a series of short dynasties produced a very mixed bag of benign, brilliant, bellicose or downright psychopathic absolute rulers. In AD 63, General Pompey captured Jerusalem, bringing back with him the Jews who would found Rome's ancient Jewish community.

Rome continued to control much of Europe, but, by AD 250, the pressure of a centralized rule had frayed the fabric of the massive Empire. In the face of repeated Barbarian attack from the north and north-east, the entire system buckled, being divided into Western and Eastern parts. It was while he was facing a serious existential threat to his army at the Battle of Milvian Bridge against Emperor Maxentius in AD 312 that the Emperor Constantine spotted the Cross of Jesus in the sky and decided that this new God should have precedence.

Constantine's subsequent decisive victory indemnified his decision and the die was cast for Christianity, adding an element to the city's make-up that would give it an eternal significance and the ability to survive the centuries. The Western part of the Empire was immediately the more vulnerable, and although the Eastern Empire, ruling from Constantinople, survived for more than 1,000 years until finally falling to the Turks, the Western Empire lost more and more territory in Spain, Gaul and Britain, before being conquered by the Barbarians in AD 476.

It was the papacy that filled a gap in western Roman power after its fall to the Barbarians, powerbroking between the Byzantine emperor in Constantinople and the various warring Germanic peoples. Treading careful paths between the various heresies (Arianism, monotheism and Nestorian beliefs), the popes ceased, in effect, to be merely Bishops of Rome, instead assuming the powers of its temporal leader. By the fifth century, the nature and status of the papacy had changed.

476 – 1000 Early Christian Rome may have officially begun with Emperor Constantine embracing Christianity through baptism just before his death in AD 337, but there were several disagreeable *volte-faces* involving ferocious persecutions and confiscations of the property of both Christians and polytheistic pagans over the next century and a half. Thus it was a gradual progression from the presence of an influential Bishop of Rome to the establishment of a fully-fledged papacy, in which the pope, in many ways, took over the role of the emperor. Gradually, the oldest families of Rome converted to the new faith and the post of its leader gained status and influence. The early

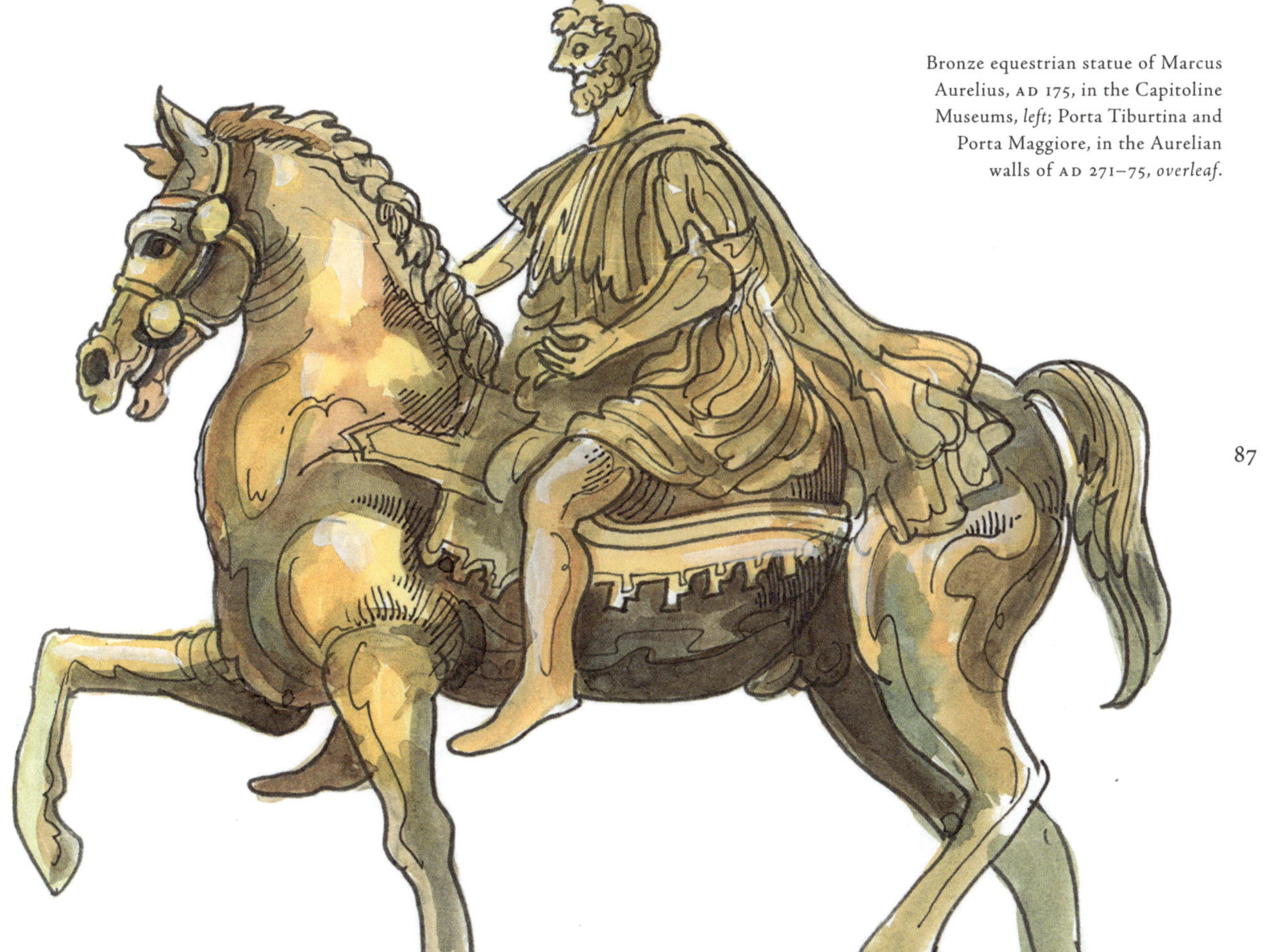

Bronze equestrian statue of Marcus
Aurelius, AD 175, in the Capitoline
Museums, *left*; Porta Tiburtina and
Porta Maggiore, in the Aurelian
walls of AD 271–75, *overleaf*.

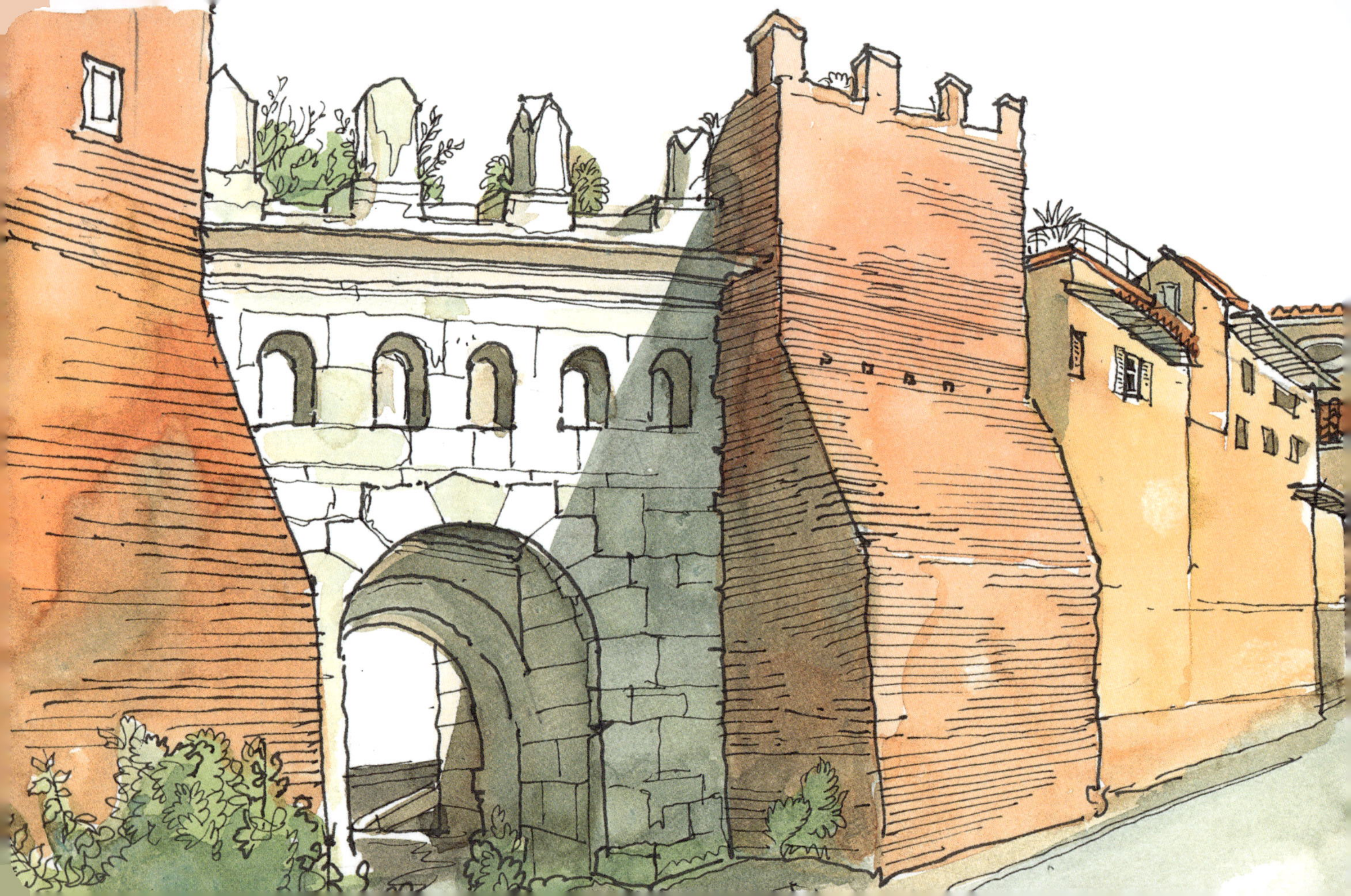

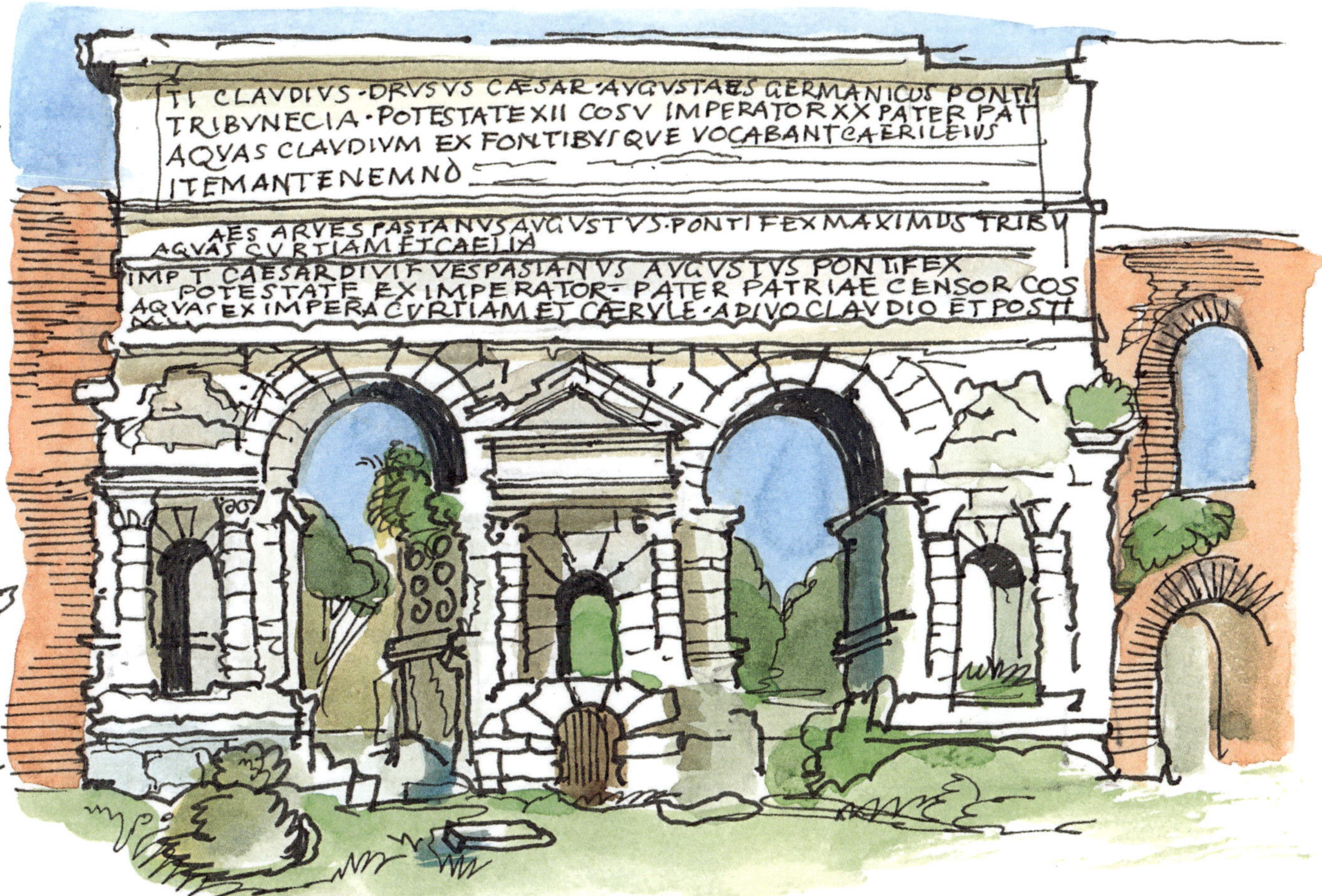
TI CLAVDIVS·DRVSVS CÆSAR·AVGVSTÆS GERMANICVS PONTII
TRIBVNECIA·POTESTATE XII COSV IMPERATOR XX PATER PAT
AQVAS CLAVDIVM EX FONTIBVSQVE VOCABANT CÆRILEIVS
ITEM ANTENEMNO
AES ARVES PASTANVS AVGVSTVS·PONTIFEX MAXIMVS TRIBV
AQVAS CVRTIAM ET CAELIA
IMP T CAESAR DIVI F VESPASIANVS AVGVSTVS PONTIFEX
POTESTATE EX IMPERATOR·PATER PATRIAE CENSOR COS
AQVAS EX IMPERA CVRTIAM ET CÆRVLE·A DIVO CLAVDIO ET POSTI

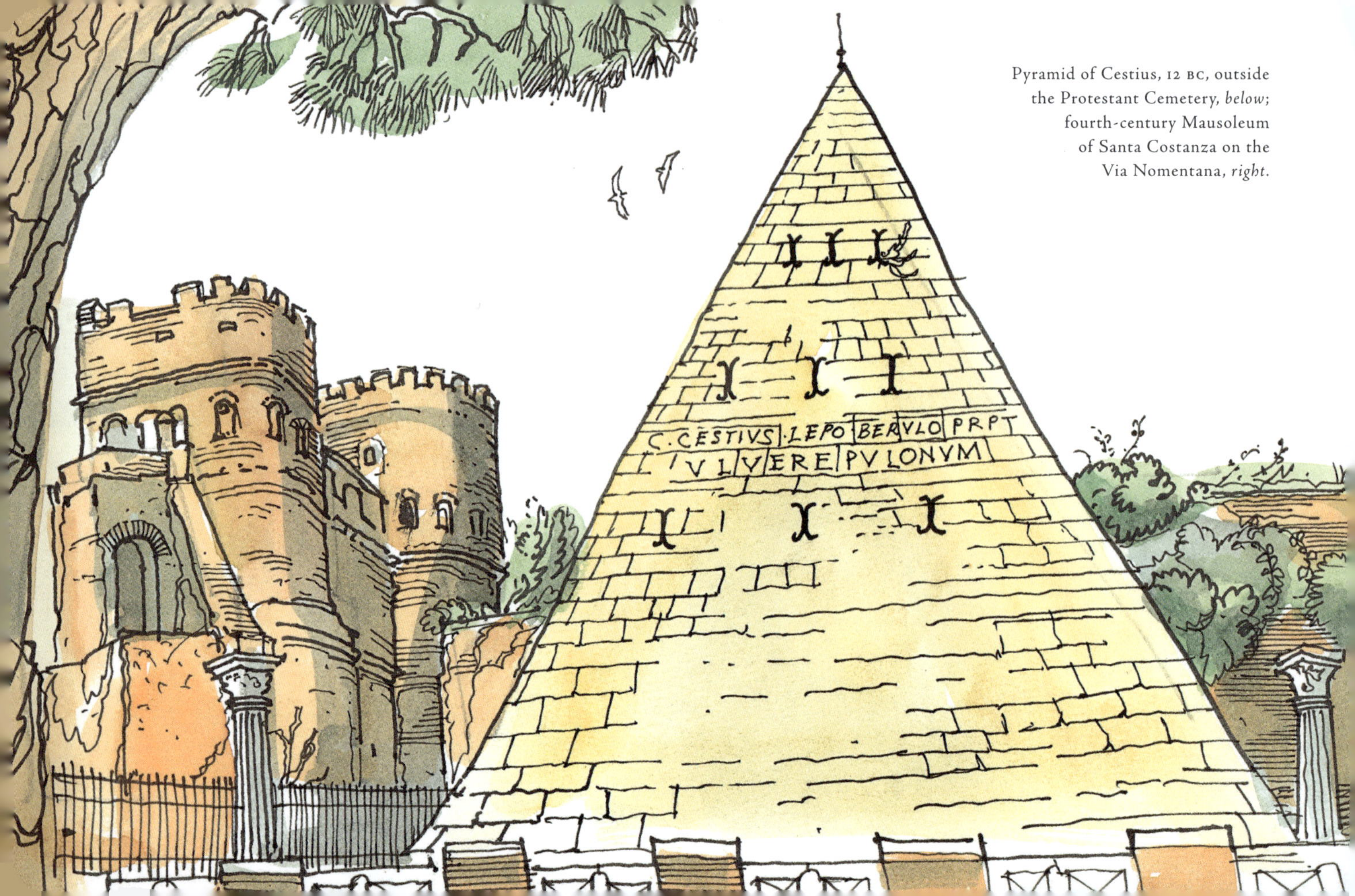

Pyramid of Cestius, 12 BC, outside the Protestant Cemetery, *below*; fourth-century Mausoleum of Santa Costanza on the Via Nomentana, *right*.

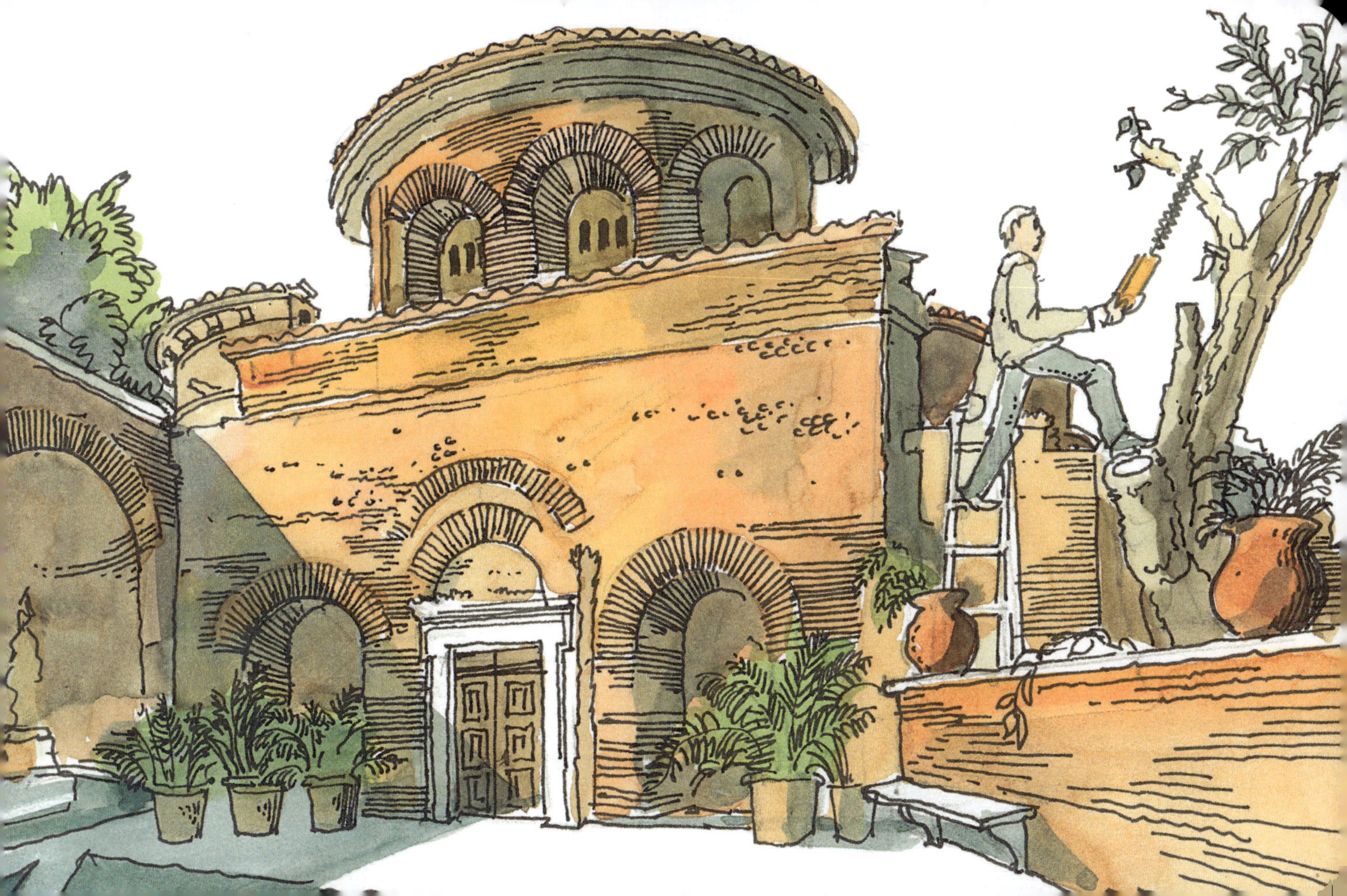

Bishops of Rome didn't all use the title pope (Papa/Father), but, by the accession of Leo I, whose pontificate lasted from 440–61, it became universally used.

This was far from a peaceful time. Alaric the Goth, a Germanic leader caught between the rivalrous halves of the Empire he wished to serve, turned against it in 410, when he sacked Rome. Following a series of Germanic attacks, another Visigothic leader, Odoacer, finally conquered the western Empire in 476, marking its demise.

It was Pope Gregory I (the Great), 590–604, himself a member of an old senatorial family of the Empire, who began to strengthen the power of Rome and its leader. Until 750, this power was almost entirely centred on the city, the wealth of which derived from PILGRIMS who wanted to visit the graves of St Peter and St Paul in the holy city. Indeed, there were many holy relics in the city, unsurprisingly considering the vast numbers of martyrs made during the persecutions.

The astonishing church of Santo Stefano Rotondo has a series of frescos representing the frightful ways that these soon-to-be saints met their end. Fire and water, GRILLING, BOILING, FLAYING and IMMURING, as well as a number of gruesome modifications, all played their part in the making of martyrs. Half a millennium later, these would prove to be the basis of Rome's *raison d'être*, both as a destination and of its income. The bodies of saints were considered efficacious in curing ills, restoring sight and lending wealth or influence. They were originally buried in subterranean vaults, or catacombs, outside the city walls, but better-known figures were brought into the city and housed in more impressive shrines and churches that bore their dedication. Associative relics were thought to do the trick, too. Thus, St Peter's chains acquired superpowers, as did St Lawrence's gridiron and the ever-growing number of fragments of the True Cross. The raging power of the new Islamic empire in the East put several key pilgrimage sites out of bounds and focused attentions on the Holy City. Later, when the Crusades turned the tide and newer pilgrimage sites – including Canterbury in England and Santiago de Compostela in Spain – gained in currency, Rome, in turn, lost out to the newcomers.

Once the Western empire had imploded and Rome was no longer its capital, it became subject to the jurisdiction of the East. Far from Constantinople, the new regional centre of Ravenna, although protected by marshes and the sea, was conquered by the LOMBARDS, another

Campanile of Santa Maria in Trastevere and the Torre de' Conti.

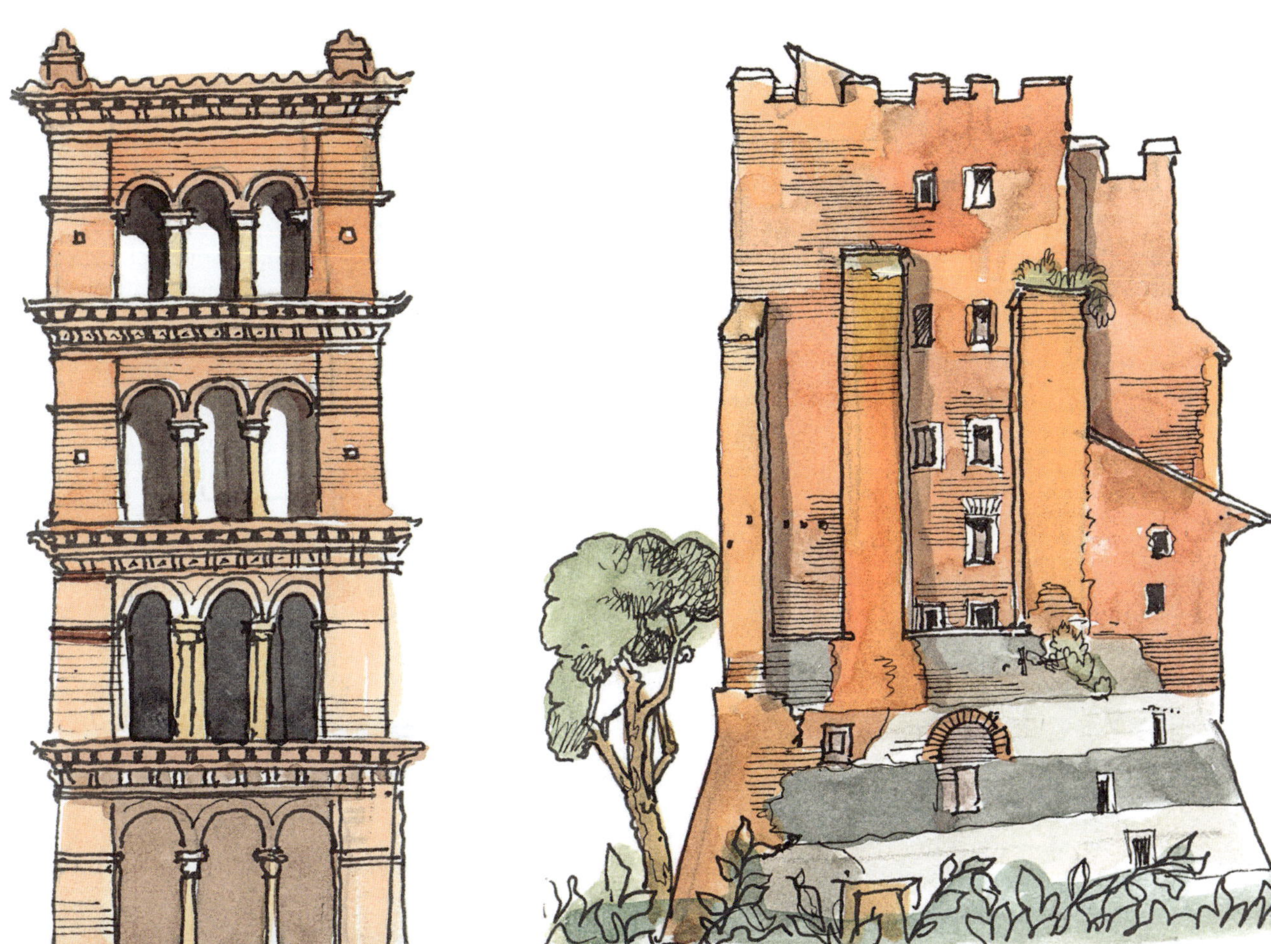

Germanic people which had, by way of Hungary, become the newest threat to the West. In 753, Stephen II was pope and, fearful that his city, too, would fall to the Lombards, sought the help of PEPIN THE SHORT, a Frank and the first king of the Carolingian dynasty. The Franks were yet another Germanic tribe, who controlled most of France and much of Germany in the eighth century, and, once they had defeated the Lombards, the zealous Pepin awarded much Frankish land to the pope. The king formed an alliance with the pope to protect this land and, fifty years later, Leo III crowned Pepin's heir CHARLEMAGNE as Roman Emperor. Thus the new German Holy Roman Empire was established with papal indemnification.

1000–1700 With the end of the Roman Empire, much of the city fell into disrepair. Visigoth attacks had cut off the aqueducts that supplied fresh water to the seven hills of ancient Rome – Quirinal, Viminal, Esquiline, Caelian, Aventine, Palatine and Capitoline. This meant that the rump of the Roman population migrated to the Campus Martius, the lowlands on the bank of the Tiber. The city was thus divided into the DISABITATO (abandoned) and the ABITATO (still inhabited). The Forum gradually sank into near oblivion. Instead of being the epicentre of an empire, it became a place where cattle and sheep were pastured. The ruins that were initially a source of amazement to pilgrims of the Dark Ages were further silted up by accretions of rubbish and dung, until only the tops of monuments were visible, causing early antiquarians to wrongly attribute various temples and other relics. Even so, early-medieval visitors could not believe that these fragmented remains were the work of mere mortals. Eventually, the destruction of monuments for use as building stone or material to feed the lime kilns did spark a desire to protect at least some of the remains, and the establishment of a new senate in 1143, a secular answer to papal government, led to some protection being granted to, for example, Trajan's Column.

Rome and its new territories, the papal states, were a constant temptation to would-be looters or conquerors. Arabs in 846 and Normans from Sicily attacked, and in the thirteenth century the Holy Roman Empire itself found itself at odds with the centre of the church. There was serious conflict between the papacy and France, which, as a major European power, much disliked taking criticism and instruction from the Holy father in Rome. So extreme did this animosity become that, in 1309, the French king Philip IV appointed his own French pope, who moved his court to Avignon in south-eastern France. Through seven consecutive popes, it remained there until 1377, during which time the entire retinue, including most of the cardinals, was French.

This had a disastrous effect on the economy of Rome. Shorn of the papal court, it found itself in financial freefall. Without the lawyers, merchants and petitioners to the Holy See, the city became no more than a small provincial capital. Finally, Pope Gregory XI, himself a Frenchman, realized that the reputation of the papacy was being compromised and decided to move the court back to Italy, forcing a schism. The return from Avignon

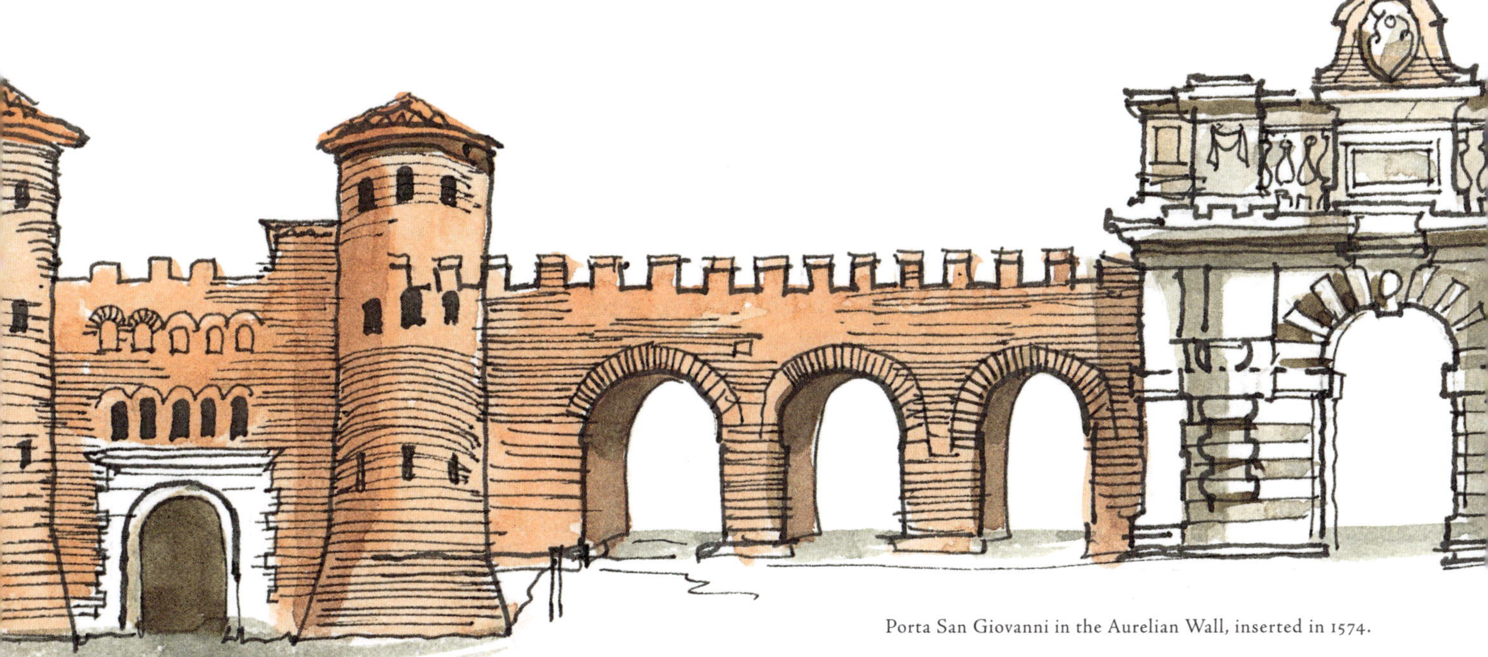

Porta San Giovanni in the Aurelian Wall, inserted in 1574.

marked a revival in Rome's fortunes, during which the development of the Tiberside city accelerated.

Ill will towards various popes was also found within Rome. The numerous powerful families were frequently at violent odds with one another and, from their strongholds in the many brick fortress towers that characterized the skyline, or in repurposed Classical ruins, they vied for power and influence, normally through the election of one of their family as pope.

Although the grim days of murderous spectacles in the Colosseum were a dim memory – no longer did ferocious lions snap up CHRISTIAN CHILDREN before lunch – an echo could be seen in bullfighting and in the races that persisted. These races were no longer held in the huge stadiums but instead in the street still called the Corso today. As well as conventional competitions between young men of the various guilds or *rioni*, this is where the Jews (we are not a race conventionally blessed with sporting prowess, baseball perhaps excepted) and the prostitutes (perhaps a better bet) would meet their challengers.

Papal Rome had many repairs to do after the return from Avignon. There were new palaces and churches to build, new streets to drive through the crumbling city. Some of this was in the area across the River Tiber, TRASTEVERE, and the neighbouring BORGO, the area around St Peter's. The Vatican had not always been the home and headquarters of the papacy. During the earliest days of the fourth century, the papal court had been installed, by the Emperor Constantine, at the LATERAN – the basilica of San Giovanni in Laterano, named after the site's previous patrician owner, was begun in 312. The whole complex took on the name PALACE in the eighth century, when fading Byzantine (Eastern Imperial) power and Lombard and Frankish rivalries demanded that the pope genuinely serve as PROTO-EMPEROR. This meant he needed a real palace, as befitted a secular ruler.

The Lateran's period as papal residence continued with a subsidiary home at the side of St Peter's. On the return from Avignon, the by then run-down Lateran required much work, so, under Pope Nicholas V from 1447, work began on a new apostolic palace at the Vatican, overlooking the Tiber. The site itself was named after VATICA, an Etruscan settlement which, in turn, had been named for the eponymous Etruscan goddess. Together with the more elevated Quirinale as a summer residence, this new complex quickly made the Lateran redundant. Today, the

Santi Quattro Coronati, an ancient basilica of the fourth or fifth century.

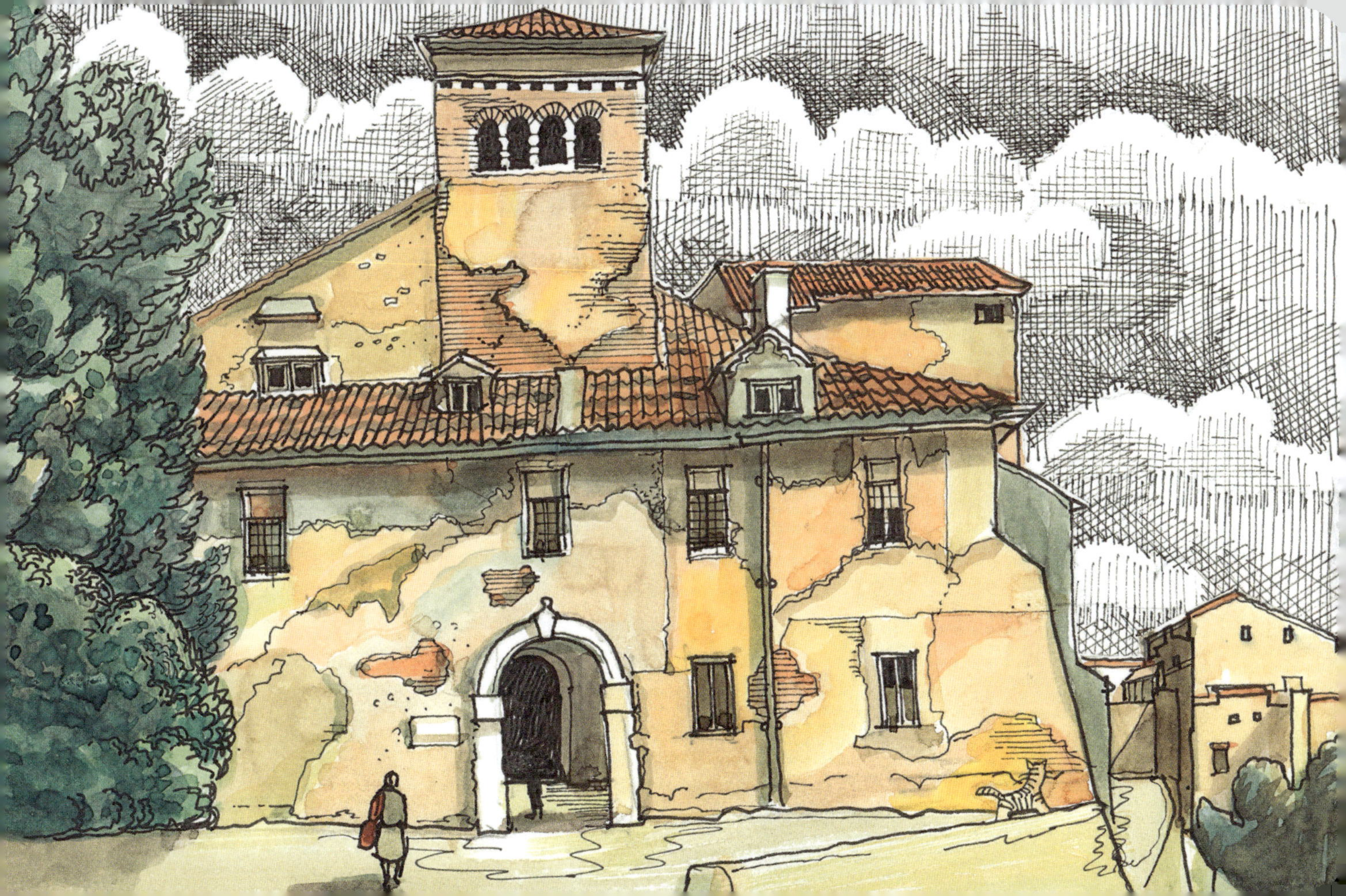

old papal residence houses a museum and diocesan offices for the city, and, whereas it was once a centre of the world, it now stands glumly as the traffic roars by.

As well as firing up violent anti-papal emotions throughout Europe and triggering England's break forever with Rome, Henry VIII's Reformation set off a series of murderous wars that moved people and ideas violently around the continent. For Rome, these reached their horrific climax with the most tumultuous of its SEVEN MAJOR SACKINGS, carried out by the Holy Roman Empire under Charles V in 1527. Although Gauls, Normans and Goths had during previous sackings stolen valuable treasure and money, that was as nothing compared with the rape, torture and killings meted out by the hungry and greedy Imperial troops and their German Landsknecht mercenaries. They abandoned a city brutally scarred and initially materially poorer, but the situation quickly improved after the pope repaired his relationship with the Emperor.

The papacy is a self-perpetuating gerontocracy. Popes are usually elected as old men and thus they succeed one another rather quickly. It can be quite hard, therefore, to work out which is which. As important as their given papal title is their family name: Colonna (Martin V), Barberini (Urban VIII), Orsini (Celestine III, Nicholas III and Benedict XIII), Medici (Leo X, Clement VII, Pius IV and Leo XI) and so on. These families represent the papal aristocracy of medieval and Renaissance Rome, as closed a shop as the electoral colleges of Venice or Genoa. They were rivals, owned great estates outside the city and intrigued one against the other. Although the Bishop of Rome himself could not marry, and thus could not officially have children, the most lavish of nepotistic gestures were almost inevitable for various relatives throughout history, and one palace or gallery or collection after another bore the name of these and other pontiffs.

Over the centuries, the backgrounds from which candidates for the papacy emerged have varied deeply, from early Christian bishops to Imperial aristocrats, from the abbots of great monastic houses to representatives of the warring noble factions of medieval Rome. Some might be archbishops, others barely Christian, being made priests only in order to take up the most powerful and lucrative position as Pontiff. Gradually, the role was professionalized and all were elected from within the Curia (the college of cardinals), but increasingly those men were from diverse backgrounds. In the twentieth century, Pius XI (died 1939) was the son of a silk manufacturer

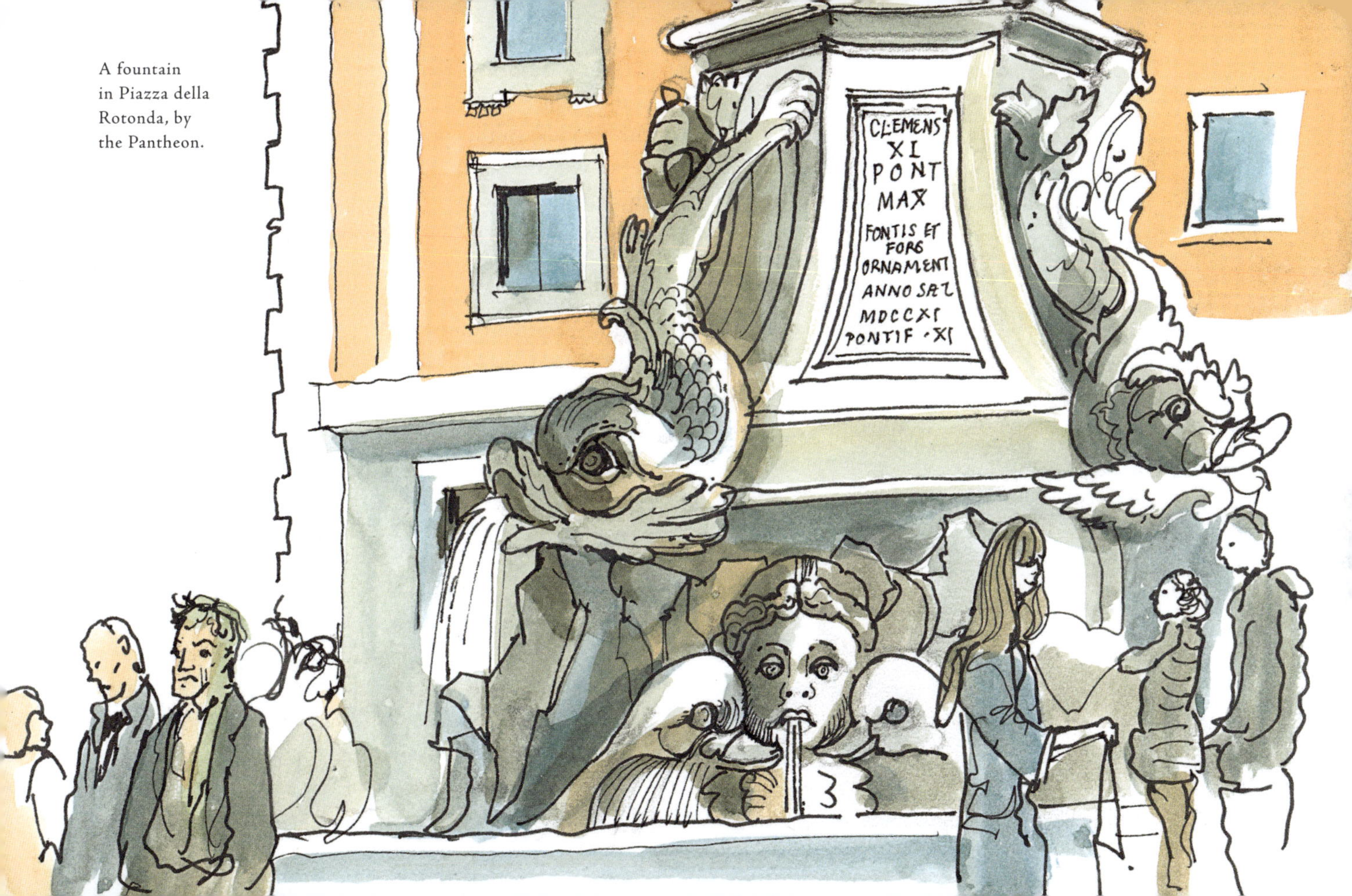

A fountain in Piazza della Rotonda, by the Pantheon.

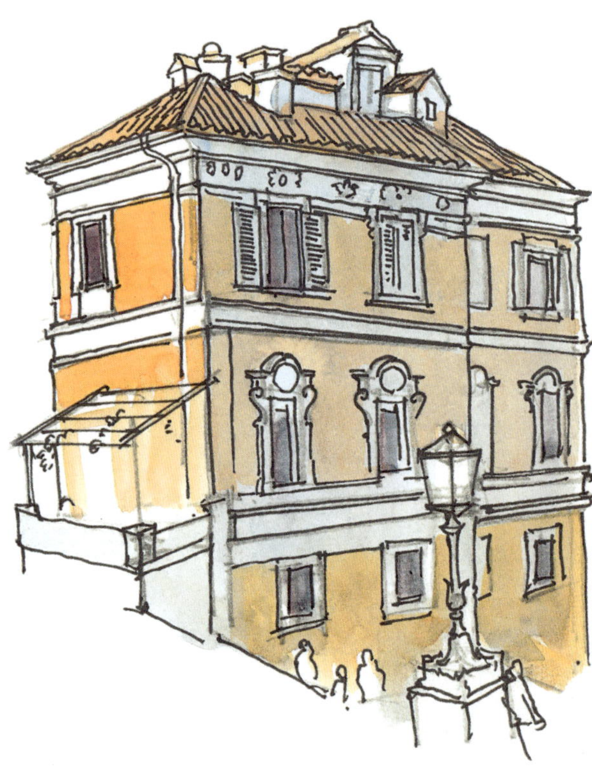

Keats' House by the Spanish Steps, where the poet
lived and died in 1821, aged only twenty-five.

(a family sunk in trade), Pius XII the son of a papal
courtier and John XXIII a poor sharecropper's son from
the north. The connections between the senatorial families
of ancient Rome and the later Catholic leaders (such as
the Colonna family) only serve to illustrate how the popes
were the emperors of medieval and Renaissance Rome and
how the contemporary idea of a pope as a purely spiritual
ruler is comparatively new.

In the aftermath of the 1527 SACK OF ROME, the
city needed high-spending popes to rebuild the city
and restore its fortunes. This expansion was funded by
the revenue from the sale of bishoprics and the many
other LUCRATIVE RELIGIOUS POSITIONS that
commanded an income. Before the English Reformation,
about thirty per cent of the English economy had been in
ecclesiastical hands, and the same economic calculation
applied throughout Catholic Europe. The church had to
rebuild spiritually, as well as architecturally, to challenge
the potentially existential disaster of the Reformation,
which had bitten hard at the finances of a church reliant
on the sale of indulgences and masses being said for the
SOULS OF THE DEAD.

The counter-reformation was this rebuilding movement,
a bravura manifestation of the grandeur and spiritual

authority of the church. This was projected through the Jesuits (1540) and the Oratorians (1575), two orders at the service of Rome that were established to spread the newly confident message. Its wounds healed, Rome regained its status and, in the sixteenth and seventeenth centuries, was the focus of a vast outpouring of artistic expression, from Michelangelo and Raphael to Bernini and Borromini, as the adventures of Spain, Portugal and Italy in capturing the huge wealth of the New World helped swell the coffers of the Vatican.

1700 – 2000 The eighteenth century is GRAND TOUR ROME. It saw a huge surge of patrician tourism that swamped the great Baroque, Renaissance and Classical city. What began as a medieval curiosity about the ancient world had, through the past two centuries, turned into an appetite for all things Roman and, indeed, by the end of the century, all things Greek. Although it began as the preserve of the highest section of northern European society, the desire to explore the motherlode of Classical culture spread widely, and soon any young man of means saw the Grand Tour as an essential part of his education. An industry and an economy developed to make this even more appealing, with guides in the form of CICERONES

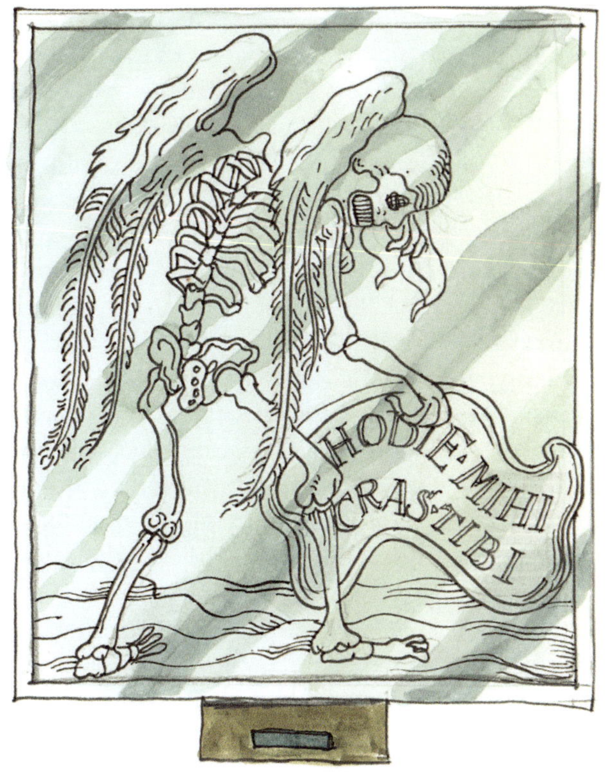

A carved panel on Santa Maria dell'Orazione e Morte,
a church rebuilt in the eighteenth century, on the Via Giulia.

and BEAR LEADERS appointing themselves to show the *milordi Inglesi* Rome's treasures. So strong was the British take-up that this title was also used to describe Dutch and German travellers, as well as denizens of the new United States of America. For some Tourists, this was a sustained and serious programme of study and research. In the case of architects like the young Robert Adam – whose visit went on to involve making lengthy and analytical drawings of Diocletian's Palace in Split – it was a profoundly important part of their professional education.

Most important of all was the need to develop 'TASTE'. Prolonged exposure to the ruins of the city and to its newer paintings and sculpture made cognoscenti of the most red-cheeked and country-reared member of the gentry. Having seen, and eaten and drunk with, as many Roman hosts and hostesses as were willing, these travellers wanted to go shopping. Whole ruins were impossible to acquire, and, unless pockets were exceptionally deep, real statuary and canvasses were ruinously expensive. Even then, the export of works of art was fiercely protected by the authorities, and subterfuge was needed to spirit away an Imperial bust or a bigger group of Classical marbles.

Enter GIOVANNI BATTISTA PIRANESI, a Venetian painter, engraver and former stage designer who adopted Rome as his home in 1740 and who made a huge series of engravings, both informative and atmospheric. The city's great ruins, the Colosseum, arches, temples and columns had mostly been unearthed, but there was still an appealing top dressing of picturesque undergrowth and vegetation. Archaically attired peasants still drove cattle through the ruins of Caracalla's Baths or grazed doomed goats among the colonnades of the Forum. These views, or VEDUTI, Piranesi captured with faultless drawing and a romanticized approach. From these recognizable scenes, he developed a series of quite invented views of imaginary classical prisons and castles with arching and vaulting all over the place. Whole sets of his works were snapped up, easily transported back to Dorset, Brittany or Utrecht, where, set in black and gold 'Hogarth' frames, they classicized the interiors of countless town and country houses.

These became a symbol of having made the Tour and an indication that the ALL-IMPORTANT TASTE had been developed. From there, it was a short step to acquiring some of Josiah Wedgwood's Etruscan and Roman wares (he even called his modern manufactory 'Etruria' in 1769), from dainty creamware tea sets with borders taken from

Verano cemetery, with umbrella pines, in the San Lorenzo neighbourhood.

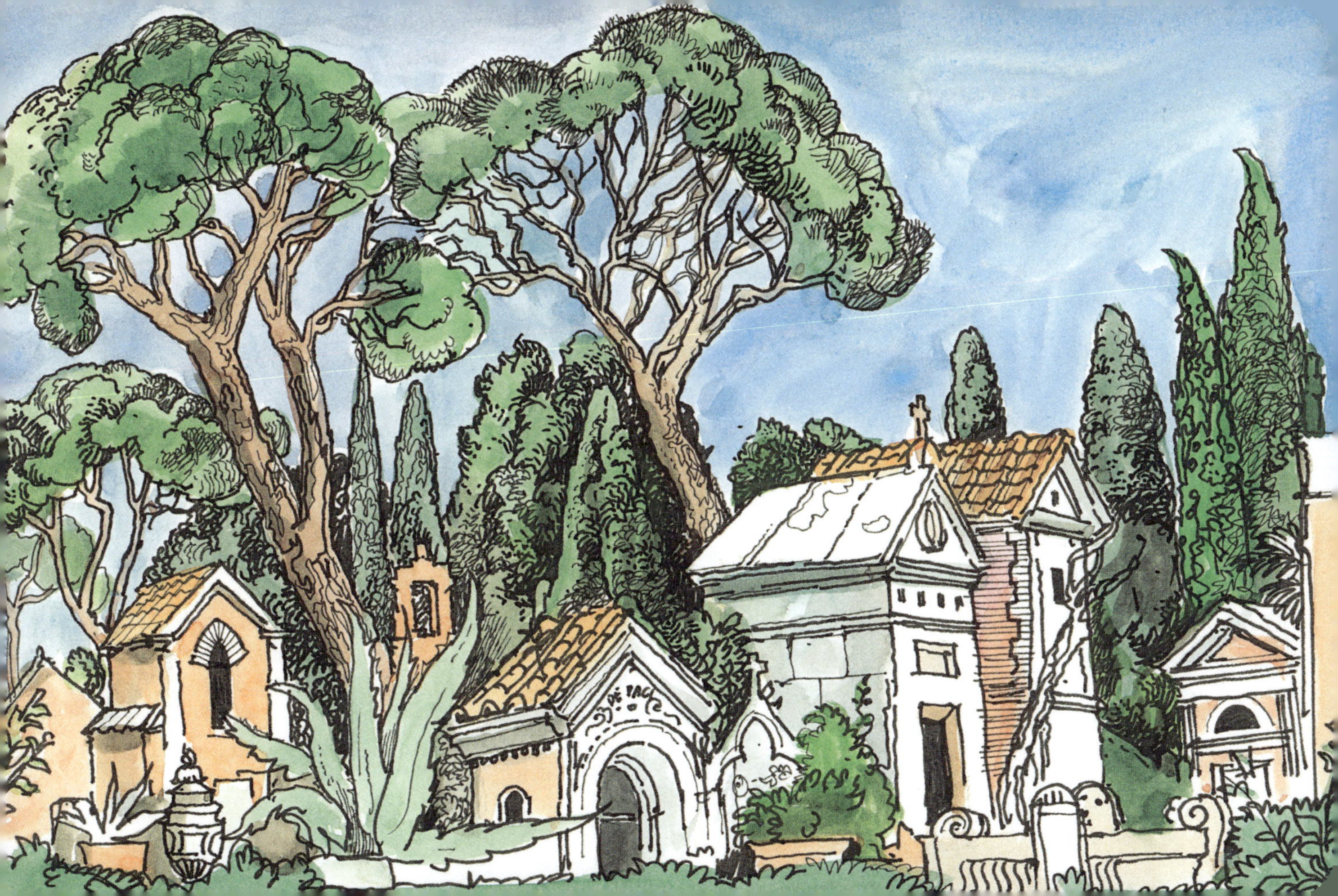
IN PACE

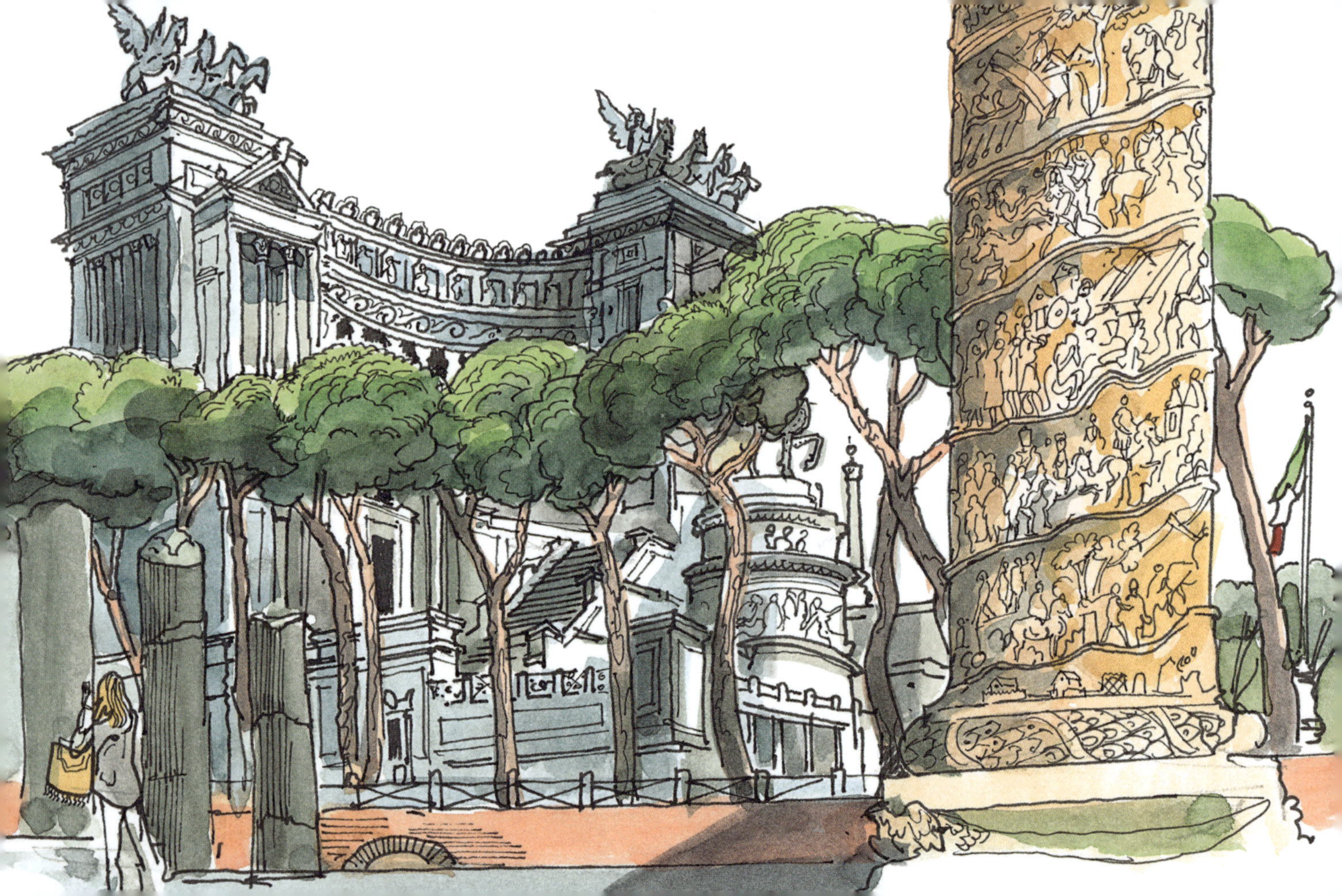

the ancient to the highest-status piece of all, a copy of the 'Portland' vase, based on a first-century piece which had made it across the Alps unscathed and settled in that Duchess's collection. This Classical taste filtered down to the newly minted middle classes, for whom, as much as for the aristocracy, the association with the Emperor Augustus or the works of Virgil and Pliny could be STRONGLY HINTED at by a Roman urn in Staffordshire earthenware. The French Revolution, however, put an abrupt stop to this pleasurable sojourning, as safe travel in war-torn Europe became all but impossible.

The revolutionary turbulence of the late eighteenth century was certainly felt in Rome. The pope was every bit as much an ABSOLUTE MONARCH as those who were losing power (or their heads) elsewhere in Europe. Napoleon Bonaparte surfed this tsunami of unrest and revolution, fighting for French military and economic superiority. France had the advantage over Italy of being one unified country, whereas the Italian peninsula was divided between the kingdoms of Piedmont-Sardinia and the Two Sicilies and the papal states, as well as the still-significant Venetian republic. To the north was the

Austro-Hungarian Empire, successor to the Holy Roman Empire. Napoleon and, indeed, the republican French were generally anti-clerical and specifically ANTI-POPE. The Italian republic was declared in 1798 after Napoleon conquered the papal states, but it was dissolved a year later when retaken by the Italians. Napoleon returned in 1805, and a new Napoleonic Kingdom of Italy was declared, which included Venice and much of north central Italy. This again fell on Napoleon's abdication in 1814, but by then the seeds of republican revolution had not merely been sown, but were putting down serious roots.

Garibaldi and Mazzini, the great NATIONALIST HEROES OF ITALY, were involved in much of the revolutionary mood that initiated the *Risorgimento*, or unification of Italy, in 1861. Despite its initial failure and the return to Austrian rule, the way was laid for Count Cavour (more diplomatic… less heroic) to broker the adoption of Piedmont-Sardinia (the house of Savoy) as a unifying monarchy for Italy. After Garibaldi's dramatic conquering of the south, the new kingdom was to include all but the still-Austrian-held Venice and papal Rome.

Venice joined the Kingdom of Italy in 1866, and, after France's failed attempt to take Rome the following year, the removal of the French emperor's troops in 1870 to fight the Prussians left the pope unprotected. Despite Pius IX's refusal to cede the city, it was promptly taken by Garibaldi, making Rome, once again, the capital of a unified Kingdom of Italy in 1871. This caused a burst of economic energy and a huge expansion of the new capital, as the apparatus of modern government required accommodation.

Following this nationalistic reorganization, the Altare della Patria or Vittorio Emanuele II Monument was started in 1885 and inaugurated in 1911. It was not really complete in all its snowy Grecian glory until 1935, when Fascism had reared its ugly head. The grandiloquent language and Busby Berkeley showy glamour could not have come at a more opportune time. The Italian dictator, Benito Mussolini, felt very WARMLY for parades and marches, in a perceived echo of his country's real Imperial past. Goosestepping conscripts could celebrate DUBIOUS VICTORIES in grubby and bloodthirsty African campaigns, and their annexations of Abyssinia and Libya, with an abundance of schmaltz towering behind them.

The career of Mussolini, Il Duce, began with the 1922 March on Rome, when he took power from parliament to popular support. Initially more 'benign' than his German ally, the filthy evil of anti-Semitism and the excesses of absolute power soon led Mussolini to head a thoroughly disagreeable violent and bullying regime. His home, Villa Torlonia, surrounded by fine cedar trees and with both a botanical garden and a small theatre in its elegant grounds, stood a few hundred metres from Villa Ada Savoia, a suburban house among the pine trees, where the king lived modestly. In 1943, summoned by his monarch late in the evening, Il Duce was told he need not be in uniform. He had all but failed to keep order in parliament that day, so had every reason to be anxious, but, buoyed up by the thought of a cocktail and a pep talk, answered the call. However, his majesty was clear: it was time to go. With the Campari unruffled in the glass, Mussolini was quietly walked to an ambulance behind the house and off to an alpine exile. Although reinstalled by the Germans briefly in 1944, he was finally captured and shot in 1945.

Late-twentieth-century Rome licked its wartime wounds. Scandals, kidnappings and economic tumults apart, Rome changed from being the capital of a poor and unindustrialized country to being one of the world's greatest modern cities, its people building, working and living among the splendours of 2,500 years of history.

Colosseo Quadrato, or Square Colosseum, 1937–42, in the EUR district.

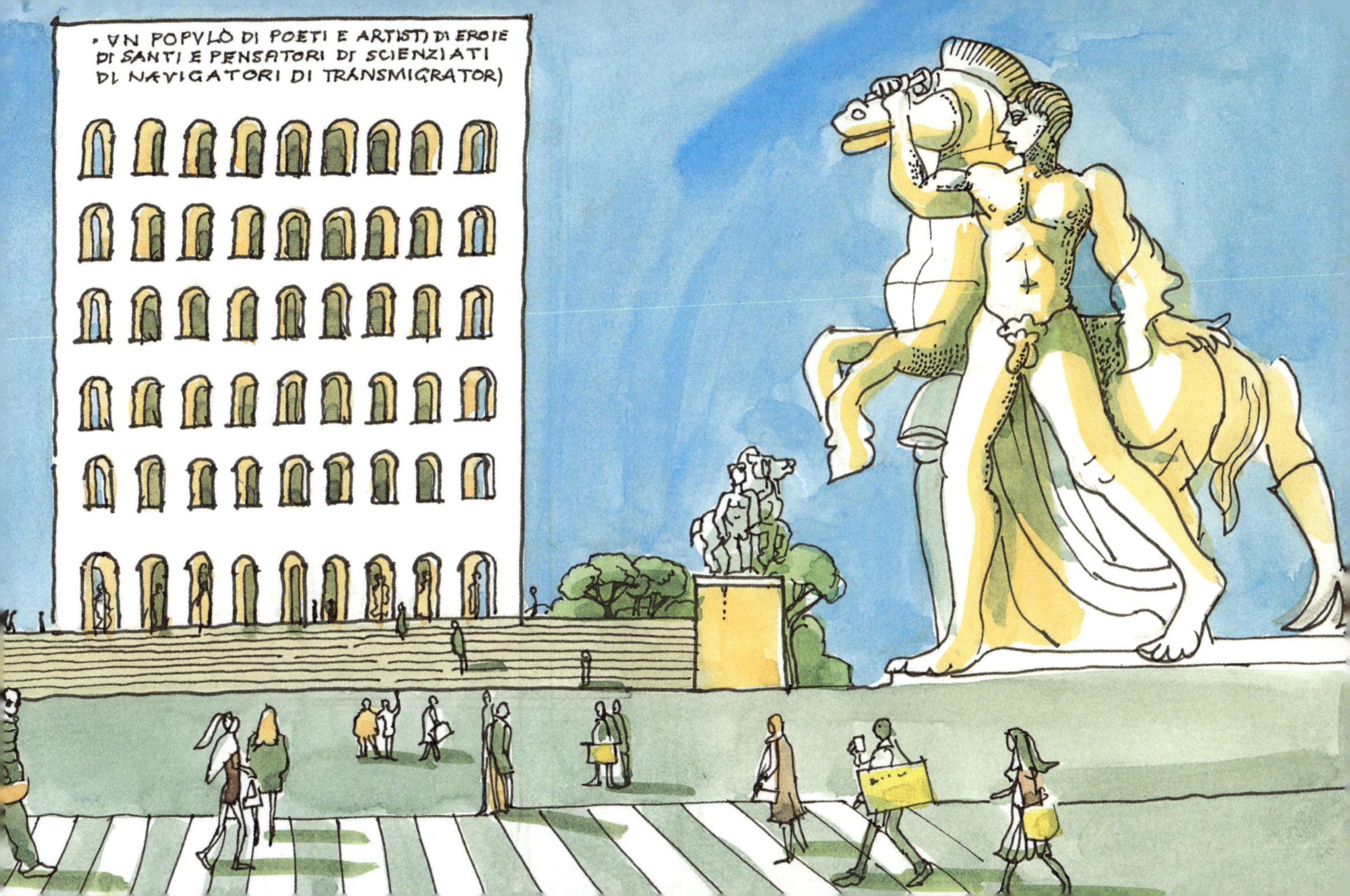

UN POPULO DI POETI E ARTISTI DI EROIE
DI SANTI E PENSATORI DI SCIENZIATI
DI NAVIGATORI DI TRANSMIGRATORI

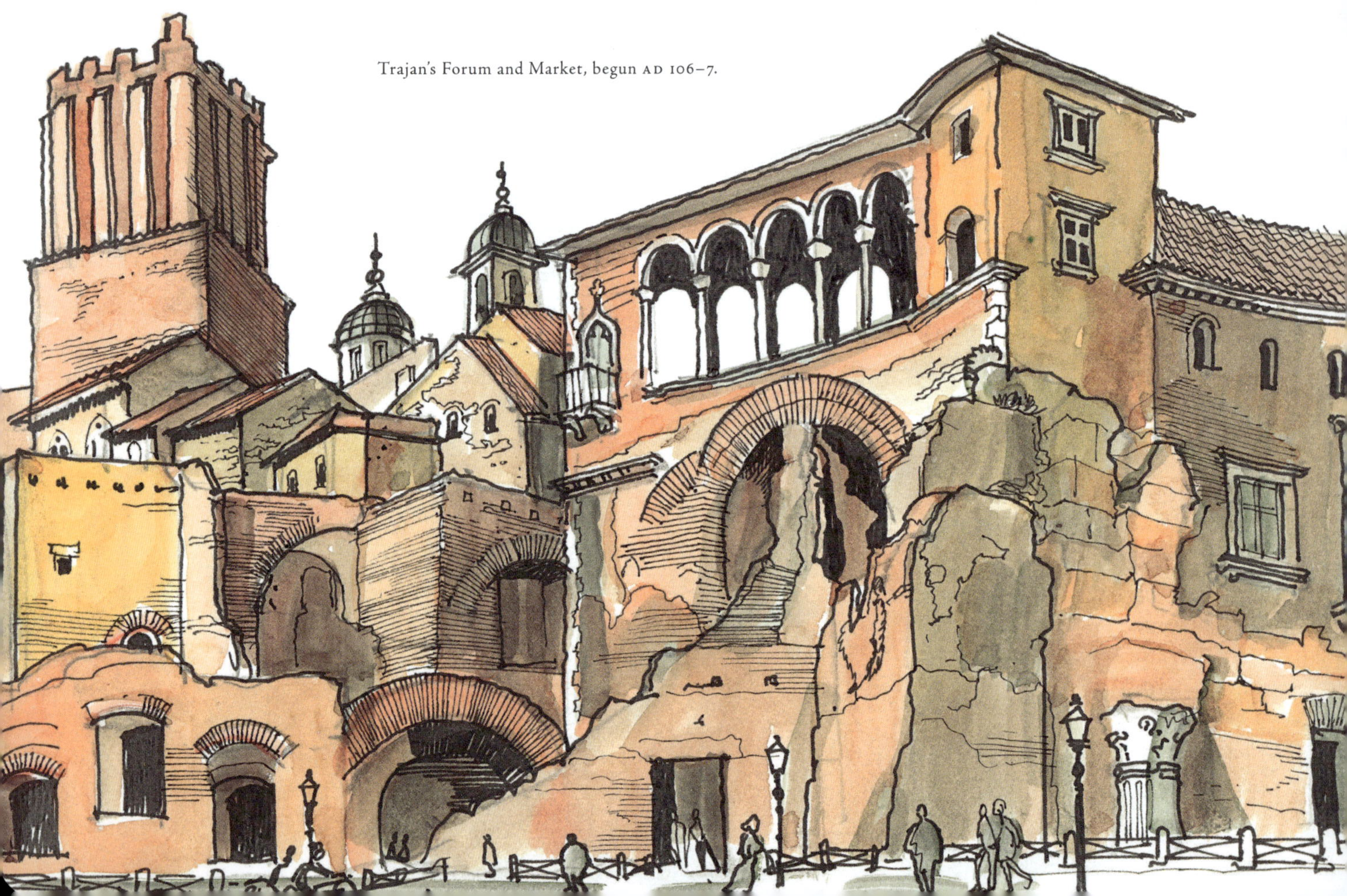

Trajan's Forum and Market, begun AD 106–7.

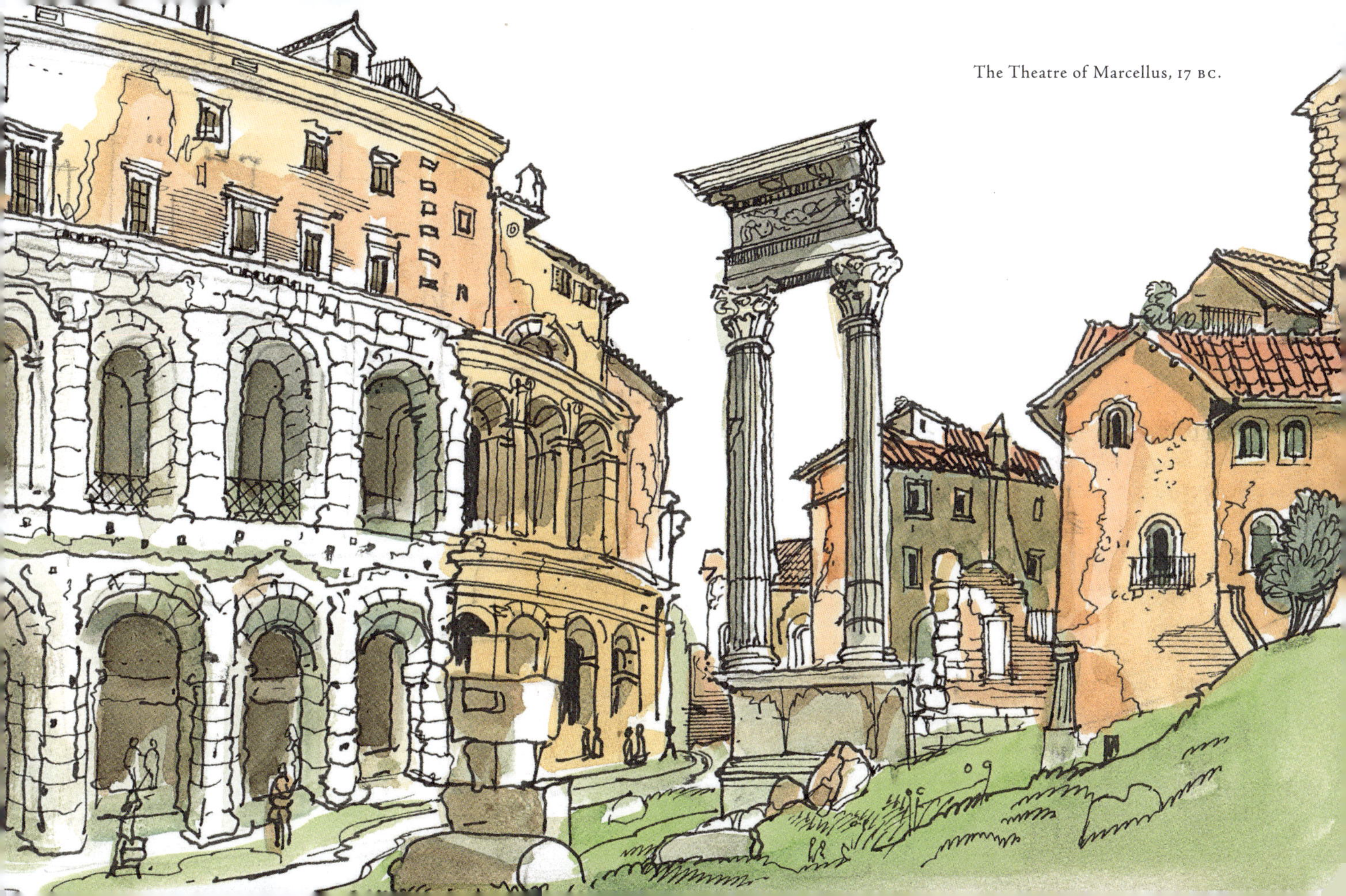

The Theatre of Marcellus, 17 BC.

Roman architecture

Rome's POWER – Imperial, spiritual or dictatorial – was expressed architecturally. Emperors threw up arches triumphal and columns crammed with narrative; popes resisted the Reformation with domes and with entablatures that wriggled like eels, and Il Duce's unforgiving repetitions and colonnades at EUR (Rome's Universal Exposition) left no room for doubt as to who was in charge. It is the general nature of architecture that a patron's dreams and aspirations may be written in stone, telling the history of a place in bricks and mortar, but the Roman version is remarkable in that these messages co-exist even if written 2,000 years apart. Also peculiar to Rome (because it had so many Classical ruins) was the degree to which it FED ON ITSELF, the Renaissance city being built from re-used columns and stones and rendered with lime made from ancient marbles fired in kilns throughout the city.

The first buildings of urban Rome, as opposed to the thatched mud huts that early settlers lived in and that were exactly like any other, were made of wood. The great Temple of Jupiter Optimus Maximus, much rebuilt, is only known from descriptions. It was characterized as primitive, clunky and low, embellished with terracotta, yet it dominated the Capitoline Hill. Etruscan sculptors, notably Vulca of Veii, produced expressive figures, acroteria (decorative pedestals) and other architectonic elements with which to embellish the giant pediment and tympanum. Its massive wooden columns were painted red and were in a bold and basic Tuscan style.

The move towards the archetypical image of ancient Rome corresponds with the rule of Octavian, known as the Emperor Augustus, who 'found Rome a city of bricks and left it a city of marble'. The temple form, the peristyle (row of columns) and, indeed, the basilica were inherited from the Greeks, who built the Parthenon in Athens in 447 BC. The three main orders, Doric, Ionic and Corinthian, also

Portico of Octavia, 27 BC, from which many triumphal processions set out.

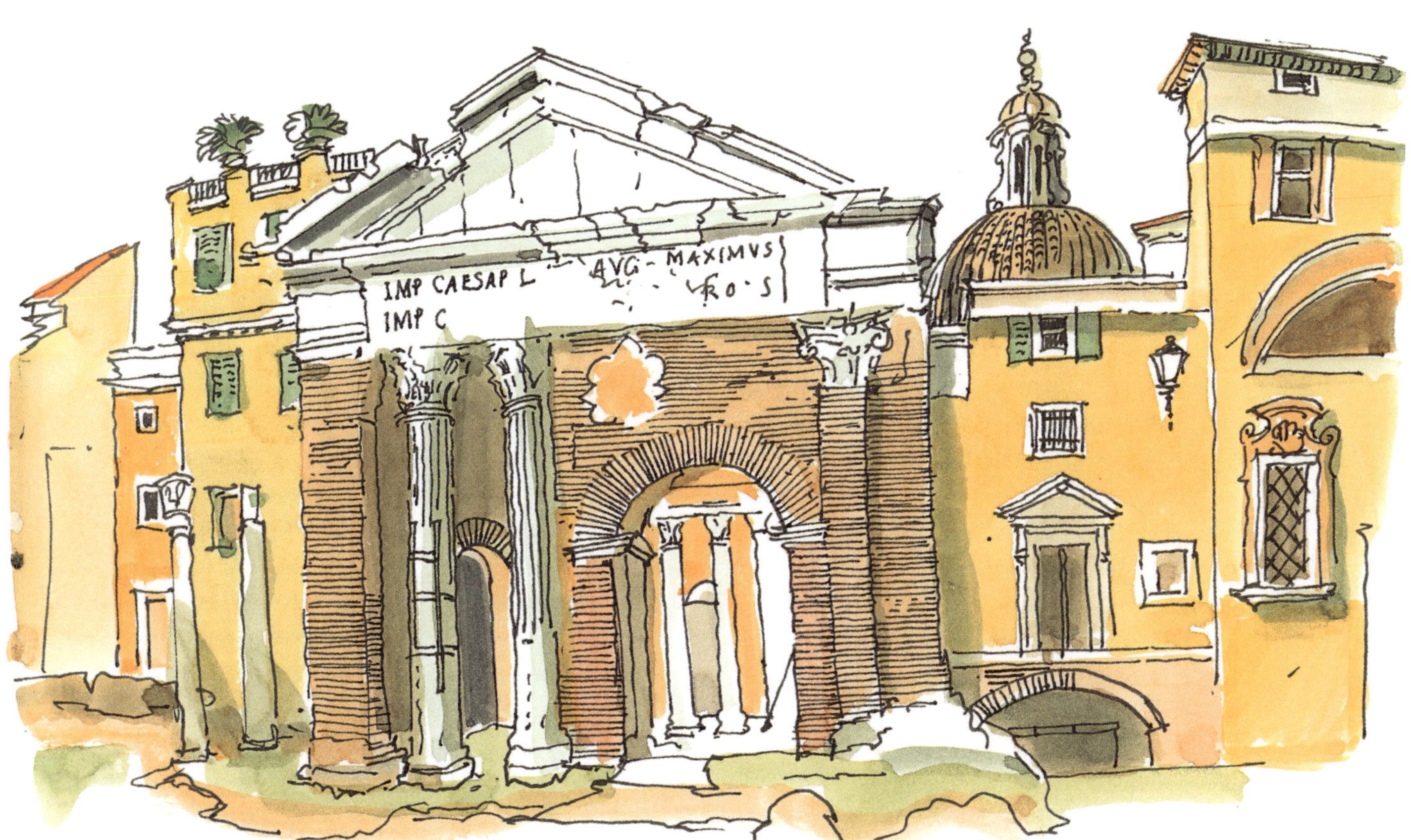

IMP CAESAP L   AVG · MAXIMVS
IMP C   RO·S

came from Greece; the more elaborate Composite order was created in Rome. Nineteenth-century philhellenes made much of the derivative nature and coarsening effect of Rome's own buildings, but they ignored two massively significant additions to the lexicon of Classical architecture.

The first of these was the ARCH, which sprang from the discovery that, by building a wooden former and laying shaped blocks, voussoirs, next to one another, the whole wedged fast with a central keystone, a wider space could be spanned than with a flat lintel. An arcade could be formed by a series of arched components or a tunnel or barrel vault made by setting a series of arches in a row, one behind the next. The Roman arch was a major advance on the post and lintel that defined the buildings of Athens, Pergamon or Corinth, and this gave rise to a totally NEW FORM: the triumphal arch. These appeared across the city, as one victorious general after another recorded his successes in marble. In the Forum, Maxentius's Basilica used barrel vaulting to dramatic effect. It is so huge that it makes imagining the complete building very difficult.

The second invention was CONCRETE. This semi-liquid building material was a game changer in terms of form, making double curves, like that of the Pantheon's dome, possible for the first time. As the best preserved and perhaps the single most impressive building from ancient Rome, the Pantheon takes some beating. Despite the fine lettering pronouncing it the work of the Emperor Agrippa, it was, in fact, the work of the Emperor Hadrian and was completed in AD 125. The building sits low in a *piazza* hollowed out from the accreted rising ground levels, so one walks down to the grandest of porticos. Two rows of eight columns support a frieze (the one with the misattribution) and tall, empty pediment. Behind, a brick-fronted concrete drum supports a dome forty-three metres in diameter, bigger even than that of St Peter's. The concrete construction allows for no windows, the only light coming through the hole, or OCULUS, in the centre of the ceiling. This format – portico under a pediment and temple under a dome – has been repeated worldwide in Classical park landscapes, such as Chiswick and Stourhead in England, and in civic buildings. The Emperor Constans II, of Constantinople, peeled off the dome's former bronze skin in AD 663 and the structure has survived minor damage, but, repurposed as a church, it has lasted for nearly 2,000 years.

In the *piazza* is an obelisk, an essential feature of Rome. More than forty-eight were imported from Egypt in Classical times and thirteen remain, punctuating the city as they rise from fountains, plinths and (with some difficulty and in one

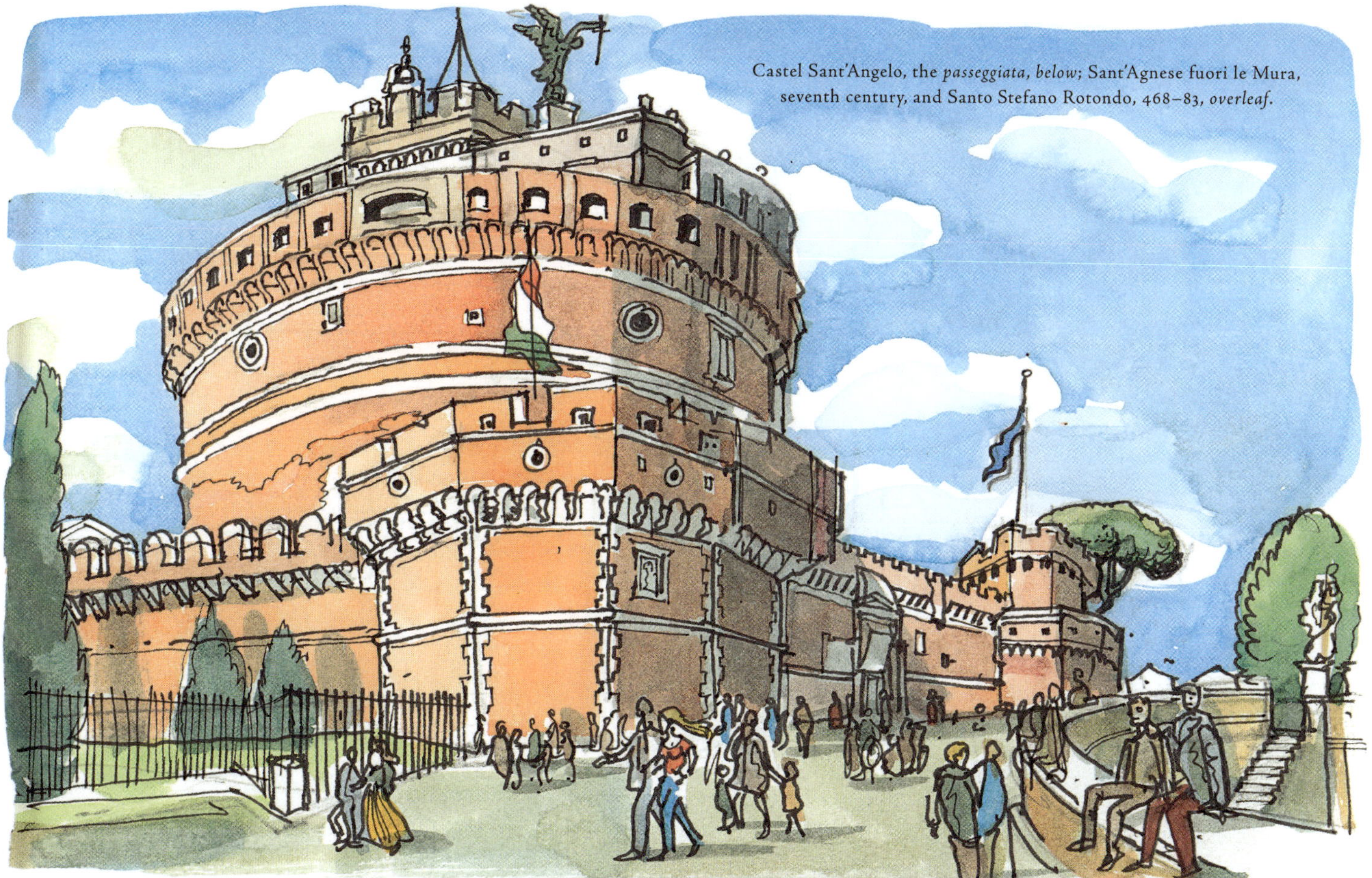

Castel Sant'Angelo, the *passeggiata, below*; Sant'Agnese fuori le Mura, seventh century, and Santo Stefano Rotondo, 468–83, *overleaf*.

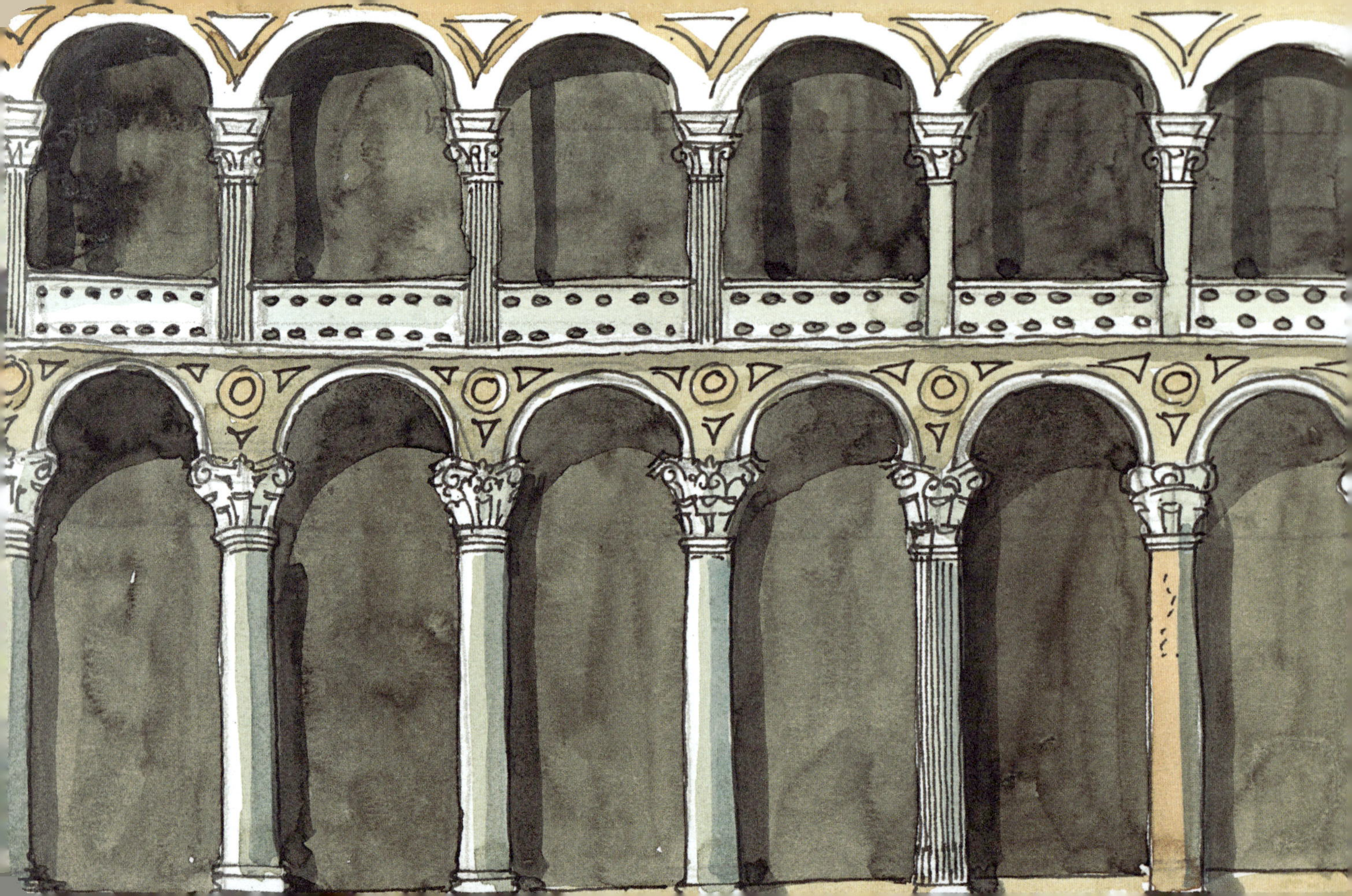

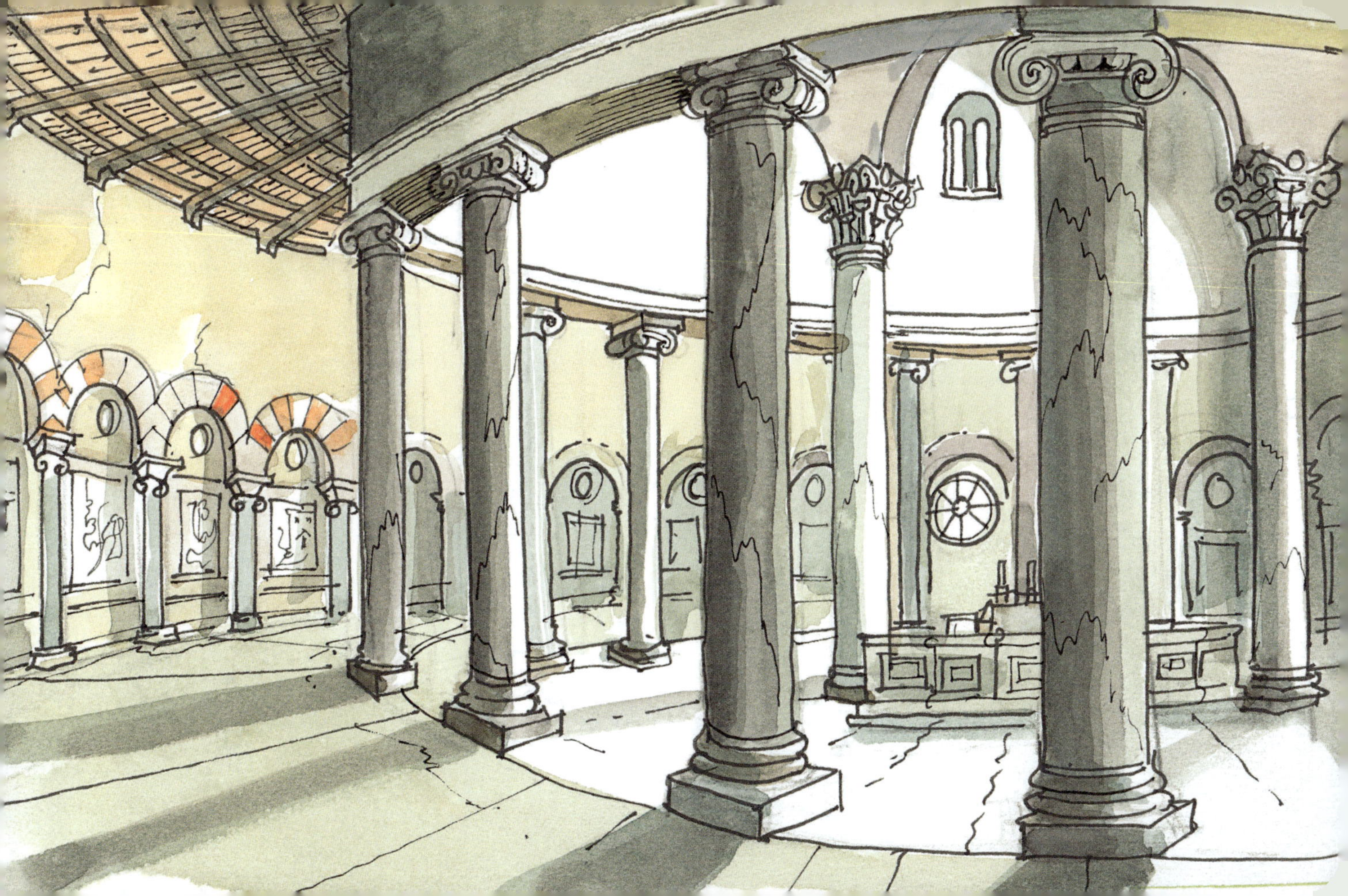

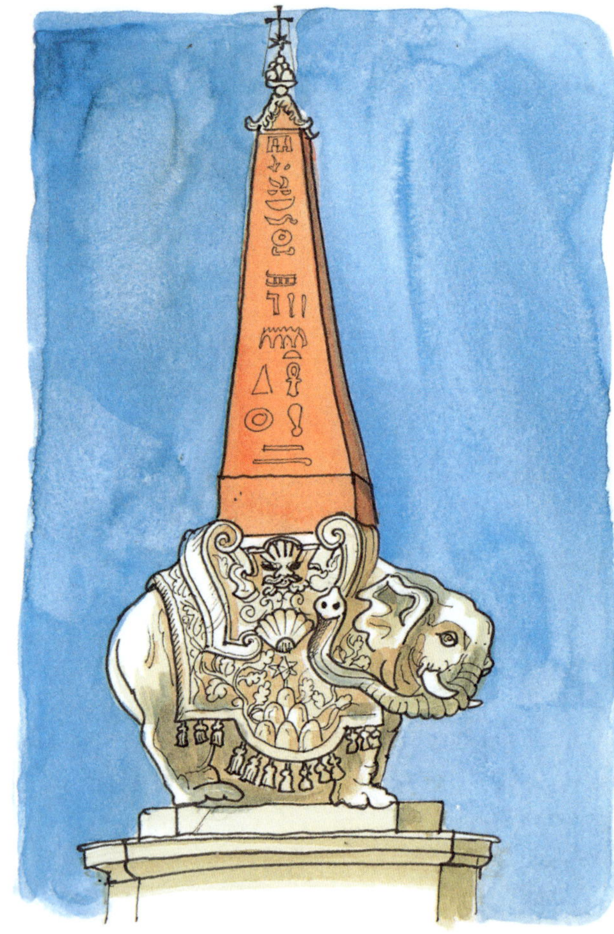

case only) from the back of an elephant. The obelisk was portable (just) and instantly recognizable and was the perfect symbol of the close, yet violent, relationship between Rome and its former rival Egypt. This found its most famous expression in the doomed but eternal love affairs between Julius Caesar, Mark Antony and the world's first *femme fatale*, CLEOPATRA, and gave rise to outbreaks of gloomy pharaonic statuary, particularly in mausolea, and, more strikingly, those Aswan granite needles that characterize the city to this day.

The buildings, paintings and monuments of Imperial Rome have a counterpoint in Edwardian Britain; indeed, in the architecture of that period Western-worldwide. Take the inclusion of high-relief sculpture in façades. This is incredibly resource-heavy and requires many thousands of man hours to produce – what's more, skilled man hours. That relies upon the confluence of two environmental conditions: first, a robust economic environment that encourages construction and, second, the availability of craftsmanship at relatively low cost. That, in turn, depends on a profoundly unequal society. In the case of Augustan Rome, this meant a very large population of

First-century elephant and Bernini's obelisk, 1667, in Piazza della Minerva.

slaves and, in *fin de siècle* Europe and America, a poorly paid and unenfranchised working class swollen by skilled immigration, for example, Italian plasterers and gilders in Edwardian Britain. The International style, by contrast, calm and undecorated, proved to be the ideal architectural language of Socialism, its components made in factories, with their systems of organized labour, which also, usefully, serve to anonymize the patron.

The sheer scale of ancient Rome is sometimes hard to understand from a row of isolated columns standing among their fallen comrades in the Forum. However massive their smashed capitals and acanthus scrolls or their granite shafts, held together by bands of steel, they are still ruins that need a fairly powerful projection of imagination to turn into a Forum thronged with toga-wearing citizens. One who possessed such imagination was the draughtsman, engraver and GENERAL FANTASIST Piranesi, the overachieving polymath who re-created the ancient city of Rome, detailing its surviving ruins and architectural details and interpreting them for eighteenth-century eyes. However, the very best way to reimagine them as they once were is to see a building itself reimagined and repurposed.

Palazzo Farnese, Sangallo, 1517, redesigned by Michelangelo in 1534.

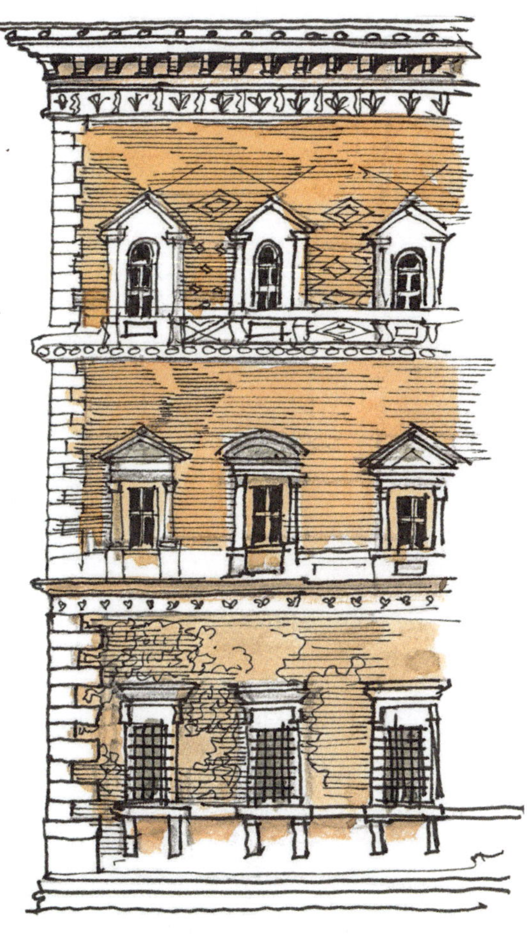

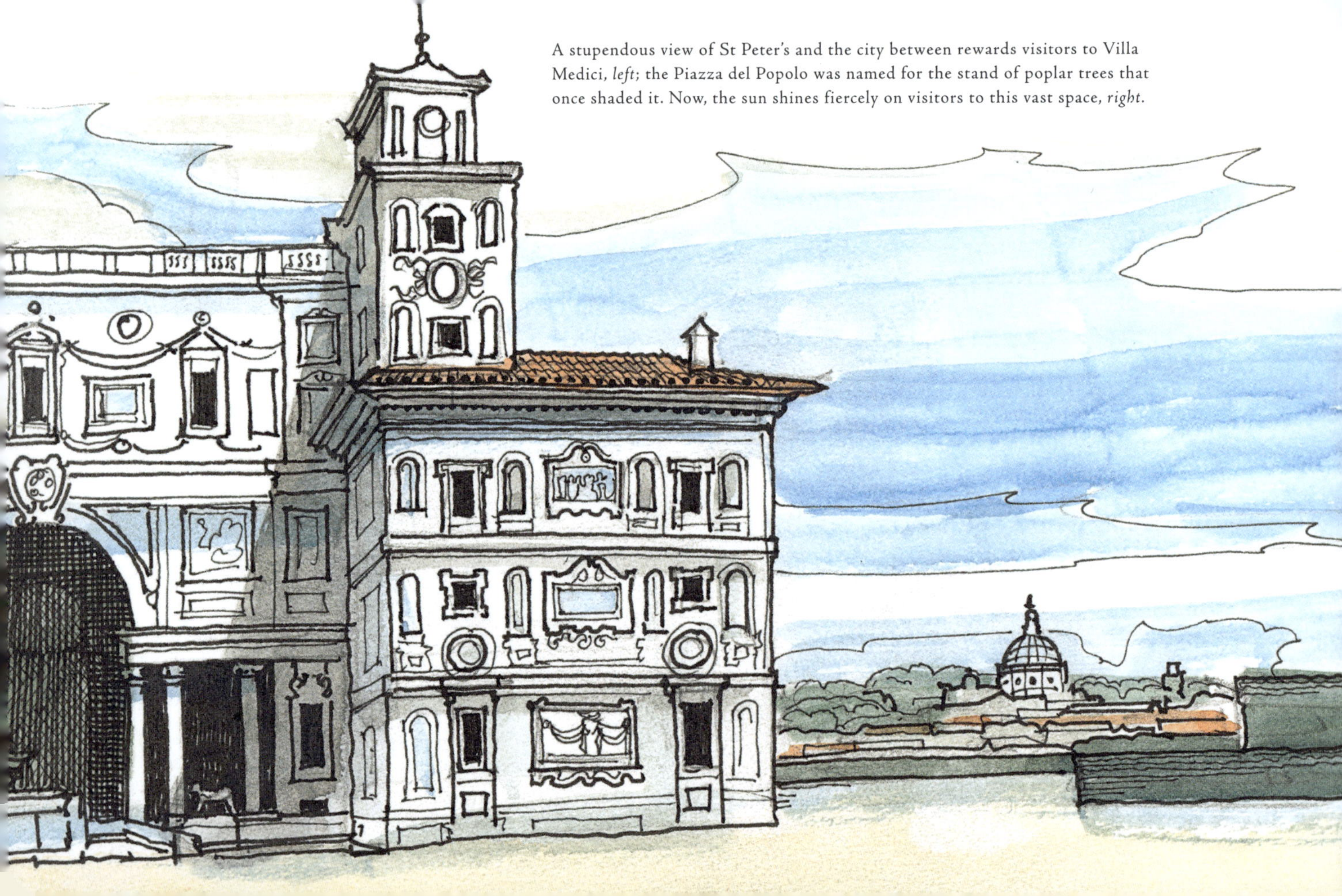

A stupendous view of St Peter's and the city between rewards visitors to Villa Medici, *left*; the Piazza del Popolo was named for the stand of poplar trees that once shaded it. Now, the sun shines fiercely on visitors to this vast space, *right*.

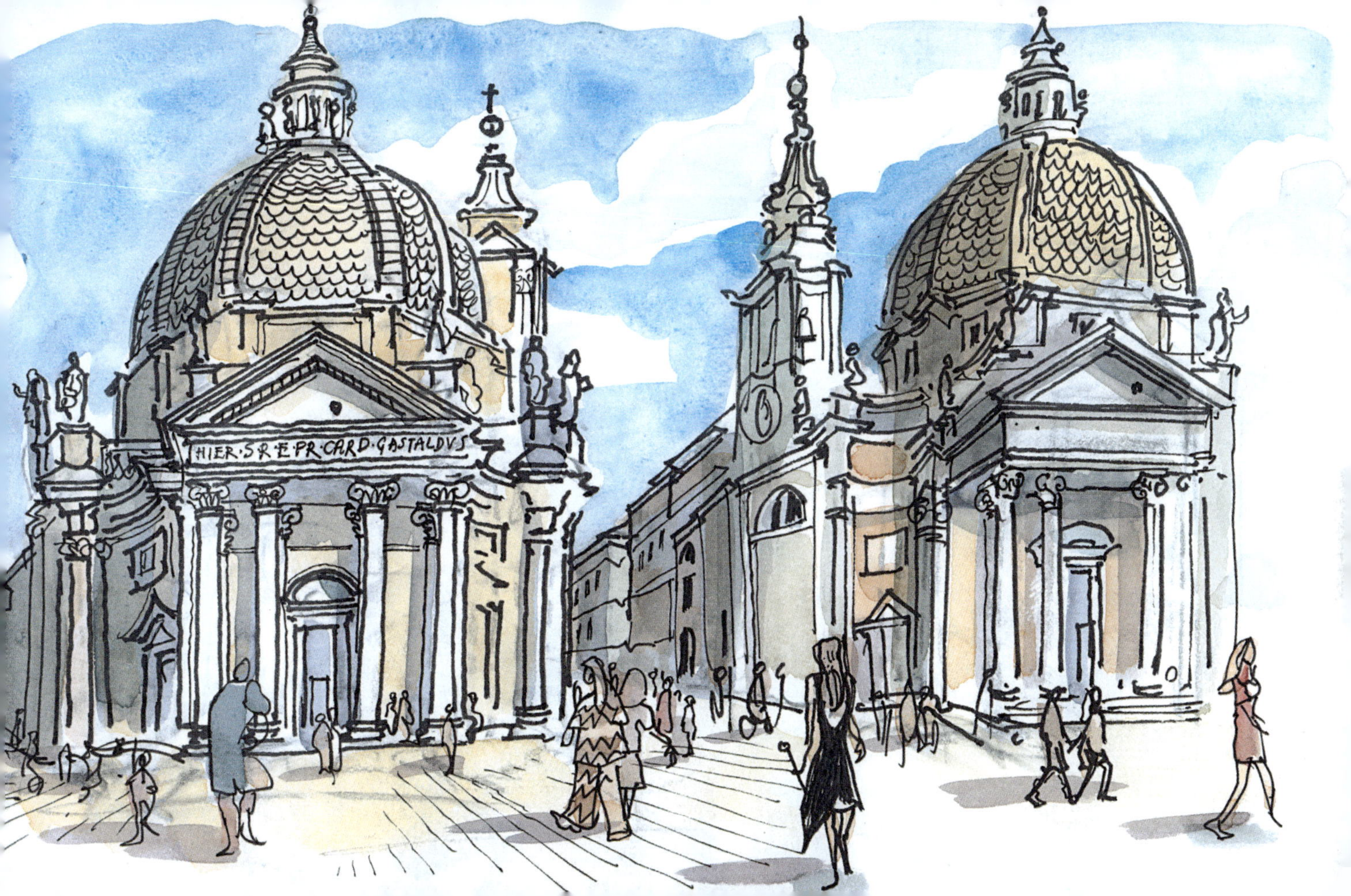
HIER · S R E PR · CARD · GASTALDVS

The Pantheon is an obvious candidate, as is the church of Santa Maria degli Angeli e dei Martiri.

When Pope Pius IV commissioned Michelangelo to design the church in 1561, he wanted not only to create a new place of worship, but to utilize one of the city's most magnificent ancient palaces. Diocletian was one of the greatest of the late Roman emperors, who stabilized for a time the already shuddering structure of the Empire. He formed a power-sharing tetrarchy (a gang of four) and achieved military victories against omnipresent threats in central Europe. To honour his triumph, a huge bathing complex was built in AD 306, complete with bath houses of various temperatures – *caldarium*, *tepidarium* and *frigidarium* – as well as other essential facilities, such as a swimming pool (*natatorium*), a gymnasium (*palestra*) and libraries. These days, following diggings, delvings and repurposing, the remains are hard to read architecturally, except for the odd piece of marble that declaims 'these were the biggest baths in the world', but it is still easy to spot DIOCLETIAN WINDOWS. These are tripartite windows built inside a semi-circular arch, and they became a device used by architects throughout the Renaissance and beyond, including the great Palladio, in whose compositions they were a key feature.

Within Santa Maria degli Angeli e dei Martiri lies Michelangelo's boldly designed Carthusian cloister, which became a charterhouse in the sixteenth century. Huge arcades enclose a garden, in the centre of which two bulls, two horses and a sheep, which once presided over the day-to-day life of Trajan's Forum, are joined by a sixteenth-century elephant and rhino. They (the beasts) sit on brick plinths, looking at a very good collection of statuary and architectural detritus displayed in each bay, or even just scattered in the cloister garth. There is so much antiquity in Rome that an arm or an ear shows up whenever any new building is embarked upon, evidence of the dramatic fall of ancient Rome in the Middle Ages.

The early churches of Christian Rome were built in basilica form, a Greek concept comprising a hall with an apsidal (semi-circular) niche at one end. Hitherto adopted for Roman law courts, this plan was perfect for the early liturgy of the Church and remained the standard form for a millennium. It also provided an ideal field for decorating in the technique imported from Byzantium: mosaic images of Christ the Good Shepherd with attendant ovines, vines and angels on deep-blue skies survive in churches such as San Clemente or Santa Prassede. In these relatively under-fenestrated buildings,

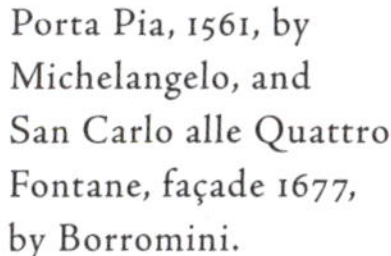

Porta Pia, 1561, by
Michelangelo, and
San Carlo alle Quattro
Fontane, façade 1677,
by Borromini.

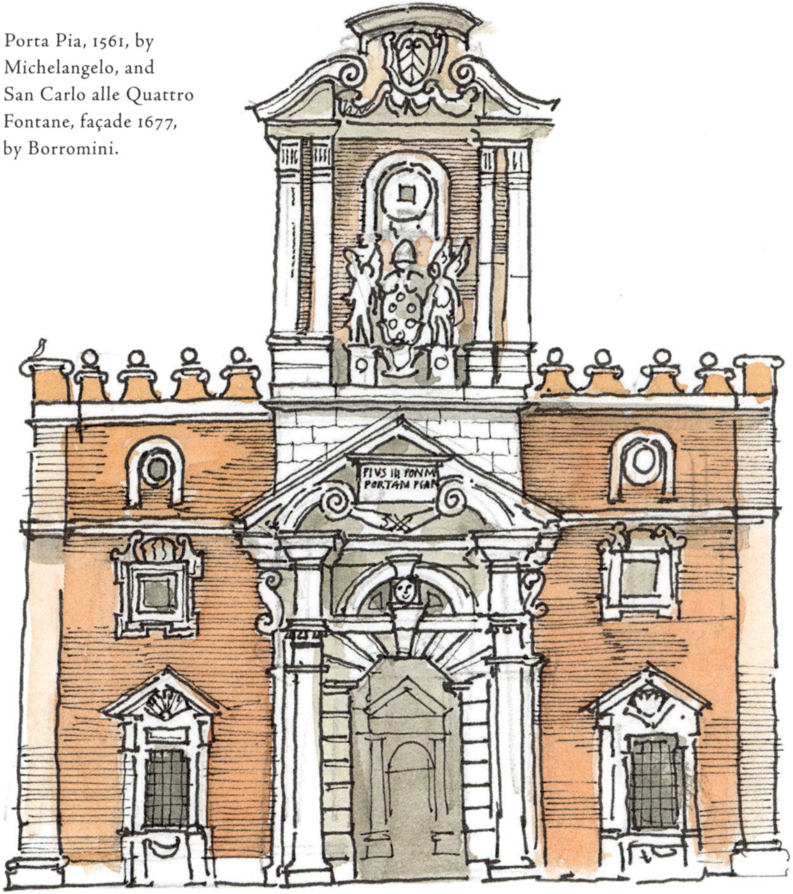

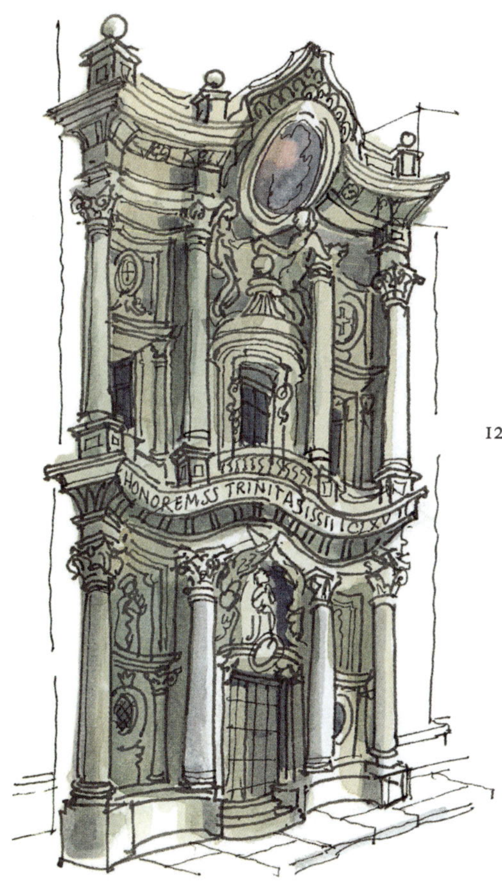

121

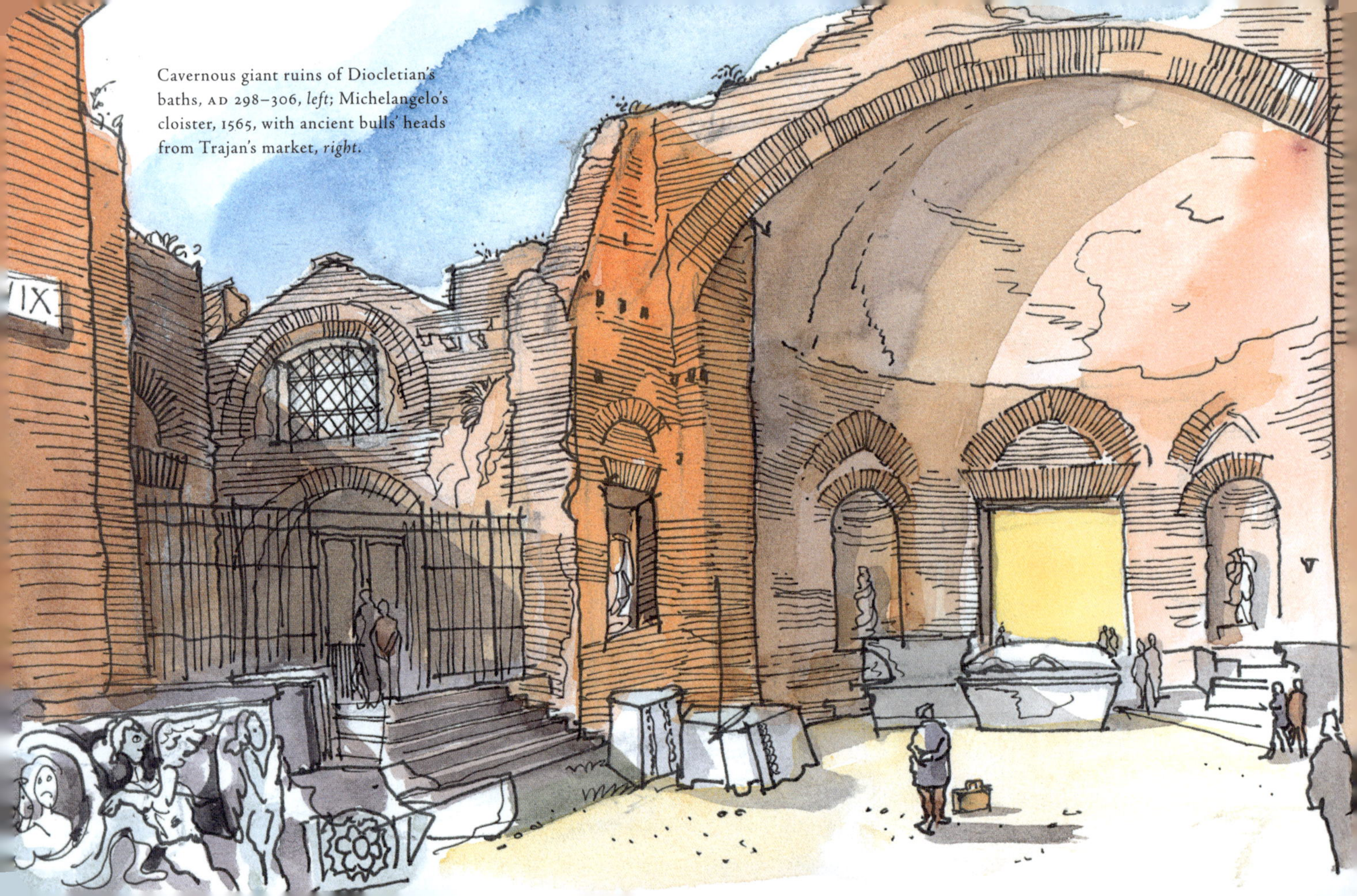

Cavernous giant ruins of Diocletian's baths, AD 298–306, *left*; Michelangelo's cloister, 1565, with ancient bulls' heads from Trajan's market, *right*.

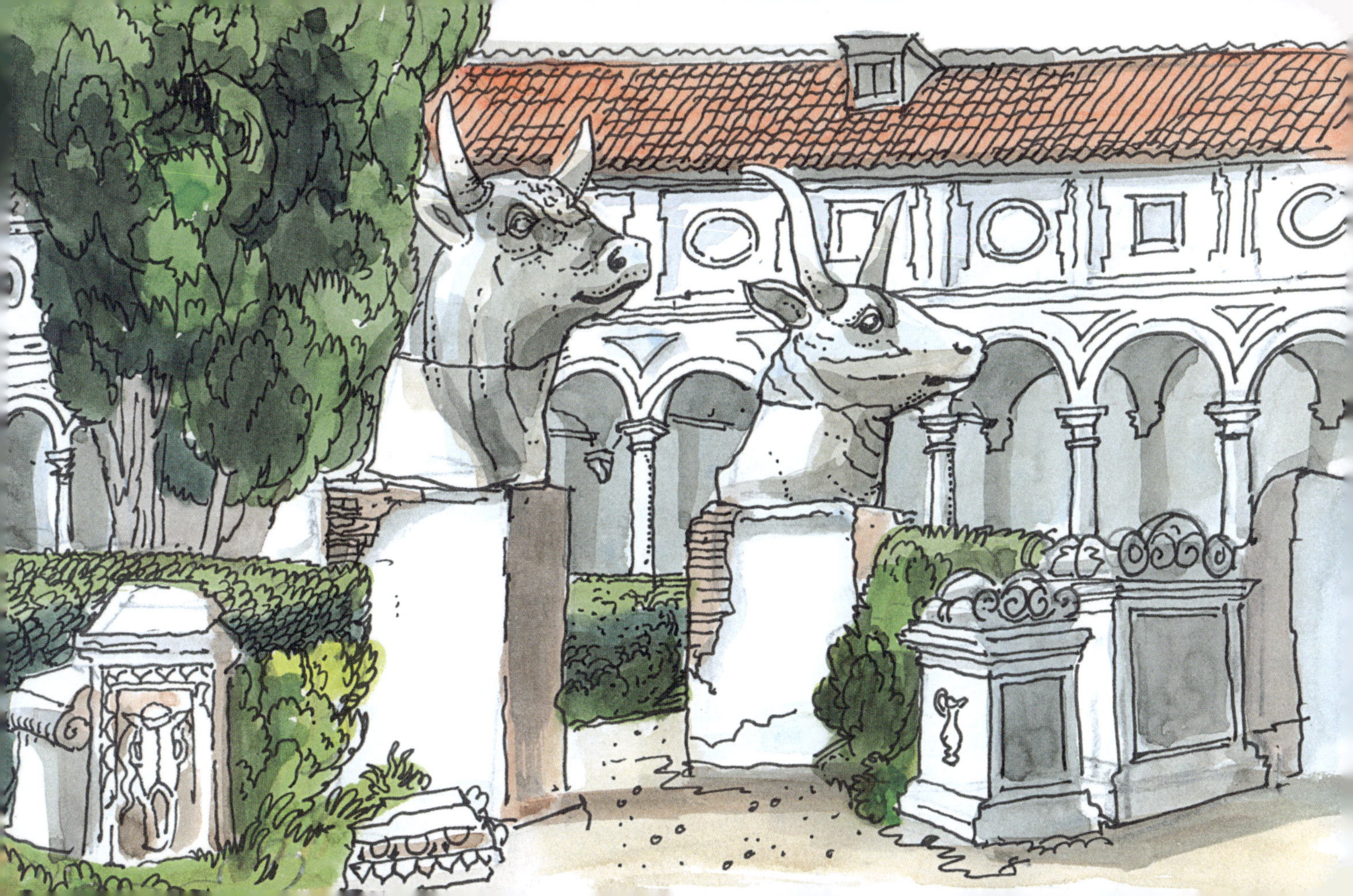

the GLITTER AND GOLD of glazed fragments light up the space and expound the message of Christianity in iconic simplification. All the great basilica churches of Rome were designed in this way and, set among the brick defensive towers, made a Manhattanesque skyline that astonished pilgrims.

Bramante's Tempietto on Gianicolo Hill is one of the city's first Renaissance buildings. It is, like the Pantheon, circular in plan and, in its miniaturized and carefully articulated way, quite as perfect. A circle of Ionic columns rings a perforated drum under a shallow dome. It is much visited by students of the Renaissance, who (like the author) struggle to do it justice with pencil and paper.

What followed was an enfloration of domes and drums that changed Rome from a city of square brick towers to something altogether more cursive and luscious. The mother of all churches, St Peter's itself, is one of the most dramatic compositions in the world, its thick-ribbed dome soaring on a drum supported by pairs of columns, its attic storey crowned by a full team of statues and, beneath a temple façade and colonnade, the whole affair embraced by two curved arms of Baroque splendour. The best of this it owes to the giant of Roman Baroque, Bernini, a tireless worker of untrammelled genius and energy.

The milky, emerald-green Tiber, which curls around the city and past the Vatican, is wholly cut off from its surroundings today. The ferocious embanking of 1876 destroyed forever the picturesque riverside views that had so entranced eighteenth- and early-nineteenth-century *vedutisti*. The mills and waterside agglomerations of essentially rural Rome were the last remnants of the abandoned city of the Middle Ages, but the river, even far from its source two hundred miles away in the APPENINE HILLS, is a powerful torrent when snow melt and torrential winter rains swell its modest flow into a destructive force, impossible to accept in a modern city. And so, walls some forty feet high embank the river and, until one looks over their parapet, the water is invisible. Stone stairs lead down to a wide, paved riverside path busy with cyclists, runners and, in its shadier areas, the sad redoubt of syringe-scattering unfortunates and rough sleepers. While at night this puts it out of bounds, on a sunny day, glimpses of Castel Sant'Angelo, St Peter's and the bridges themselves are still good views. The river's colour is characteristic, and its ruffled surface hints at greater

Oratory of San Filippo Neri, 1637–50, Borromini, *right*; Santa Cecilia in Trastevere and Palazzo Colonna, Antonio del Grande, 1700, *overleaf.*

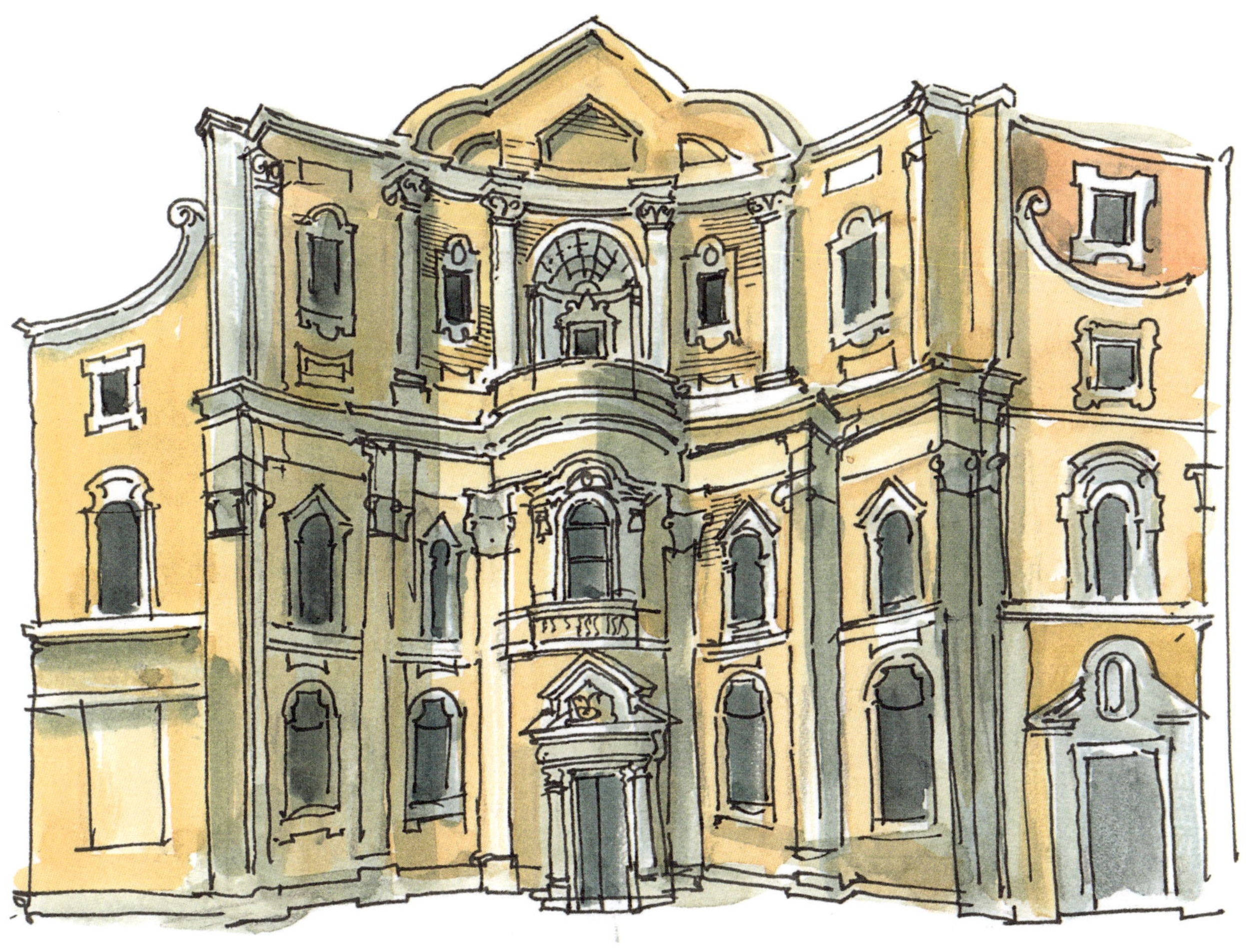

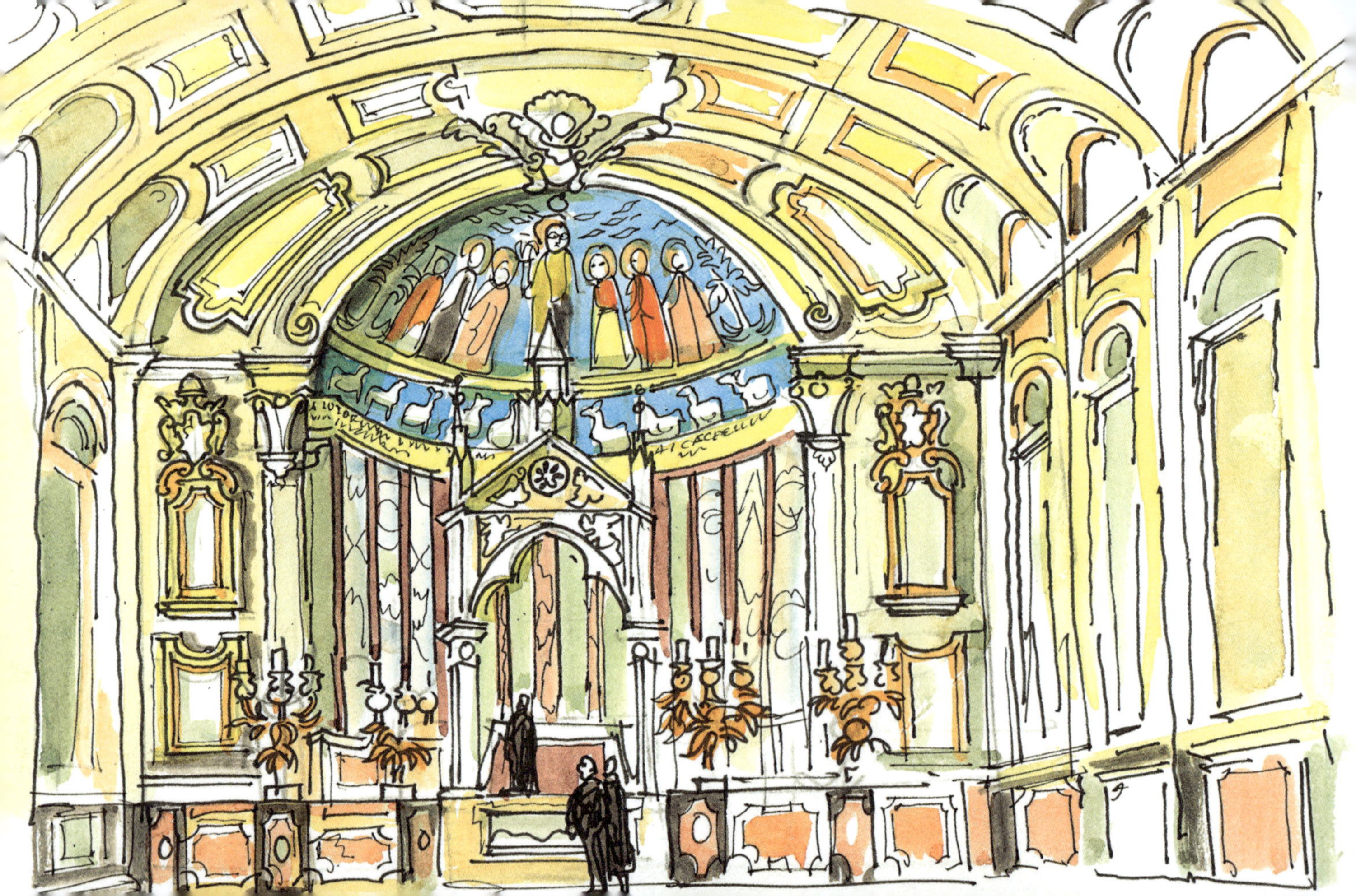

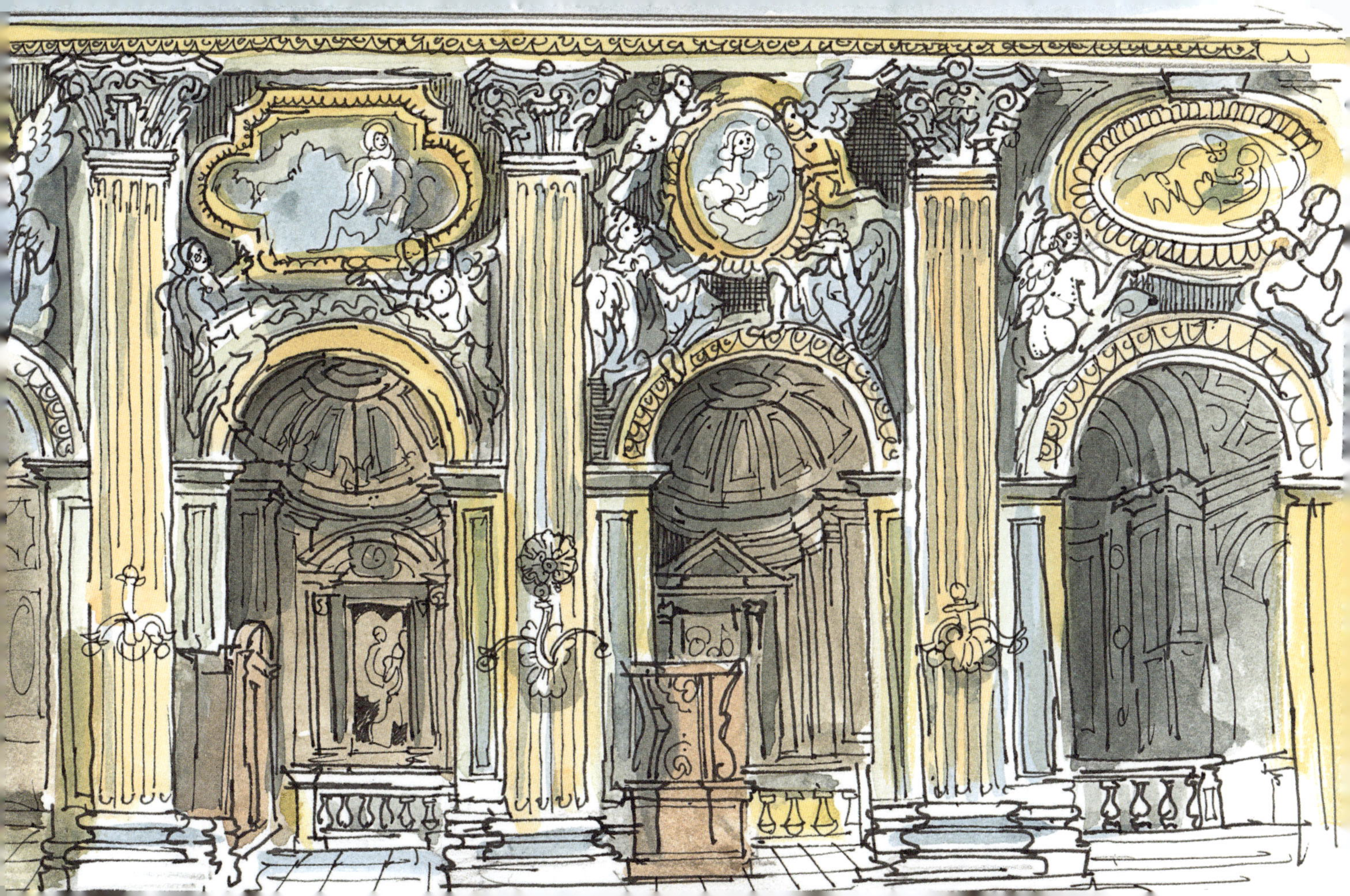

Two Baroque churches:
Santa Maria di Loreto
and Santi Luca e Martina.

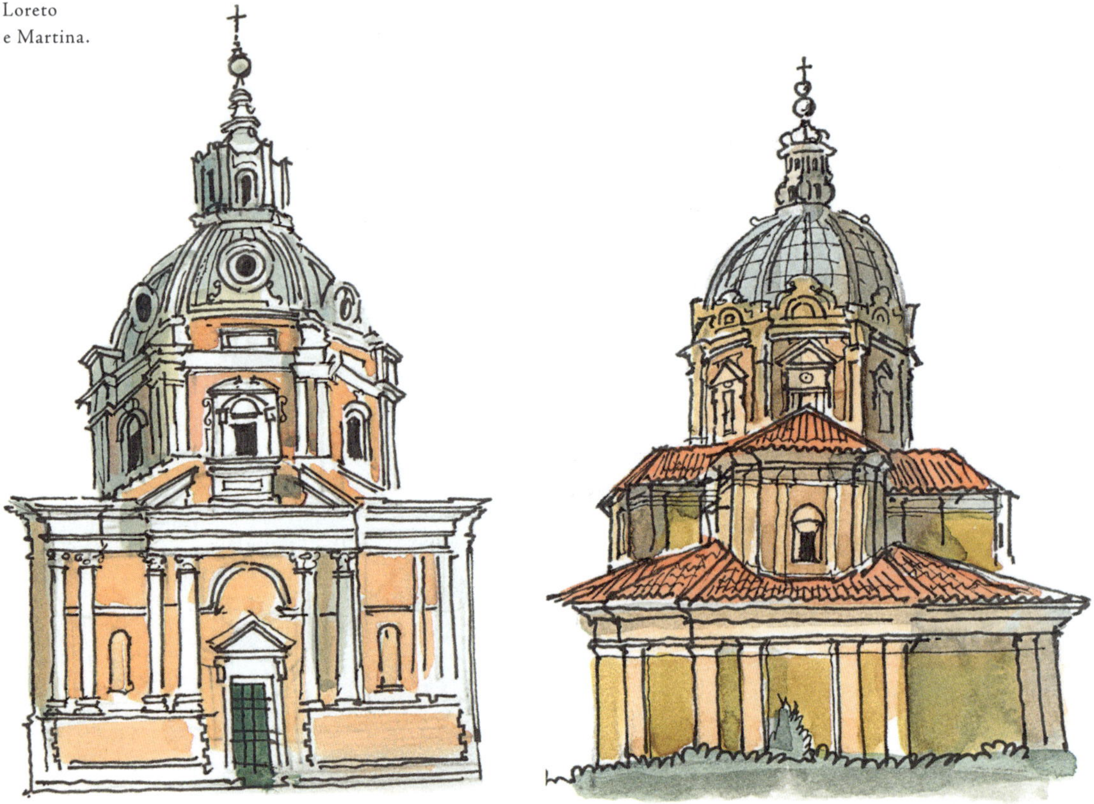

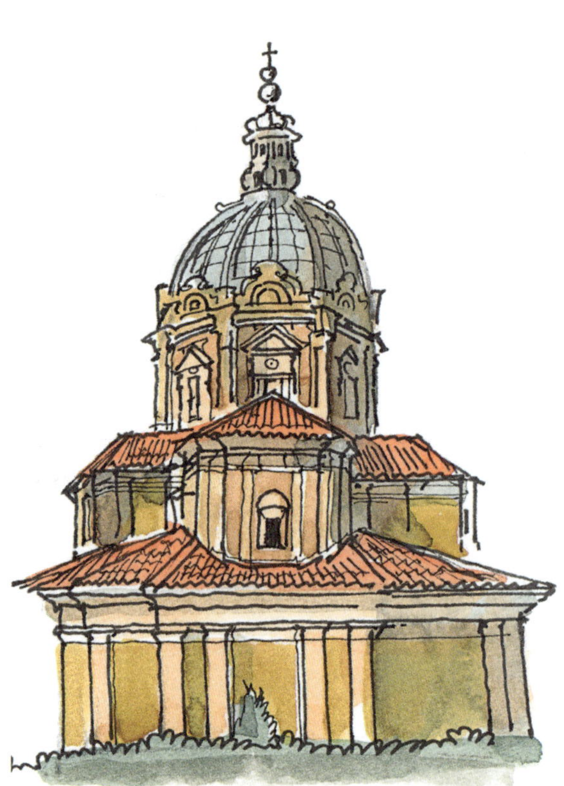

swirling depths than its shallow edges imply, deep enough to consume the victims of invasion and internecine battles, as well as huge quantities of Roman archaeology abandoned from the ages of Horace to Hitler.

The great churches are a mixed bag. St Peter's and its extraordinary Baroque complex is unbeatable, and Santa Maria Maggiore is huge and ancient, glittering with gold, but as for San Giovanni in Laterano… There is no point pretending this is a charming or lovely church. The Lateran papal palace next door is splendid and orange and perfectly detailed, with lions in its decorated cornice and a coat of papal arms of grandeur and elegance, but in the church itself a dead hand is at work. It doesn't live up to the promise of Galilei's 1735 giant-scale coffered narthex, the pilasters seem not to be supporting the roof, and the detailing is coarse. Borromini designed the niches for the supersized saints, but they themselves are all later and slightly undistinguished. Yet the exterior is splendid and, seen from far away, the eleven Baroque saints seem to dance in the wind over a solid country-house façade.

The same cannot be said of any elevation of San Paolo fuori le Mura. This is Rome's most oppressive and lifeless church; with not a breath of the numinous, not a trace of humour or bravado, merely a feeling of profound gloom.

There is a reason: it was entirely consumed by flames in 1823. The pope of the day dreamt on his deathbed that St Peter's would be burnt to the ground (he was never told how acute his premonition was). His successor decreed that it should be rebuilt, and, by 1854 it was completed with much global assistance. The malachite altar was a gift of Tsar Nicholas I, and, like its Russian contemporary, St Isaac's cathedral in St Petersburg, it has the DEAD HAND OF NEO-CLASSICISM, the chilling thoroughness of the nineteenth century and a deep unloveliness throughout. Augustus Hare, the nineteenth-century travel writer, described it as a charmless railway station, but he is too kind: it has none of a station's nobility of endeavour. A fire in 2023 would rather have resulted in a painstaking and loving restoration and might have retained some of the refined grace of the HAPPILY SURVIVING adjacent cloister. This elaborate, beautiful and dainty Gothic building, with elegant mosaiced barley-sugar columns and charming cloister garth, only serves as a reminder that to be thorough and muscular is not necessarily wise or kind. The last shred of reality to survive within the church is the

Breathtaking grandeur in the galleries of Palazzo Colonna;
Borromini's San Carlo alle Quattro Fontane (completed 1646), makes
you gasp with its contorted plan and unexpected turns, *overleaf*.

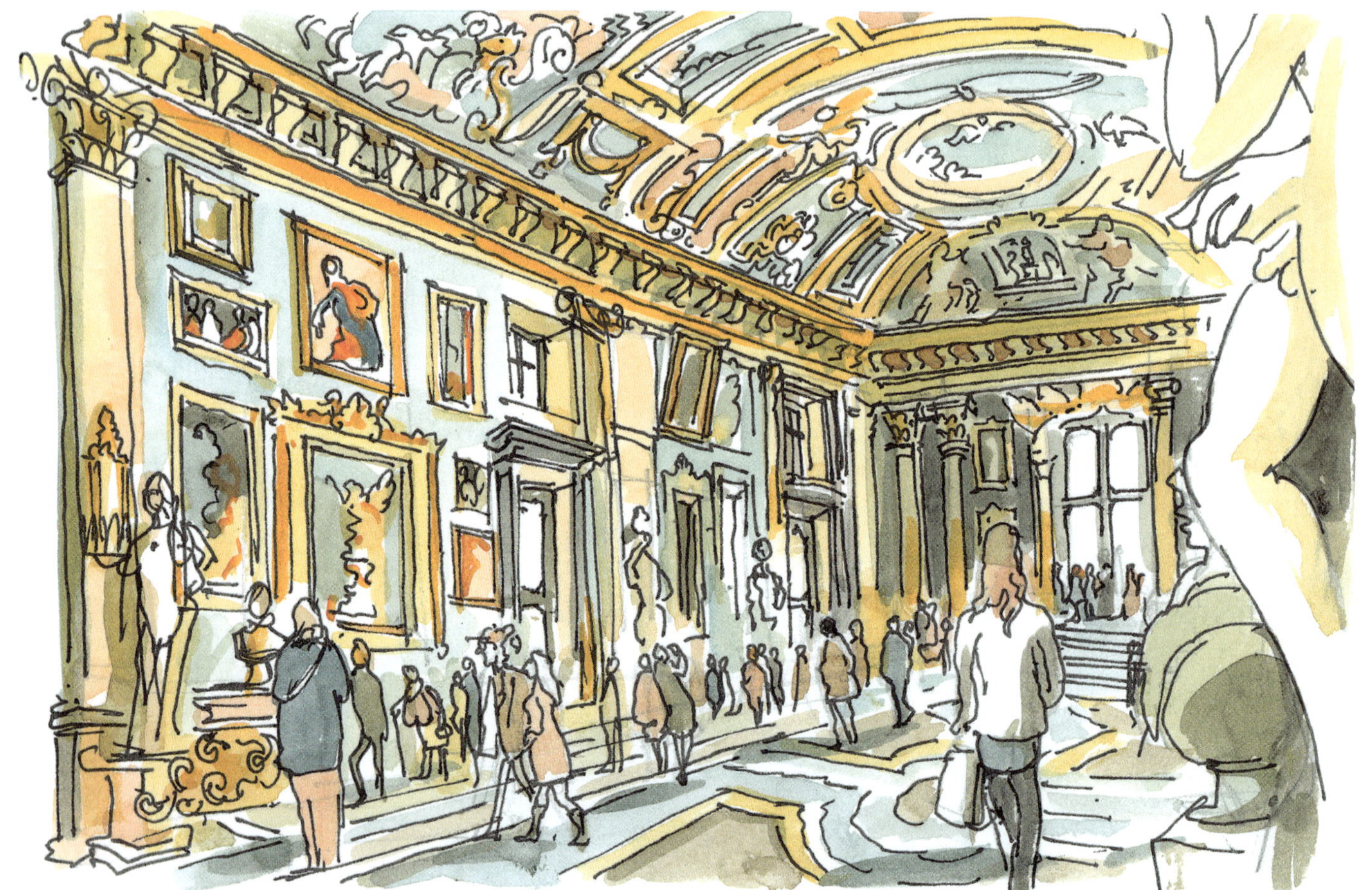

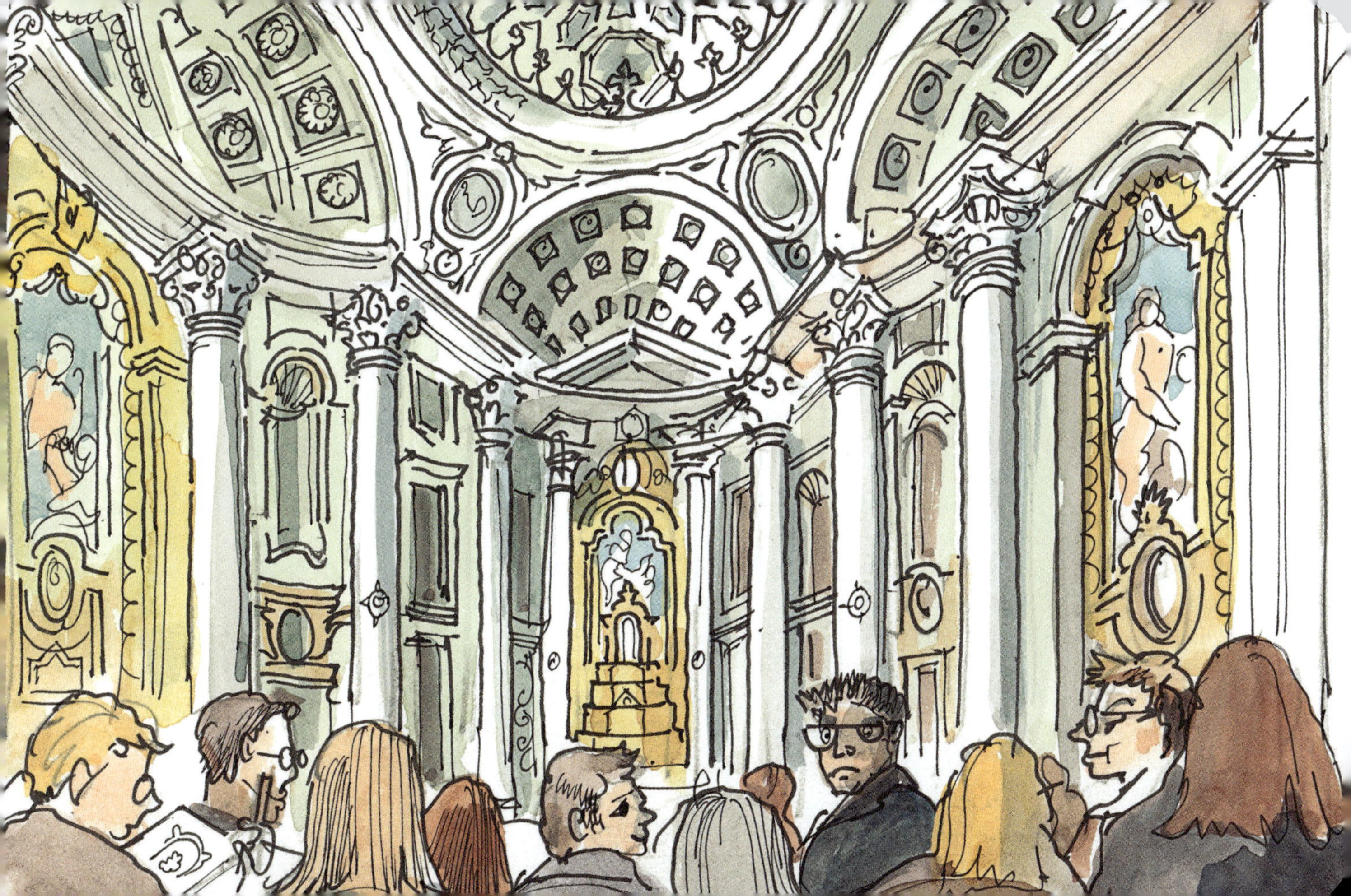

central tomb of St Paul. A curiously unimpressive rough-hewn hole in the stone floor, it is a place of pilgrimage.

The great palaces of the PAPAL ARISTOCRACY, the families from whom for nearly one thousand years the Bishops of Rome were chosen, were frequently built to aggrandize a close relation of a pope, often themselves a cardinal. There is a long list of these great buildings that are open to the public: Colonna (the family produced a pope and many cardinals and claim descent from the Julio-Claudian dynasty); Pamphilj (yet another pope, Innocent X); Barberini (Urban VIII); Medici; Farnese; Borghese; or Altemps (the Austrian nephew of Pius IV, hence the un-Italian name).

Many of these families originated in other parts of Italy but came to Rome to be at the centre of the papal court. The appointment as a cardinal, let alone as pope, was a life-changingly lucrative opportunity, not to mention a chance to consolidate political family power. The villas and *palazzi* of the papal aristocracy were the manifestation of these enormous fortunes and, as well as amassing the greatest of collections of paintings and sculpture, these grandees were the great patrons of Rome's architects. Borromini and Bernini were both employed at the Barberini palace and each produced a pen-bafflingly

complex, yet elegant, staircase, part of an interior that is easier to love than the rather massy façade.

The Palazzo Spada shares with the Medici and Borghese palaces a form that is a deeply characteristic expression of the humanist Renaissance passion for painting and sculpture. Yet they are great stacks of buildings, alternately over- and under-fenestrated. This, strangely, is a Gothic approach to the elevation of a building: that function is reflected in appearance, for example, rooms needing more light might have large windows, whereas those that don't do not. This is profoundly un-Palladian. Indeed, the contrast between the roughly coeval façade of Borromini's Palazzo Spada and Scamozzi's set design for Teatro Olimpico in Vicenza is interesting. Both are rich in sculpture and carved decoration, but, in Scamozzi's model, they are ordered into an architectural system, with niches and aedicules, a defined geometry making the sculpture subordinate to the architectural whole. By contrast, in the Roman example, the marble crowd has got the upper hand and the building seems to be falling into place behind them.

Ruskin, that rabid Renaissance-loathing Goth of the nineteenth century, might have been confused here, for, although the buildings are clearly Classical in language, the supremacy of individual creativity and craftsmanship

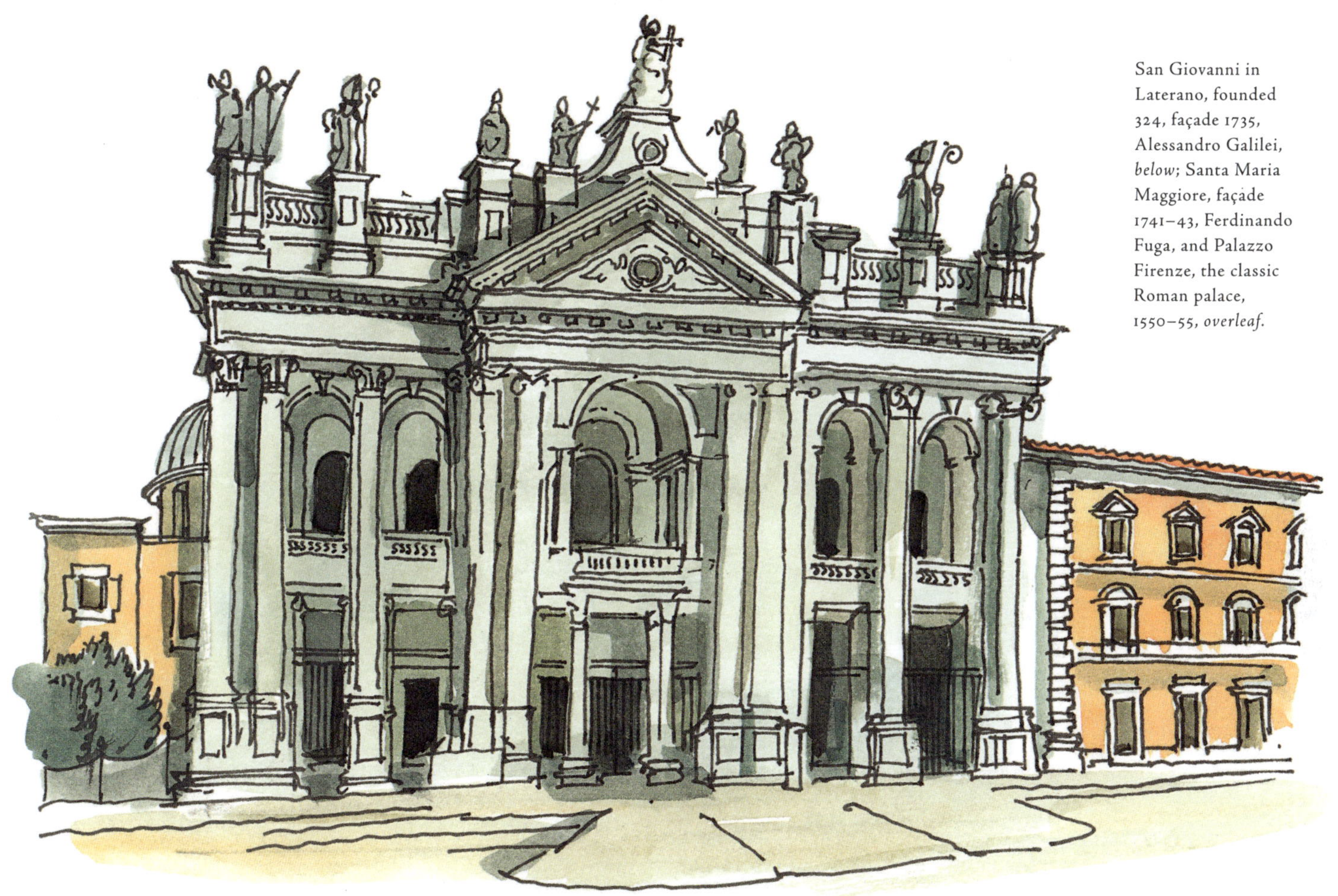

San Giovanni in Laterano, founded 324, façade 1735, Alessandro Galilei, *below*; Santa Maria Maggiore, façade 1741–43, Ferdinando Fuga, and Palazzo Firenze, the classic Roman palace, 1550–55, *overleaf*.

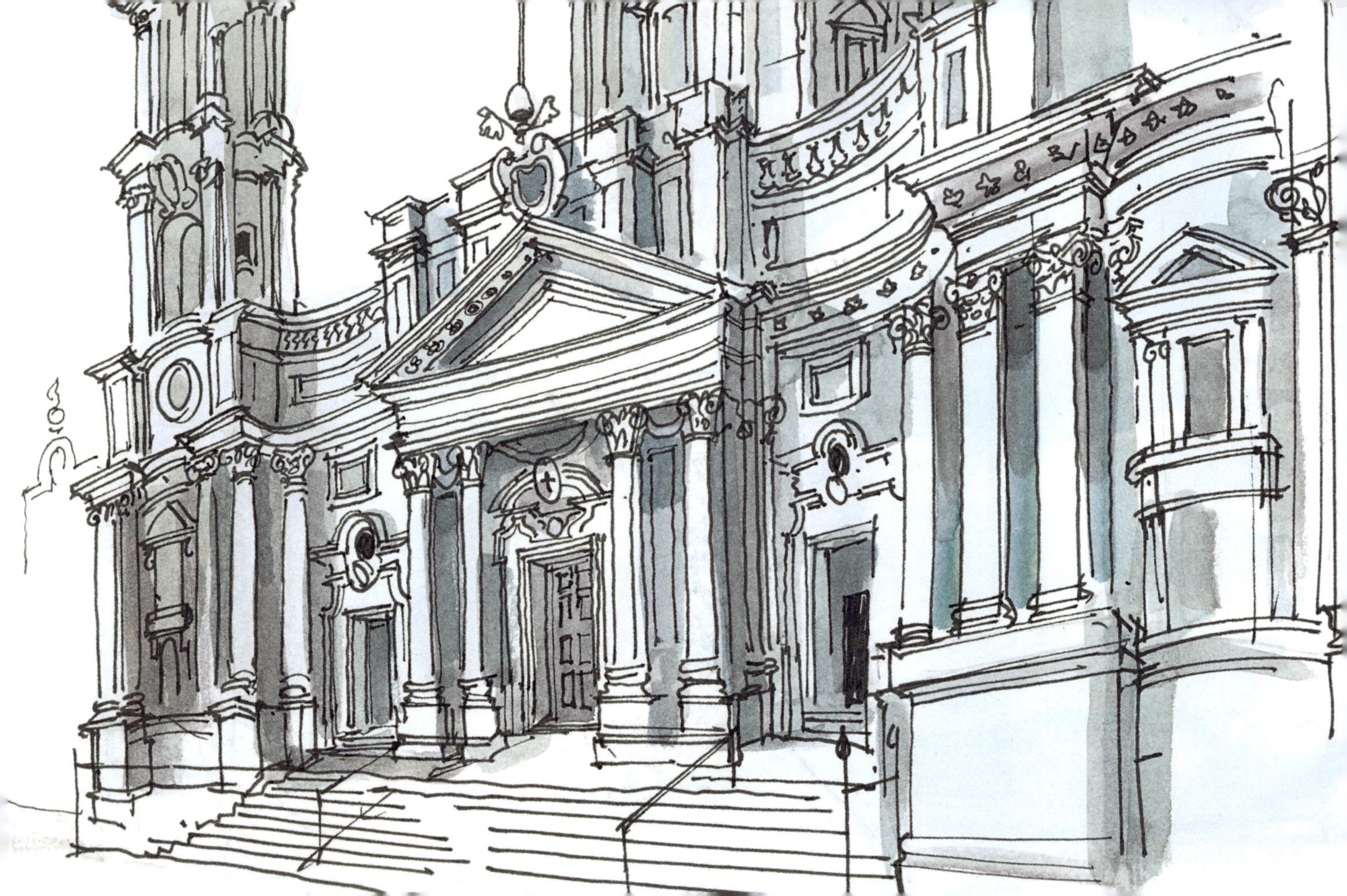

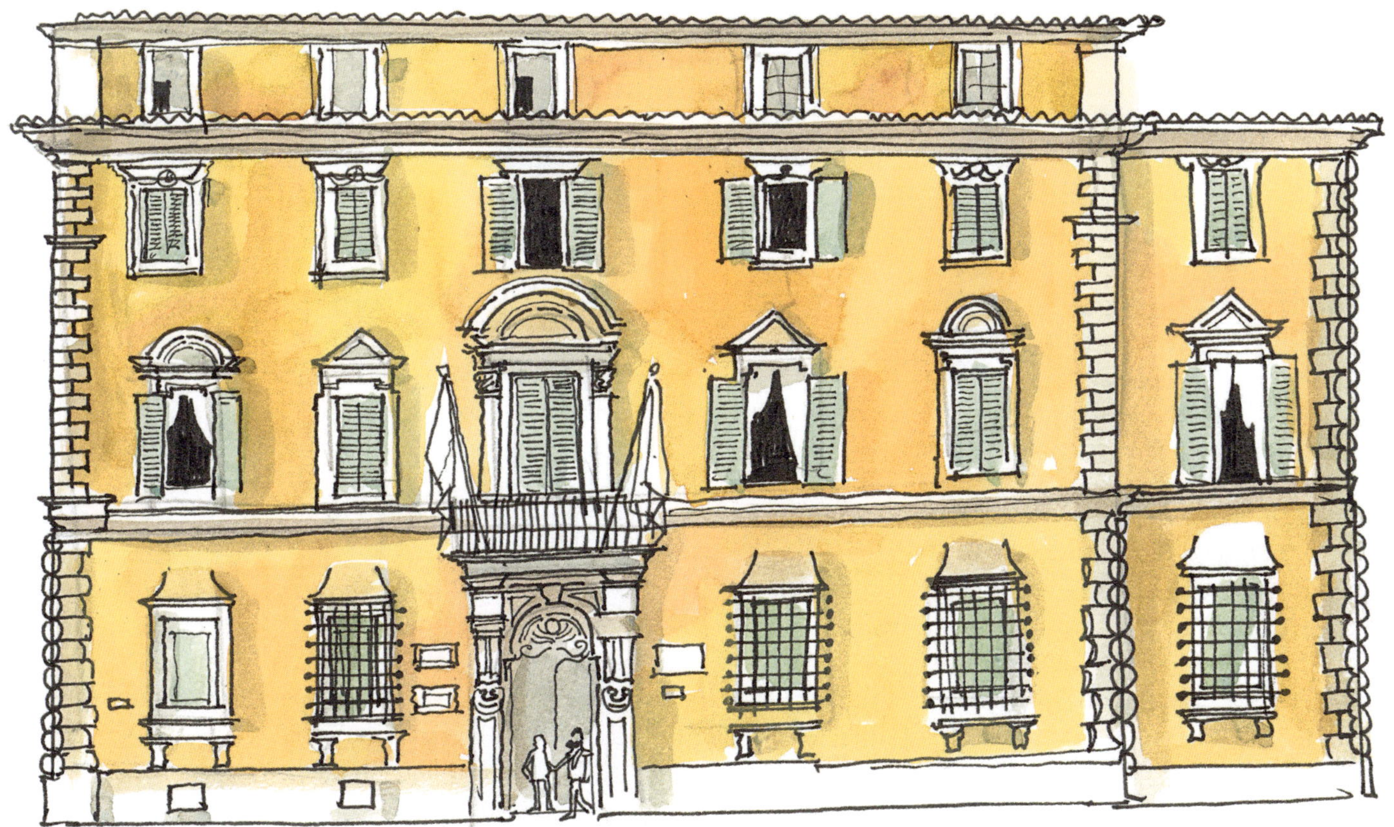

in the great elevations of these buildings must have assuaged his anger at the lack of Gothic arches and tracery.

An architectural lure hinted at in the external elevation is Borromini's perspective colonnade at Palazzo Spada. The whole concept and the *trompe-l'oeil* effect (of reducing the size of a receding arcade to give the impression of a tunnel far deeper than its true dimensions) either excites or… doesn't. If the latter, it is extraordinarily boring, unless, like Scamozzi's great *scaenae frons* in Vicenza, it happens also to be a thing of beauty. This Roman version feels a rather bleak contrivance, and the statue at the back, alleged to finally baffle the simple-minded viewer, is charmless and fails entirely to do this because… it could be any size. To add insult to injury, the whole tawdry little set is taped off, so the one main pleasure, viz, PHOTOGRAPHING ONE'S FRIEND as a GIANT or DWARF, is denied.

If the Spada leaves you a little unsatisfied, you could go for a slap-up visual feast at the Palazzo Colonna (on a Saturday morning only, for this great complex is still a princely home and is otherwise closed, except for guided tours). When the doors are flung open, it is with grace and a charming welcome that is yet insufficient to prepare one for the *tour de force* that is the main galleries. They GLITTER with mirror and gilt and have an extraordinary collection of paintings on the silk brocade walls. Working through the tapestried throne rooms, you walk into a garden which, although only metres from the centre of the city, rises in green terraces with switchback paths and clipped dark-green ilex that lead you up the Quirinal Hill. Equally stimulating visual treats are to be found in the Palazzo Altemps, with its heavily decorated first-floor loggia, or in the red silk state rooms of the Palazzo Pamphilj.

These palaces housed not only many generations of one family, but also retainers and assorted hangers-on. To have a lot of dependants was perceived as a symbol of high status. They would be housed in various levels of grandeur, with state rooms below and modest family pensioners in the attics or nether parts.

An eighteenth-century addition to the city is the Protestant Cemetery, a cool and bosky escape from the traffic of central Rome built immediately behind the stark and beautiful Pyramid of Cestius. To be buried in the cemetery there, you have to be non-Italian and non-Catholic, a wide net that scoops up several hundred expatriates, none more notable than the poets Shelley and Keats. The latter's rather primitively carved tablet has this

San Francesco a Ripa in Trastevere, Onorio Longhi, 1603.

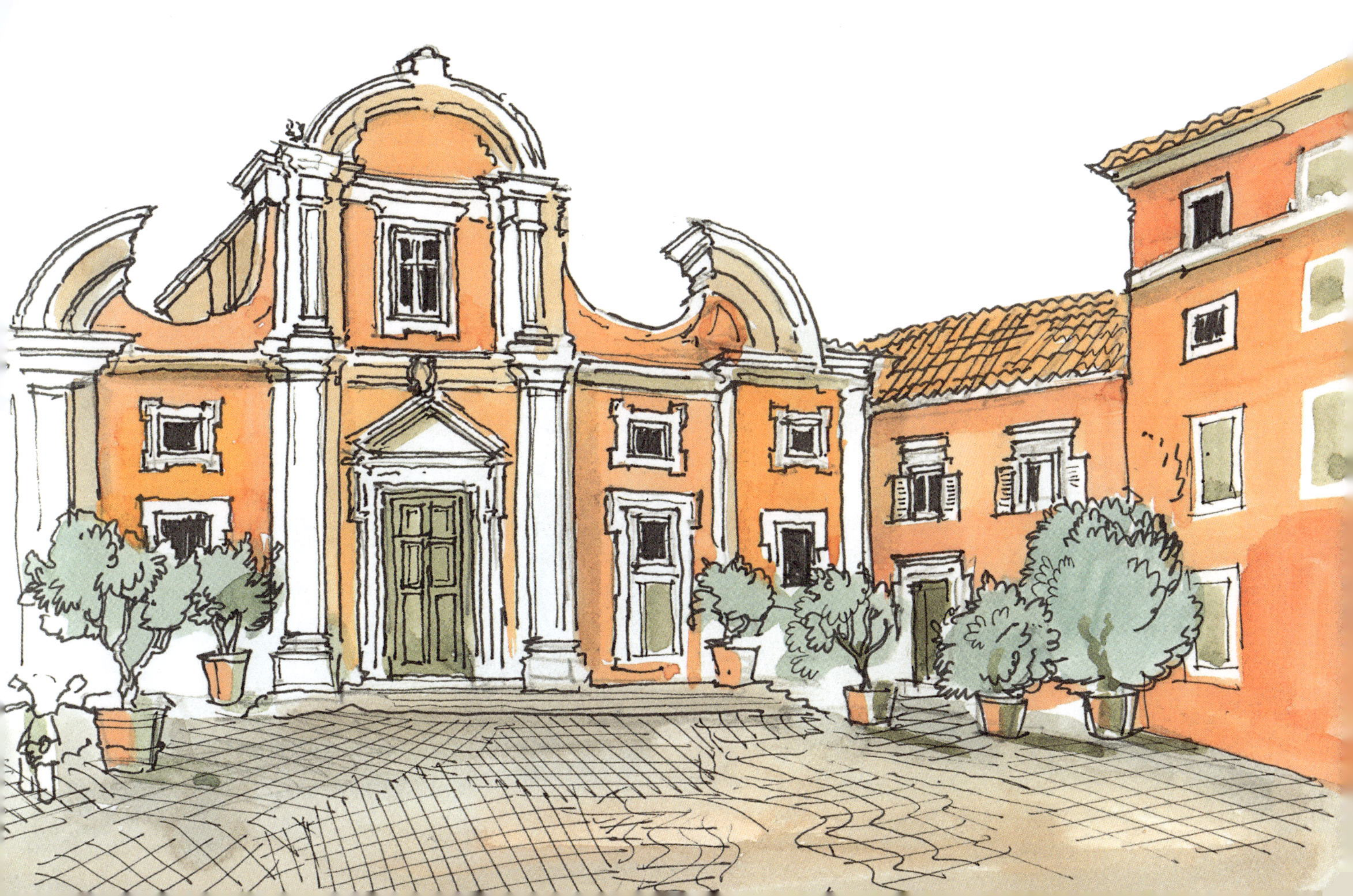

sad inscription: 'This grave contains all that was mortal of a YOUNG ENGLISH POET who on his deathbed in the bitterness of his heart at the malicious power of his enemies desired these words to be engraven on his tomb stone: Here lies one whose name was writ in water.'

The nineteenth century saw a frenetic building boom, as Rome's adoption as capital of the new Italy urgently required houses of parliament, law courts and opera houses, arcades and leafy squares indistinguishable from those of Turin or Milan, Budapest or any other European capital. The construction drew in a new population from outside, and they, too, needed housing. Whole new neighbourhoods grew up, such as Testaccio, in which both industrial and domestic development colonized previously open land close to the city centre. Here is to be found the grand but supremely gloomy Mattatoio, the former abattoir that, with dramatic sculptures of twisting bulls and contemporary art exhibits in the pavilions where pigs once squirmed, is unable to slough off the unhappy associations with its former life.

The Vittorio Emanuele II Monument is the child only a mother could love. It is massive, overbearing and sets jangling the already confusing components of the Capitoline Hill. In its favour, unlike so many of the allegedly 'iconic'

buildings thrown up in the world's capitals in the past fifty years, it is at least profoundly ARTICULATED, catching the changing light to emphasize its masses. Perhaps in an age when jingoistic nationalism has a bad name – one part of the complex is called 'the Altar of the Fatherland' – it's hard to imagine how very significant the entity of the newly United Kingdom of Italy was in 1885, when this building was initiated. It wasn't completed until 1935, by which time a whole new order of Imperial ambition under Mussolini was in place, so it must have seemed a prescient investment in national pride. A new age of processions could pass before this assemblage of ancient Roman and Greek components, but freeing a site large enough meant the wholesale destruction of a huge area of medieval and even Classical Rome and, in creating the large Piazza Venezia below, the architects made as disagreeable a traffic feature as any in London, Berlin or Paris. The monument's historicist detailing may be erudite and its huge bronze quadriga impressive, but it rears its massive head at the end of so many views of the city and, in doing so, compromises them.

Santi Domenico e Sisto, 1633, *left*, and Santa Barbara dei Librai, Campo de' Fiori façade, which was restored after a fire in 1634, *right*.

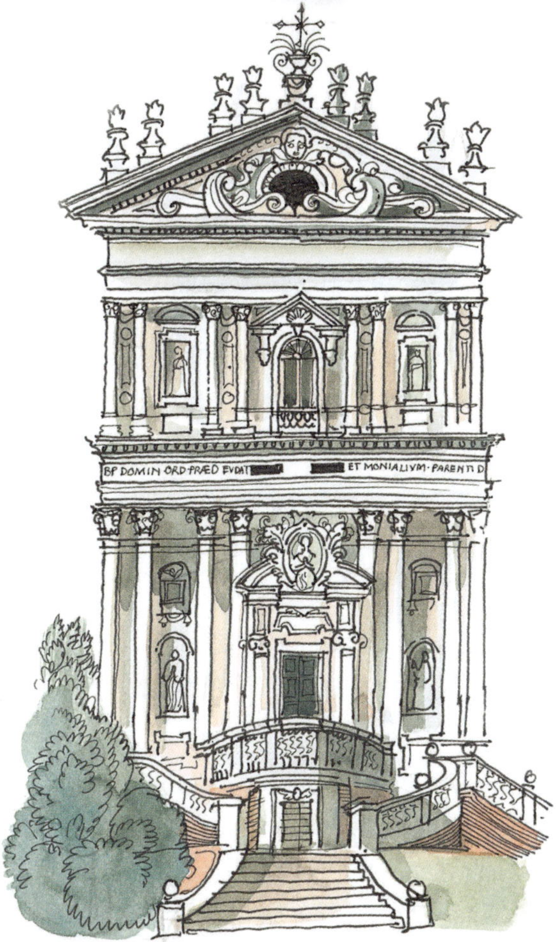

BP DOMIN ORD PRÆD EVDAT
ET MONIALIVM PARENTI D

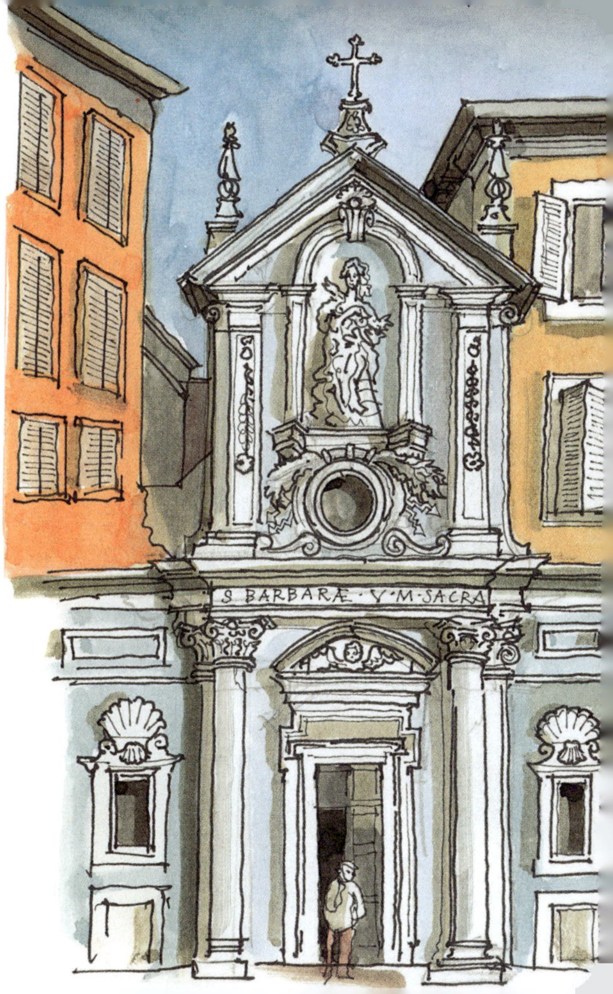

S BARBARÆ V M SACRA

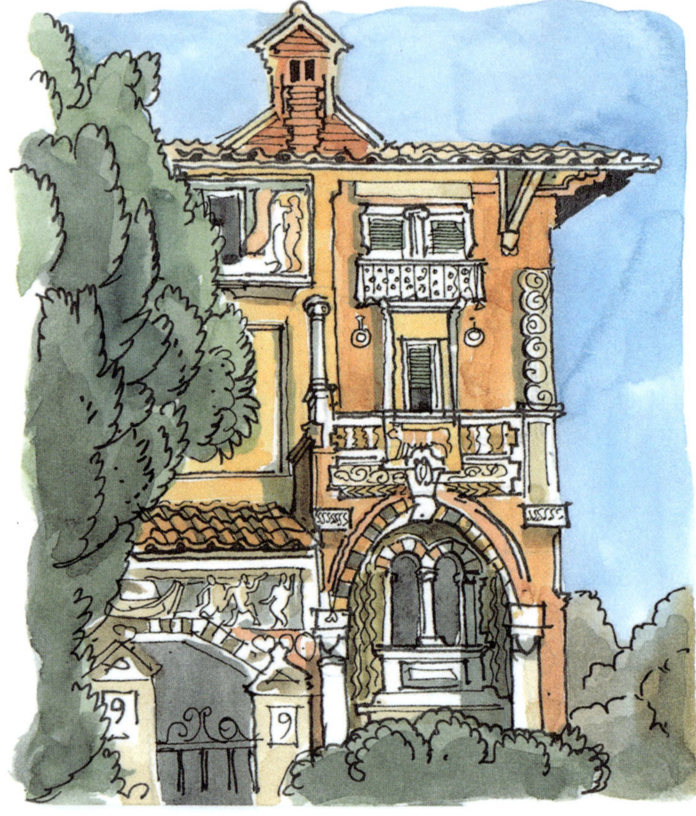

Coppedè quarter, 1927, named after the architect Gino Coppedè.

In suburban Rome, just off Via Nomentana, is a very particular group of buildings. Quartiere Coppedè is named after its eponymous designer, whom Rome guides compare to Antoni Gaudí (1852–1926) in Barcelona, but, although they are contemporaries, they are chalk and (soft) cheese. Where Gaudí's Modernism slips around in amorphous vegetative forms and detail on standard-issue commercial terraces or careers all over the frankly odd Sagrada Família, the Florentine architect and designer Gino Coppedè (1866–1927) is painstakingly historicist, mashing up sgrafitto naval scenes and mythological reliefs with heavy carved corbels and Italianate eaves. There is glorious asymmetry and stacked balconies, chimneys and (in a limited palette of terracottas, creams, browns and reds) MUCH USE OF COLOUR. More than anything, the strange Art Nouveau designer feels most like Carlo Bugatti (1856–1940), whose inlaid furniture braided together the decorative languages of cultures from around the world. The Art Nouveau outbreak that bulged its way out of the straitlaced nineteenth century was known in Italy as the STILE LIBERTY, named after the London store whose proprietor Arthur Lasenby cornered the market in Belle Époque bohemian housewares. This group of half a dozen streets of villas and apartment buildings is definitely worth the (slightly long) walk.

Although Adolf Hitler may have produced a few inept daubs before he rose to power, the Italian leader of the 1930s had no such pretensions. At least in the early days of his reign, IL DUCE's political party was closely allied with the Futurist movement, and, as it was essential to be aligned with the popular Fascist party, he had plenty of nominal support among architects and designers. Mussolini's grand projects ranged from huge and rather destructive town planning changes, such as the Via dei Fori Imperiali that blithely bisected the most important archaeological site in the world, to the grand Termini station and the futuristic new Roman city, EUR. Il Duce's vison of a new Roman empire stretching from Albania and Croatia to Egypt and north Africa may not have been realized, but he did introduce a new architectural language to the city.

This was his own rather martial and practical Modernism known as rationalism. The Colosseo Quadrato at EUR, for example, is extraordinary. Huge in scale, with brutal super-sized statuary guarding the entrance, deep-punched arched windows and an arcade beneath, the tower speaks eloquently of megalomaniacal control. Similarly to Speer's stadium in Nuremberg, the excitement of seeing such a grand project realized and SURVIVING is tempered by underlying horror at its human cost. From its windy podium, it looks down Imperial-scale avenues lined with splendid shade-casting magnolias. Less-distinguished blocks line these boulevards, but, beyond, vainglorious porticos in utterly simplified order front echoing muralled exhibition halls and a brilliant museum of popular culture, with exhibits that range from faintly pornographic advertisements for water-melons to models of ships and ancient tools and jewels.

There are refreshingly few contemporary buildings in central Rome. Those yearning for steel and glass wax lyrical about the banal box, designed by Richard Meier, that houses Augustus's Altar of Peace, the Ara Pacis (it is disagreeably hot when the sun is out and adds little to the urban scene). Meier is one of the Greats of Modernism and one of Le Corbusier's most productive followers. Those bold revolutionary theories are intellectually robust and lead to stylish, spare architecture, but that is a bit of a tinkling cymbal with Castel Sant'Angelo and St Peter's as close neighbours. The world's cities are full of GRANDS PROJETS, but the international style is correctly named, and those architectural ICONS vary little in appearance whether in chilly Norway or the blistering Emirates. The gruesome goosestepping of EUR is quite enough and suitably distant from the centre to be a second, parallel, Rome, modest in acreage, but Titan in scale.

Architectural detail

Rome is supremely decorative. Less was LESS to ancient Roman eyes, and elaborate decoration inside and out was desirable. The ARA PACIS is covered with both narrative propaganda and lavish arabesques (if we can call them that, given that Islamic art hadn't yet been thought of), acanthus scrolls and palmettes that reticulate and interlock to form the most complete and decorative scheme. It is constructed decoration, not decorated construction, utterly superficial, *ars gratia artis*, but, in this temple to a human God, is perhaps the highest-status piece of decorative design in the whole of Rome. Mixed with cornucopic festoons as lavish, as deeply carved and as realistic as those of Grinling Gibbons 1,700 years later, the bucrania ARE real ox heads, and the marble ribbons DO flutter between composite pilasters.

The COMPOSITE order was Imperial Rome's great contribution to the vocabulary of Classical architecture, in which each Order describes the vertical relationship of plinth, column, capital and entablature. The Doric, Ionic and Corinthian orders were, as their names indicate, fully developed imports from Greece – named after the places Doris, Ionia and Corinth – but the Composite, in which the volutes of the Ionic are combined with the acanthus leaves of the Corinthian, and the Tuscan, a modest elaboration on the simple Doric, are purely ROMAN. Indeed, the relaxation of the inflexible orthodoxies of the Greek orders is a characteristic of Roman architecture, continued with ROLLICKING, ROILING ENTHUSIASM by the Renaissance and Baroque builders of the city, who played fast and loose with the orders. Elaborations are not purely decorative: the fleuron (the squiggle in the top centre of a capital) was replaced by a BEE when symbolizing the glorification of the Barberini, typical of the general incorporation of family badges and armorial devices into architecture. The other components of the capital, too, were manipulated and added to, producing a whole lexicon of derivative forms, some of which barely nodded to their Attic forebears.

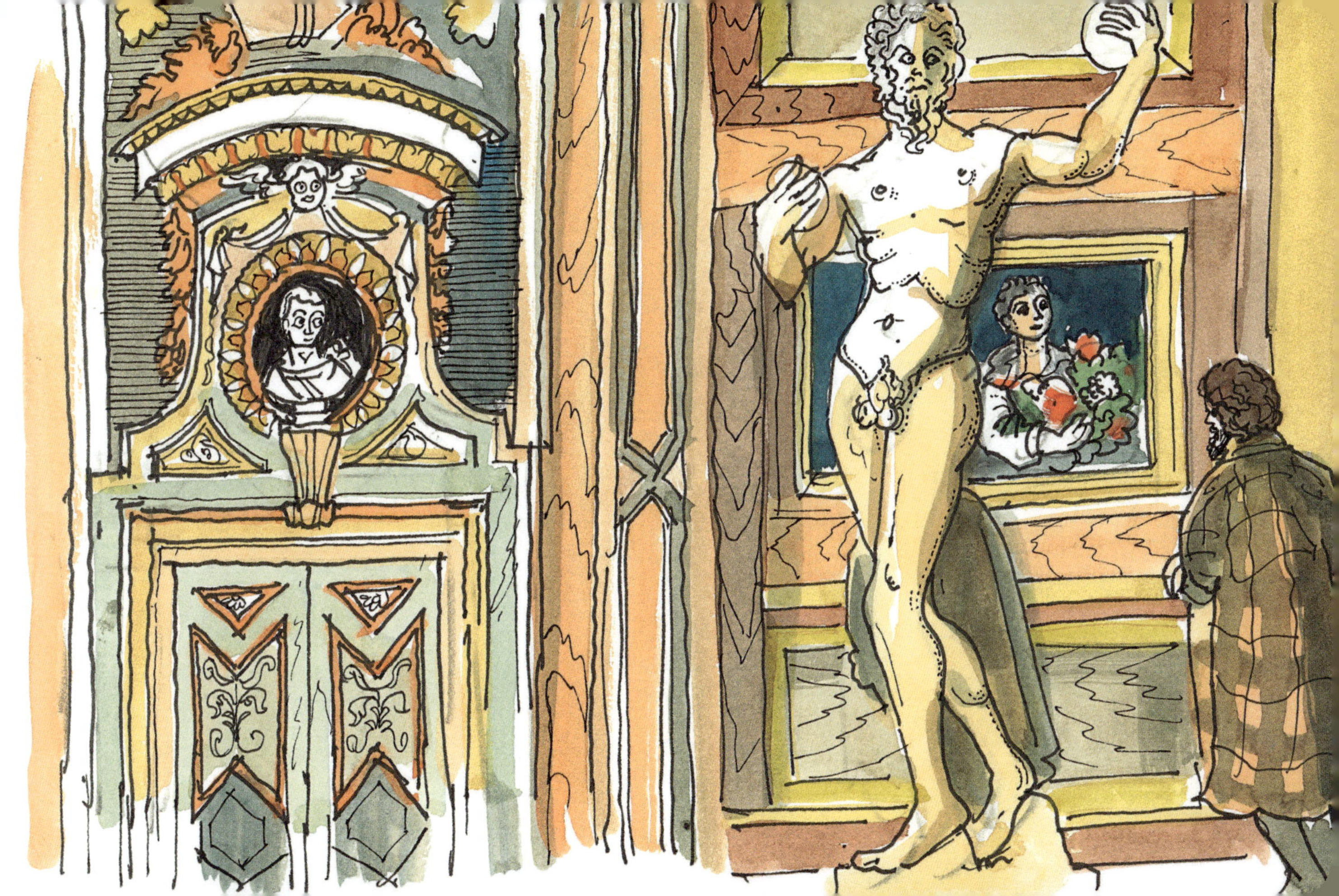

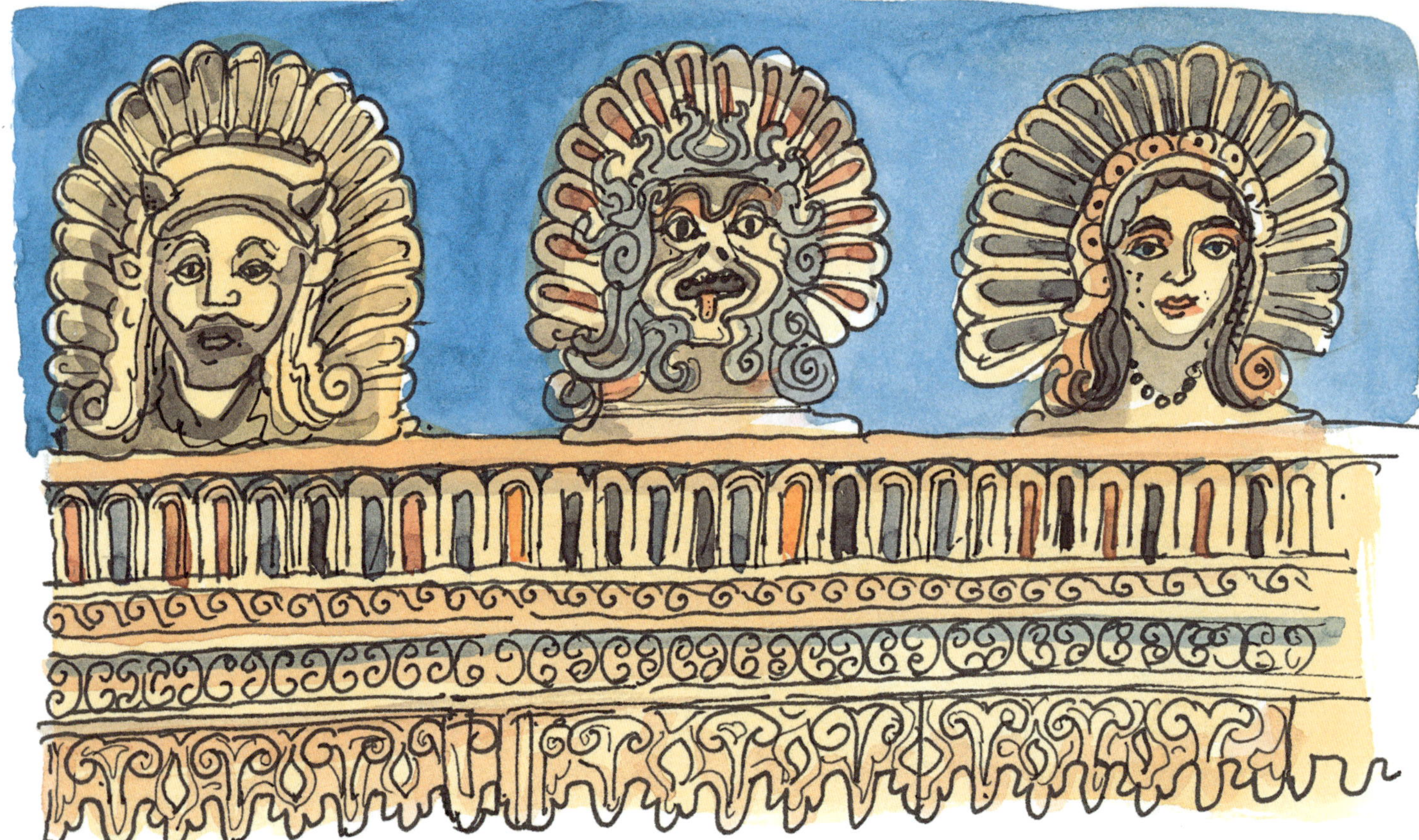

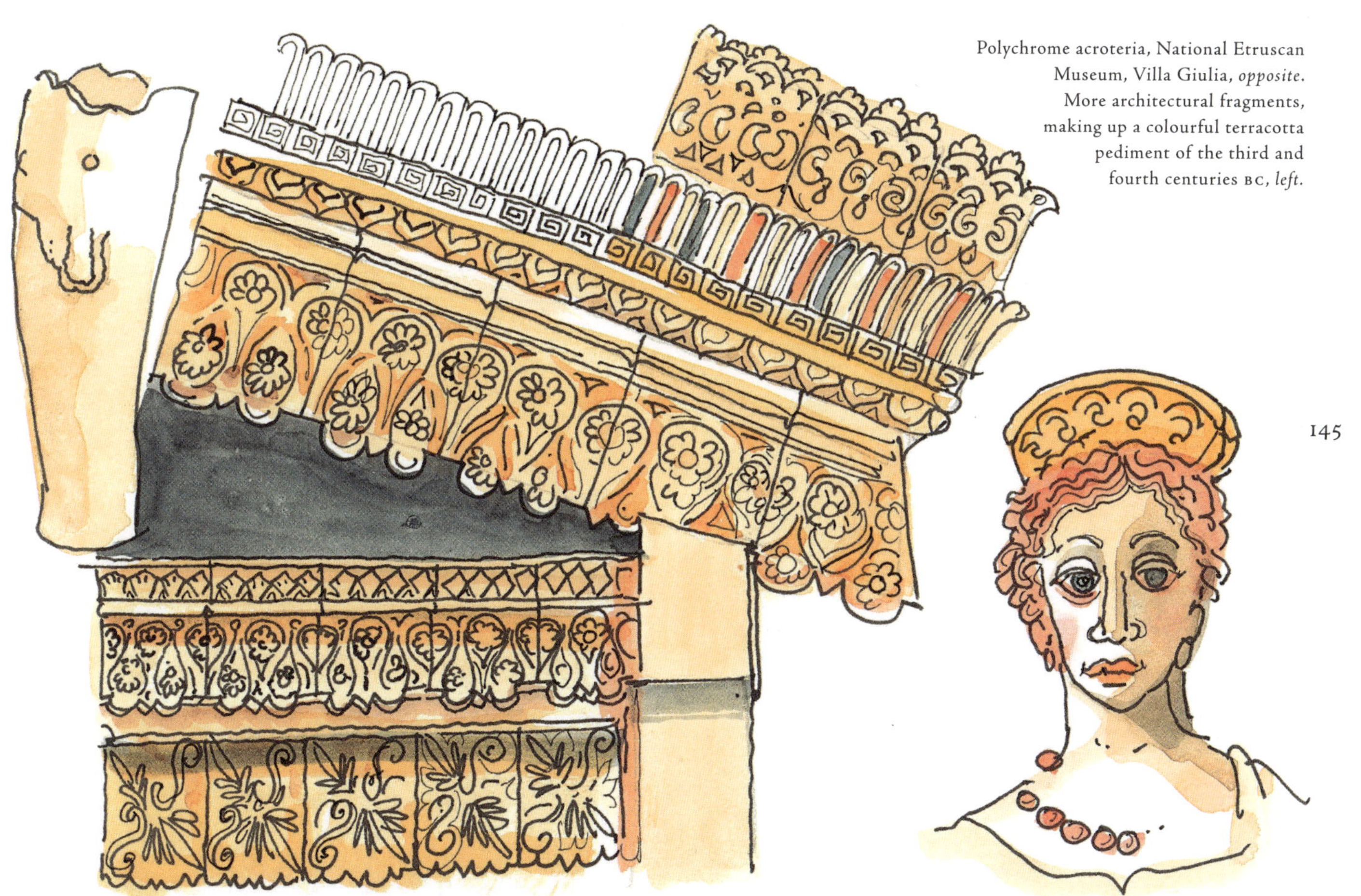

Polychrome acroteria, National Etruscan Museum, Villa Giulia, *opposite*. More architectural fragments, making up a colourful terracotta pediment of the third and fourth centuries BC, *left*.

145

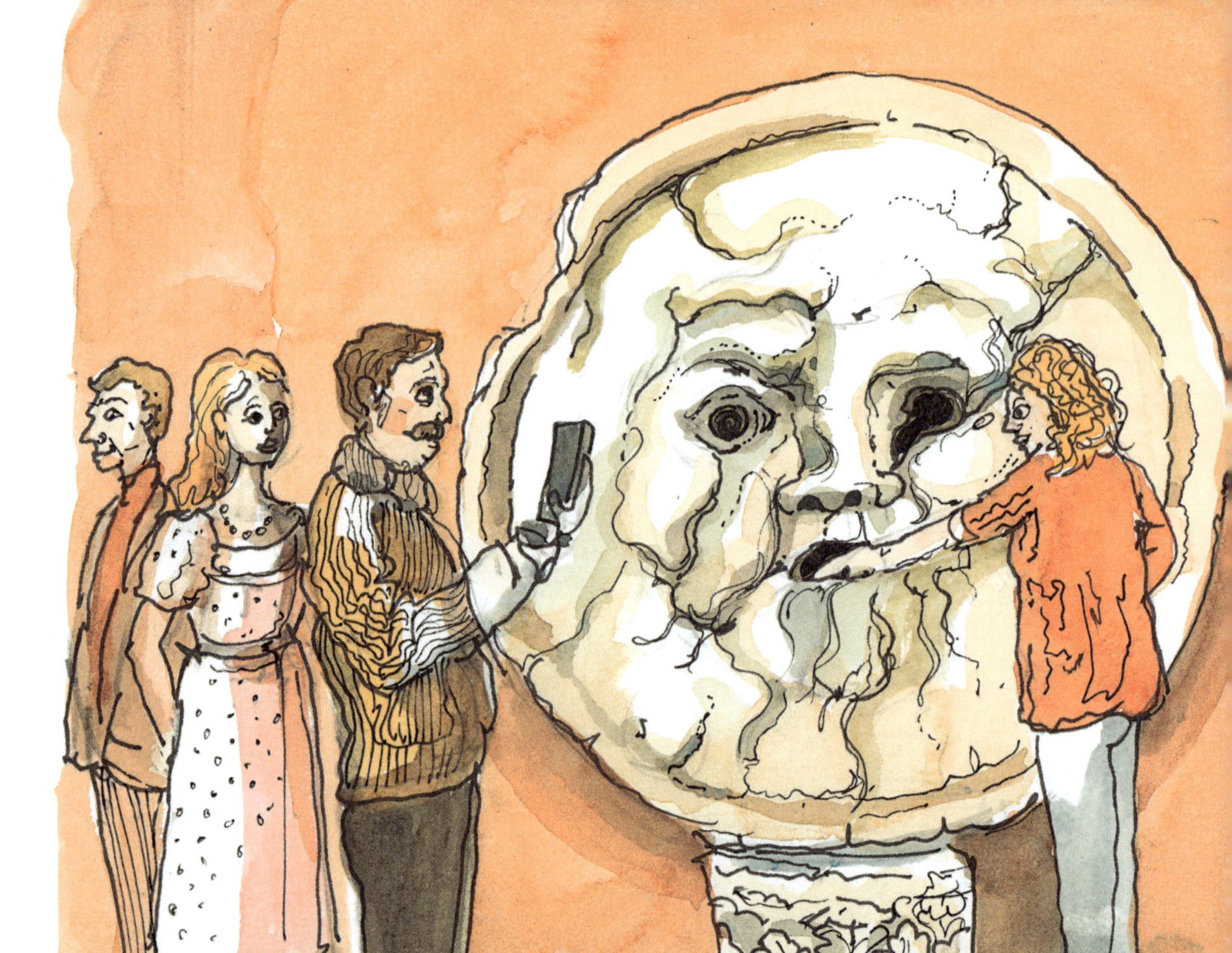

Bocca della Verità,
in the narthex of
Santa Maria in
Cosmedin, second
century BC.

NARRATIVE carving played a dominant role in the decoration of the great buildings of Rome. We imagine this as sharply carved marble bas-reliefs, but the earliest buildings were decorated equally opulently in coloured terracotta. This could be seen in the astonishingly rich Etruscan museum in the VILLA GIULIA, where some of these have been pieced together: bits of tympanum and cornice, incorporating residual components in rich colour and with generous moulding. Influenced by the Greeks, the Etruscans made lavish use of the acroterion, the fanned-leaf form of finial, and the anthemion, another element inspired by plant forms, to enhance their grand wooden structures. Later work was, indeed, of marble, and Greek craftsmen were imported, willingly or as slaves, to produce work as complex as the Solomonic strip cartoon wrapping Trajan's Column or the more flamboyant trophies of armour that emblazon each face of its plinth. From these carvings, early antiquarians began to understand simple details of the ancient world, including furniture, armour, ships and OUTFITS that have not survived the centuries as well as buildings. One source for identifying the costumes of nineteenth-century statuary is the English designer Thomas Hope's *Costumes of the Ancients*, published in 1812, which records the clothes worn by the conquerors of Europe.

Rome's later glories are Baroque, not Renaissance. It is in the sinuous, the reversing and embellishing and the downright wilful ignoring of orthodoxy that Bernini, Borromini and their followers and rivals defined the appearance of papal Rome. Even door- and windowcases illustrate this development, in which a basic form first acquires refinement in a line of raised or incised detail. This is followed by a simple lobe that differentiates top from bottom or, if used on both ends, lends formality and dignity to the composition. The introduction of scrolls begins a process of elaboration, during which the simple hole in the wall becomes utterly subordinated to the frame, in due course leading to blind windows where there is no hole and the frame is nothing but a division on a façade. The doorcase offers yet more scope, with the basis of a temple front as its decoration.

This opened the way for a similar escalation in lawless elaboration, as pediments were bent and curved, broken and chopped, stilted and generally awarded an almost endless list of variants, again decorated with heraldic badges and insignia, both secular and religious. Not content with these alterations to the elevation of the door-way, the masters of the Baroque even curved the ground plan for increased balletic drama and dynamism.

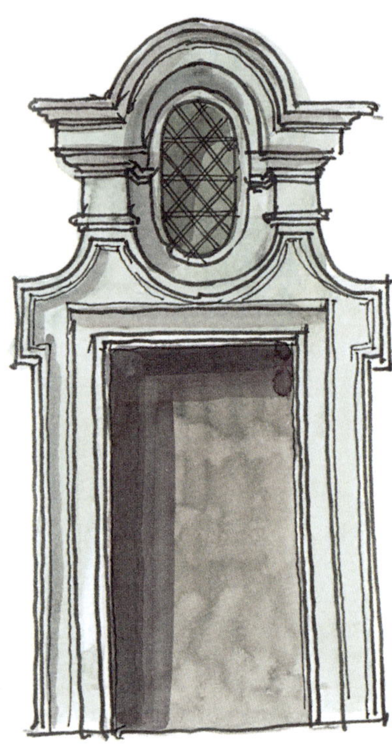

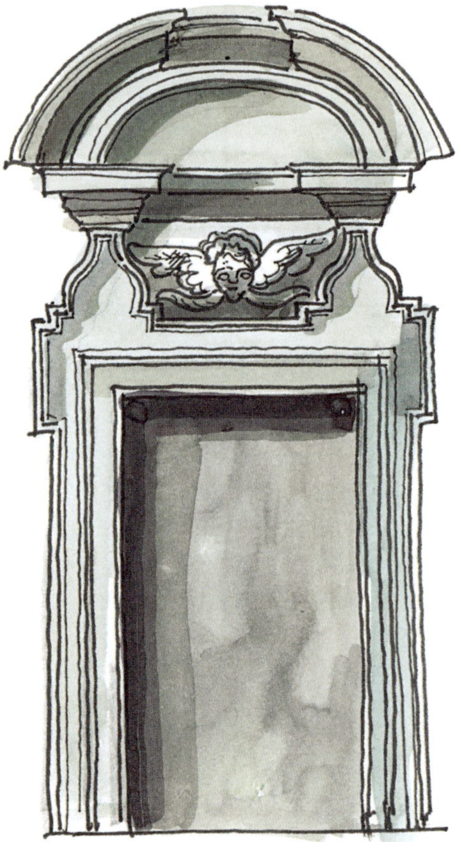

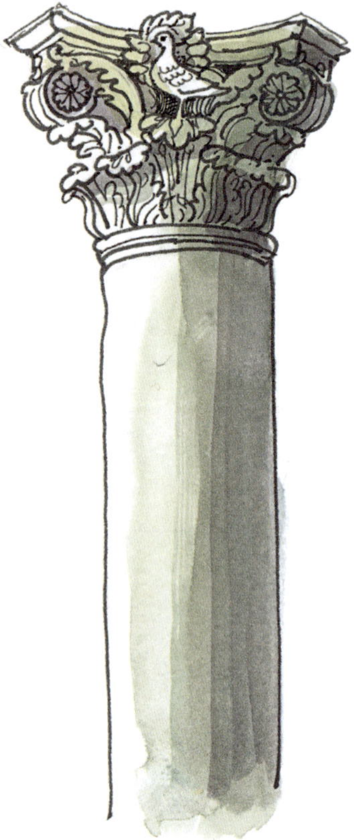

Baroque doorcases of the seventeenth century
and a Romanesque Composite capital.

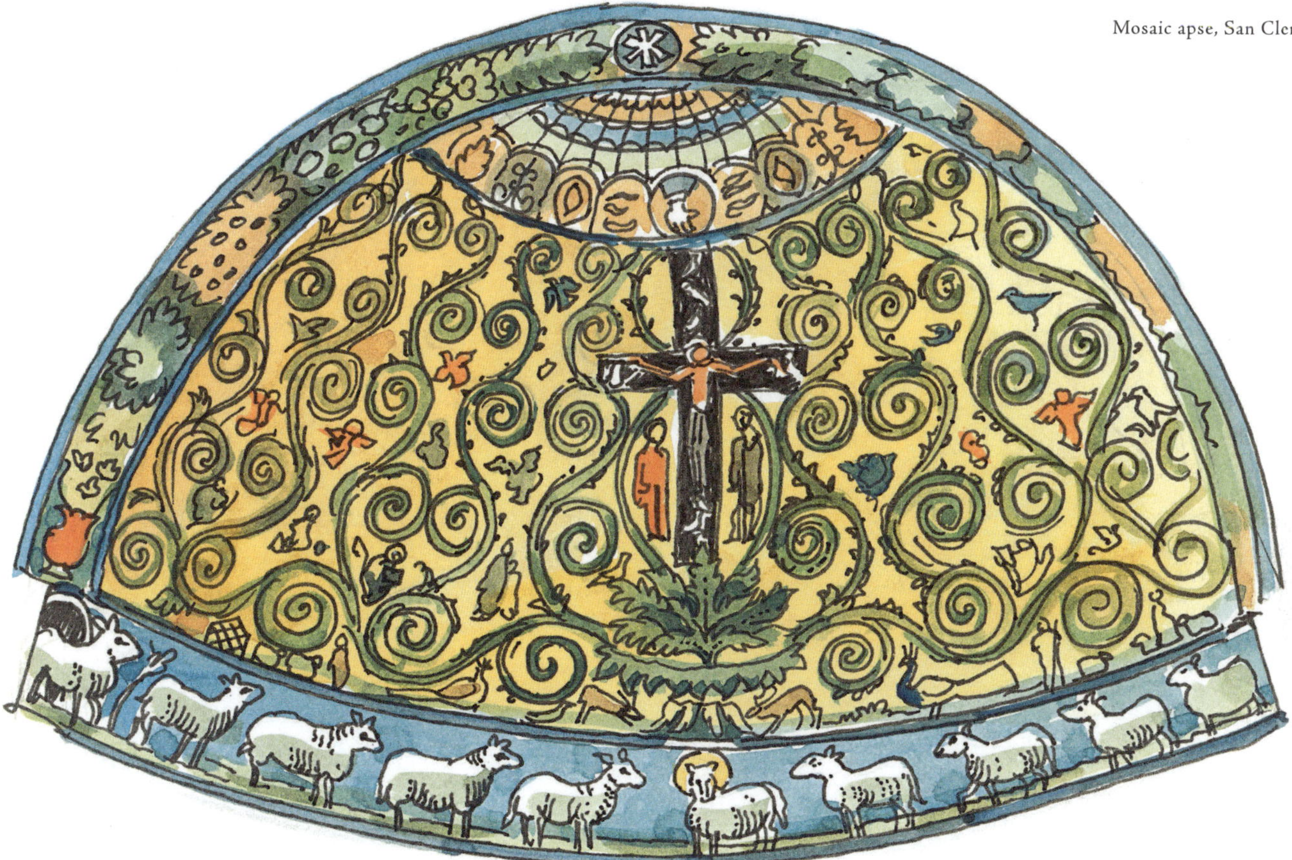

Mosaic apse, San Clemente.

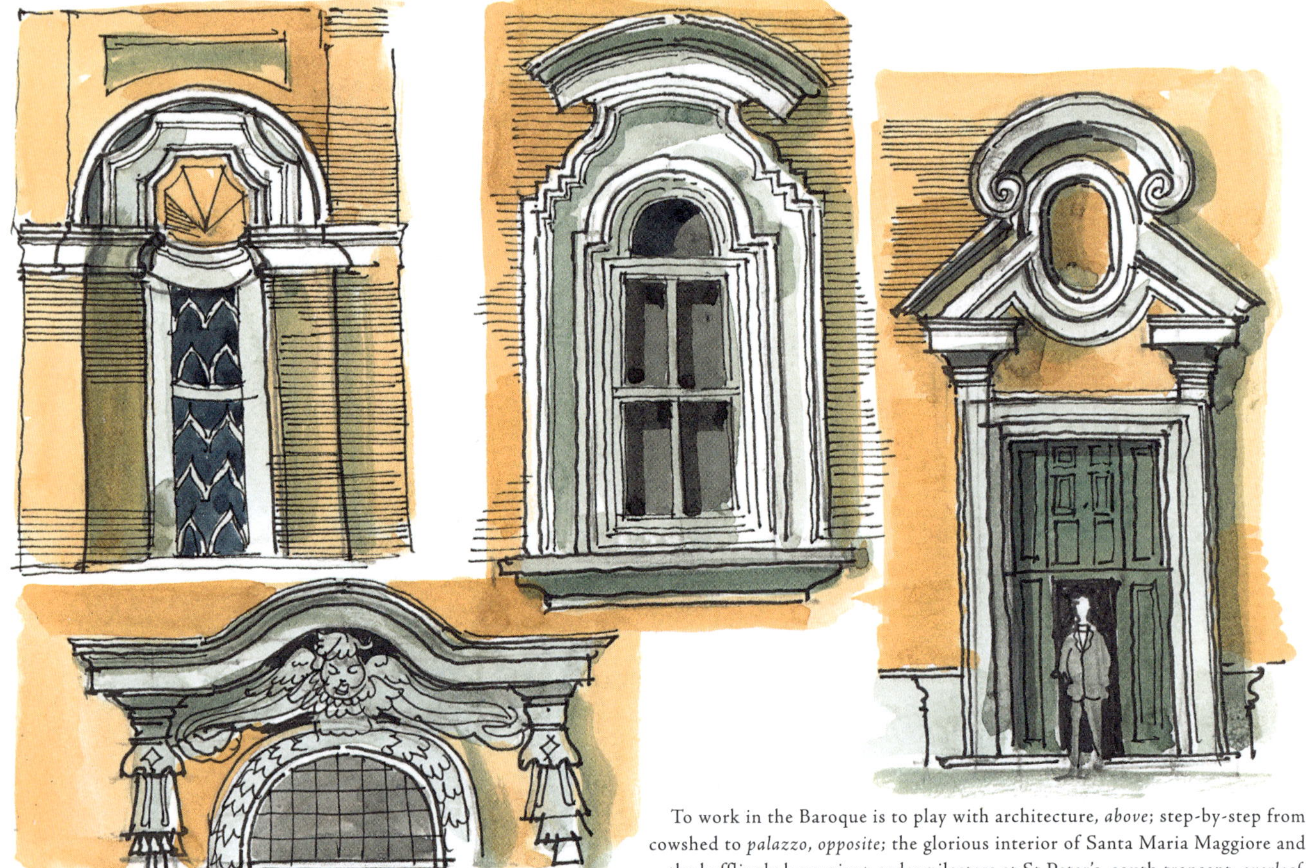

To work in the Baroque is to play with architecture, *above*; step-by-step from cowshed to *palazzo, opposite*; the glorious interior of Santa Maria Maggiore and the bafflingly huge giant-order pilasters at St Peter's, south transept, *overleaf*.

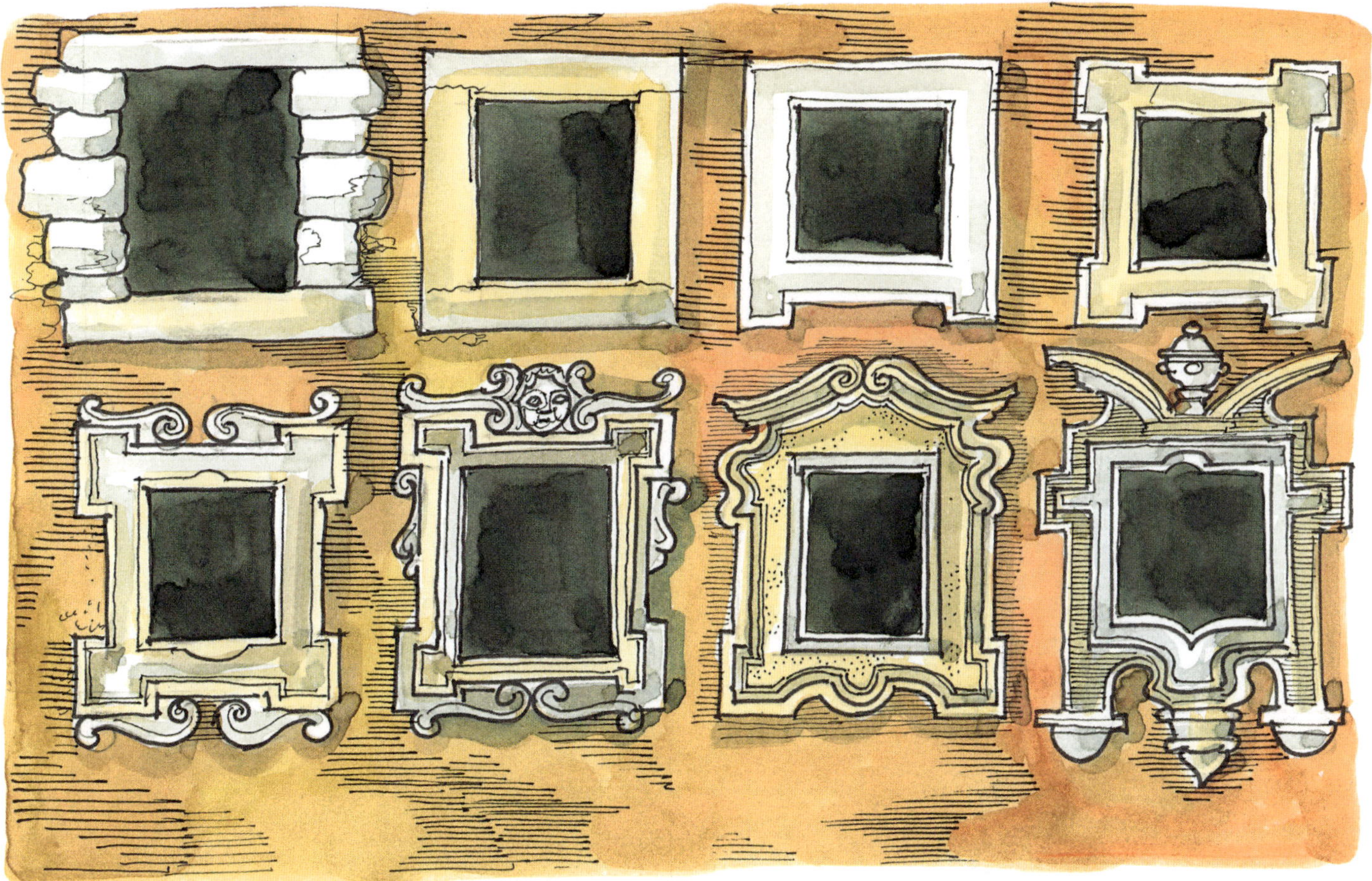

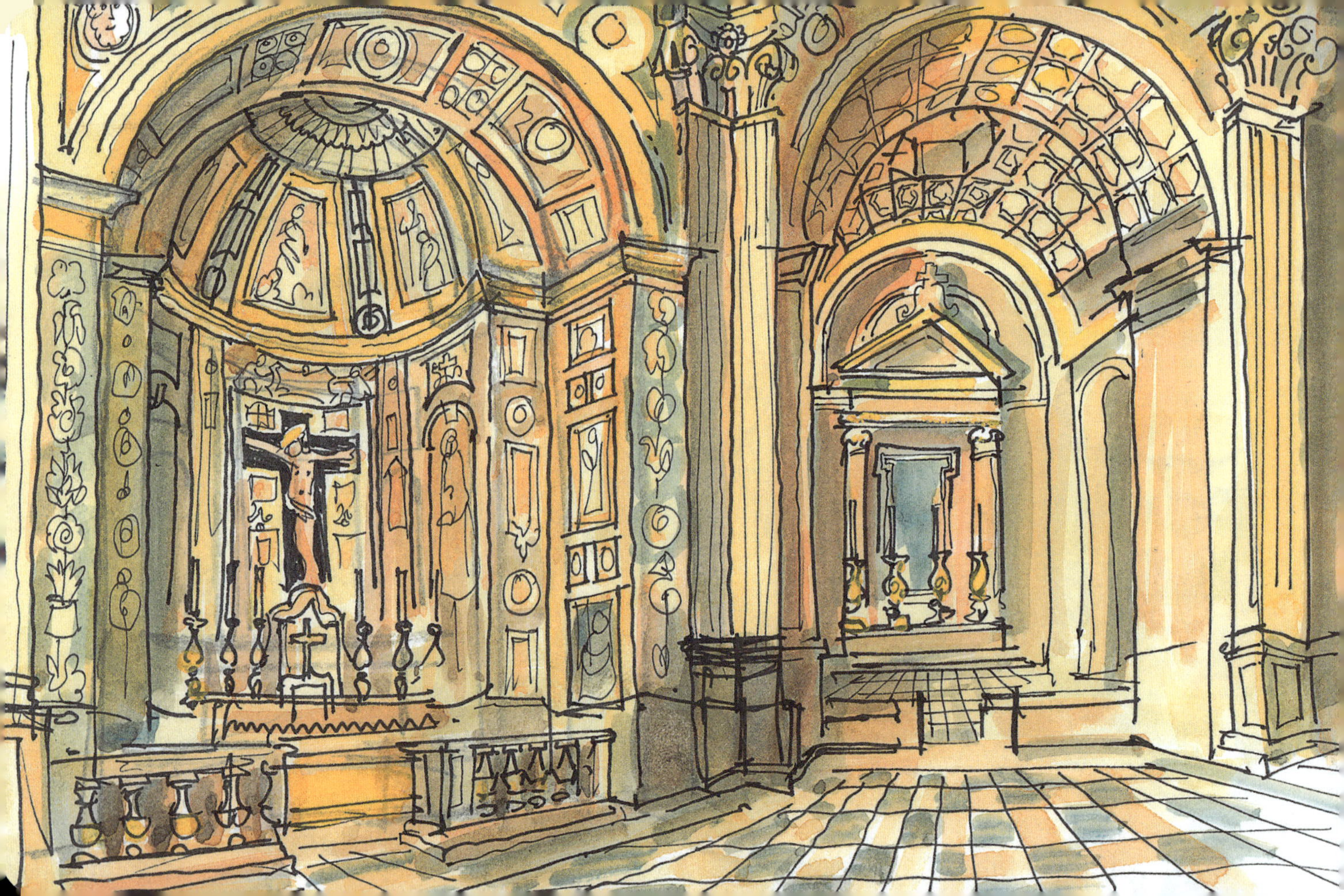

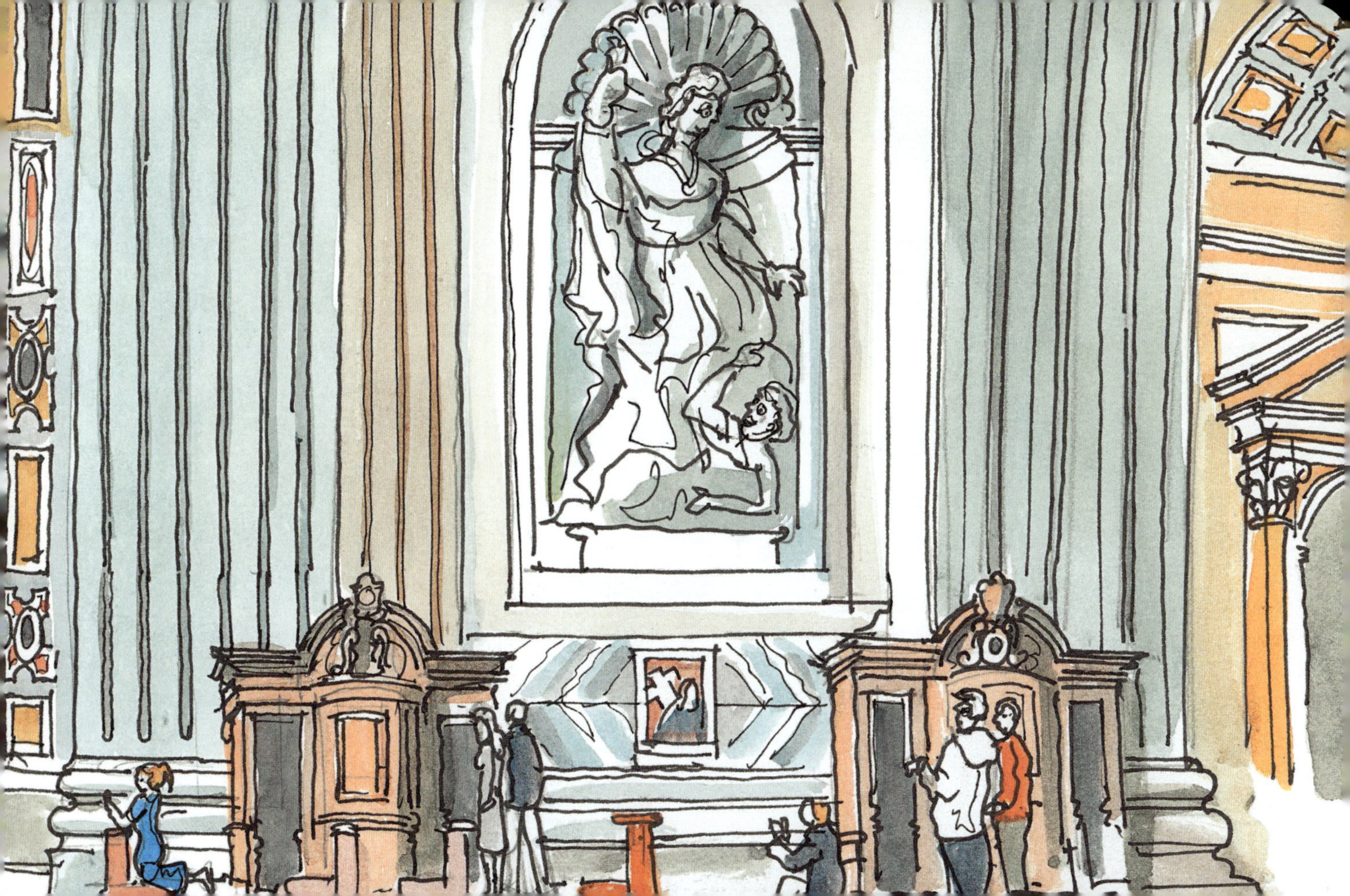

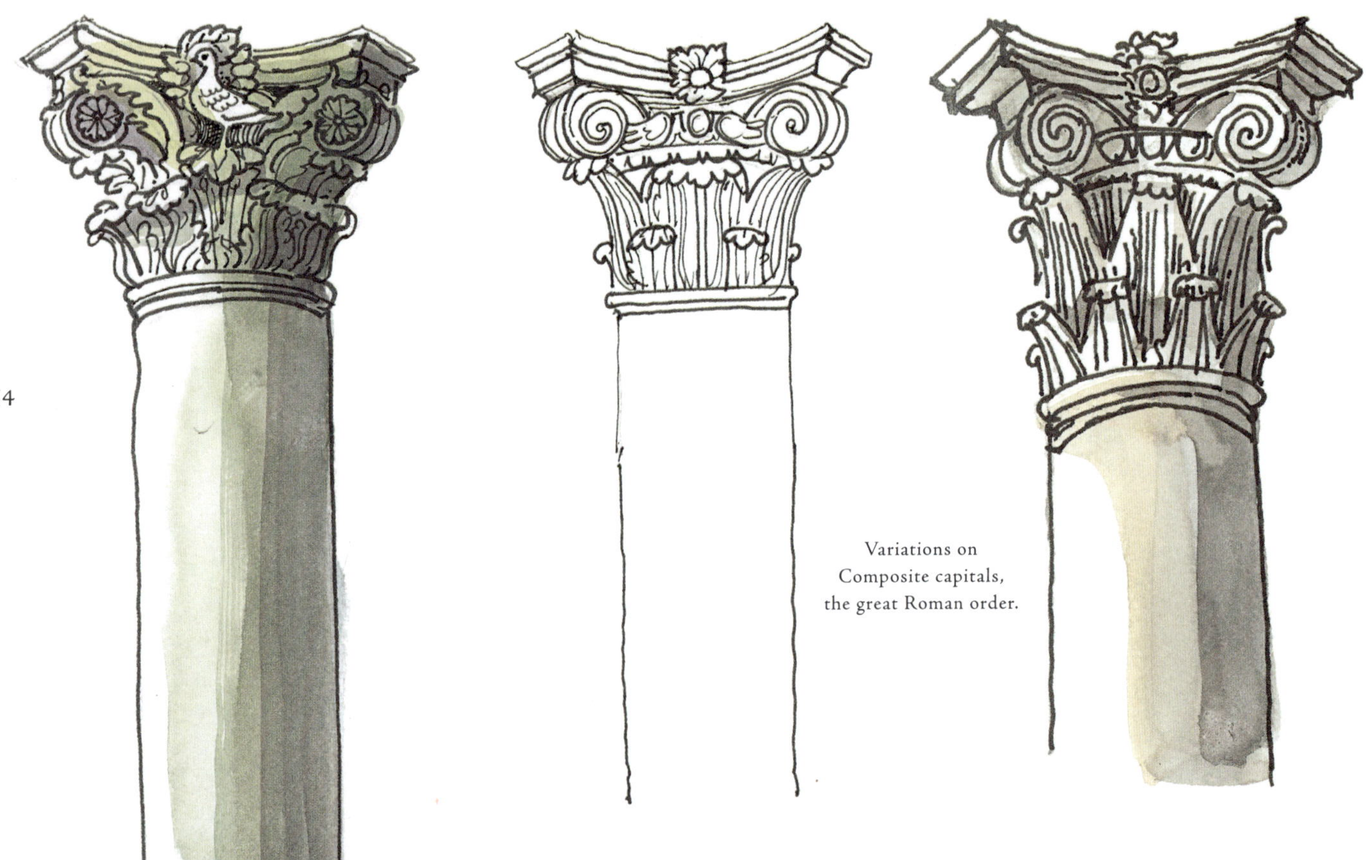

154

Variations on
Composite capitals,
the great Roman order.

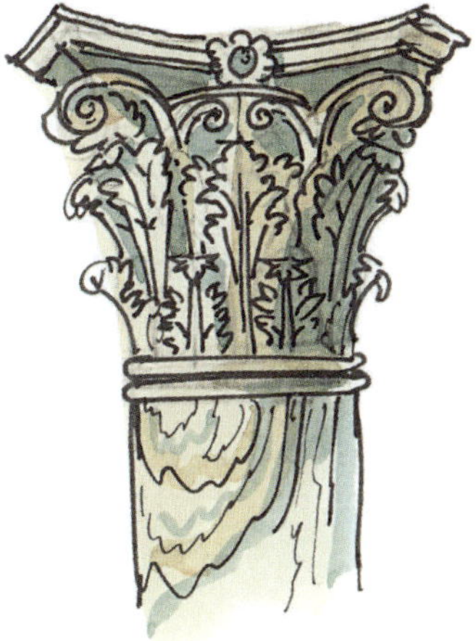

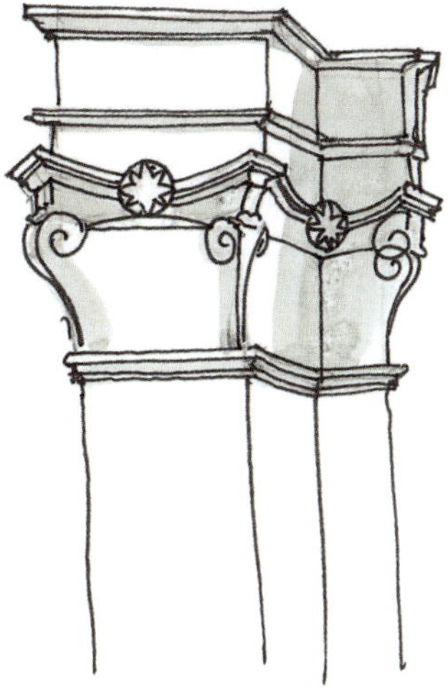

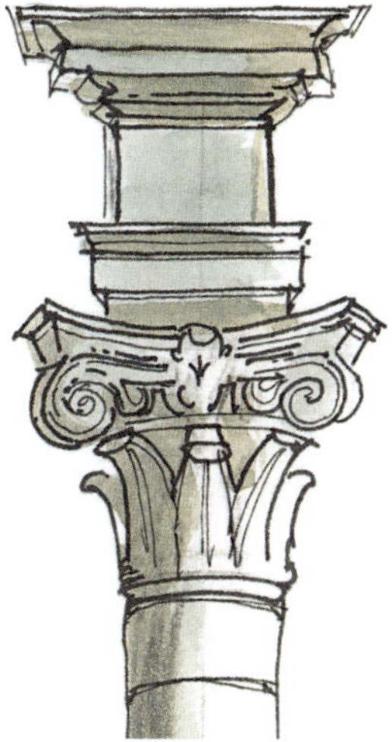

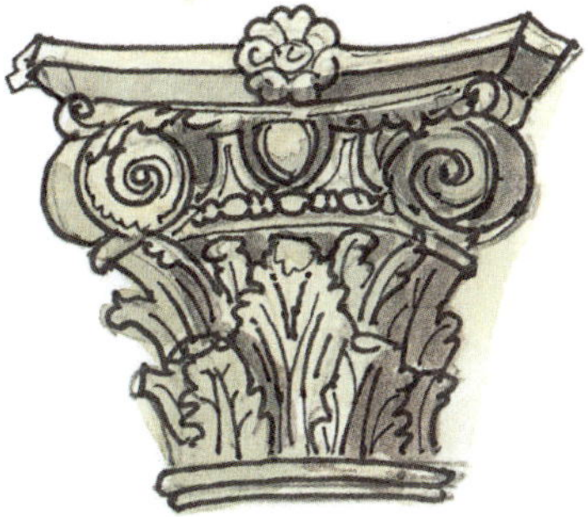

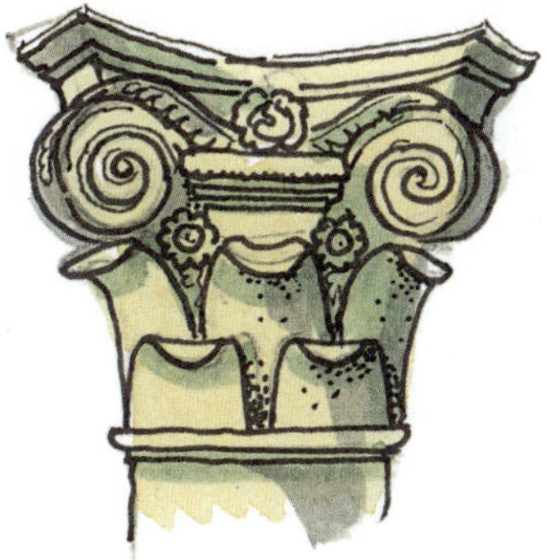

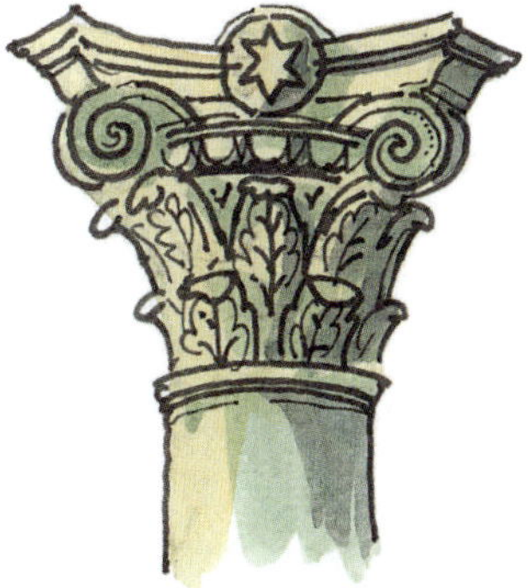

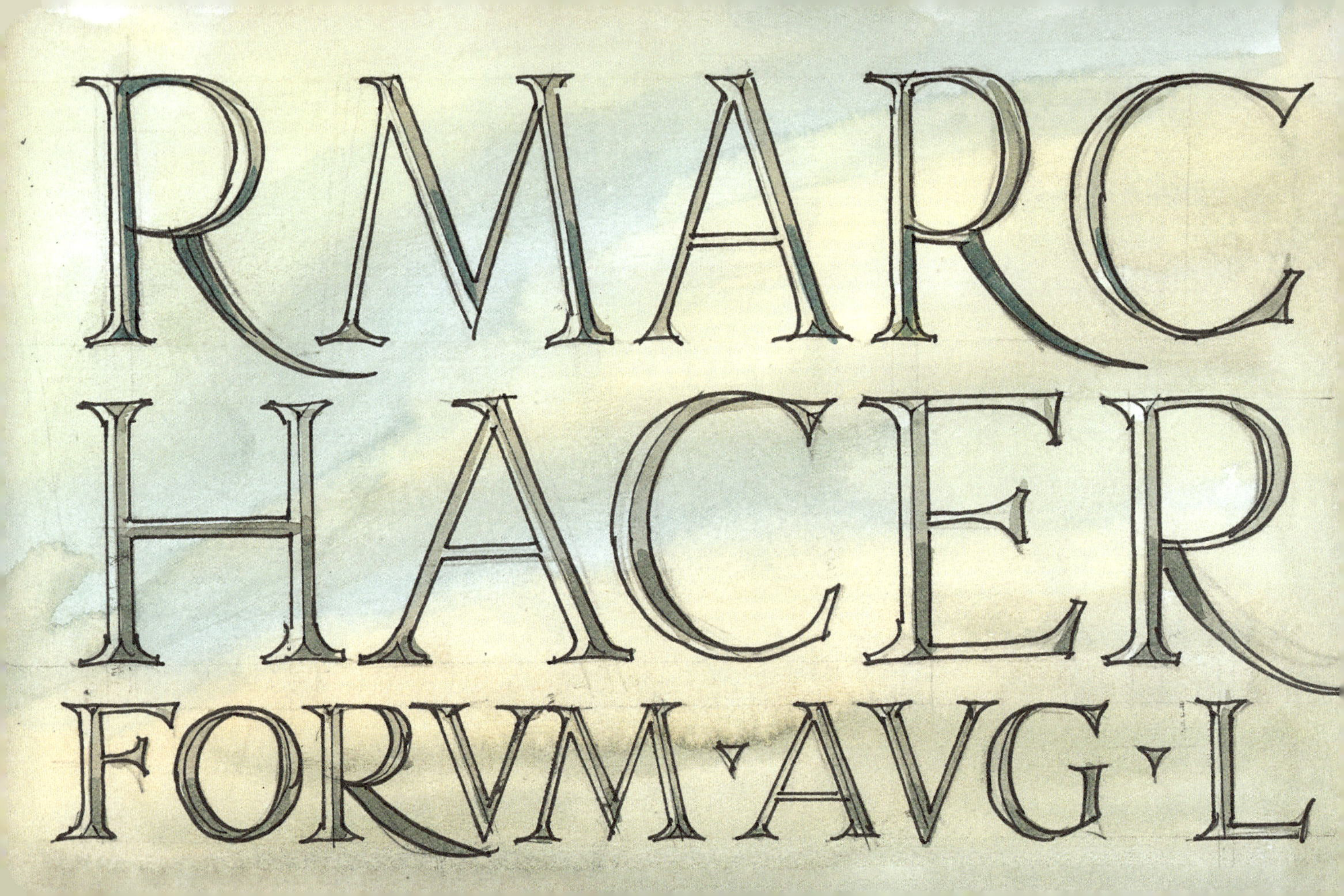

R MARC
HACER
FORVM · AVG · L

GLOVES
ANGELL
SERMONETA
ALIMENTARI

Sculpture and painting

A DAMASCENE CONVERSION. Feeble to admit, but I have never had much interest in sculpture, seeing it as a subsidiary art form to, in order, Music, Painting, Architecture, Writing and even Poetry (I'd probably add flower arrangement, ornamental pastry work and cake decoration, too). Hitherto horrified by the idea of a sculpture park, and sidestepping exhibitions with great care, I had not in any way anticipated a VOLTE-FACE to be one result of spending time in Rome.

But Rome is a city of statues. So many groups of gods, demigods, vestal virgins and heroes lined the parapets and pediments of the ancient city that they were an intrinsic part of its fabric. Ancient taste was for the Greek, and villas, palaces and courtyards were decorated with copies of Hellenistic statues. Seeing room after room of statuary finally infected me, and suddenly I developed a raging thirst for bronze gladiators, snowy-white marble naiads or gilded cupids, only to be truly slaked when slumped in front of Bernini's heart-quivering modelling of crisp linen or wind-twisted foliage. All at once, the challenge of creating in unyielding limestone a character of complex and intense emotion became THE THING. Indeed, it soon became hard to really focus on any but the most lurid paintings, which seemed... hopelessly two-dimensional.

And anyway, Rome is all about the sculpture. Not contemporary single-issue sheets of rusting steel, nor the organic snails lovingly carved in Purbeck marble that sit on a garden plinth... Here, it is the real thing and, whether in a gallery, garden or as part of an architectural composition, whether a portrait, a narrative scene or a depiction of a Classical ideal, it is minutely observed, beautifully carved and often more than two thousand years old. It is also often broken, a fragment of torso and thigh, a noseless head or a mythological subject impossible to parse from the back half of a horse, a vestal virgin's shift or a few frowning centurions' heads, yet this seems not to matter.

It is quite impossible to ignore this second marble population of Rome cavorting along a seventeenth-century

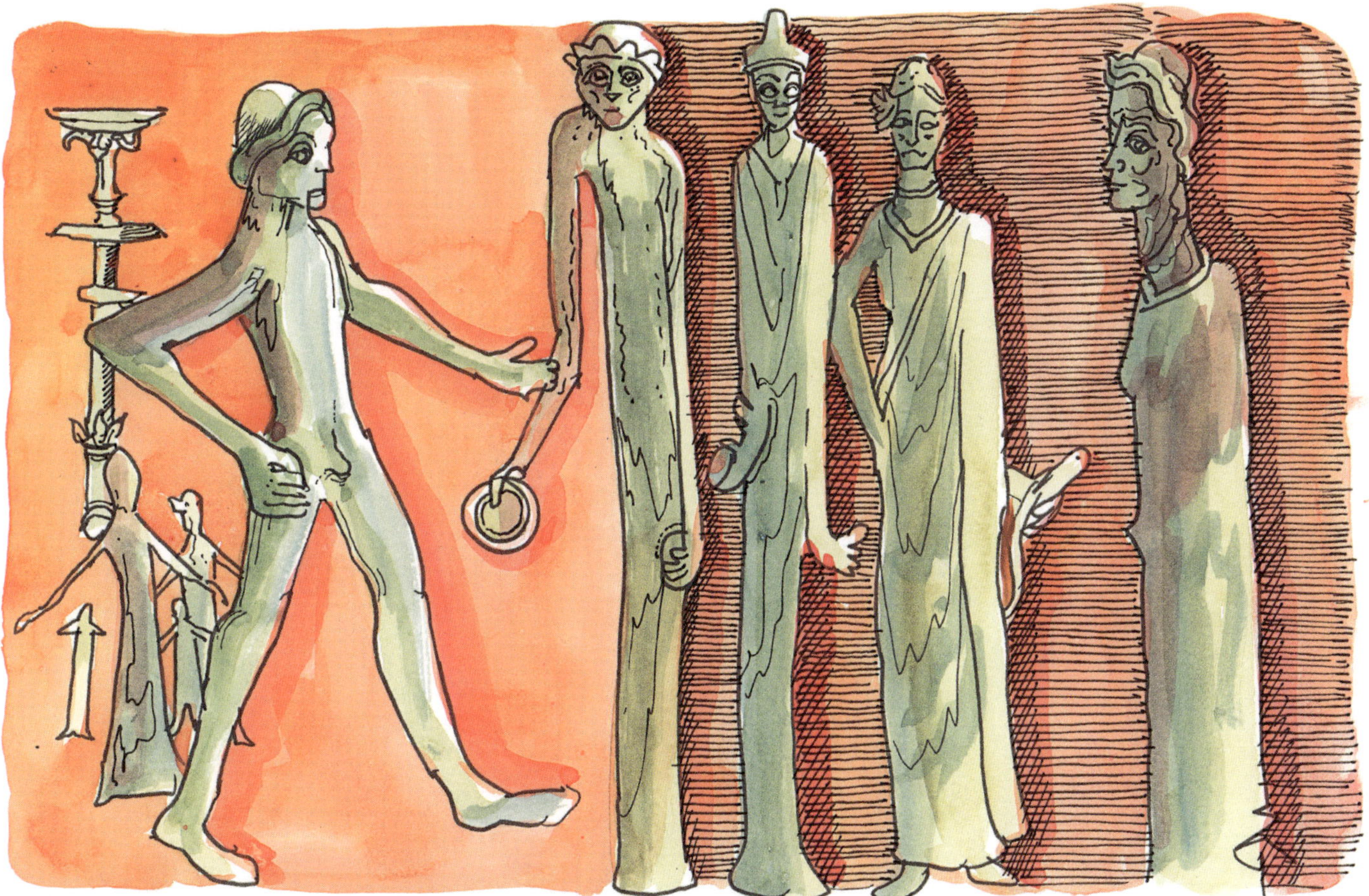

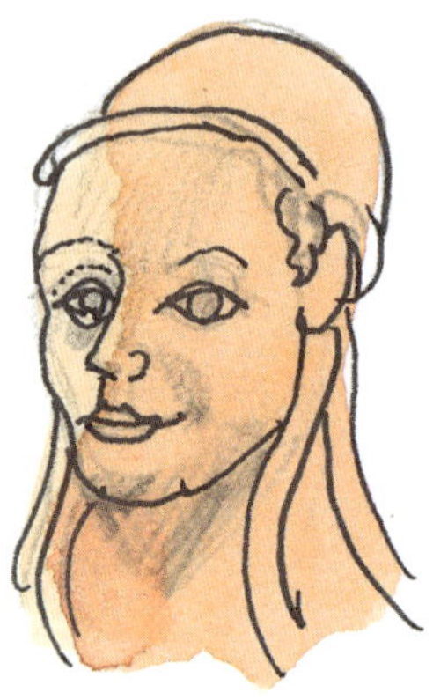

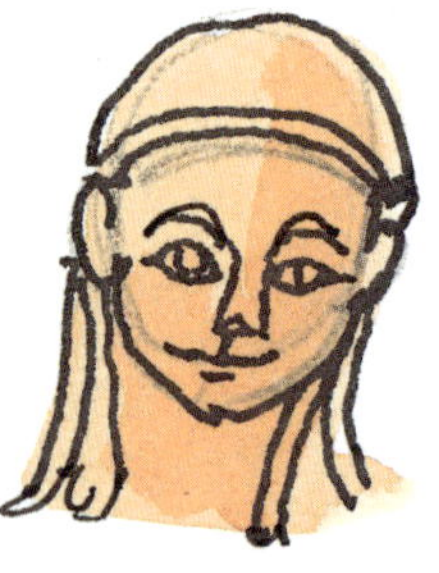

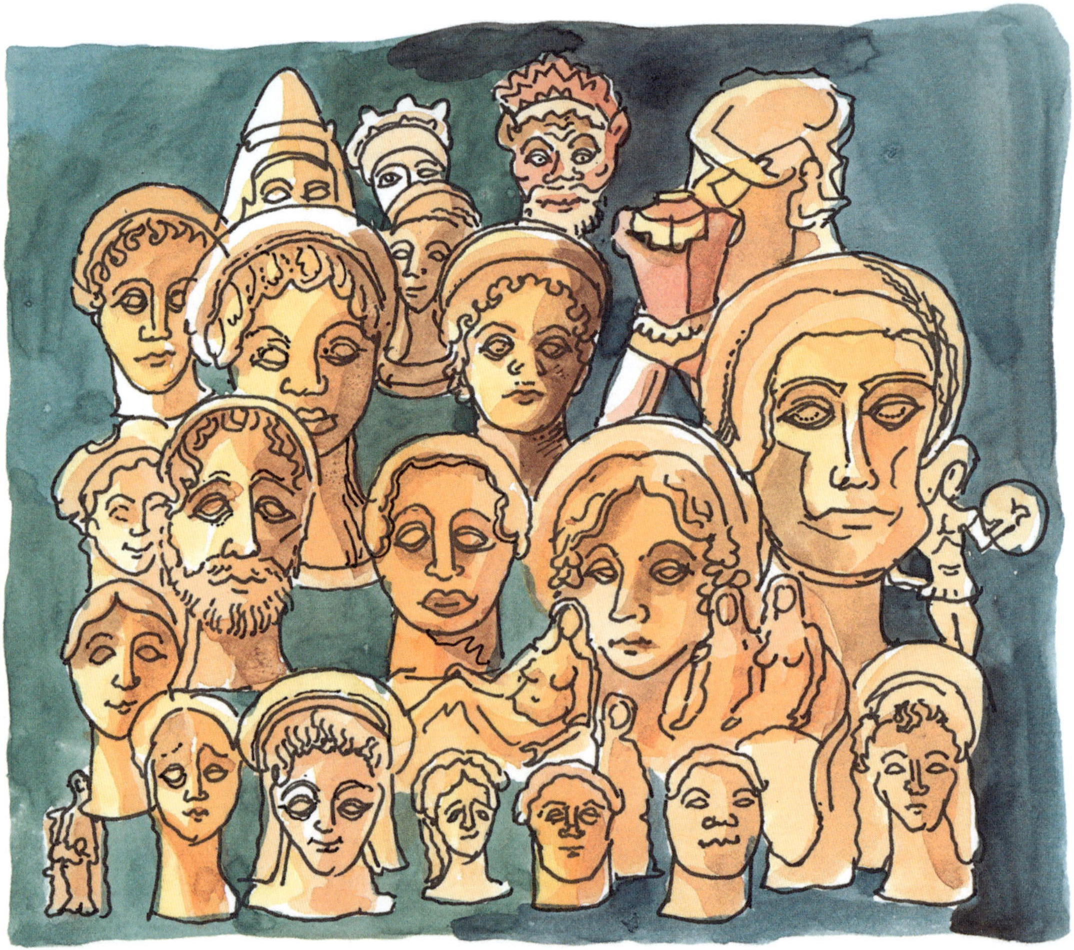

pediment, recording the thrashing of the Dacians or standing sentinel in front of a tightly clipped bay hedge.

This three-dimensional enthusiasm started early, with the great Etruscan sculptor Vulca, popular in the days of the kings, who produced the huge terracotta figure of Apollo for the Temple of Portonaccio and the statue of Jupiter in the Capitoline Temple for the first Etruscan king, Tarquin. The Etruscans were influenced by the Greeks, both as sculptors and in the production of pottery, but there was always a steady flow of statuary from Greece straight to Rome. The works of Phidias and Praxiteles, the Greek masters of the fourth century BC, were in demand both directly and as models to copy. The giant horses in the Quirinal *piazza* are just that: first century AD reproductions of ancient models.

The passion for ancient sculpture raged feverishly during the Renaissance, and aristocratic grandees became serious collectors. More oversized Renaissance figures stand sentinel in the towering courtyard of the Palazzo Spada, and the Villa Medici has as its inner face a patchwork quilt of 'ROMANITAS', fragments carefully fitted together to make a cogent architectural composition. But it is the figures that define Roman sculpture, muscular men or epicene beauties, redoubtable matrons, impossibly

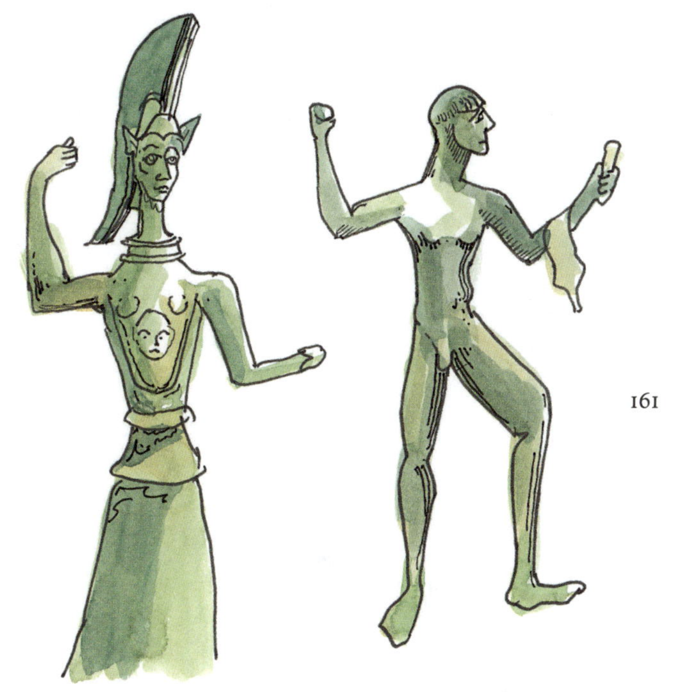

Etruscan terracotta busts, third century, *left*; more bronze stick men, *above*.

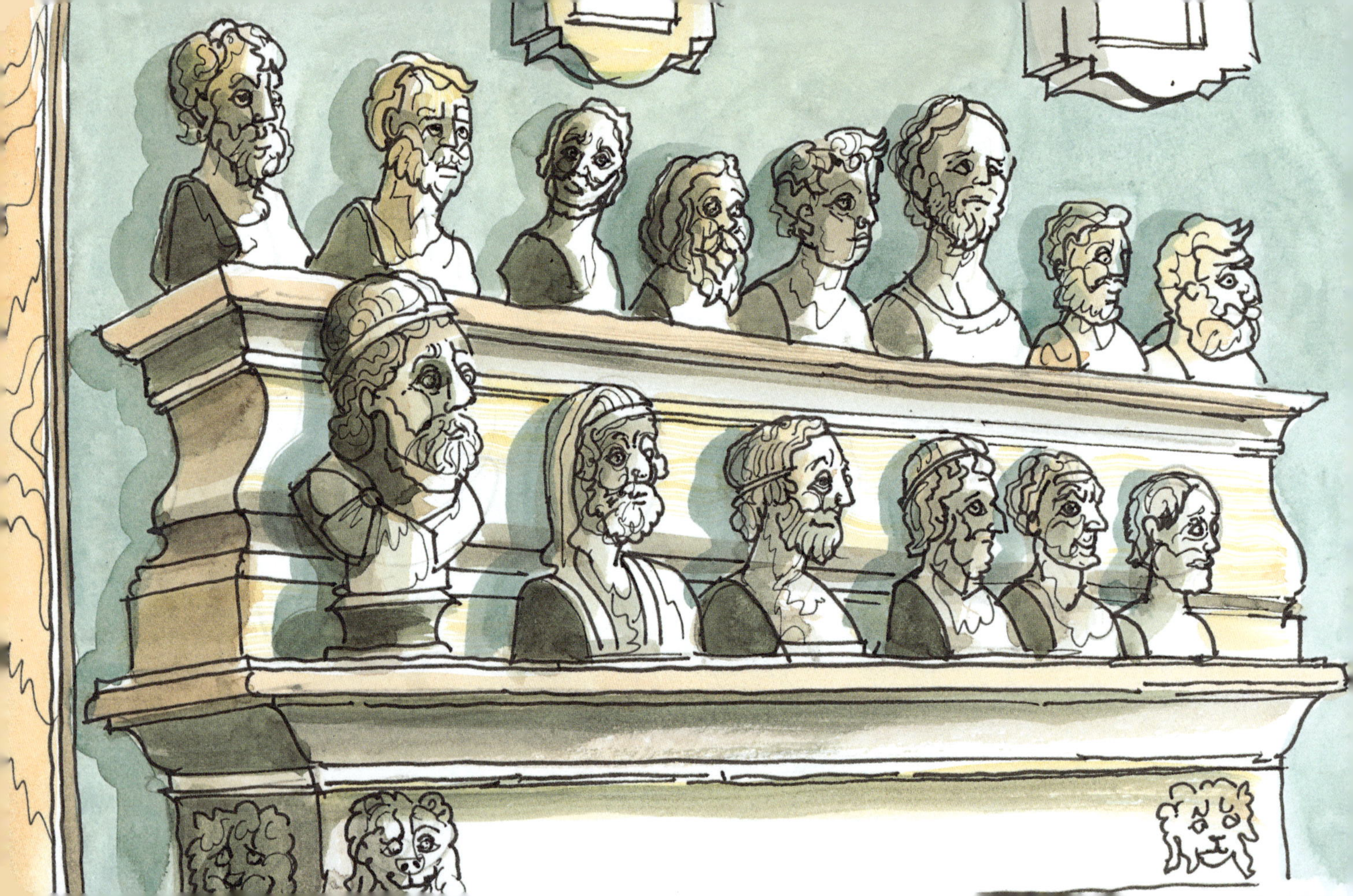

beautiful young women and even a hermaphrodite lying asleep, revealing their unusual arrangements within the parameters of classic beauty. From them, we learn what people wore when they went to war or lounged in the *triclinium*, see how the finest lawns hung or breastplates crackled and, most of all, what they LOOKED like. Whereas statuary in the early centuries was iconographic or at least deeply idealized, the work of the later Imperial era explored the SPECIFICS: noses and brows, cheekbones, eye sockets and chins. Thus we can see and almost feel the face of Augustus, Julius Caesar or Nero.

Much of what is best in Rome is held in the Palazzo Massimo alle Terme. Even on a Sunday afternoon, this extraordinary museum is quiet. An English mother and her resentful daughter, a deeply intense middle-aged German and I walked round the three floors of this externally slightly off-putting nineteenth-century museum. Inside, it is anything but. An exhausting staircase leads first to a forest of helms and busts all carefully explained and so close as to be especially engaging (although noisily alarmed). Following a tip off, I went straight to the second

Selection of philosophers' busts, Capitoline Museums, *left*;
the Sala degli Animali (Hall of Animals) Vatican Museum, *overleaf*.

floor, to LIVIA'S GARDEN. Here, this empress, wife of the great Augustus, had a large room covered in the most subtly painted garden scene. Beyond a foreground of trellis and a hurdle fence, there is a row of realistically painted fruit trees, among them citrus and pomegranates. Through these flit birds – long-tailed tits and jays, thrushes and finches. Behind, more carefully painted greenery gradually loses focus, adding depth and canny realism.

Other rooms have more architecturally decorative schemes, sophisticated in design and delicious in colour, but with a filter imposed by their stilted figures and with a slightly less developed and formalized style of drawing. Floors of all sorts of mosaic are shown in each room, some almost cartoon-like with unsophisticated imagery, others subtle, geometric and intricate. The middle floor has as its principal attraction two astounding bronzes. The SEATED BOXER fixes you with sightless eyes as he rests his gloved hands, the green, brown and gold patches of the heavily patinated bronze giving life to what is already a powerful and utterly believable figure. Across the room, a standing man leans forward with the support of a tall staff. Physically impressive, both the men have a heavily defined musculature. The viewer has a most direct response to these two sportsmen, one that easily straddles two

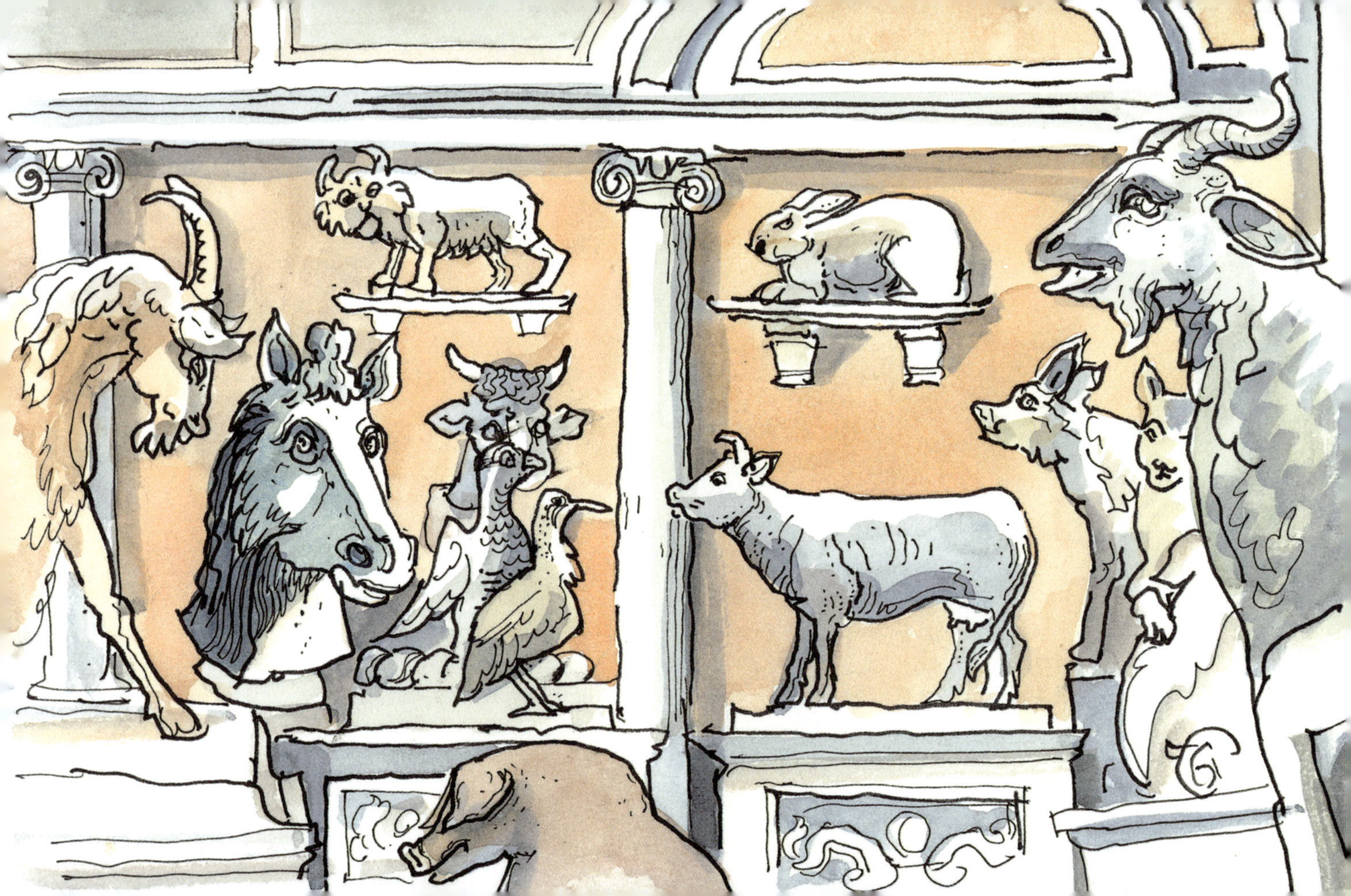

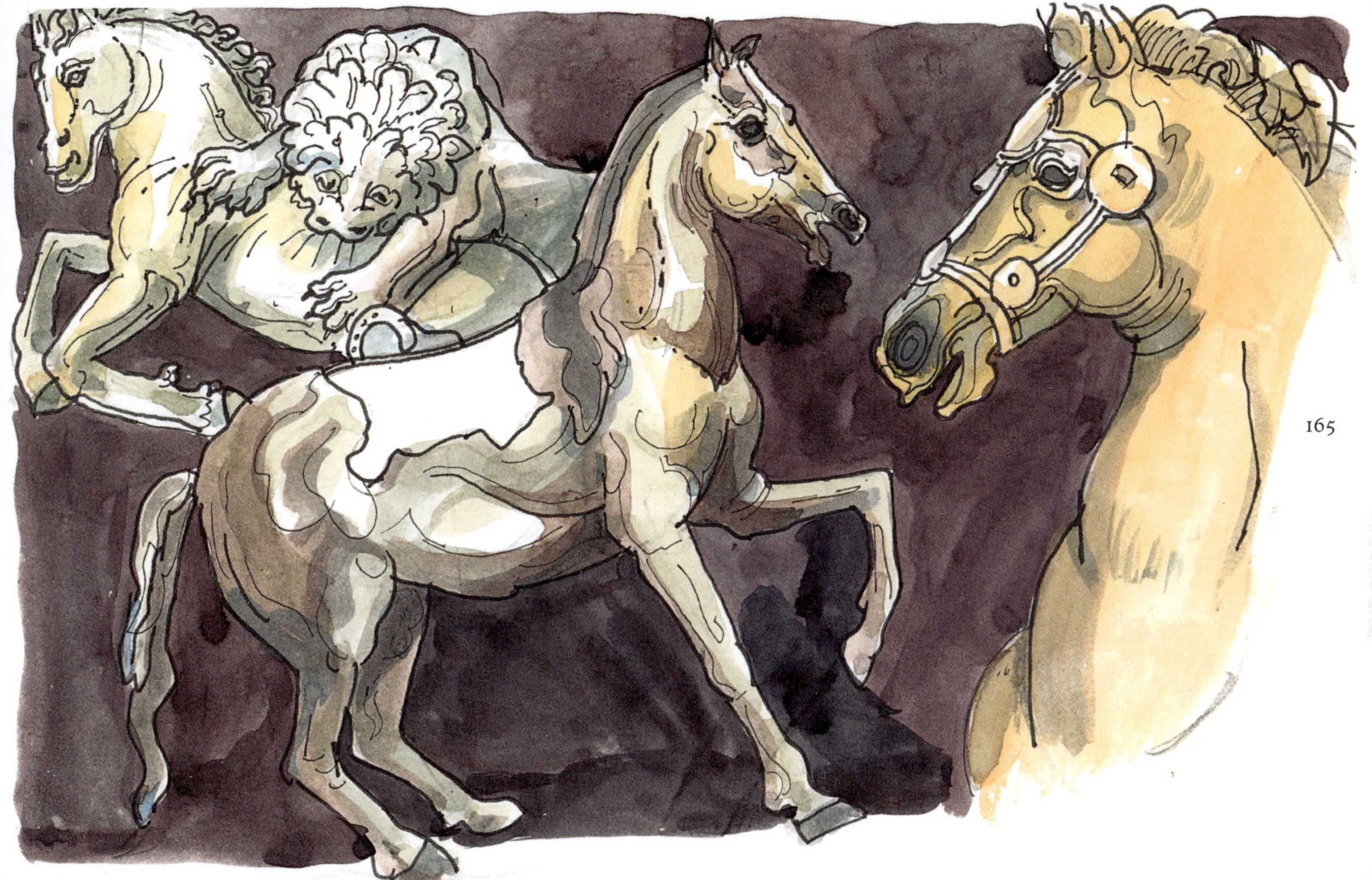
165

millennia. It is exciting that they are alone in a darkened space, so there is absolutely no distraction from their eyeless sockets, and the conversation is entirely with their poise and bodies.

Whether in stone inlays, mosaic or micromosaic, fresco, bronze or marble, this museum manifests the sophisticated levels of craftsmanship in ancient Rome over its 1,200-year life and shows that, while the masters of the Baroque took the treatment of physical expression and swirling material to stratospheric levels, there was a full and lavish articulacy thriving a millennium and a half earlier.

Many of the city's other great works are in the Villa Borghese. For more than a century, this has been a national gallery, and it contains internationally significant works, including three of Bernini's most notable sculptures: *Aeneas, Anchises and Ascanius* (escaping from Troy); *Apollo and Daphne*; and *The Rape of Proserpina* (Persephone). If you are not inclined to be moved by sculpture, the latter may be the work to convert you. Pluto, king of the underworld, grasps Persephone, dragging her to his gloomy realm to be his wife. One strong hand rests around her slender waist, as the other grips her marble thigh, moulding her muscles as she writhes in his lethal grip. It is beyond lifelike and hard to walk away from. Less emotionally engaging, but still an

unthinkably skilled bravura performance, is the Apollo and Daphne group, in which the nymph's smooth skin is gradually hardening into the bark of the laurel tree she will become. It *is* laurel bark and the laurel leaves are cut into the smooth block of marble with baffling realism and carefully articulated crispness, echoing Bernini's treatment of rocks throughout the city's fountains. Most extraordinarily, he began this work aged twenty-three.

Set against this brilliance, Canova's cool neo-Classicism does seem a bit... COOL AND NEO-CLASSICAL. Yet his reclining Venus is, in fact, a portrait of a real person, Napoleon's sister Paolina, by then the wife of Camillo Borghese. Completed in 1808, this statue unsurprisingly caused comment, even though, despite her revealed upper body, there is something chaste and forbidding in her partial nudity. Like a country-house visitor drawn from grandiose state rooms to the more domestically resonant kitchen below stairs, the viewer – well, at least this one – is more drawn to the loving care addressed to the pillows between her and the elegant bed on which she lies than to her undeniably smooth skin and idealized features.

Fresco in the Villa of Livia, wife of Augustus, 39 BC, *right*; Hellenistic statues: *Seated Boxer* and his standing cousin; Piazza Navona fountain, *overleaf*.

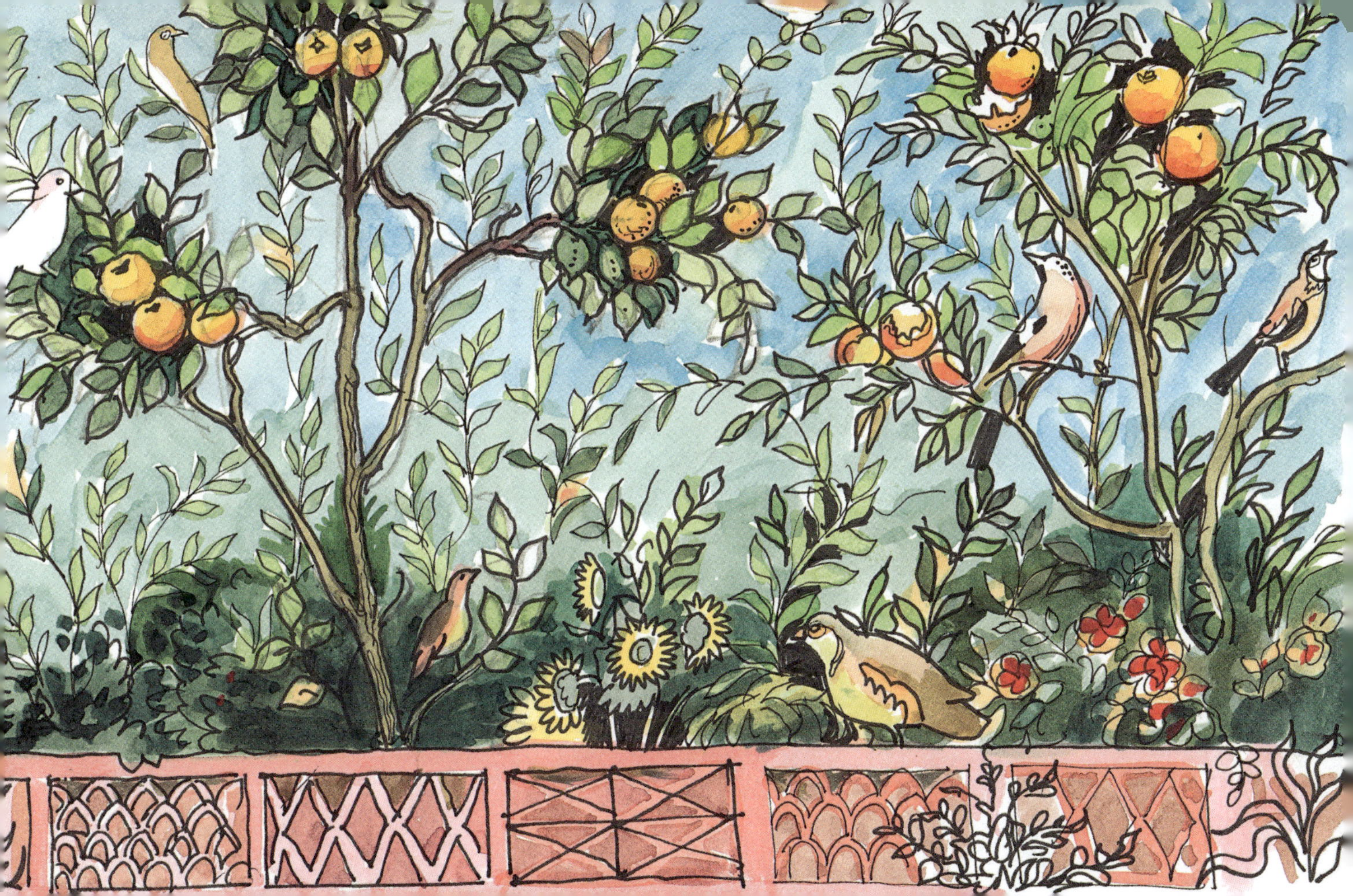

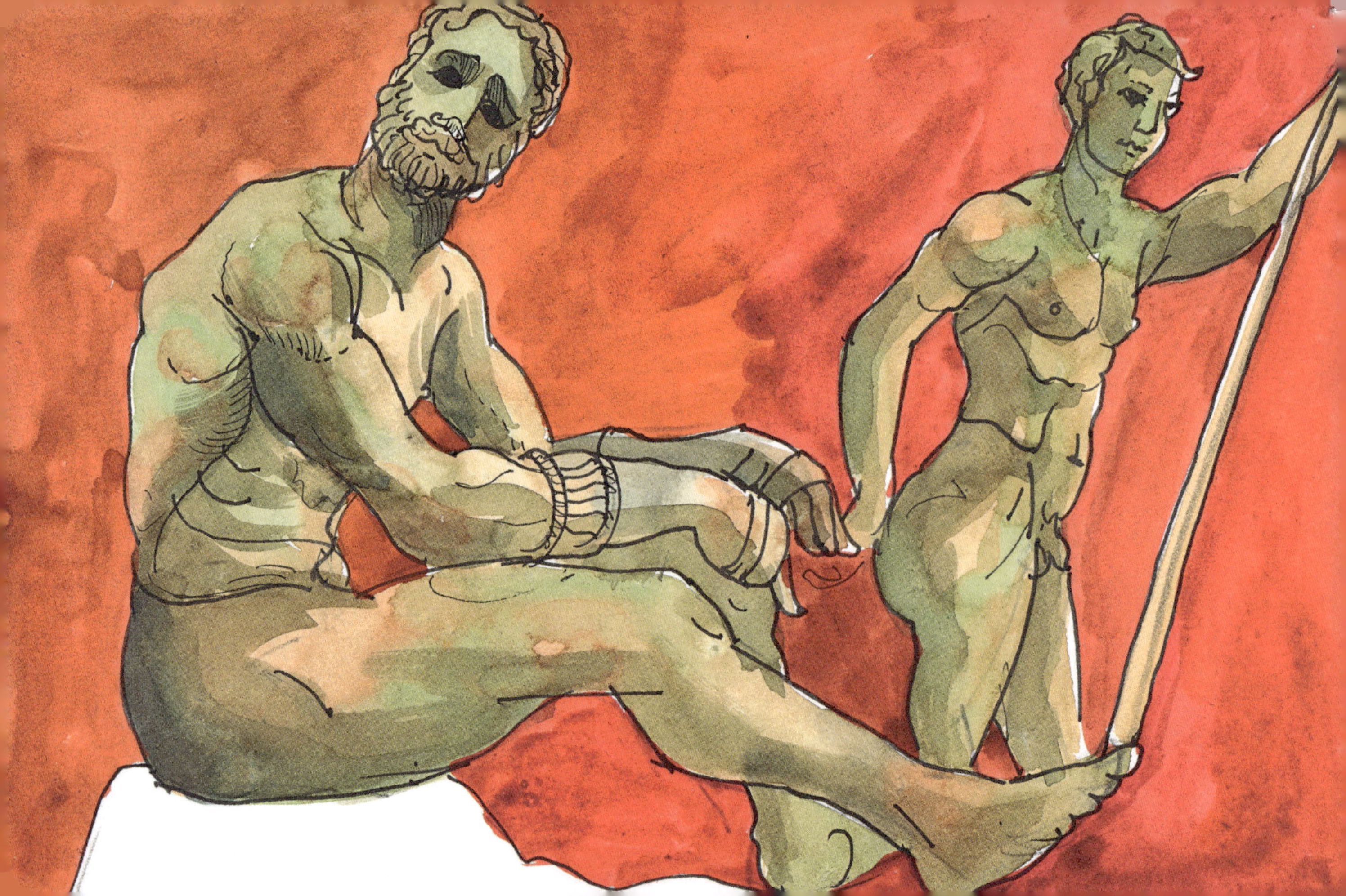

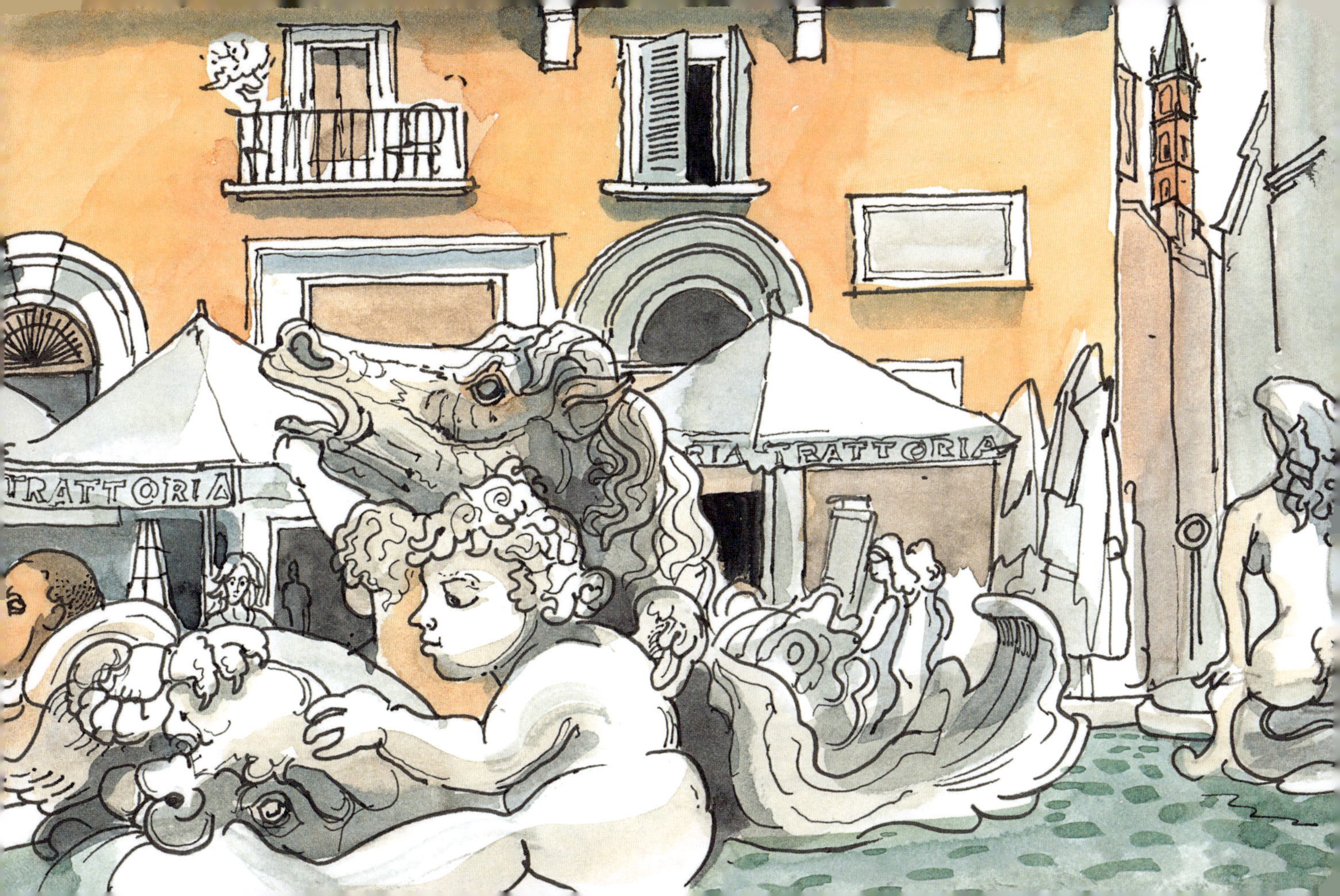

TRATTORIA
RIA TRATTORIA

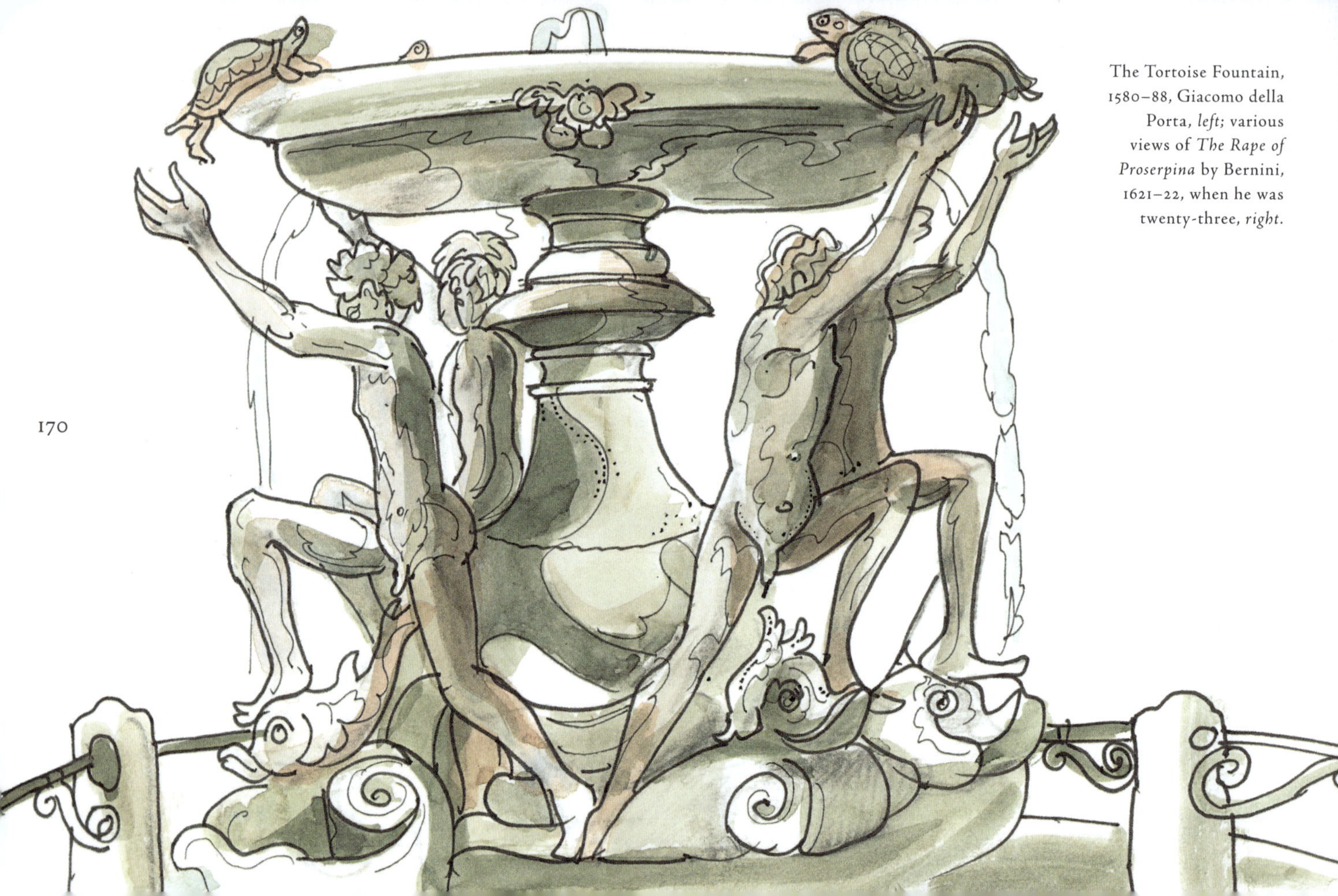

The Tortoise Fountain, 1580–88, Giacomo della Porta, *left*; various views of *The Rape of Proserpina* by Bernini, 1621–22, when he was twenty-three, *right*.

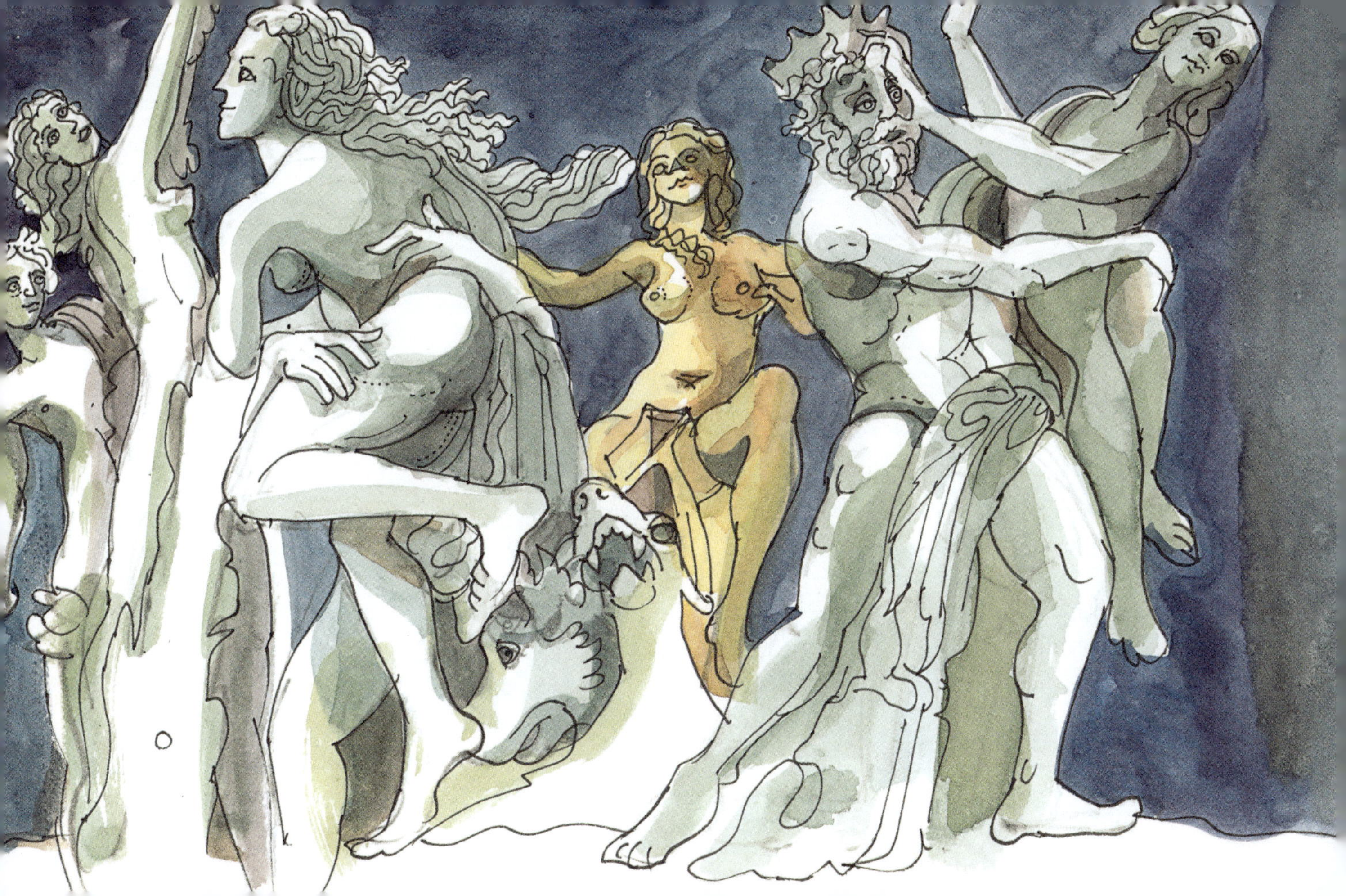

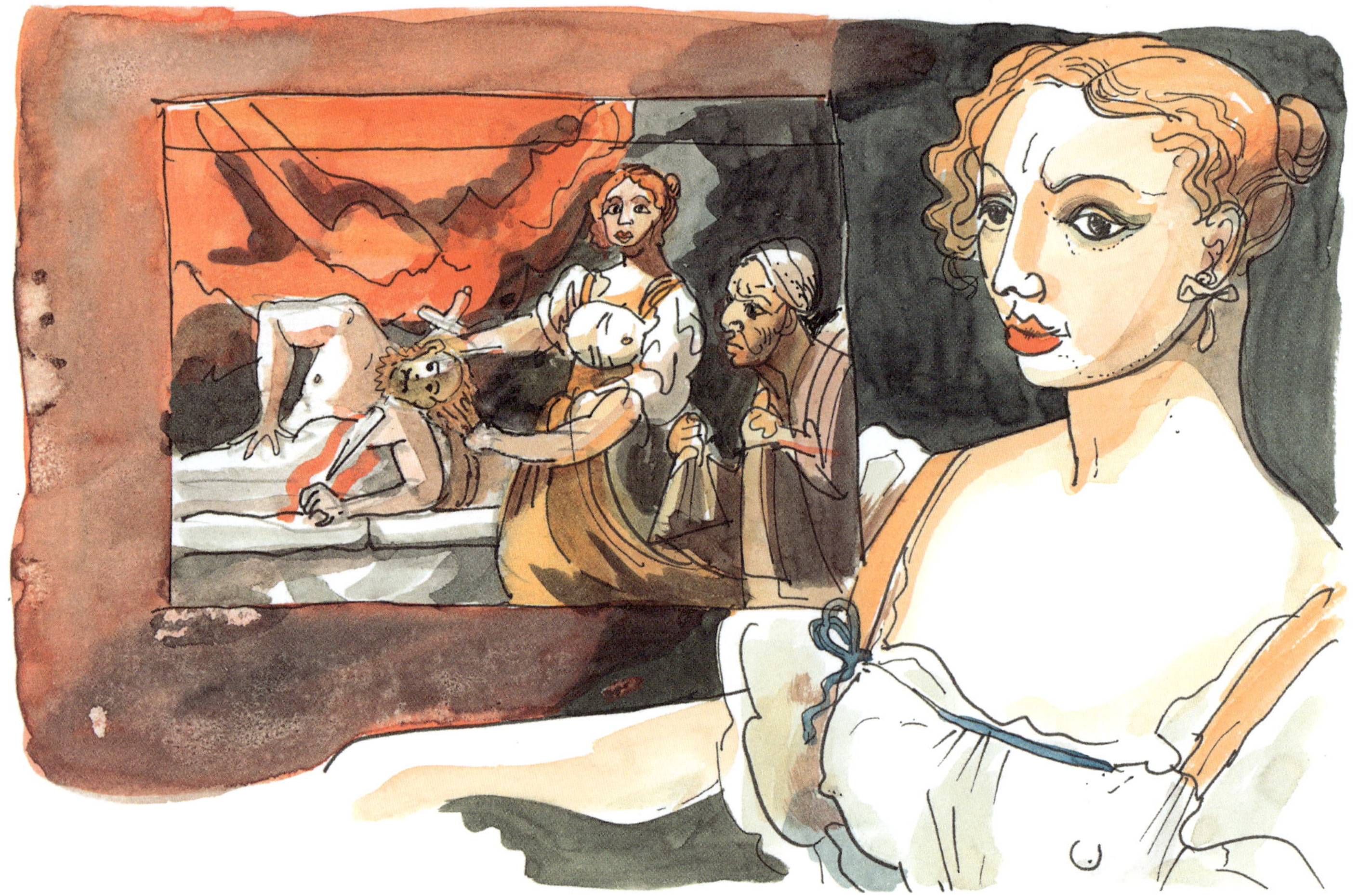

The gallery also has stupendous paintings: by Raphael (*Deposition*), Titian (*Sacred and Profane Love*) and Guido Reni (countless), but perhaps most famous and adoringly visited are those by Caravaggio. Two great works to study: *David with the Head of Goliath*, a successful exercise in chiaroscuro, the lopped bonce all but invisible in the murky shadows as the muted light of victory illuminates the King of Israel alone, and *Young Sick Bacchus*, an unspeakably gloomy self-portrait of the artist as a very unwell young man. He was, indeed, extremely ill for part of his time in Rome.

If you had to do one piece of deep cultural sightseeing and one only, the Capitoline Museum(s) is head and shoulders above the rest. Not only does it have both ancient and Renaissance works, it has archaeology, architecture and… VIEWS. What one piece sums up the very best of the Roman Empire? Well, a good case could be made for the partially gilded, supersized equestrian statue of Marcus Aurelius Antoninus Augustus, emperor from AD 161 to 180. He was one of the 'GOOD' emperors, following Antoninus and Hadrian. While renowned as a Stoic philosopher, he was a powerful soldier, and the statue

Judith Beheading Holofernes, Caravaggio, 1599, Palazzo Barberini.

was erected in his honour following a number of successful campaigns against the warlike and generally bolshy Germanic tribes. We get to see it twice, once in faithful reproduction raising its hoof on Michelangelo's robust plinth in the Piazza del Campidoglio, and then again in the sheltered conditions of the glazed garden of the Palazzo dei Conservatori. Here, the supersized rider and steed are plinthless. (It is hard to decide whether taking them down to eye level, thus making them far easier to see, makes up for the bathetic and utterly incorrect sloping slab on which they prance.) This is a remarkable work. More than lifelike, it is heroic, THE STALLION OF ALL STALLIONS and the strong, barrel-chested Emperor, a giant among men (and, on his death, among gods). Marcus Aurelius was the most powerful man in the world, and the weight and solemnity of this portrait, combined with the free-flowing folds of his cloak and tunic, show him to have been both human and immortal. An idea of his formerly completely gilded surface can be gleaned from the neighbouring, shining statue of Hercules clasping his knotty club.

Another way in which the statue of Marcus Aurelius reflects the inheritance of the Caesars is the rather patchy way it was moved from the Forum to San Giovanni in Laterano, where its fictitious identity as Constantine, the first emperor to adopt Christianity as the state religion, led to its survival when other equestrian bronzes felt to be HEATHEN were melted down for their metal. It subsequently made the move to the Capitoline, seat of Roman government, in 1538, and was installed by Michelangelo in his dignified Renaissance composition.

But the Capitoline Museums are no one-trick pony. They have the finest collection of paintings and classical sculpture of all, with a smattering of Bernini, including the imposing seated marble portrait of Urban VIII, all swirling clerical vestments and substantial worldly power. The museum complex is divided into three. One initially enters the Palazzo dei Conservatori, where a suite of palatial rooms is grandly frescoed. Subsequent rooms reveal ancient Greek horses and a bull, Bernini's snake-curled Medusa and, alongside Marcus Aurelius, the all-important Lupa. This is the she-wolf that suckled the infant brothers Romulus and Remus, who founded Rome. The wolf is fifth-century BC, whereas the babes are Renaissance interlopers, but whether she is *the* wolf or not, she remains extremely ancient, profoundly LUPINE and fierce.

Stairs down lead to the Epigraphic corridor, full of deeply engraved Roman tablets. If, like me, you are excited by the lettering of the ancient world (an arcane and special interest, I concede), this is a Holy Grail, but assuming not it is the corridor leading to a long underground Roman arcade, a remnant of the Classical Capitoline Hill complex. The view out of the central arch looks straight down the Via Sacra from one triumphal arch to the next. The last part of the museum, the Palazzo Nuovo, is a gallery *par excellence*. One show-stopping set piece follows another: the Hall of the Emperors, the Hall of the Philosophers and the chandeliers in the Hall of the Galatian. On the lower floor, a giant prone river or ocean god, the Marforio, is slumped beardedly in his fountain among gloomy Egyptian monoliths and a good snarling lion.

The palace complex itself, built on top of the remains of its ancient predecessor, is a powerful, site-specific composition, with its subtly asymmetrical arrangement of rooms housed in three Renaissance blocks. Michelangelo was commissioned to build it by the Farnese Pope Paul III in 1536, fulfilling the papal desire to create a courtyard grand enough to impress the incredibly powerful Holy Roman Emperor Charles V (king, duke and everything else, from Holland and Austria to Mexico and his New World territories). Replacing a fairly fortified medieval

La Fornarina, Raphael, 1518–19, Palazzo Barberini.

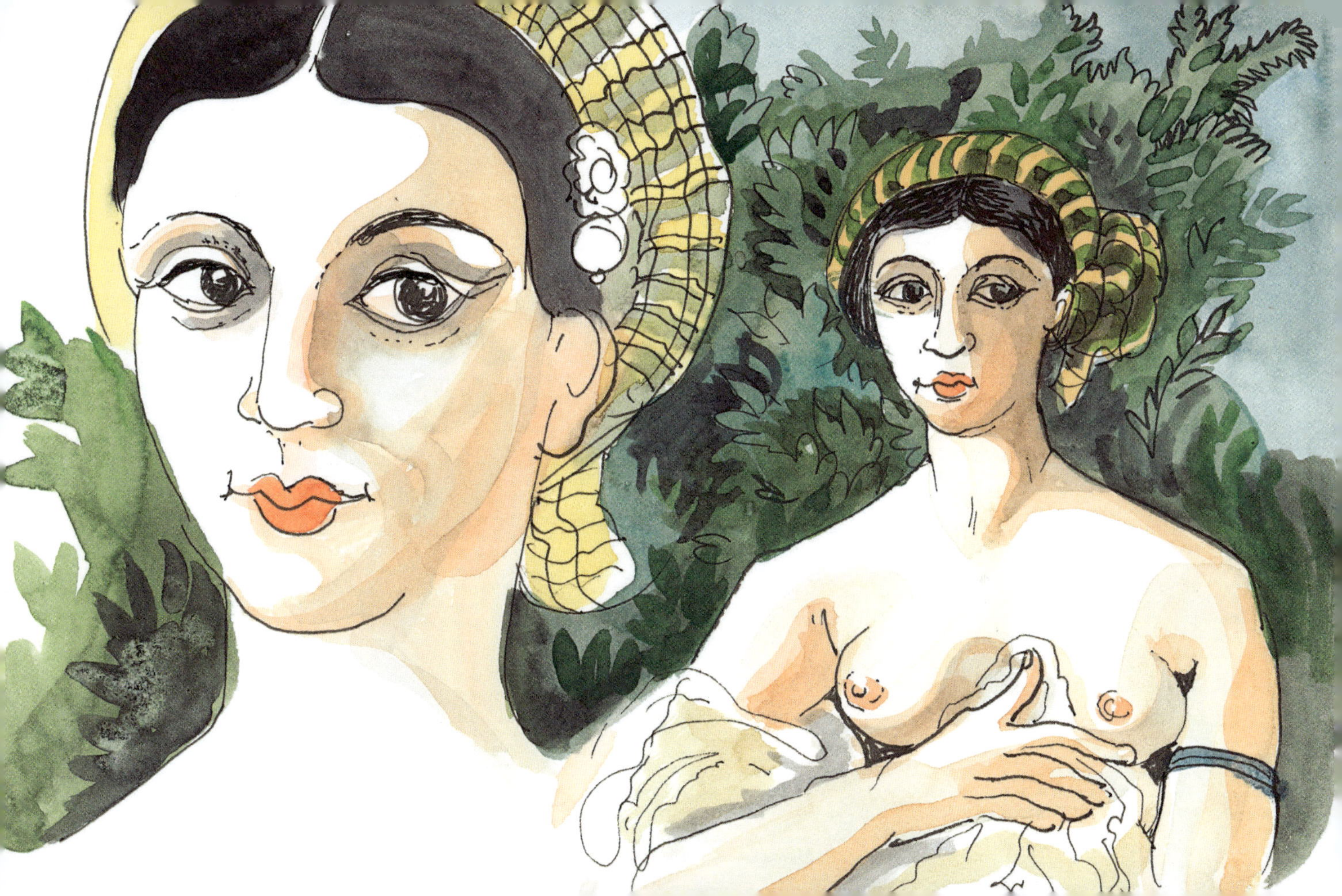

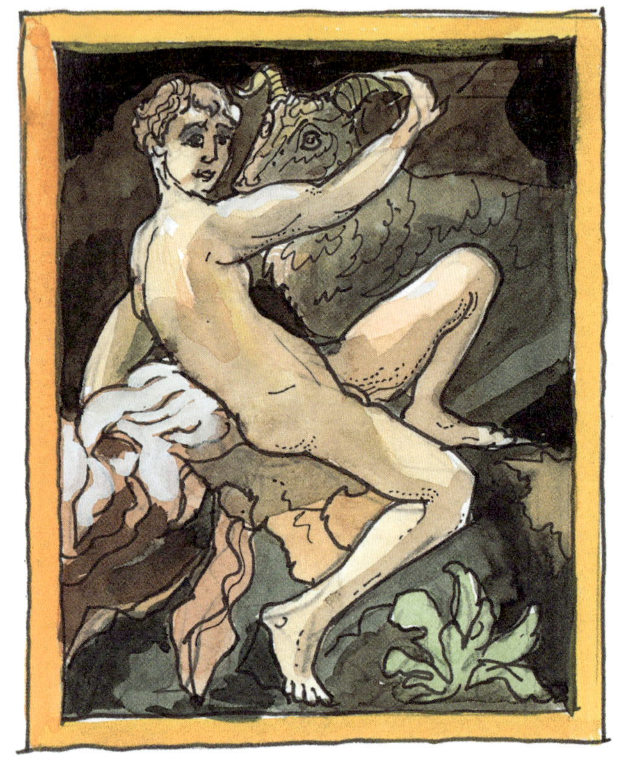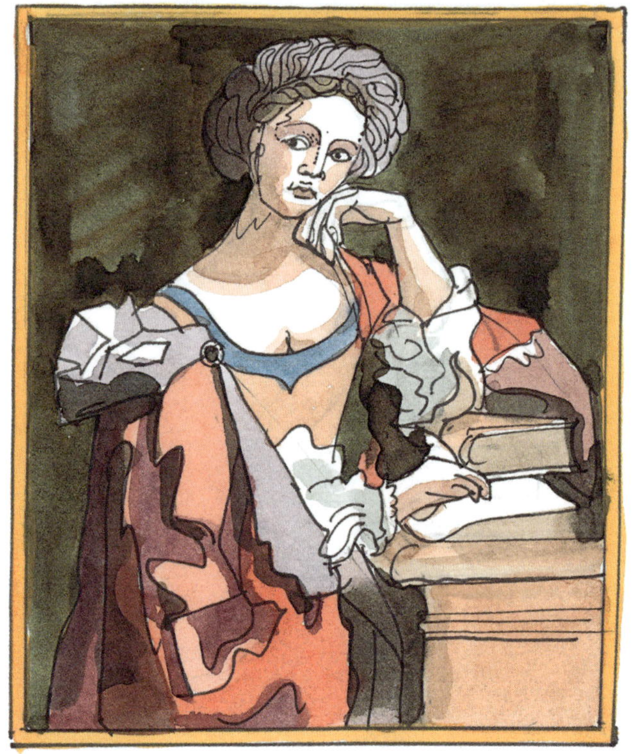

Caravaggio's *John the Baptist*, as a shepherd boy, appears twice… the original hangs in the Capitoline Museums and a copy is in the Galleria Doria Pamphilj, *left*; Guercino's *Persian Sibyl* of 1647, *right*.

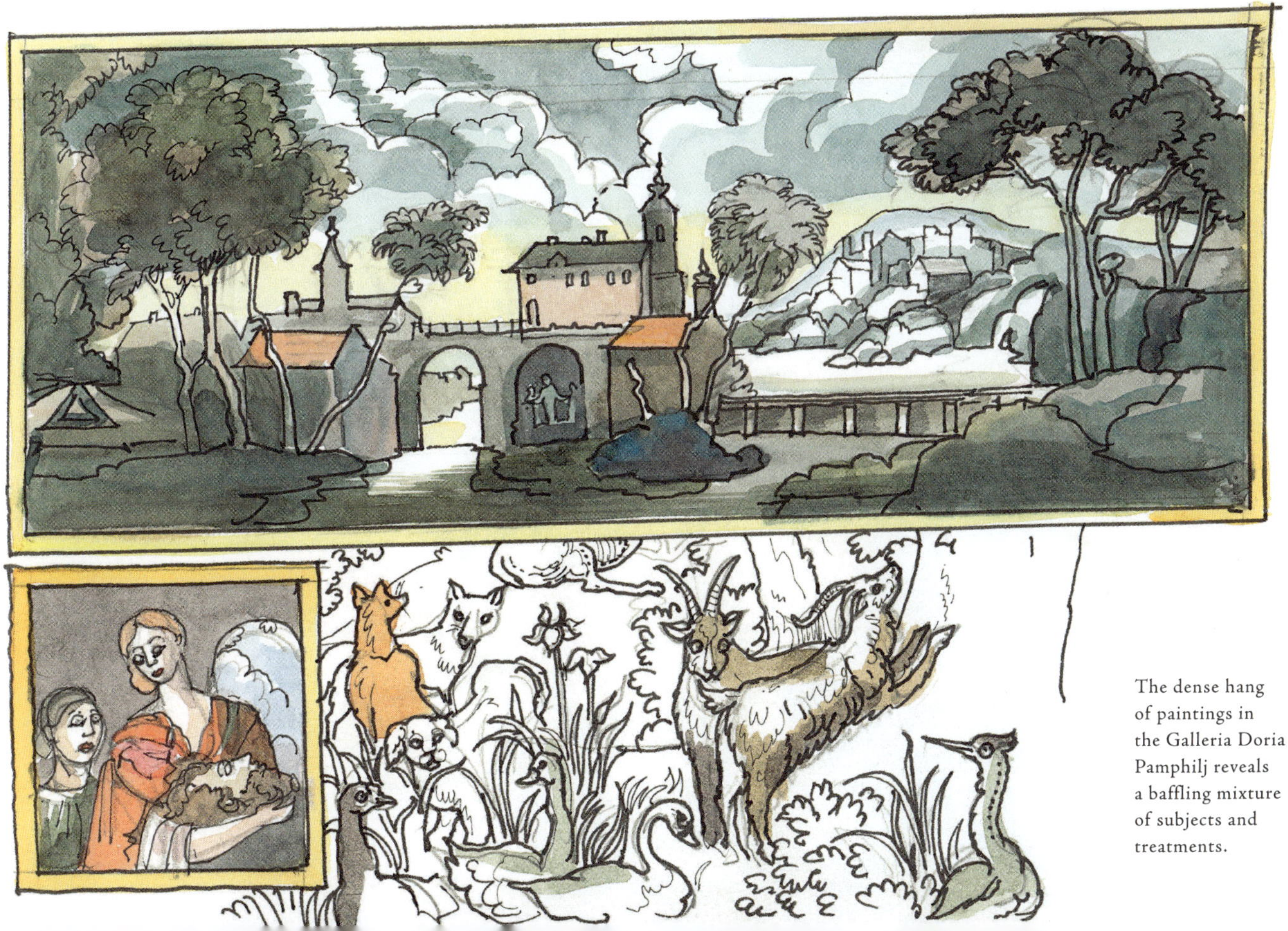

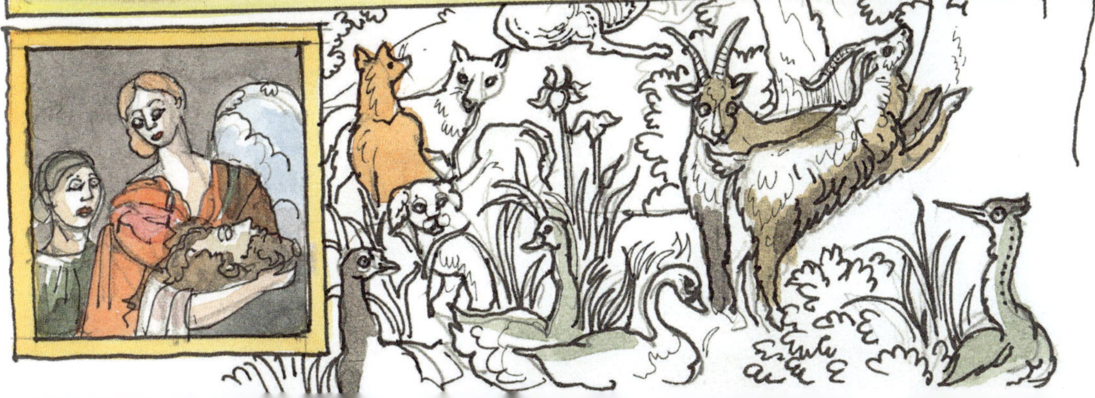

The dense hang
of paintings in
the Galleria Doria
Pamphilj reveals
a baffling mixture
of subjects and
treatments.

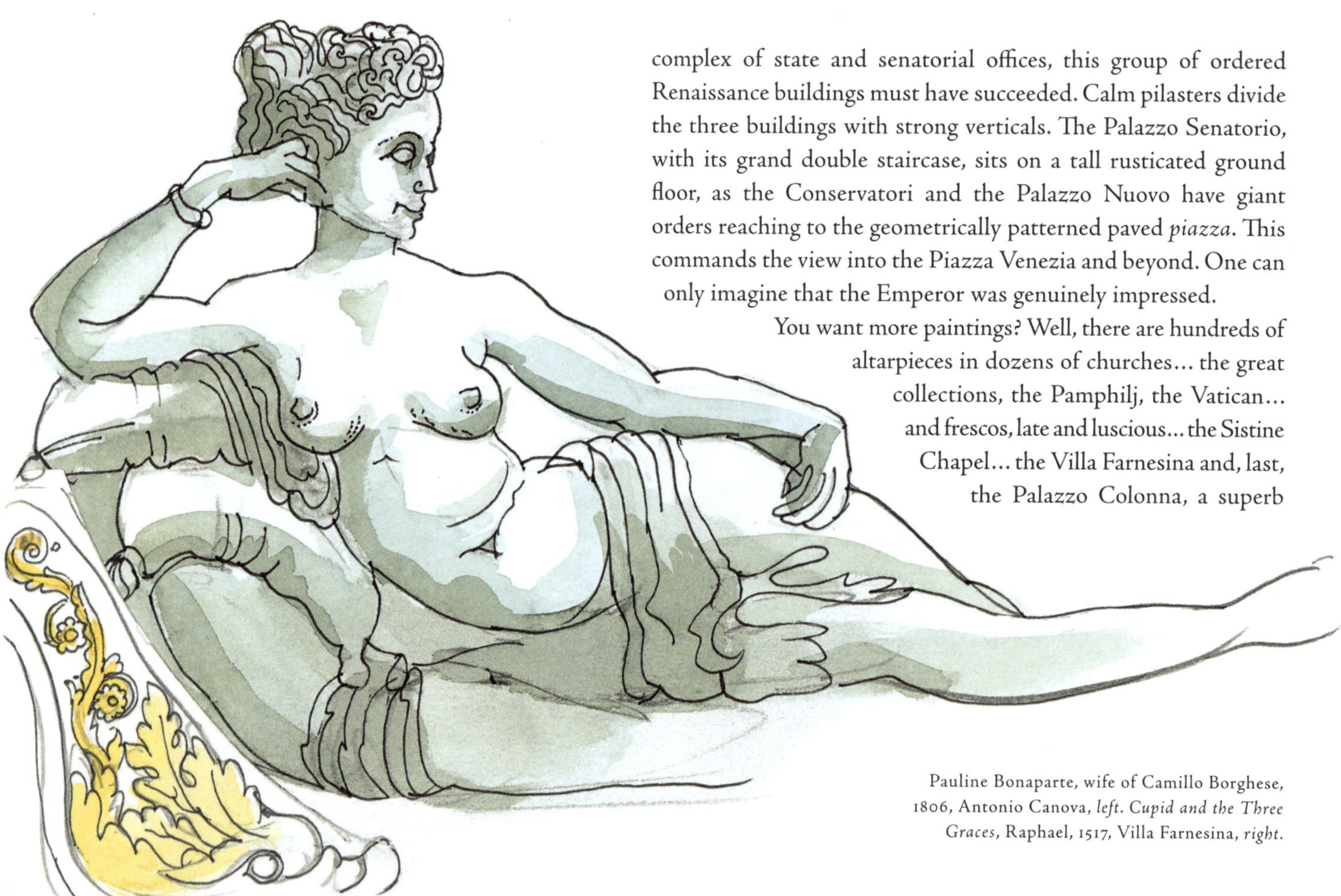

complex of state and senatorial offices, this group of ordered Renaissance buildings must have succeeded. Calm pilasters divide the three buildings with strong verticals. The Palazzo Senatorio, with its grand double staircase, sits on a tall rusticated ground floor, as the Conservatori and the Palazzo Nuovo have giant orders reaching to the geometrically patterned paved *piazza*. This commands the view into the Piazza Venezia and beyond. One can only imagine that the Emperor was genuinely impressed.

You want more paintings? Well, there are hundreds of altarpieces in dozens of churches… the great collections, the Pamphilj, the Vatican… and frescos, late and luscious…the Sistine Chapel… the Villa Farnesina and, last, the Palazzo Colonna, a superb

Pauline Bonaparte, wife of Camillo Borghese, 1806, Antonio Canova, *left. Cupid and the Three Graces*, Raphael, 1517, Villa Farnesina, *right.*

final flourish to a stay in Rome. The kindly guard smiles as one visitor after another ACTUALLY GASPS as they enter the grand gallery of this most central of princely palaces. Firmly closed for most of the week, the doors are thrown open to the general public on Saturday mornings, and the interiors and huge gardens are an astonishment. The great gallery must be the best room in Rome. Four massive decoupage-obscured gold mirrors break up a thickly hung collection of A-list paintings: Bronzino, Carracci and Tintoretto rub distinguished shoulders behind Classical busts and figures on absurdly grand swirling-gold consoles. Marvelling guests slide over mirror-smooth marble floors and on into a series of the grandest rooms. One of the best, the throne room, is hung with very heavily stitched and decorative embroideries, with peacocks, hoopoes and partridges nestled among the formalized foliage and flowers. Carracci's 'bean-eater' is a remarkable portrait of a very hungry man attending to a rather solid kind of lunch.

Nearby, in the Palazzo Spada, the collection of the eponymous cardinal is hung in three rooms of palatial splendour and ranges from the astoundingly dramatic death of Dido by Guercino to a rather strange painting of a badger and two guinea pigs. Roman art starts with a wolf – and ends with a guinea pig.

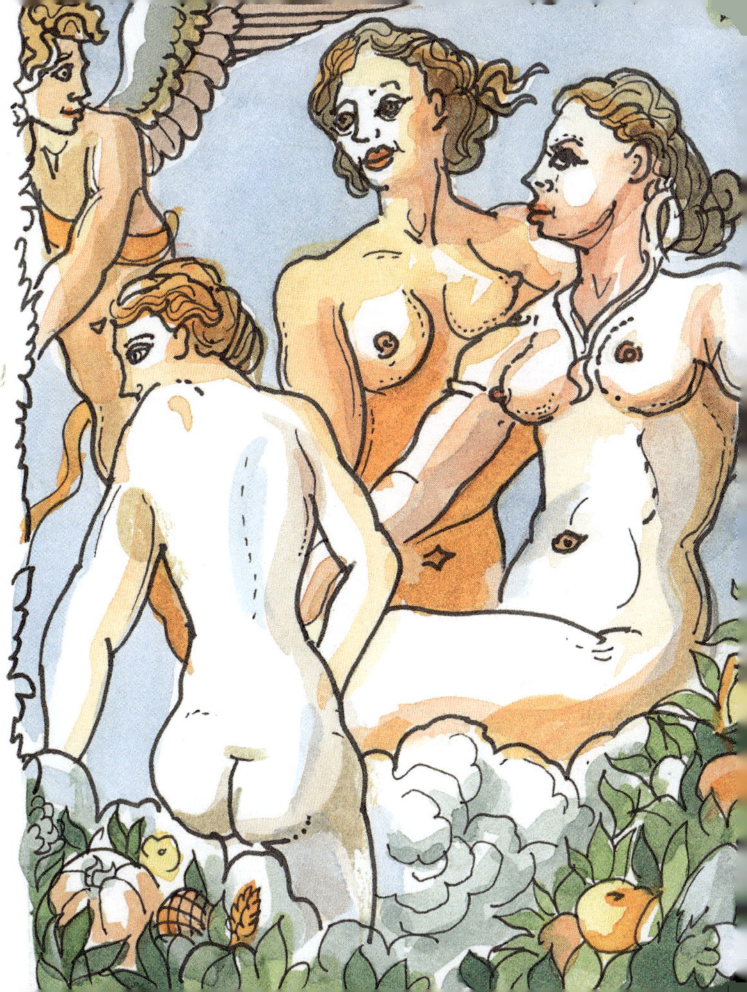

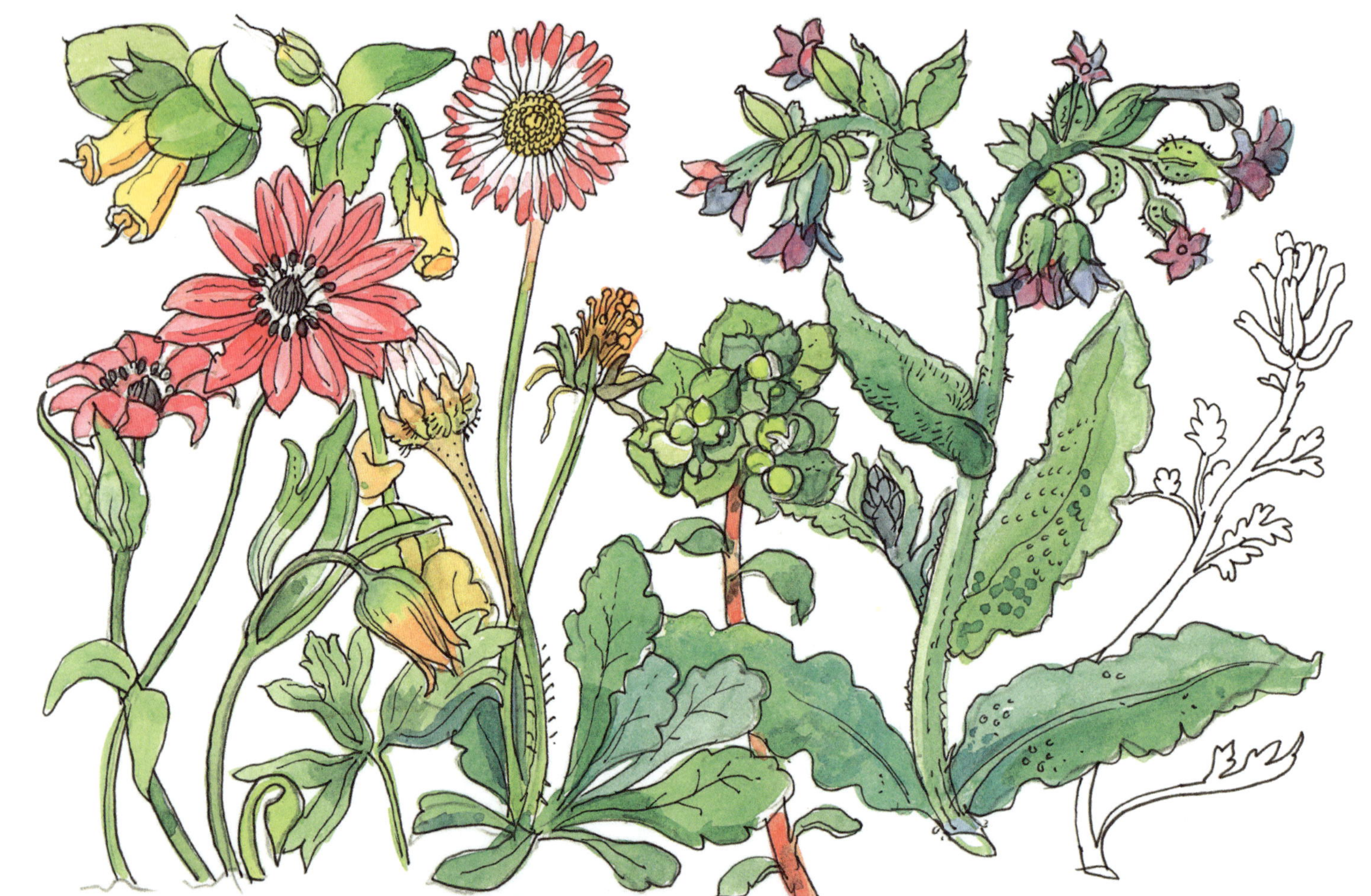

Nature and gardens

Villa Borghese, Rome's Central Park, is on the edge of the old city. Its umbrella pines and ilexes are a background to, and not a feature of, urban views. Crossing the central ring road beyond Piazza del Popolo or looking over the walls of the Villa Medici, you enter a new world of grass and deep-green shadows. It is scattered with buildings and a large lake, a zoo, temples and, somewhat surprisingly, a replica of Shakespeare's Globe Theatre, erected in 2003 to celebrate the hundredth birthday of the gardens being open to the public. The tree cover characterizes the space, most of all the umbrella or stone pine (*Pinus pinea*), with long, often mildly leaning trunks and reticulated pinky-orange bark. The pines grow tall and branchless until they fan out, supporting a shallow domed mushroom of long-needled green canopy. The gardens are also full of evergreen holm oak (*Quercus ilex*), frequently subject to rigorous

pruning, and are criss-crossed by wide avenues and paths, some of which lead to the villa itself. This white Renaissance edifice was built in 1607 by Scipione Borghese, after he had been made a cardinal by his uncle, Pope Paul V. This is a suburban villa, not a city palace, with a small number of showy rooms that lead from one to another.

Rome itself isn't rich in nature, despite the dramatic recent news that families of wild boar, once shy and retiring creatures in the forests of the Maremma, have become emboldened enough to enter the city. Perhaps encouraged by a general lack of hunters and a rise of liberal feelings towards our fellow creatures, they can occasionally be spotted weaving through the rush-hour traffic of outer Rome or scuffling for food among restaurant bins, with stripy babies following their shaggy brown parents. More surprisingly, a small pack of wolves have taken digs near the Leonardo da Vinci airport, close to the city centre. All this is part of a gradual recolonization of less intensively managed parts of Europe, in which these large animals,

March wildflowers at Ostia Antica, *left*; ceiling in Santa Costanza, fourth century, and bird-filled wall in Villa Medici, 1570, Jacopo Zucchi, *overleaf*.

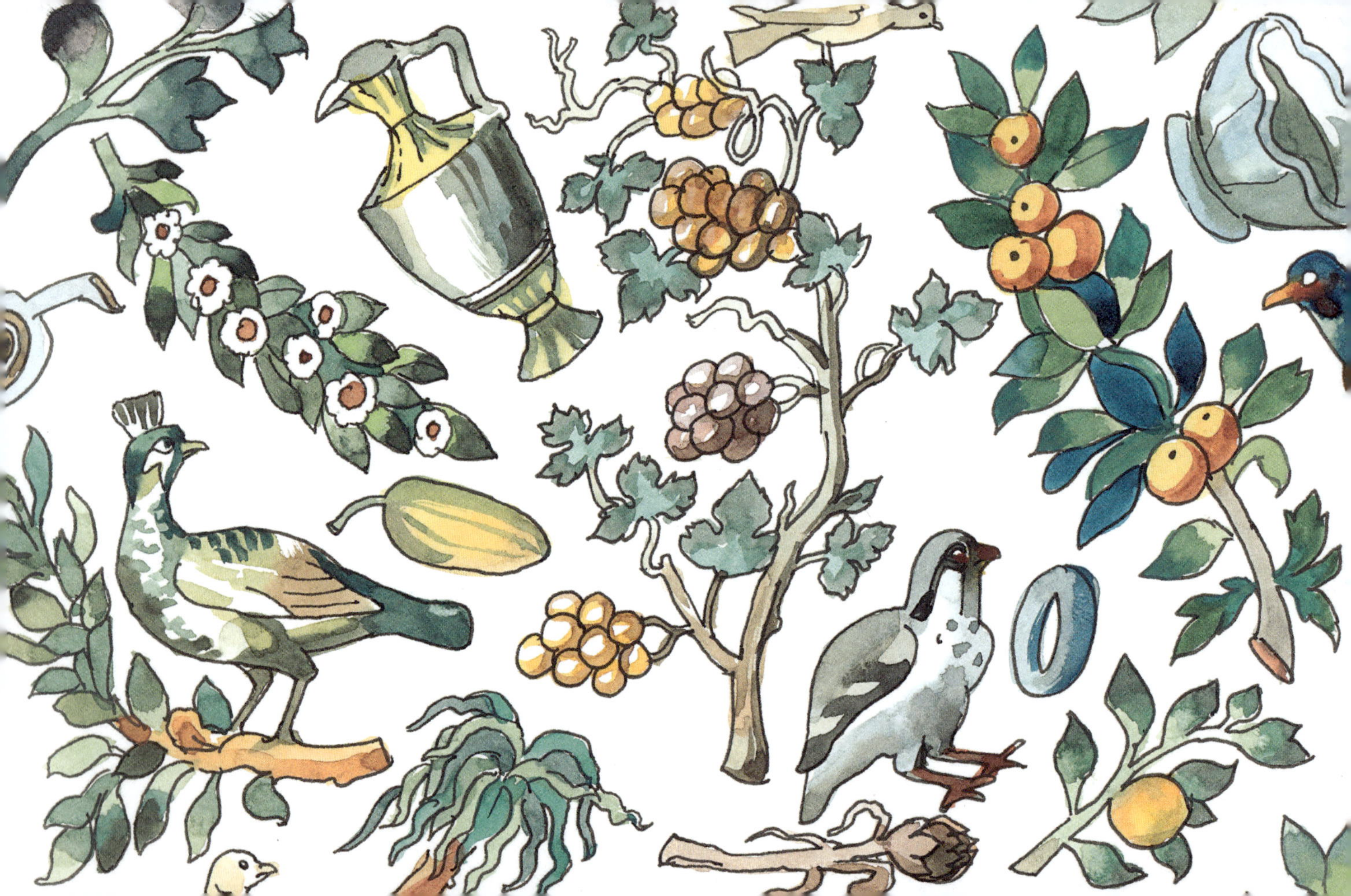

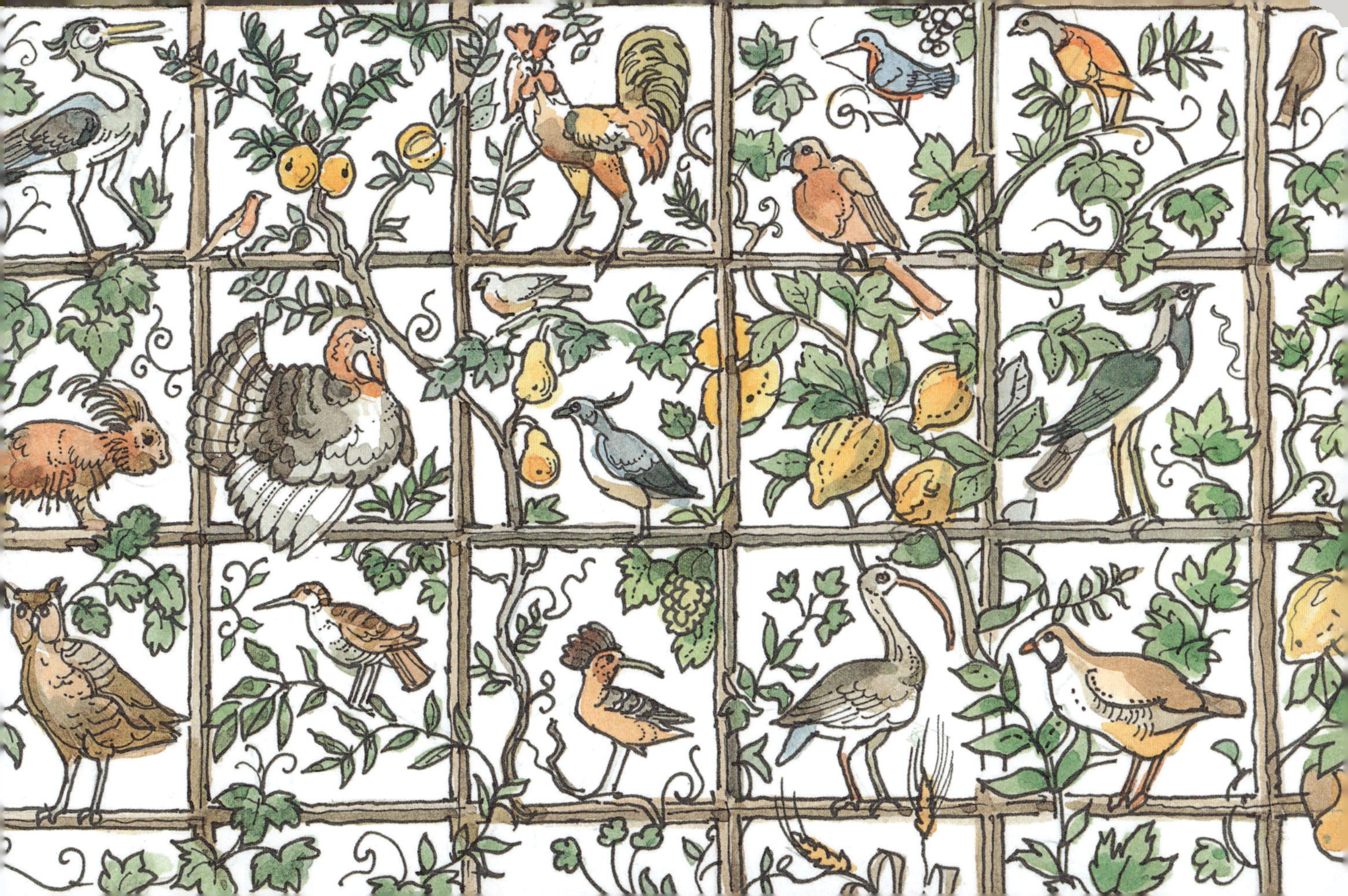

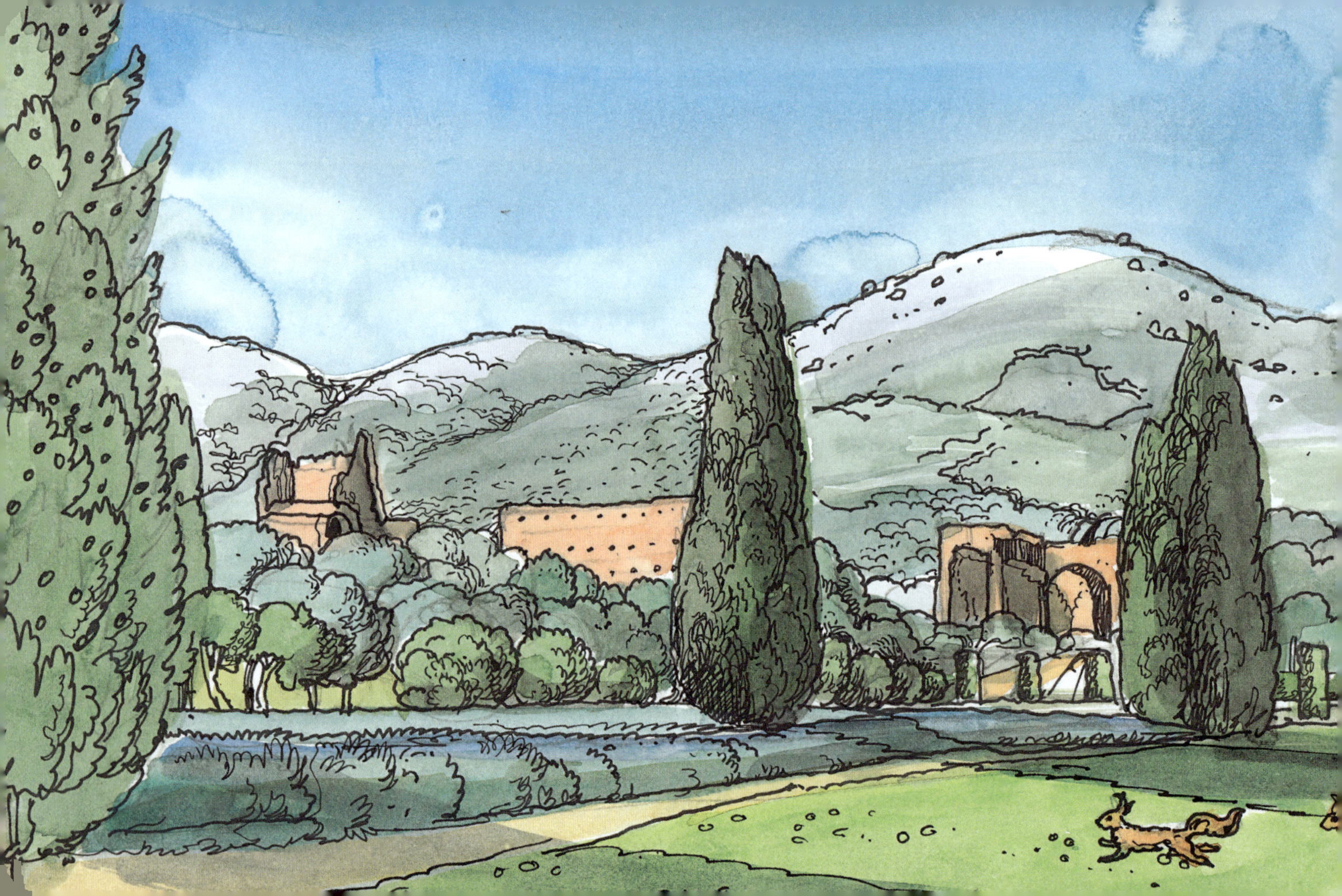

as well as jackals and bears, are gradually reclaiming their rightful place in the ecosystem.

Hooded crows hop among the acanthus (real or marble) throughout the city, and smart black redstarts (easily recognizable as robin-sized birds in charcoal grey with bright and showy chestnut underparts) nest among ruins and in useful holes in buildings medieval or Baroque. Grey wagtails, moorhens, yellow-legged gulls and the odd desultory mallard cruise the Tiber, which is also home to COYPU. These large Jack Russell-sized South American rodents were originally escapees from fur farms but are now naturalized in Europe's rivers. Prodigious eaters of arable crops and industrious burrowers into river and canal banks, they were branded noxious pests and were eradicated from Britain by the 1980s. In Rome, they seem more desirable and, when spotted, are alarmingly large water rats LOLLING on a rock.

By far the most striking component in the city's fauna is a new introduction, or rather two. Parakeets have become both numerous and potentially a cause for concern. There have been small populations of these birds for more than fifty years throughout Europe, ostensibly escapees

Red squirrels, Hadrian's Villa, *left*; parakeets and hooded crows, *overleaf.*

from aviaries or even, potentially, intentionally released. It was initially thought that they could not survive the chilly European winter, but either that was wrong or they have grown thicker feathers. Flocks of them shriek happily as they whirl and dive amongst the pines of the Giardini Borghese. As recently as 2000, they were a relative rarity, but now the city has more than five thousand of these elegant and tropical Asian birds, completely transforming the evening soundtrack of the city.

They are not alone. A completely different parakeet, the MONK, comes from Argentina and, although less numerous, is easily seen, as are its nests. It lives colonially (next to its companions) in huge messy stick nests metres across, normally in cedar of Lebanon trees. There are particularly good colonies in the approach to the mournful visitor centre in Ostia Antica. The colossal nests have made monks unpopular in Britain and the US, as they have caused electricity pylons to collapse under their weight. The English population is no more, and in certain states of America they are banned even as domestic pets. There is much talk of their displacing native species (woodpeckers and nuthatches), but there is no evidence that this has actually been the case. Perhaps they are actually a benign and colourful addition to the urban landscape.

185

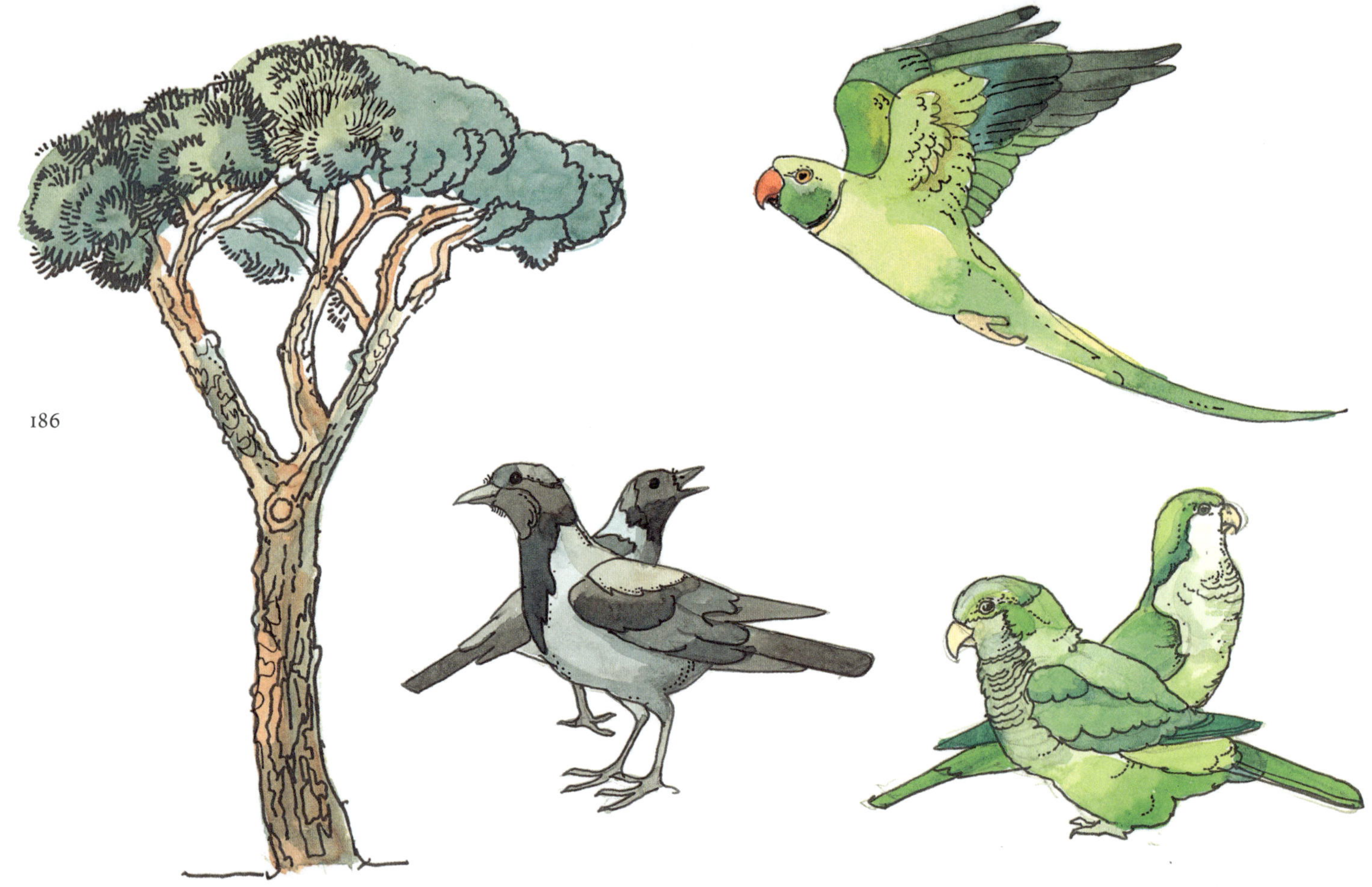

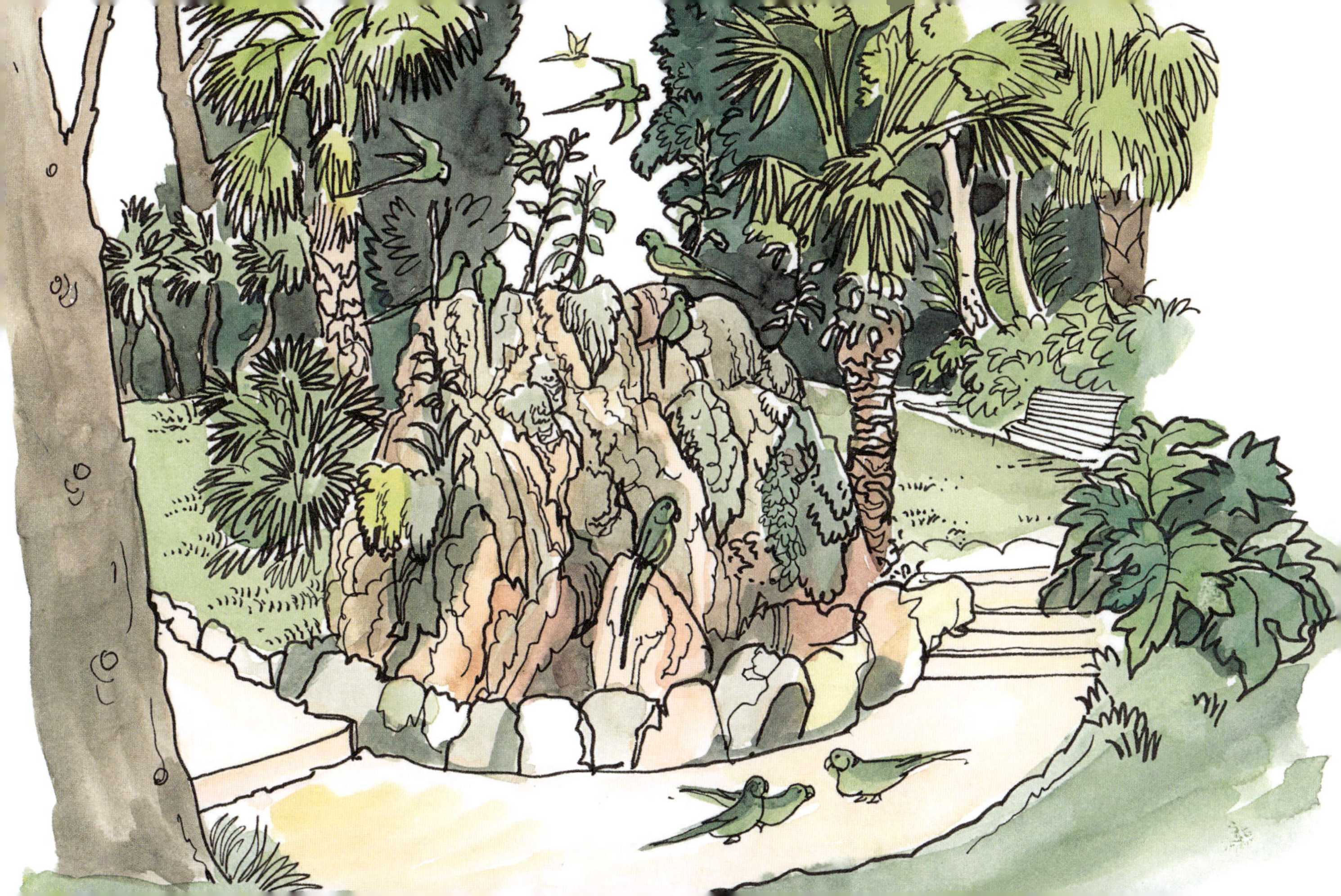

Eating and drinking

Ancient Roman cooks wrestled with lampreys and fretted that their dormice would not be fat enough for the senators' dinner, tempting the sulky rodents with hazelnuts and almonds. There may have been supply-chain problems with asses' milk for the dairies in Trajan's Forum, and perhaps the garum for sale next door may have been losing its efficacy, not smelling sufficiently of rotting anchovies… But the days of stuffed udders and teats and peacocks tucked inside boned swans are well and truly over. Instead, a series of less esoteric specialities are characteristic of Roman kitchens.

Italy is long and thin, stretching from the Alps in the North to the near-African climate of Sicily. When it is snowy in the Val d'Aosta, the waft of lemon blossom is drifting through the orchards of Sicily, so fresh, summery treats are always only a lorry ride away. In the capital city, therefore, it isn't at all surprising that there's a huge variety of veg coming to town every day, varying of course with the season. The beginning of the year sees a lot of rather firm, and no doubt cleansing, bitter greens appearing in stalls and shops. Generally called cicoria, they are a slightly tough kind of salad, but are healthy-feeling and delicious when cooked. Related, but more tasty, is puntarella, a pale-green, self-blanching kind of chicory that fills the markets in early spring. Its classic preparation is complicated, with individual shoots being pulled through a wire sieve and the resulting curling pieces kept in a bowl of iced water, being adorned with a characteristic anchovy-rich dressing. As early as February, zucchini flowers with their baby fruits attached are available in every stall, shop and even supermarket, ready to be stuffed with ricotta and sweetest new peas, then deep fried. Throughout Italy, it is notice-able how even small local supermarkets have a full selection of even quite unfamiliar vegetables, artichoke hearts carefully prepared or forced white asparagus, none with the

Vegetable stall in the Campo de'Fiori, *right*; a cornucopia of fresh vegetables from the market, *overleaf*.

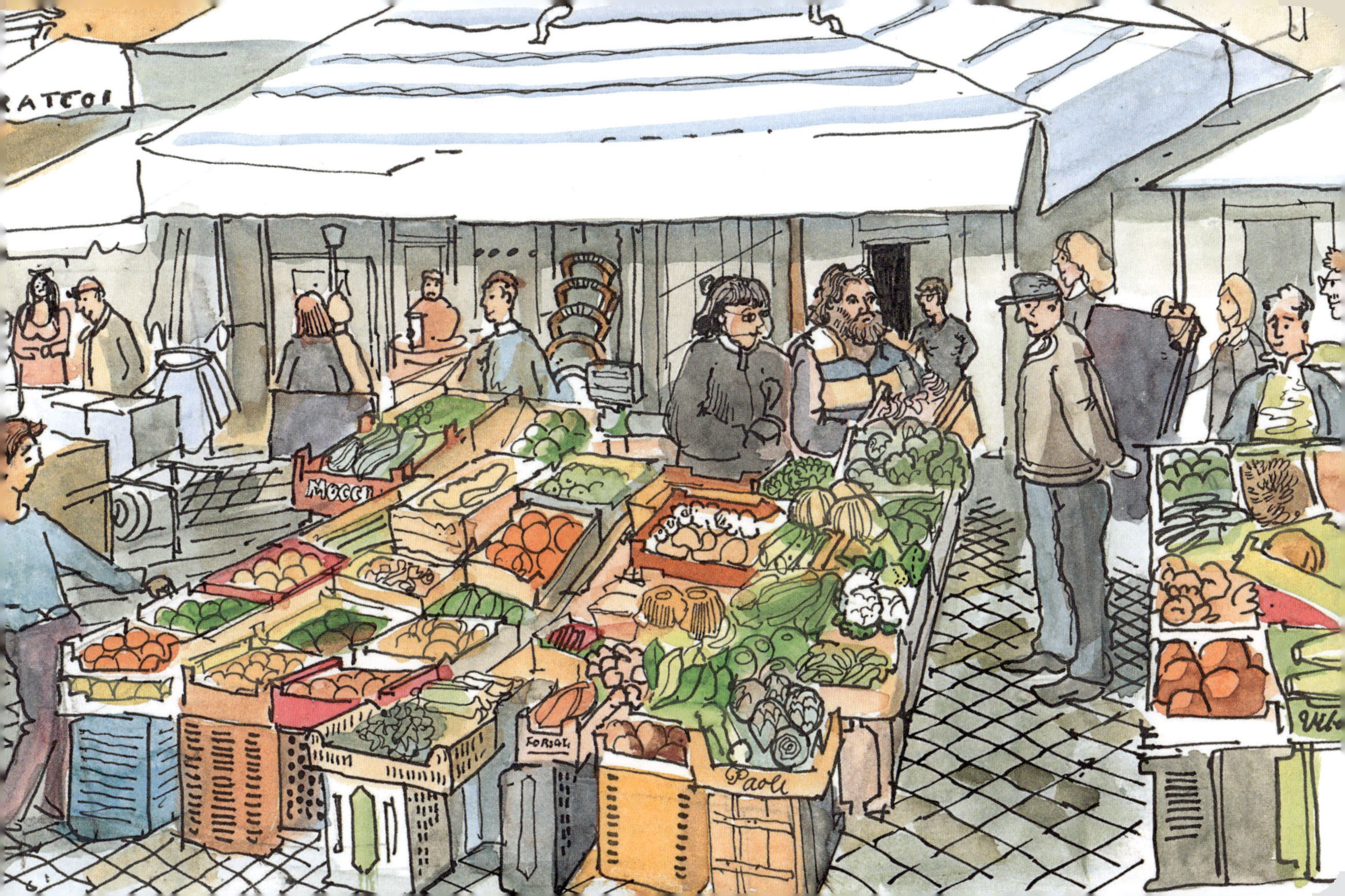
RATEOI
MOCCI
FORSAL
Paoli

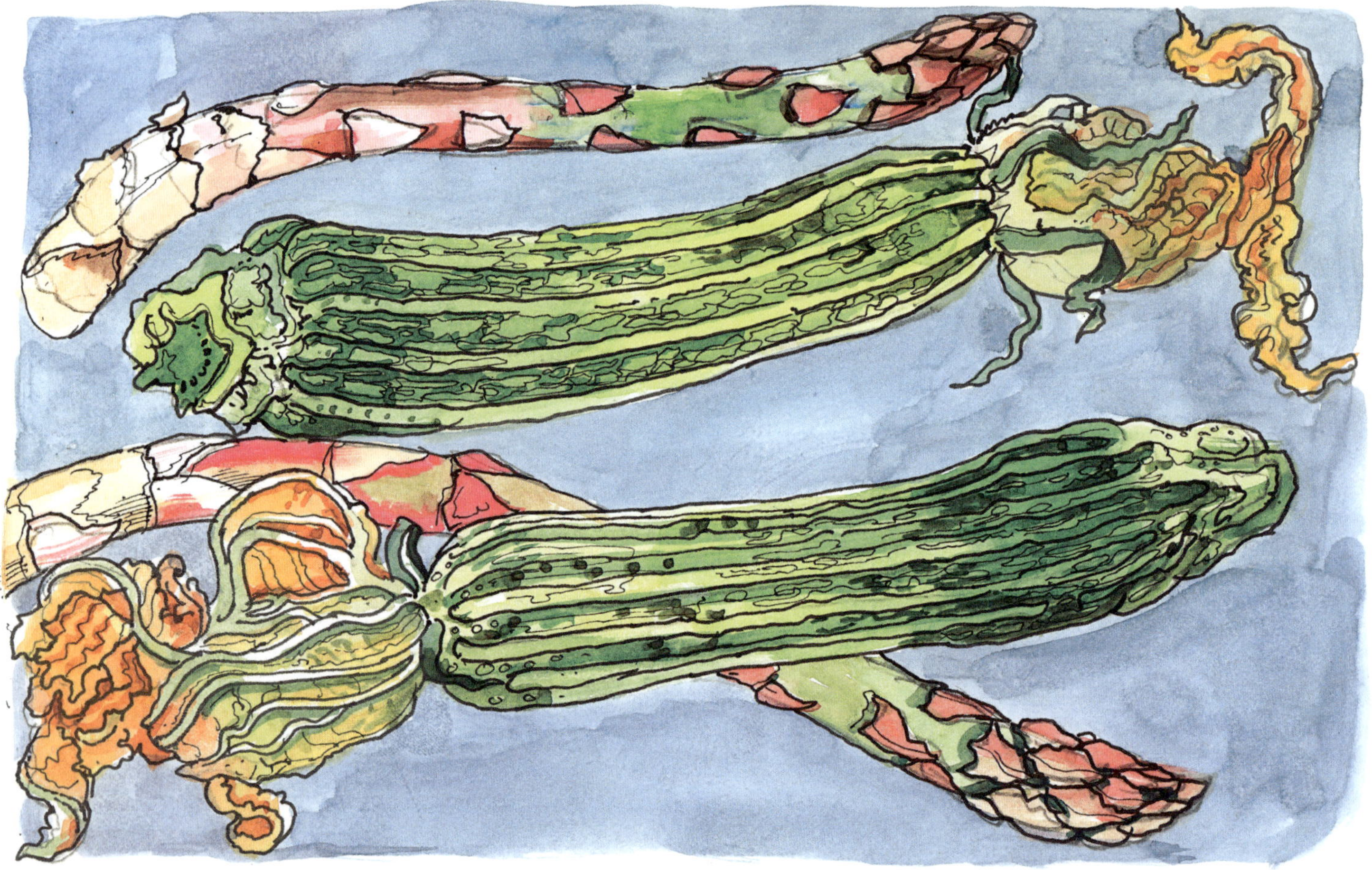

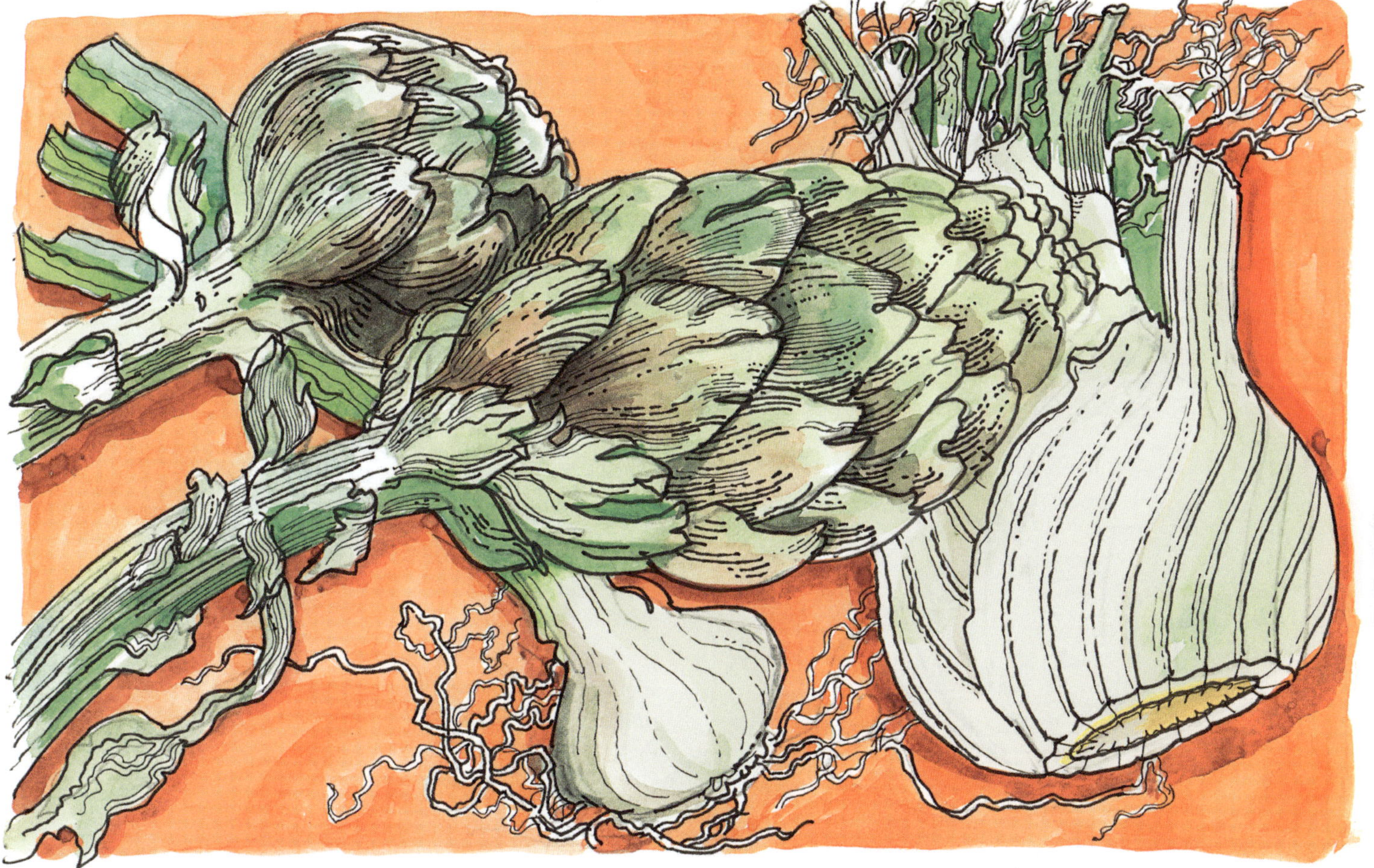

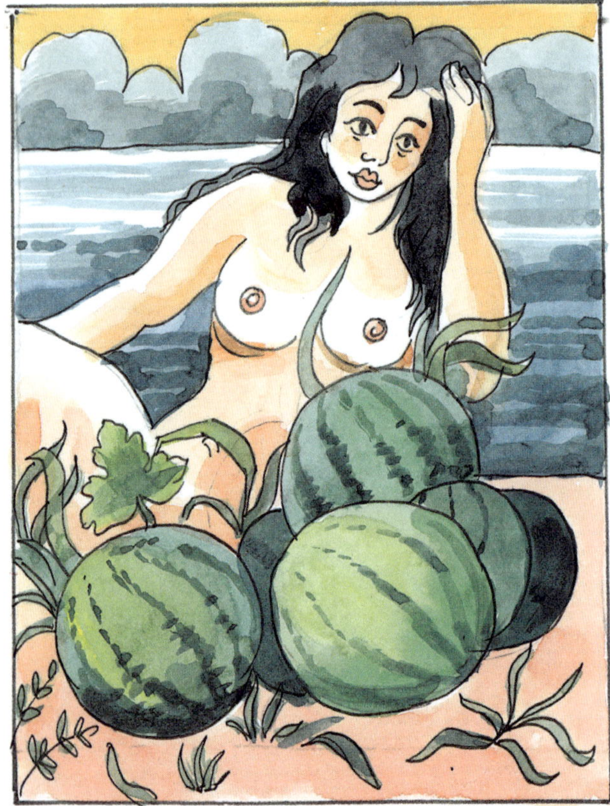

Florentine trade sign to attract melon lovers in the EUR folk museum.

shiny, anodyne, regimented boredom of produce favoured by their northern European equivalents. In Italy, TASTE and QUALITY are PARAMOUNT, rather than flawlessness of skin or consistency of zucchini length.

The vegetable that is most definitively Roman is the artichoke, in season from Christmas to Easter. It comes in many shapes and sizes, some small enough to be eaten whole and some massive globes to be pulled apart, but the most frequently sold are middle-sized and tinged deep violet, varieties like Violetta di Chioggia, di Romagna or di Provenza or, better still, di Mammole. Some are stuffed (*alla romana*) and others deep fried (*alla giudia*).

For *alla romana*, you must have young, plump globe artichokes. Peel the stems and leave them 6cm long. Chop off the last 2cm of the flowering end and break off a couple of layers of scales. In a bowl, mix garlic, parsley, mint, black pepper, lemon and olive oil to make a rough paste and work it into the gaps between the artichoke's scales. Lay the prepared chokes stalk up in a lidded pan, pour in a shallow pool of water, then cover and cook for twenty-five minutes. This is the quintessential Roman spring starter, in restaurants or at home.

Alla giudia is slightly harder to do, but still perfectly possible. Clean the artichokes, removing the leathery outer scales, peeling the stalk and taking out the hairy choke in the middle with a teaspoon (one of my favourite kitchen tasks). Keep the prepared chokes in acidulated water (that is, with lemon juice in it) to stop the chokes discolouring in an unappealing fashion. Heat the sunflower oil in a middle-sized pan and, when it is around 160–190 degrees Celcius, pop the artichokes in for ten minutes or until golden. Take them out, drain them on some newspaper and, when bearable, open them up like a flower before returning for a final five mins to crisp up. With this ancient JEWISH ROMAN dish, you eat the whole artichoke.

Pasta and pizza dominate the menus of most *trattorie*. The classic pasta dishes are *carbonara*, *alla gricia* and *cacio e pepe*. A real Roman *carbonara* is a thing of beauty, yellow with egg yolk and scattered with fried shreds of either bacon skin or *guanciale*. This is cured, unsmoked pork cheek, and it is the key component in these dishes. Importantly, cream does NOT get a look in. *Alla gricia* is made with no egg, just guanciale, pecorino and black pepper. *Cacio e pepe* is the most Roman of all and relies on lavish quantities of pecorino cheese, made from the milk of the long-legged sheep that roam the stubbles in the winter and march off into the hills for the hot summer. These are all sauces suited to spaghetti, *bucatini* (hollow, but thin,

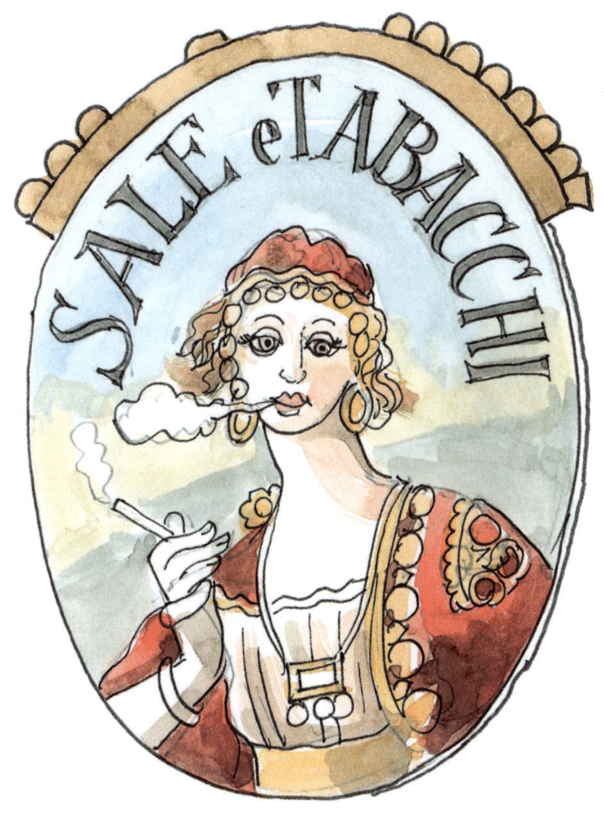

Keeping smoking glamorous in the folk museum.

193

spaghetti) and *tonnarelli* (square-section, thick spaghetti), but never short pasta.

Pasta *is* the great Roman staple. Despite the fabled NOODLE-LADEN return of Marco Polo in 1295, pasta is known from historical accounts to have been made in Etruscan kitchens as early as the fourth century BC, and recipes exist from the first century AD for a proto-lasagne in Rome, although the sheets of raw pasta were baked dry and not boiled first (rather like modern, pre-cooked lasagne sheets). By the thirteenth century, it had already become a staple and, by the following century, dry pasta became an easily portable commodity to be exported or cooked on sea voyages. During the eighteenth century, mechanized production began to develop in Naples, and the modern commercial business was quickly developed. *Pastasciutta* (dry pasta) became an industrial product made for consumption worldwide. Sepia photographs of extensive racks of spaghetti drying in the Mediterranean sun make one's own rather forlorn experiments seem paltry, but the ability of flour to absorb delicious egg conjures up some wonderful meals.

Accounts of Roman meat cookery and supply seem barely to mention beef, focusing instead on lamb and, most of all, pork and its many by-products, but all species are represented in the great love of offal-eating. *Trippa* (tripe) *alla Romana* appears on most menus and several more esoteric internal organs make a variously welcome appearance: *animele* (sweetbreads), *cervelli* (brains), *coda alla vaccinara* (oxtail stew) and, lastly, *rigatoni con la pajata* (calves' intestines). This final Roman treat is fairly strong stuff and, unless you are one of those who yearn for hodge or chitterlings, is perhaps one to pass over...

The reason for this emphasis on offal or, as it is slightly euphemistically referred to in the United States, 'variety meats', is rooted in the historical function of the Testaccio area across the Tiber. This now-fashionable and happening part of town was once the site of the largest abattoir in Europe, next to the colossal 2,000-year-old rubbish dump made entirely of discarded amphorae, large single-use earthenware vessels used for importing olive oil from around the Mediterranean. The oil was originally used not only for cooking, but also for the oil lamps that illuminated all Roman rooms, which explains the unthinkably huge scale of this tip.

In the later Empire, the dole, both of corn and meat, to the Roman population was a vital component in

The most popular bar in Trastevere.

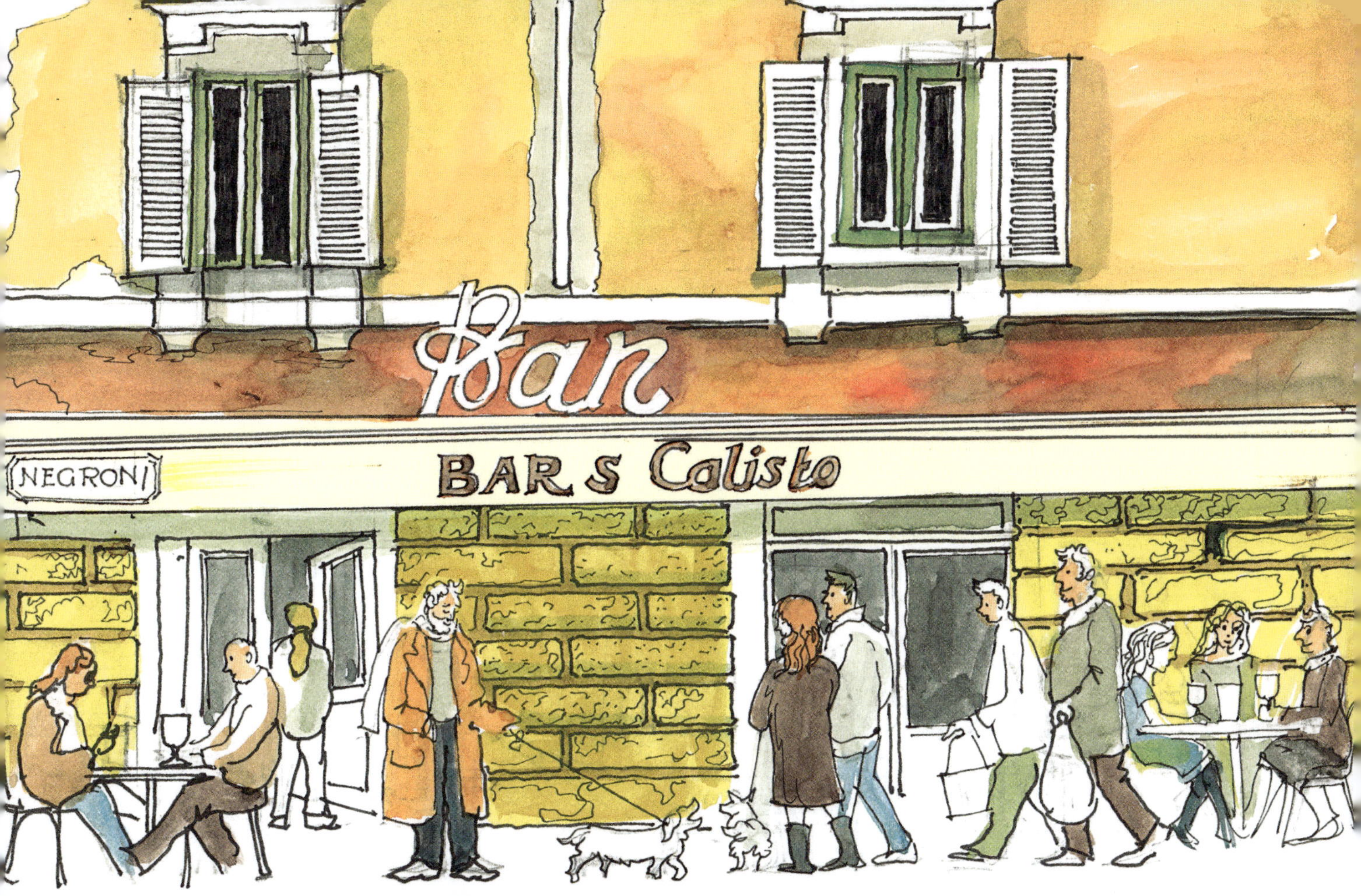
Ban
NEGRONI
BAR s Calisto

maintaining the peaceful running of the city. The quarters of each beast were divided between the strata of society in descending order, from aristocrats, via clerics to citizens and, finally abattoir workers, who received the least desirable share, or 'fifth quarter', of each beast. This allegedly led to a habit that has died hard as the basis of Roman cookery. Although this need not have lingered on, it remains the case that offal is the cheapest cut of any animal and that all animals contain it, so imaginative ways must be found to make it delicious.

There are specific areas of town rich in Chinese or Indian restaurants, but they are the exception. Food in Rome is clearly both Italian and Roman and, although the variation may be limited, the food itself is uniformly delicious. My favourite *trattoria*, one in which I ate at least twice a week for two months, is called Osteria dei Colli Emiliani, on the Via Tiburtina in San Lorenzo. It is the least snazzy *trattoria* imaginable, with uncurtained plate-glass windows looking onto the busy everyday street. The décor is profoundly unexceptional, yet, by that sensible, unselfconscious workaday scheme of tiles and formica and wood, it has become special. The decoration is also fairly subfusc, with a few old photographs and paintings, but the whole place is spotlessly clean and presided over by a neat and polite proprietor, with a small group of middle-aged cooks just visible stage left. Arriving at 7.30pm (with my book), I found the place invariably empty, but, as I progressed from soup (*ravioli in brodo*) to a dish of risotto (or *trippa*) and some green beans or *cicoria*, the whole place filled with a fairly regular clientele; men alone or in twos or threes, the odd young couple and then an office party or a family. It is not a tourist *trattoria* and isn't in a tourist area, but it *is* Roman. I felt utterly welcome there, eventually heading for the same table beneath a rather odd stoneware water jar on a shelf each time. Perhaps settling on 'your' restaurant is one of the sleights of hand by which one can feel at home, not on holiday; a commitment of some kind even if the proprietor of the selected establishment is unmoved by your loyalty. I have little interest in restaurants with experimental dishes of tripe or pig's cheek. The REAL THING DONE WELL is the epitome of eating abroad, and finding a restaurant with the right dowdiness, unsympathetic lighting and huge popularity is my aim.

Although pizza is Neapolitan, that source is only a short trip along the coast, and the Romans do it well. It is the perfect mid drawing-day treat and, in good bars, you can literally buy your slice by the inch, indicating which side of the mushroom you want the knife to fall. This is by far the least wasteful and most pleasing way to do it – and, yes, also allows me to have small slices of two types, lest I seem gloomily austere. I had a neat and nice kitchen in my lovely apartment, too, and, every other night, I made a plate of vegetables – tiny thin beans, pale zucchini, Sicilian potatoes and a salad. It has taken me years to realize how much I love shopping for vegetables abroad and how pleasing it is to unpack those thinnest plastic bags on returning home and put the food on to cook.

As regards liquid refreshment, the utter pleasure of a negroni seems central to drinking in Rome, and the internet bristles with ten-best-bars-for-a-negroni-in-Rome articles. There is a (false, I am sure) feeling that the bitter Campari taste makes for a slightly healthier cocktail… almost good for you? What is certain is that it is a better and more delicious start to the evening than a sweet and confected Aperol spritz. At the other end of the spectrum, equally delicious and genuinely GOOD FOR YOU, is a spremuta, either orange or lemon. There's a bar in Piazza Santa Maria in Trastevere that has hundreds of oranges awaiting their fate, their super-fresh juice drunk while looking at the façade of a church built in AD 350. Maybe *that's* the best drink in Rome.

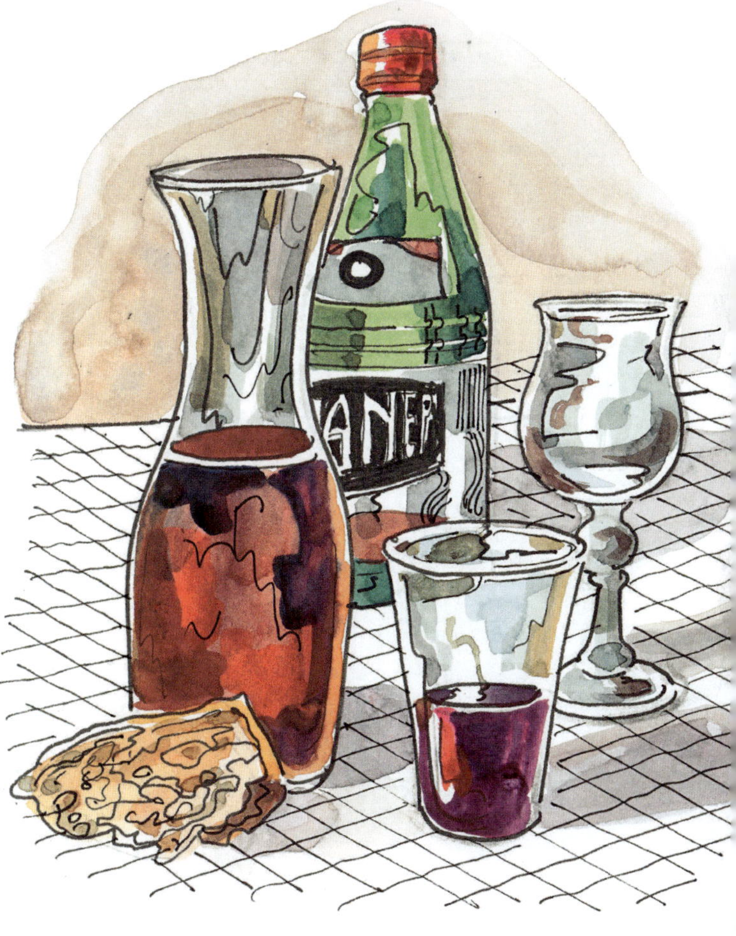

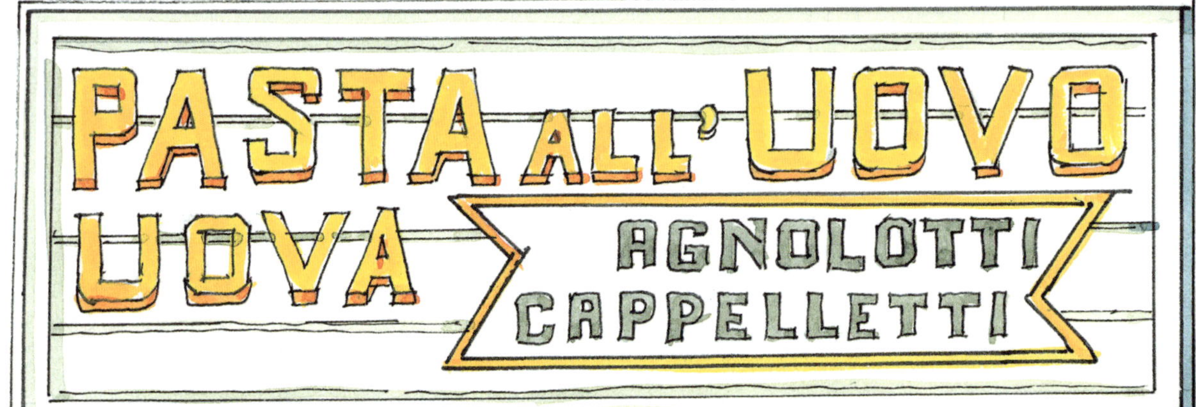

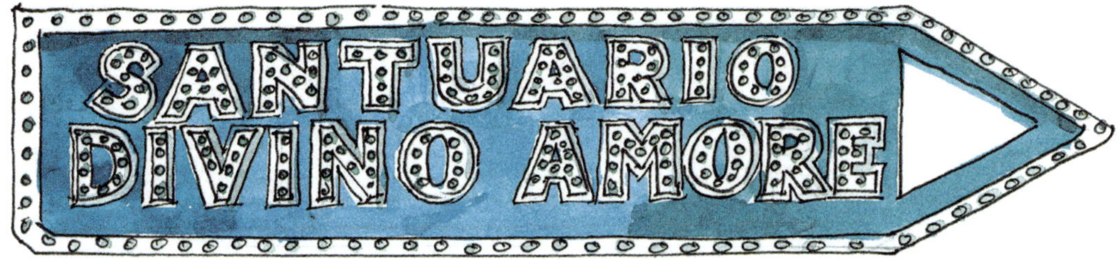

Rome has the most stylish shop signs in Europe, of all styles and periods.

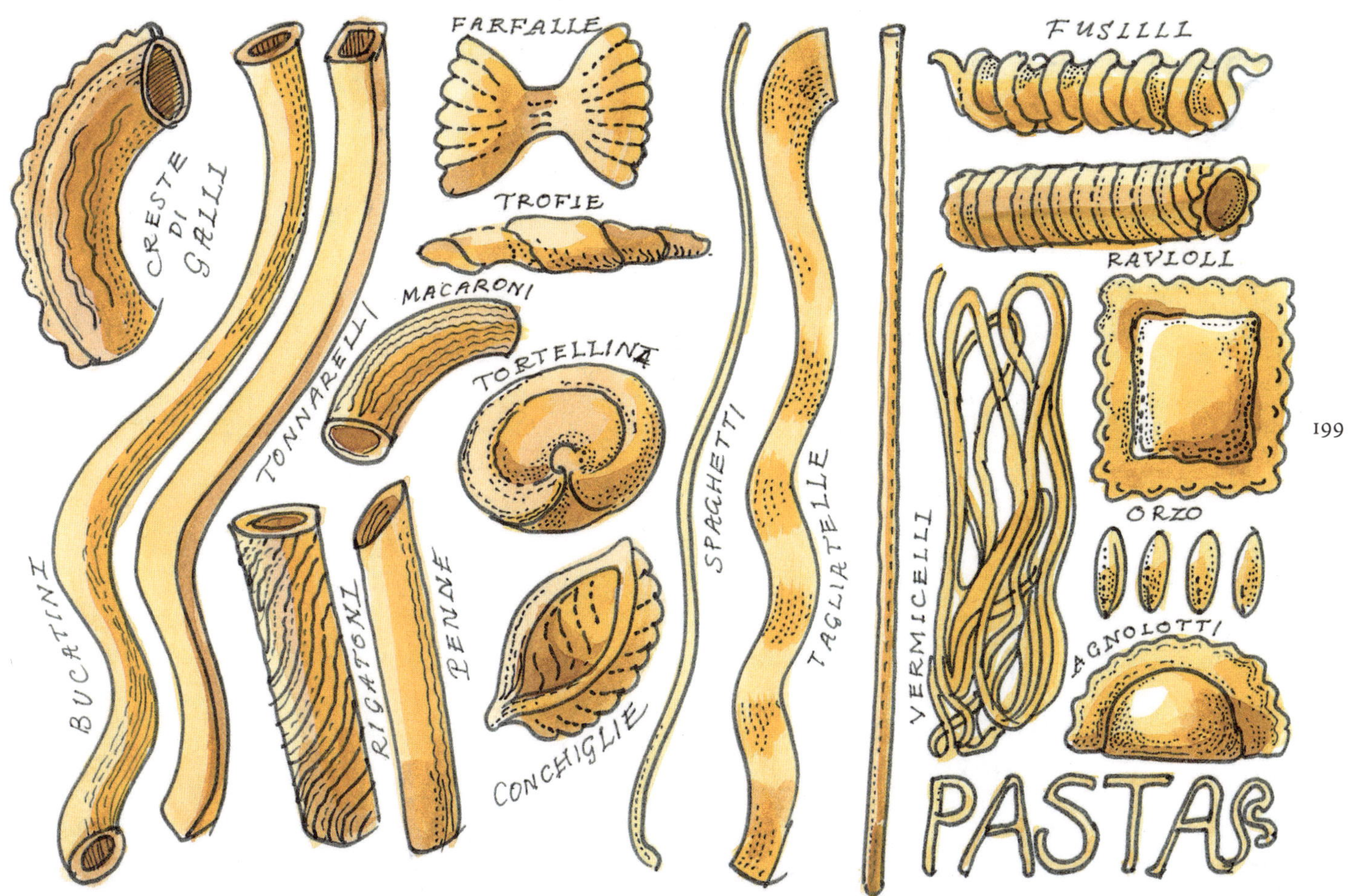

FARFALLE
FUSILLI
CRESTE DI GALLI
TROFIE
RAVIOLI
TONNARELLI
MACARONI
TORTELLINA
BUCATINI
RIGATONI
PENNE
CONCHIGLIE
SPAGHETTI
TAGLIATELLE
VERMICELLI
ORZO
AGNOLOTTI
PASTAS

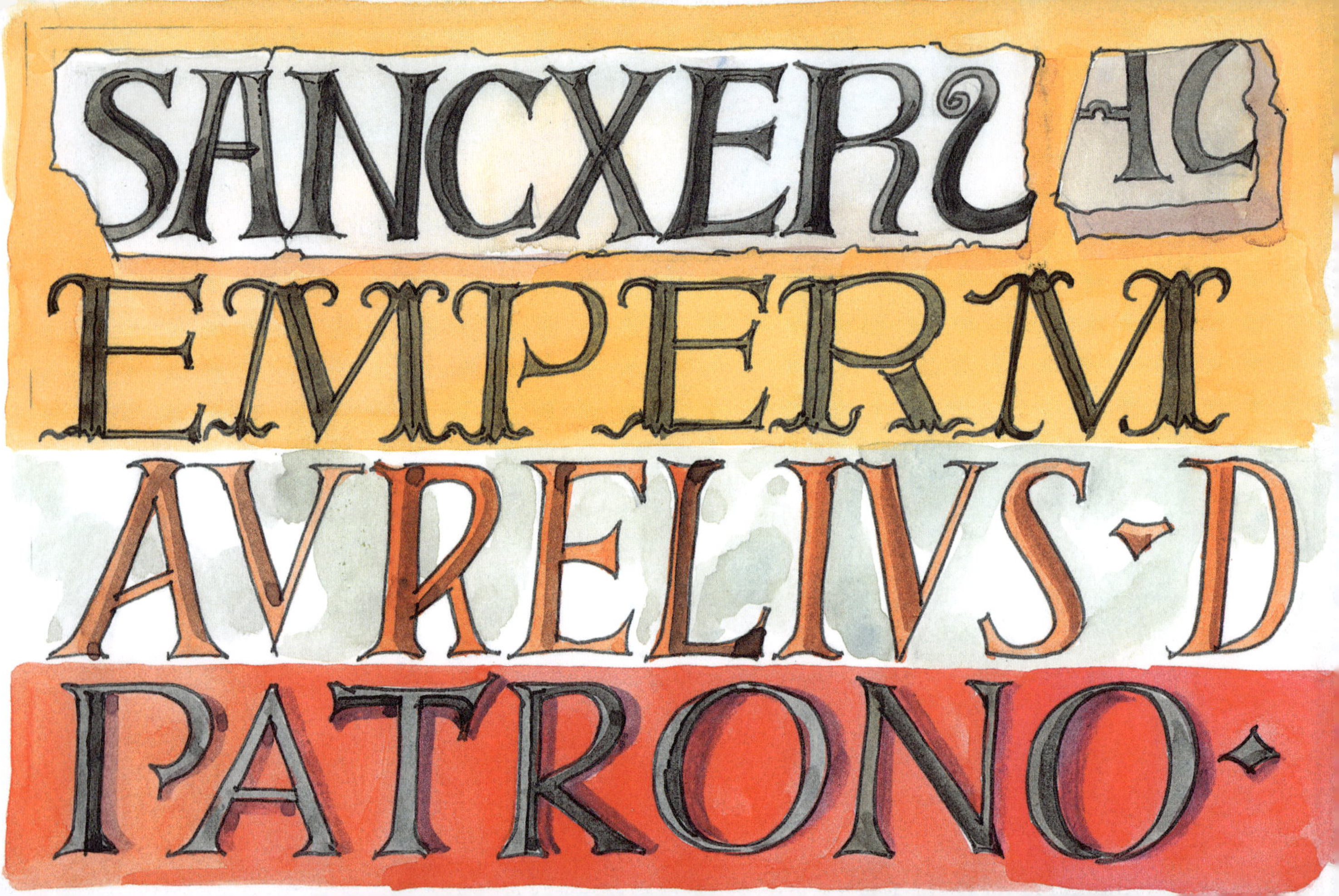

SANCXERIS AC
EMPERM
AVRELIVS·D
PATRONO·

BAMBOLE

FILATELIA

BARBIERE

TRATTORIA

Some books you might read

The Roman bibliography could be endless, as there may not be a city more written about, not least because it has been important for so long. Some of these are reads for a winter evening, but, in the pursuit of some understanding of the core of the city, *The Roman Forum* by David Watkin (Profile Books, 2009) is unbeatable.

Robert Hughes's *Rome* (Weidenfeld and Nicolson, 2011) is a rollicking good read. The Australian cultural commentator is un-modishly straight speaking in his enthusiasms and dislikes. His far-from-encyclopaedic but colourful narrative is chronological and starts a hundred balls rolling. Equally personal is *An Elephant in Rome* by Loyd Grossman (Pallas Athene, 2020). Again, not academic, but exceptionally well researched: he throws light on the all-pervasive genius of Bernini. Matthew Kneale's *Rome: A History in Seven Sackings* (Atlantic Books, 2017) is full of adventure and fact, and Matthew Sturgis's *When in Rome* (Frances Lincoln, 2011) is thematic and full of documented commentaries.

I was genuinely in the dark about the history of the papacy and even about its global significance over two millennia. The shroud of mystery was pulled aside by John Julius Norwich's *The Popes: A History* (Chatto and Windus, 2011), which is magisterial in its breadth, but also in its willingness to skip whole areas to focus on the genuinely significant, interesting or egregious pontiffs. On the same general theme, Bernard Green's *Christianity in Ancient Rome* (Bloomsbury, 2010) is academic and complex, but absolutely not a hard read. It covers a relatively obscure moment and, in terms of the early church and the Roman Jews, is also very interesting.

A much admired guidebook is Georgina Masson's *The Companion Guide to Rome* (Companion Guides, 1965). It is authoritative and I have it in the version revised by John Fort (2009). It is a bit thin on jokes (such lighthearted bits that do get in are Fort-isms), but that is really only a sign of my own feebleminded obsession with jollity. It is invaluable. In my Venice book, I was able to suggest Deborah Howard, whose *The Architectural History of Venice* (Batsford, 1980) is impressively comprehensive. I didn't find a book to rival that, but Masson-Fort is your best equivalent.

Some things you must do

Visit the BATHS OF DIOCLETIAN and Michelangelo's cloister. They are less frequented than other Roman archaeological sites, and the cows' heads among the box and cypress trees in the cloister are unmissable.

Gird your loins and book a day at THE VATICAN. The Sistine Chapel may be hard to see without binoculars, but the museums, with everything from early Italian paintings to pope-mobiles, are comprehensive and thrilling.

Walk under the umbrella pines of the BORGHESE GARDENS before diving into the gallery for the pleasures of Bernini and Canova in the series of rooms inside.

Sit in CAMPO SANTA MARIA IN TRASTEVERE and drink a spremuta in front of the ancient church that you are about to visit.

Brave the broiling glass case of the ARA PACIS to see the Altar of the deified Augustus and, on its marble walls, the finest and most elegantly refined carving in ancient Rome.

Book a visit to the VILLA MEDICI and get one of the best big city views from the ilex-lined parterres. Visit the pavilions, some of which used to house Prix de Rome winning artists. The best of them are decorated in some of the most charming murals of birds ever seen.

If you are in the city on a Saturday, visit the PALAZZO COLONNA close to Piazza Venezia. Open to the general public once a week, it is eye-poppingly lavish in its paintings and sculptures, and has the best of all the city's gardens.

Climb to the CAPITOLINE MUSEUMS and visit every room, because they are so varied and so full of ancient Rome, from bronze horses to philosophers' heads all racked up. The view down into the Forum is the best in the entire city.

Walk along the VIA APPIA ANTICA. It is bucolic, with lambs under the umbrella pines and a stone pavement 2,300 years old. Along the route lie tombs and villas and catacombs. It is shady and deeply picturesque.

206

Acknowledgements

To spend February and March in Rome is the most terrific pleasure. When the garden at home is a gloomy wet mire, and spirits are correspondingly low, then to flee to the Mediterranean spring makes the soul SING. For all that I must first thank Richard Atkinson, my publisher at Penguin Press, for continuing to support and commission me, and my well-travelled and informed agent Caroline Dawnay and her assistant Kat Aitken for making this happen.

Richard has behind him a remarkable team of clever women and men – Millie Andrew and Sam Fulton, Maddie Watts and Shauna Lacy – while the most egregious errors and oversights in the text have been ironed out and smartly re-folded by Octavia Pollock. Matt Young has expertly reordered the less focussed drawings from the original sketchbooks and turned them into an actual BOOK.

While I was in Rome, I was treated with extreme kindness by Marella Caracciolo under whose balcony full of PERFECT LEMON TREES I talked about my new discoveries. But most of all I must thank my friends Nick and Kirsty whose generosity made my stay in San Lorenzo delicious, and supremely comfortable. Soho Rome became my home, and its affectionate staff my friends. Thank you all.

Previous trips to Rome have always been such a pleasure, albeit often all too fleeting; first driving madly round the city with Askandar Samad in 1979, then with Max and Wefe Deliss, several times with Emma Bridgewater, with Gabriel Langlands, Mark and Georgie Rowse. However, first and foremost, Rome to me is Margaret Rice's city. My bold, kind, brilliant daughter spent two years working, studying, helping, playing and making friends in this extraordinary place, and it is to her that this book is dedicated x

Matthew Rice, Bampton, February 2023

PARTICULAR BOOKS

An imprint of Penguin Books

UK | USA | Canada | Ireland | Australia
India | New Zealand | South Africa

Penguin Books is part of the Penguin Random House group of companies whose addresses can be found at global.penguinrandomhouse.com

Penguin Random House UK
One Embassy Gardens, 8 Viaduct Gardens,
London SW11 7BW

penguin.co.uk

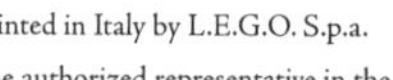

Penguin
Random House
UK

First published 2023   002

Text and illustrations copyright © Matthew Rice, 2023
The moral right of the author has been asserted.

No part of this book may be used or reproduced in any manner for the purpose of training artificial intelligence technologies or systems. In accordance with Article 4(3) of the DSM Directive 2019/790, Penguin Random House expressly reserves this work from the text and data mining exception.

Printed in Italy by L.E.G.O. S.p.a.

The authorized representative in the EEA is Penguin Random House Ireland, Morrison Chambers, 32 Nassau Street, Dublin D02 YH68

A CIP catalogue record for this book is available from the British Library.

ISBN: 978-0-241-59443-8

Penguin Random House is committed to a sustainable future for our business, our readers and our planet. This book is made from Forest Stewardship Council® certified paper.

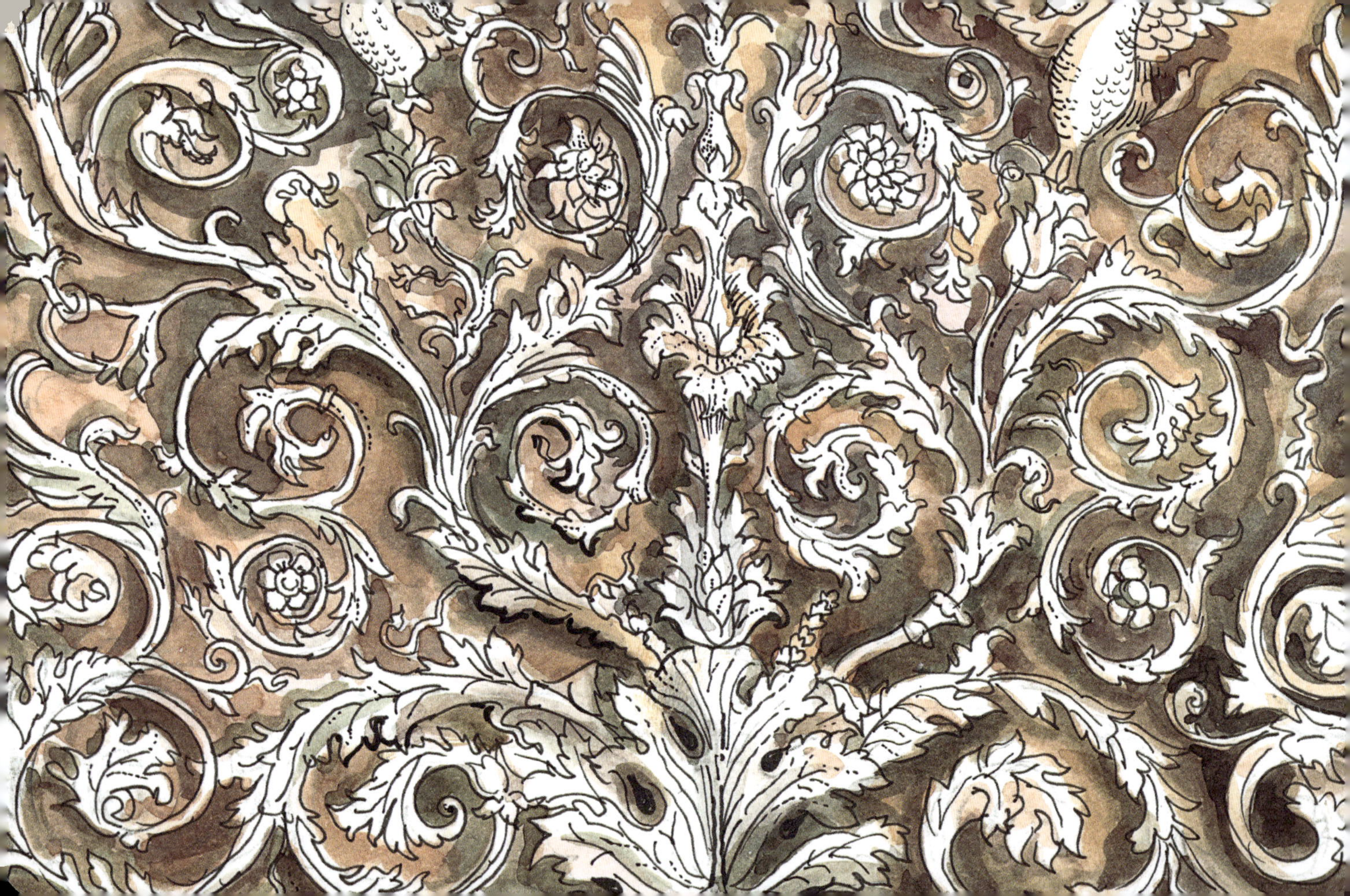